POETRY AND LETTERS
IN EARLY CHRISTIAN GAUL

Poetry and Letters
in Early Christian Gaul

Nora K. Chadwick

BOWES & BOWES LONDON

First published in 1955 by
Bowes & Bowes Publishers Limited,
3 Henrietta Street, London, W.C.2

Made and printed in England by
STAPLES PRINTERS LIMITED
at their Rochester, Kent, establishment

To the Memory

of my Husband

HECTOR MUNRO CHADWICK

PREFACE

WHEN I was made a lecturer in the Early History and Culture of the British Isles I found myself embarrassed by the almost total absence of contemporary sources of information for the period between the departure of the Romans and the establishment of the Saxon kingdoms. Much material is available in written records from Ireland, Wales, and Brittany, both in Latin and in the vernacular; but, apart from the fact that the texts involve a knowledge of at least two difficult Celtic languages in addition to Latin of unclassical type, the texts themselves are all relatively late, and of very unequal value.

In these circumstances it seemed natural to me to turn first to Gaul, a neighbouring Celtic country which has a wealth of contemporary records, all in Latin, and of a high quality. The Roman system of education still prevailed in Gaul, and ensured that the writers of these works had critical standards and literary ideals like our own. They are writing, moreover, of events of their own time, national and international. They had acquired from the Romans the custom of keeping chronicles of contemporary affairs, some of which are our only source of information for the events which they mention. Above all, these Gallo-Romans had adopted extensively the habit of letter-writing, and of forming collections of letters for publication. These letters are written both by private individuals and by important public men, often ecclesiastics, and in them we live again through the period of the great invasions of Franks, Burgundians and Visigoths, and through what is perhaps the most momentous period in Western Christianity.

It seems to me that from many points of view these contemporary records of Gaul in the late fourth and fifth centuries offer a sounder basis for the understanding of our own contemporary history than the later British traditions relating to the same period. This is especially true in regard to the early British Church and the *Lives* of the saints. But it is not only as a background that Gaul is a valuable field of research for the reconstruction of the

7

history of early Britain. There is hardly a writer mentioned in my book who has not something to tell us which has some bearing on the history of our country. Both directly and in-directly it seems to me that Gaul must be our starting point for a study of the history, as distinct from the pre-history, of the British Isles.

Yet, while the contemporary records for Gaul are extensive and varied, and of exceptionally high quality, a large propor-tion have never been translated into English, and even of the original texts many are not easily available. Moreover the period as a whole has hardly received the attention which it merits from those scholars best equipped to interpret it. Clas-sical scholars tend to pass it by as being too late for their inter-ests. Historians regard it as an interlude of decline and dis-integration. Theologians concentrate on the more specialized issues of the time, the history of the Creed, the liturgies, heresies, and above all, on the great Fathers of the Church. The general history of the period has hardly been fully appreciated. *Life and Letters in the Fourth Century*, written in 1901 by the late Dr Glover, is not concerned primarily with Gaul, but with the whole Roman world of the fourth century. Sir Samuel Dill's *Roman Society in the Last Century of the Western Empire*, written in 1898, is not confined to Gaul, and, as its name implies, is con-cerned with wider issues than the intellectual life alone. A num-ber of books on the period have been published in France in recent years which I have been following with care. But so far as I have been able to ascertain, none covers comprehensively the subject of the present book.

I must conclude with a confession. My book on the intellec-tual life of Gaul in the period of the Barbarian invasions was, indeed, originally planned as prolegomena to a study of early British history; but the truth is that while reading what was written in Gaul at that momentous period I have fallen in love with my subject. The personal records of the great Gaulish officials and bishops, of the pioneers of monasticism, of the men of letters and the country gentlemen, have drawn me insensibly into their lives and into the great events in which they were in-volved. Men brought up like ourselves in the classical tradition, they faced the political and military crisis with a reserve of strength, an ungrudging public spirit, a balanced judgment and

an appreciation of literary and spiritual values, which are congenial to the modern mind. To me personally the people of Gaul
in the fifth century seem more like ourselves in their mental
outlook than any other people at any other period of history.

There has been a heightened interest and a special poignancy
in reading these very personal writings of a period which is so
tragically like the ordeal through which France has recently
passed. In the writers of the fifth century we again watch populations dispersed, cities sacked and burnt, the citizens given
over to forced labour, or massacred and left unburied; sickness,
robbery, and starvation rife; the churches roofless, their doors
unhinged, and choked with brambles. We see the landed gentry
setting up temporary houses for their homeless tenants, or themselves striving to grow a few vegetables for their miserable
livelihood, or snatching eagerly a few moments from defence
measures to read the Classics they have loved all their lives. And
we hear the beleaguered Auvergnians, while reduced to eating
grass plucked from the crannies of the walls, crying that they
are ready to endure yet greater hardships rather than suffer a
dishonourable peace. And after the dreaded peace had come:

'Everyone is saying that things were better during the war
than they are now in peace-time.'

How strangely familiar it all seems to us now! A generation
ago our historians and critics had a ready sneer for the appeal
of Salvian for relief-funds for the Church and the poor, and his
burning indignation at the thoughtless luxury of the rich was
looked upon as fanatical; but for us the words 'charity', 'relief',
'destitute', have lost their abstract sense, and have now a more
personal ring. We ourselves have acquired a quickened sense of
human misery, and are in a better position to understand the
intellectual life of fifth-century Gaul than was possible at any
time before the second European war; and now, more than ever
before, a fresh study of the period has become imperative.

The substance of the present book was given in courses of
lectures delivered in the University of Cambridge during the
years 1949–1953. I am grateful to Miss M. A. Hennings, who
has made the Index. I am especially indebted to Professor
Jocelyn M. Toynbee, who read the work in its early stages and
encouraged me to publish it. I also gratefully acknowledge help
in a number of ways from my friend the Rev. Owen Chadwick,

who has also read the proofs. Mrs MacQueen's fine Latin scholarship has saved me from many pitfalls. To all these scholars I am deeply grateful for criticisms and corrections, and it is hardly necessary for me to add that I alone am responsible for such errors and shortcomings as may still remain. I am, like many of my colleagues, unable to express my debt to Professor Bruce Dickins in a neat formula. I have had from him so much help in so many ways. I will only add that without his help and encouragement this book would never have been published.

NORA K. CHADWICK.

Cambridge,
   November 1954.

TABLE OF CONTENTS

CHAPTER I

The Intellectual Background
and
The Priscillianists

In the closing years of the fourth, and throughout the fifth century Gaul is the meeting point of some of the most important currents of thought in the intellectual history of Europe and the Mediterranean lands. The ancient world, the classical world of Greece and Rome, is still the present world at the time when our period opens with the great Gaulish personality of Ausonius, and his no less famous pupil St Paulinus of Nola. And when the curtain falls, shortly after 475, the Bishop of Auvergne and prince of letter writers, Sidonius Apollinaris, has just closed the volume of Menander which he has been reading with his son. At the beginning of the period the great senator Symmachus is corresponding with Ausonius, linking ancient with modern times by still organizing gladiatorial combats for the birthday celebrations of his son; and before the close we shall find Claudianus Mamertus carrying on a little academy on Platonic lines in Vienne at no great distance from Marseilles, taking part with a handful of others, scholars like himself, in what has been called a 'Little Renaissance'. The ancient world still lived on in Gaul.

But Gaul was no conservative backwater. New influences were pouring in from the East, political, cultural, religious. The popular movement of the native population of Coptic Egypt, fostered by St Athanasius, the great adversary of the Arians generally, is already making itself felt in Aquitaine in the polished and charming writings of Sulpicius Severus. The reputation of the Desert Fathers of Egypt, and the hermits of the Cyrenaic coasts, has reached Italy and southern Gaul before the close of the fourth century, and is arousing a spirit of emulation. The arrival from Dacia, and establishment in Gaul, of St Martin, a monk of military origin and no great family distinction, and his election as Bishop of Tours, mark a widening of the basis of episcopal recruitment, which has hitherto tended to draw its bishops from the great territorial magnates who represented the old Roman administrative system in Gaul.[1] Even more important is the new spirit in religion which St Martin introduced – the mysticism characteristic of the East, combined with asceticism and a life of devotion set apart from the 'daily round'.

Interesting cultural changes are also in progress. The vogue of the Greek novel is making itself felt, and is believed to have stimulated the growth of stories of miracles which – sparse at first – come to play a more and more important part in the new literary genre of hagiography. The rise of ecclesiastical biography is itself a new and important element of the literary life of the period, and here we may trace the influence of Alexandria. The *Life of St Antony*, now generally accepted as the work of St Athanasius, written between 356 and 362,[2] formed the model for the biographies of the saints in the West, and undoubtedly inspired Sulpicius Severus's *Life of St Martin*.

But the most interesting feature of the intellectual life of the period is the rise and spread of letter-writing in Gaul. The habit developed rapidly, and from the extensive collections which have survived we are able to make the acquaintance of the Gauls as individuals, men and women alike. We learn to know them as personalities, to follow their daily routine; their relations one with another. We accompany them abroad and into their homes. We learn of their religious convictions and habits, their friendships and their bitter enmities, the nature of their intellectual life, and – a rare privilege – of their sense of humour. We can trace the whole pageant of their life, public and private. We become the audience of the great drama of this most dramatic epoch, and the letters are our main source for a period which is of the greatest importance for the future of European thought. These letters are not confined to Gaul:

---

[1] On the subject of local bishops at this period, see R. Laprat, 'La Carrière ecclésiastique de Saint Germain', in a collection of essays published by Le Bras and Gilson, *Saint Germain d' Auxerre et Son Temps* (Auxerre, 1950), p. 160, and note 27 ad loc.; cf. also H. G. J. Beck, *The Pastoral Care of Souls in South-East France during the Sixth Century* (Rome, 1950), p. 6 ff.

[2] The work is translated into English by A. Robertson in the series *The Nicene and Post-Nicene Fathers*, Vol. IV (New York, 1903), p. 188 ff; and by R. T. Meyer (London, 1950).

some of the most interesting were probably written by Britons abroad to their families at home.[1]

The rise and spread of letter-writing in the West was facilitated by the quick and regular means of communication. The Roman roads were still functioning, and of special importance for Gaul was the great west-east route from Bordeaux through Arles, to Milan and Aquileia and on through Sardica to Constantinople. St Paulinus in Campania corresponded annually with friends in Aquitaine, and his more occasional correspondence radiated out in all directions. St Jerome from Syria corresponded with men and women living on the Atlantic seaboard, as well as with the whole Mediterranean world.

Some of the most interesting letters of the time were written by women. We shall find the ladies Hedibia and Algasia of Bordeaux sending letters to St Jerome[2] in Bethlehem by the priest Apodemius[3] (cf. p. 35). Artemia, a near relative of Hedibia, flees to Palestine on the Barbarian invasion of Gaul, and again Hedibia writes to Jerome, begging him to use his influence with Artemia's husband, Rusticus, who has refused to leave his estates in Gaul and accompany his wife. We still possess the letter which Jerome wrote to Rusticus at Hedibia's request,[4] though the answer of Rusticus is unknown.

Parcels and books were no less rapidly distributed. St Jerome in Bethlehem regularly borrowed books from his friends in Europe, and his letters from the Syrian desert are full of references to books which he was returning to the owners, or again to books which he wished to borrow for his own use. St Paulinus of Nola writes to St Augustine[5] about his five books against the Manichees which he has received from Bishop Alypius; and he writes to Alypius himself, sending him St Jerome's version of

[1] See C. P. Caspari, *Briefe, Abhandlungen und Predigten* (Christiania, 1890); English translation by R. S. T. Haslehurst, *The Works of Fastidius* (London, 1926). For a brief account of the contents of the collection the reader may refer to *Studies in Early British History*, edited by N. K. Chadwick (Cambridge, 1953), p. 210 f.

[2] For the established text and translation (French) of St Jerome's letters see the recent edition by J. Labourt (Budé Series), Paris, 1949 ff., as yet incomplete. For the sake of convenience I have given references throughout to the collection in Migne, *Patrologia Latina*, Vol. XXII.

[3] For Jerome's reply to Algasia, see his letters, *Ep.* 121. For his correspondence with Hedibia, see pp. 15, 35. For some account of Hedibia and her circle, see A. Thierry, *Saint Jérôme* (Paris, 1875), p. 412.

[4] St Jerome, *Ep.* 122.

[5] Paulinus, *Ep.* 4 (Ed. G. de Hartel, Vienna, 1894; cf. also Migne, *P.L.*, Vol. LXI).

the *Chronicle* of Eusebius which Alypius had asked him to obtain
for him in Rome.[1] St Augustine himself also sends his own
works to Paulinus by his letter-carrier in response to his request.[2] To Sulpicius Severus Paulinus sends his work, the
Defensio Theodosii.[3] We shall see (p. 306) how, in the middle
of the fifth century, Sidonius Apollinaris sends copies of
Eusebius and Varro to his friend Namatius, the admiral of the
Roman fleet, patrolling the Straits of Dover against Saxon
pirates. Elsewhere again we see Sidonius laughingly pillaging
the luggage of the priest Riocatus who had been commissioned
to procure the works of Bishop Faustus of Riez and to take them
to Britain (or possibly Brittany). Books were eagerly sought for
and read with a passionate interest similar to that aroused in
the eighteenth and nineteenth centuries by fiction. Even towards the close of the fifth century Bishop Ruricius, Bishop of
Limoges, was still borrowing books from friends and monastic
libraries.[4]

The increasing facilities for communication and travel, and
the rise of the great Christian centres in the East, were awakening curiosity about the eastern Mediterranean lands, Egypt and
the Holy Land especially. St Jerome from his cell in Bethlehem
received visitors from Britain, which is described in a letter
from St Paula and her daughter Eustochium in Bethlehem to
Marcella in Rome as *divisus ab orbe nostro*;[5] and early in the
fifth century we read in the *Lausiac History*[6] by Palladius of
Britons visiting Palestine. We possess a letter, dating probably
from the fifth century, written by an unknown traveller, probably a Briton, who had set out to make a pilgrimage to the
Holy Land, but who had changed his plans and decided instead
to go to Rome. He tells us that he has been influenced in this
decision by the arguments of a very holy lady of Sicily, who
is evidently a religious devotee, for the writer has decided
to confide to her care the little daughter who accompanies

---

[1] Paulinus, *Ep.* 3.
[2] St Augustine, *Ep.* 27 (to Paulinus; Migne, *P.L.*, Vol. XXXIII).
[3] Paulinus, *Ep.* 28.
[4] H. G. J. Beck, *The Pastoral Care of Souls*, p. 10, and references.
[5] St Jerome, *Ep.* XLVI, 10, translated in part by A. Stewart, *The Letter of Paula and Eustochium to Marcella about the Holy Places*, A.D. 386. (The Palestine Pilgrims' Text Society, London, 1896), p. 10.
[6] For an account of this work, and some references to editions and translations, see p. 144, n. 1.

him, in order that she may be trained as a religious recluse.[1]

From the fourth and fifth centuries we have a number of diaries and itineraries[2] which claim to have been written by *peregrini* ('pilgrims') from western lands, Gaul, possibly also Spain, or even conceivably Britain. The earliest is that of an unnamed pilgrim from Bordeaux which gives the principal stages on the land route from Bordeaux to the Holy Land by way of Constantinople in 333.[3] One of the most interesting of these itineraries is written by a woman, who relates her tour of the holy places of Egypt and the East. She came perhaps from at least as far west as the valley of the Rhône, to which she makes reference in her text.[4] The name of the writer is again unknown, and the only text which we possess is incomplete. The author was formerly identified with St Silvania or Silvina, the sister-in-law of Rufinus, Prefect of the East under the Emperor Theodosius the Great; but this identification is now generally rejected. The writer may possibly have been a certain Etheria or Eucheria,[5] referred to in a letter of the seventh-century abbot Valerius of north-western Spain as having made a pilgrimage to the 'Holy Places', and as being herself 'sprung from the farthest shore of the western sea, the ocean'.[6] If we could accept the identification the lady would presumably be Spanish. The identification is nevertheless still a matter of some uncertainty.[7] The itinerary, whoever the authoress, claims to be

[1] The letter is one of a number of anonymous treatises, dating probably from the fifth century, which were discovered by C. P. Caspari (cf. p. 15).

[2] For a caution against accepting all that they relate as based on personal knowledge, see H. Delehaye, *Les Légendes Hagiographiques* (Brussels, 1927), p. 40 ff. Cf. also W. Telfer, *Journal of Theological Studies*, Vol. XXXVIII (1937), p. 397 ff.

[3] *Itinerary from Bordeaux to Jerusalem*: '*The Bordeaux Pilgrim*', translated by Aubrey Stewart (P.P.T.S., London, 1887).

[4] Edited by W. Heraeus, *Silviae vel potius Aetheriae Peregrinatio ad Loca Sancta* (Heidelberg, 1929); also by E. Löfstedt, *Philologischer Kommentar zur Peregrinatio Aetheriae* (Uppsala, 1911; reprinted without alteration, 1936); translated under the title: *The Pilgrimage of S. Silvia of Aquitania to the Holy Places* (c. A.D. 385), by J. H. Bernard (P.P.T.S., London, 1891); and later, under the title: *The Pilgrimage of Etheria*, by M. L. McClure and C. L. Feltoe (London, 1919).

[5] For a note on the forms of the name, see Dom. G. Morin, 'Un Passage énigmatique de S. Jérôme contre la Pélérine espagnole Eucheria?', *Revue Bénédictine*, Vol. XXX (1913), p. 174.

[6] *Extremo Occidui maris Oceani littore exorta* (Migne, *P.L.*, Vol. LXXXVII, col. 424). Valerius was the biographer of St Fructuosus, a famous Spanish saint of the seventh century.

[7] For some discussion of the writer's identity, see McClure and Feltoe, op. cit., p. viii; T. R. Glover, *Life and Letters in the Fourth Century* (Cambridge, 1901), p. 133 ff.; Dom. G. Morin, loc. cit., and the references there cited; D. Brooke, *Pilgrims Were They All* (London, 1937), p. 91 ff.

addressed to sister nuns at home, and it must have been greatly enjoyed, for the extent of the author's travels and her intellectual curiosity and naïve delight in all that she saw, especially the fine views, are very compelling. The narrative is all the more racy owing to the credulity of the writer and her artless colloquial Latin, and the reader's interest never flags for a moment. The itinerary is also especially valuable today for its appendix describing the daily offices and the liturgical ceremonies and feasts of the Church at a time for which our information is scarce.

We know from incidental references that many other ladies both from the East and West made similar pilgrimages of which we possess no itineraries or diaries. Reference has already been made to St Silvania or Silvina, the sister-in-law of Rufinus, who was formerly identified with the writer of our anonymous itinerary. Palladius[1] gives a brief but very interesting note on a pilgrimage which she made to Egypt in company with himself and the elder Melania, in which he stresses her devotion to Biblical studies and her intense austerities. We have seen also that the unnamed writer of the letter from Sicily is accompanied by his young daughter who is to be trained as an ascetic. Later we shall see the poetess Euchrotia, wife of the orator Delphidius of Bordeaux, journeying to Rome with her daughter Procula in company with Priscillian, the Bishop of Avila. St Jerome felt it necessary to warn the Spanish lady Furia against the moral dangers of such pilgrimages and journeys.[2]

These cultivated and independent ladies of the Roman provincial world were in no way unique at this period, when Roman women in general enjoyed a high status. Many shared the desire to go on pilgrimage, and to see for themselves the holy places of the East. In her own day perhaps the most outstanding of these noble pilgrims was St Melania,[3] a Roman lady of Spanish extraction, known as Melania the Elder to distinguish her from her grand-daughter, the Younger Melania. She had become acquainted with St Jerome while he was living in

---

[1] *Lausiac History*, Cap. 55.

[2] *Ep.* 54, *Ad Furiam* (Migne, *P.L.*, Vol. XXII, § 13). Morin makes the interesting suggestion that our pilgrim is the lady whom Jerome has in mind in his cautionary observations. See *Revue Bénédictine*, Vol. XXX (1913), p. 174 ff.

[3] St Melania the Elder figures prominently in contemporary letters and other writings. Among our chief sources of information are letters of St Jerome and St Paulinus; the *Chronicle* of St Jerome; and the *Lausiac History* of Palladius.

ascetic retreat at Aquileia, and also with Rufinus, who had been one of the same group; and on the death of her husband she resolved to adopt the ascetic life. About the year 372 she set out for Egypt, where she was joined by Rufinus of Aquileia, the friend and later the enemy of St Jerome. Shortly afterwards she left for Palestine, where she established a community of virgins on the Mount of Olives. Here she was visited by Evagrius, and was in touch with many of the most eminent ecclesiastics of the day, chief of whom was Rufinus, much of whose literary work was done under her auspices. In 397 she again visited Italy, accompanied by Rufinus; but in 408 she finally left Italy, travelling first to Sicily and then to Africa and on to Jerusalem, where she died forty days later in her old community on the Mount of Olives.

In the following century the growing love of travel and pilgrimage, and of the asceticism which was closely bound up with them, received a great stimulus in Italy, as in other areas, from the invasion of Alaric. The girl Demetrias, a beautiful young heiress of one of the wealthiest and noblest families in Italy, adopted the ascetic life as a professed virgin, and left Italy for Africa with her mother and her grandmother, just in time to witness the burning of Rome as they set sail. Both St Jerome[1] and Pelagius[2] wrote elaborate addresses to her on the ascetic life, and St Augustine, having read that of Pelagius, sent a letter later to her mother, Juliana, warning her against the writer.[3] The letter of Pelagius was written in 413. In 414 we find the Younger Melania, and her husband Pinianus in Bethlehem with St Jerome and the younger Paula, grand-daughter of the founder of the convent, and now herself in charge of it. Like Demetrias they had left Italy on the invasion of Alaric, and, after a severe ordeal in Africa, had passed on to Palestine, where they adopted the ascetic life. A letter from Pinianus, his mother Albina, and his wife Melania, written to St Augustine, probably from Jerusalem, in support of Pelagius on the ground

[1] Jerome, *Ep.* 130.
[2] For the text of the letter, see Migne, *P.L.*, Vols. XXX, col. 15 ff., XXXIII, col. 1099 ff.; cf., also G. de Plinval, *Pélage* (Lausanne, 1943), p. 26, n. 2 for further references. De Plinval justly calls this address by Pelagius 'l'un des joyaux de la littérature chrétienne' (p. 245).
[3] Augustine, *Ep.* 188 (to Juliana); Migne, *P.L.*, Vol. XXXIII. For a fuller account of Demetrias, and of the texts of the letters cited above, see de Plinval, op. cit., p. 242 ff. A brief account in English is given by D. Brooke, op. cit., p. 197 ff.

of their personal knowledge of his (in their opinion) orthodox views, called forth Augustine's *De Gratia Christi* in 418.[1]

Many of the great Roman ladies who had not shared the desire of these religious devotees and refugees for foreign travel and settlement in the Holy Land showed themselves no less inspired by Christian devotion to asceticism and a secluded life. I have already referred to the 'very holy lady' in Sicily to whom an unknown writer ascribes his decision to visit Rome instead of going on to the East, and to whom he confides his little daughter that she may be trained as a religious devotee. In the preceding century the great Roman lady Albina had been deeply impressed by the teaching of St Athanasius on his visit to Rome in 340, and had turned her palace on the Aventine into a religious retreat for a community of virgins. Her friend Lea had also placed herself at the head of a community of noble Roman women.[2] Their examples were soon followed by others, some of whom lived retired lives of prayer in their own homes.[3] Among the most illustrious of these ascetic women was Albina's daughter, Marcella, whose life of devotion to the poor and to Christian asceticism, and whose noble death during the sack of Rome, are among our most precious recollections of these early days. Not even the persuasions of her old friends St Paula[4] and Eustochium, or her old master St Jerome, could induce her to leave Rome and join them in the Holy Land.

For many years before her departure for the East, St Paula also had converted her house in Rome into a religious retreat for herself and her daughters and household dependents, and for a number of other young girls whom she took under her charge, so that St Jerome described it as a kind of 'domestic church'. But pilgrimage was in the air, and in the spring of 382 she left Rome with her daughter Eustochium, setting sail for the East, via Cyprus. St Jerome has left us an account of the journey,[5] which took them from Antioch through Lebanon southward, through the coastal cities to Jerusalem, thence through Egypt

---

[1] *De Gratia Christi* (Migne, *P.L.*, Vol. XLIV, col. 364 ff., cap. 40).
[2] See Jerome, *Ep.* 23.
[3] See Jerome, *Ep.* 24; Palladius, *Lausiac History*, cap. 37, 41, 54 ff.
[4] Jerome, *Ep.*46. For translations (English and French) of this letter, cf. p. 16.
[5] Our chief source of information for St Paula's life and travels is contained in Jerome's letter (*Ep.* 108) to her daughter Eustochium on her mother's death. See also the translation of this letter by Aubrey Stewart, *The Pilgrimage of the Holy Paula* (P.P.T.S., London, 1887).

westward to visit the ascetics in the desert of Nitria. On their return to Palestine they settled finally in Bethlehem, where they founded a monastery for men and a convent for women, in the former of which St Jerome settled and in which his most important literary work was done. Both Paula and Eustochium already had a good knowledge of Greek, to which they now added that of Hebrew also. We owe much of Jerome's work on Holy Scripture to their trained help and devotion and to the stimulus which they gave him.[1] The number of books which he dedicated to them is remarkable, 'though not', as Haarhoff remarks,[2] 'when we consider that they inspired the translation.'[3]

The Romans had developed a fine system of education at both the high school and the university stage, and the women evidently shared to some extent in the educational privileges enjoyed by the men. We shall find Ausonius consoling his grandson for his sufferings and fears under school discipline with the reminder that his father *and mother* had endured all this in their time. The ladies of Aquitaine in particular impress us by their personality and efficiency in letters. Their part in the upbringing of the young Gaulish boys was evidently an important one, and their status as educated women was high. One of the most remarkable instances is that of the *sacra virgo*, the Christian lady Eunomia,[4] daughter and pupil of an eminent professor of Bordeaux, the famous panegyrist Nazarius,[5] and, according to St Jerome, his equal in eloquence.[6]

The earliest schools of learning[7] known to us had been in Eastern Gaul. Autun was certainly the most ancient of such centres and already in 21 B.C. the most flourishing. Here, so

---

[1] See e.g. the second Preface to his translation of the *Psalms* (Migne, *P.L.*, Vol. XXIX, col. 118.
[2] *The Schools of Gaul* (Oxford, 1920), p. 208.
[3] For an account of the convent of St Paula and Eustochium at Bethlehem see F. Lagrange, *St Paula* (English translation by the Benedictines of Talacre, London, 1938) – an illuminating little book.
[4] *Laus domnae Eunomiae sacrae virginis* (*Anth. Lat.*, Teubner Series, 767). cf. Prosper, *Chron. Min.* I, 452: *Eunomia Christiana virgo.*
[5] *Nazarius rhetor insignis habetur*, Jerome, *Chron.*, s.a. 324. Migne, *P.L.*, Vol. XXVII, col. 673.
[6] *Nazarii rhetoris filia in eloquentia patri coaequatur*, Jerome, *Chron.*, s.a. 336. Migne, *P.L.*, Vol. XXVII, col. 679.
[7] For general works on Roman and sub-Roman education, see M. Roger, *L'Enseignement des Lettres Classiques d'Ausone à Alcuin* (Paris, 1905); T. J. Haarhoff, op.cit.; C. Jullian, *Histoire de la Gaule*, Vol. VIII (Paris, 1926).

Tacitus tells us, grammar, eloquence and poetry were studied; Greek had held at that time a place almost as important as Latin. There had been another school of learning at Marseilles. Others schools at Lyons, Arles, Vienne, Toulouse, Limoges, Reims, and Trier achieved their importance somewhat later. The masters, sometimes Greek by origin, were highly esteemed, particularly at Autun.[1] By the fourth century the chief centres of education had moved from south-eastern Gaul to Trier and Bordeaux, and the latter became the most important centre of learning in western Europe.

The Gauls were eager to profit by the excellent education provided for provincials under the Roman government. The teaching in the schools had, of course, been carried on in Latin from the time of the Conquest, and by the fifth century Latin had become the universal language in Gaul among the educated classes. The most zealous propagandists of Latin were the Gauls themselves. To govern Gaul the Romans depended largely on members of the Gaulish aristocracy, who had eagerly adopted Latin culture and sought to raise their own mental and spiritual life to the intellectual level of Rome.

An interesting measure of the progress of Romanization is the adoption of Latin names. At first the Gauls kept their own names, but used them as surnames; then, in a generation or two, the surname tended to be eliminated. Caesar mentions two members of the tribe of the Aedui who bore the Gaulish name *Eporedorix*. One of these became *Gaius Julius Eporedorix*, according to an inscription in Bourbon-Lancy; but his son called himself *Gaius Julius Magnus*. His grandsons were *Lucius Julius Calenus*, and *Gaius Julius Proculus*.[2] The survival of Gaulish elements in place-names (e.g. *Paris* from the tribal name *Parisii*, and *Trier* from the tribal name *Treveri*) is too well known to require illustration here.

Gaul had a long native tradition, and pride in this tradition inspired in her people a deep sense of the value of education, which combined with economic causes to produce the intellectual pre-eminence of the country in the closing days of the Empire. During the early fourth century Roman culture was

---

[1] See Thevenot, *Les Gallo-Romains* (Paris, 1948), p. 73 f.

[2] ibid., p. 69. We can also trace the reverse process in the sixth century. See H. G. J. Beck, *The Pastoral Care of Souls*, p. 8.

moving westward, and in the second half of the same century, and throughout the fifth, Gaul was the principal intellectual area of the western Empire. It was in Gaul that the traditions of the ancient world retained their fullest vitality. The native element in this Gallo-Roman culture is difficult to estimate, because contemporary Gaulish writers, themselves members of the aristocracy, deliberately cultivated the outlook and intellectual interests of Rome, and appeared to care little for their ancient native traditions. Yet earlier Celtic influences are undoubtedly strong in the native Gaulish character and background, and have left their impress on the literary style of the period, as will become clear in the following chapters.

In the meantime it will be well to bear in mind that, apart from the big towns on the great rivers, notably Trier, Bordeaux, and the cities of the Rhône – which were often ancient tribal capitals developed on Roman lines – the country was still largely agricultural, while great areas remained under forests. The landed gentry were devoted to agriculture to an astonishing degree, and delighted to take an active, personal interest in the management of their country estates. Very often after a busy political or official career in the Roman civil service in Britain, Italy, or Africa, they would return thankfully to their own country houses and lands, to end their days in the agricultural pursuits they loved so well, much as Scotsmen do today. Among such people old customs die hard.

It has been suggested that the schools of learning which were established under Roman influence in eastern Gaul carried on an ancient Celtic tradition, created in the distant past by the Druids, who are said to have surrounded themselves by pupils or disciples drawn from the young nobility. It is further suggested that the selection of Autun by the Romans as an educational centre was dictated as much by the fact that such Druidical 'seminaries' had existed there as by the ancient alliance of the Aedui with Rome, and by the rôle assigned to them in the Romanization of Gaul.[1] Certain it is that this was precisely the area in which reactionary native sentiment made itself felt at the latest date, and that the Druids are stated to have fostered anti-Roman elements.[2]

[1] See Thevenot, loc. cit.
[2] See Tacitus, *Histories*, IV, 54.

But in the period with which we are concerned the Druids were long past, and their organization was little more than a memory. Perhaps at all times the high intellectual pretensions attributed to the Druids by classical writers may be regarded as belonging rather to the best native elements in the country as a whole than to a single class. But in any case what we learn of the Druids' equipment is interesting as giving us something of a picture of the ancient cultural life of pre-Roman Gaul. Especially significant is their interest in the stars and the heavenly bodies and in the nature of the physical universe; their traditional oral learning, handed down, like the *Vedas* of India, in the form of oral poetry; their training of the young Gaulish nobility, which lasted, we are told, over a period of sometimes as much as sixteen years. Even if we do not accept these statements entirely *au pied de la lettre*, they indicate a tradition that the training of the Gauls in poetry and eloquence at the hands of the Druids was long and arduous. Except for public and private correspondence, which is said to have been carried on in the Greek alphabet, the learning of the Druids and the education of their pupils was wholly oral.[1] This is, of course, in accordance with what we know of education and culture among backward communities elsewhere, and is in no way exceptional.

These precious glimpses of ancient native culture are significant in view of the later history of the Gaulish intellectual life under the Empire, and the high reputation which Gauls enjoyed for excellence in poetry and also for eloquence, both in forensic oratory and in extempore speaking generally. It is important to remember that even in the period which we are about to study, intellectual intercourse was still carried on extensively by word of mouth throughout Gaul. This must have given to eloquence and the art of composing extempore speeches a value far beyond that which we accord to them today. In legal and political affairs above all the art of public speaking was essential, since all propaganda had to be carried on by this means. Public speaking fulfilled the function of leading articles in the modern Press, and of our political pamphlets and broadcasts. A training in rhetoric, or in the art of polished public speaking, was widely taught by the most brilliant men in the Gaulish schools, and it was an essential acquisition for anyone

[1] Caesar, *De Bello Gallico*, VI, 14.

who hoped to hold office in the higher branches of the Roman civil service.

The native element in the culture of the Gauls is perhaps more apparent in their proficiency in poetry and eloquence than in any other intellectual field, and their natural gifts seem to have responded readily to the stimulus of the Roman rhetorical training. It has been noted that Gaulish eloquence was celebrated even before the Roman Occupation.[1] Tacitus represents the Roman general Cerealis as addressing Gaulish tribesmen, and declaring that arms, not eloquence, have always been his own profession, adding, however: 'words are held in higher esteem by you'.[2] It was doubtless to establish a healthy rivalry in this art that Caligula established an oratorical contest in Greek and Latin oratory at Lyons.[3] The Gaulish cities furnished from early times many of the most famous orators of the Roman world. Narbonne produced Montanus, who flourished under Tiberius, while Domitius Afer, the rhetorician from Nîmes, who belonged to a younger generation, was famous throughout the reigns of Tiberius, Caligula, Claudius, and Nero. Afer was the teacher of Quintilian, who mentions several of his books on oratory. Perhaps the most famous of the Gaulish rhetors of the second century is Favorinus of Arles, a philosopher by profession, and something of a Greek scholar.

The high esteem in which poetry, or perhaps rather eloquence, was held by the Gauls in the second century is admirably symbolized by the picture of the Gaulish Ogmios, the god of poetry, given by the Greek prose writer Lucian, a native of Samosata in Syria, who seems to have held a post as rhetor in Gaul, shortly after the middle of the century. In his little prose vignette entitled *Heracles, An Introduction*, Lucian relates that one day, apparently somewhere near the Atlantic coast of Gaul, he stood looking at a picture. The subject is an old man, bald and white-haired, and with a dark and wrinkled skin, who is drawing after him a crowd of men by little chains of gold and amber of great beauty, one end of which is attached to their ears, and the other to the tip of his own tongue. The people

---

[1] See Sir S. Dill, *Roman Society in the Last Century of the Western Empire* (Second edition, reprinted London, 1933), p. 406. Dill refers to Juvenal I, 44; XV, 1.

[2] *Histories* IV, 73.

[3] Suetonius, *Caligula*, 20.

follow him eagerly, praising him and trying to keep 'abreast with him. Seeing his astonishment at the picture, a Celt of France who spoke Greek excellently – an interesting detail – explained that the picture represented Heracles. He added that in Gaul Heracles rather than Hermes is identified with eloquence,[1] because Heracles is far more powerful than Hermes, and the Gauls believe that Heracles was a wise man who achieved everything by eloquence, his principal force being persuasion.

It was in the fourth century that the eloquence of the Gauls, and their proficiency both as practical rhetoricians and as teachers of rhetoric, reached their fullest development. Sulpicius Severus refers to this eloquence as generally recognized, and St Jerome himself also speaks of it on more than one occasion, referring to 'the richness and splendour of Gaulish oratory', and to the Gauls themselves as 'fertile in orators'.[2] It was during this century that the chief centres of Gaulish culture had moved from the ancient homes of learning in Marseilles and Autun in the east to Bordeaux in the west and Trier in the north. The great Roman statesman and letter writer of the second half of the century, Symmachus, was himself educated in Gaul, and trained in public speaking by a Gaulish professor of rhetoric, 'an *alumnus* of the Garonne',[3] and he is at pains to find a tutor for his son who shall have had a similar training.[4] Ausonius himself was a famous Professor of Rhetoric at Bordeaux, which had now become the chief rhetorical school in the Empire. His own teacher, Tiberius Victor Minervius of Bordeaux, had a brilliant career at Rome and Constantinople.[5] Of some twenty-five professors of Bordeaux celebrated by Ausonius, less than half a dozen were aliens, while Bordeaux supplied professors for the Chairs of Rhetoric at Narbonne, Poitiers, and Toulouse.

Gaulish mastery of polished speech and eloquence, especially

---

[1] An important reference to Hercules Musagetes occurs in the panegyric of Eumenius of Autun, *Pro Instaurandis Scholis*, 7, 8 (*XII Panegyrici Latini*, ed. Baehrens, Leipzig, 1911, p. 252, f.). Cf. further, S. B. Platner, *A Topographical Dictionary of Ancient Rome* (Oxford, 1929), p. 255. See also p. 25 above.

[2] Migne, *P.L.*, Vol. XXVI, col. 355.

[3] *Senex Garumnae alumnus, Symmachus* (ed. O. Seeck, Berlin, 1883), IX, 83.

[4] ibid., *Ep.* VI, 34.

[5] Ausonius, *Commemoratio Professorum Burdigalensium*, 'Poems commemorating the Professors of Bordeaux', Poem I; (cf. p. 32).

on the more technical side, is admirably exemplified in the surviving prose compositions of the panegyrists.[1] Most of the pagan prose panegyrists were connected with Gaul, and their work offers relatively favourable specimens of the genre, necessarily stereotyped from the nature of its subjects and of the occasions on which it was employed. Such occasions were chiefly civic and public, such as the visit of an emperor to a great city; the anniversary of the accession of the emperor, which was celebrated every five years and marked by a public speech in his honour, though the emperor was not necessarily present in person. Again, the birthday of the city of Rome was kept every year, and public speeches were often delivered on the occasion.

Both the poetical and the prose panegyrics which have survived are valuable sources of information for the history of their period. The specific allusions introduced in them to contemporary events, conditions, and persons place us in direct touch with great public affairs as these affect individual cities and communities. Especially interesting are the pictures which we get of the University and town of Autun in the period after its disgrace and eclipse as a result of the rebellion of the Aedui, and of the general disturbances of the latter part of the third century. It is in the anonymous panegyric on the victorious Emperor Constantius,[2] delivered on the first of March 297,[3] that we read of the grateful thanks of the citizens of Autun to their emperor for the rebuilding of their houses and restoration of their temples. Here, too, we are given the information – surely of especial interest to ourselves – that the restorations were carried out by workmen imported from Britain as a result of Constantius's reconquest.[4]

No less interesting is the panegyric of Eumenius of Autun, *Pro Instaurandis Scholis*[5] ('On the Restoration of the Schools'), delivered before the governor of the province in the spring of

---

[1] For the text, see W. Baehrens, *XII Panegyrici Latini*, and a more recent text and French translation by E. Galletier, *Panégyriques Latins*, Vols. I, II (Paris, 1949, 1952).

[2] Baehrens, *XII Panegyrici Latini*, p. 232 ff.; Galletier, *Panégyriques Latins*, p. 71 ff.

[3] See Galletier, op. cit., p. 68.

[4] It has been suggested that these are the workmen who had completed the chief forts of the Saxon Shore under Carausius and who had carried out the later restoration of the Wall under Constantius (Donald Atkinson, 'Classis Britannica', in *Historical Essays in Honour of James Tait* (Manchester, 1933), p. 1 ff.).

[5] Baehrens, p. 248 ff., Galletier, p. 103 ff.

298.[1] The period of victory and of consequent peace had em-
boldened the families of the high nobility to settle once again in
Autun, and under Constantius the public buildings took on
once more their ancient splendour and the statues were re-
erected. We get an interesting reference (caps. 7, 8) to a temple
of Heracles and the Muses which is said to have been erected
in 187 B.C. by M. Fulvius Nobilior, the friend of the poet
Ennius, after his campaign in Aetolia and his victory in Ambracia, because he had learned in Greece that Heracles was a
musagetes. Eumenius tells us (cap. 7) that Nobilior had had the
statues of the whole choir of the nine muses brought from
Ambracia and placed under the protection of Heracles, and he
makes this the text of a tactful request (cap. 8), and at the same
time of graceful thanks, to the emperor who has judged fit to
lend his royal strength and support to the re-establishment of
the ancient splendour of the university, and has thus become,
like Heracles, a champion of the arts, and especially of the art
of rhetoric. But what is the bearing of the passage on Lucian's
story (cf. p. 26) of the picture of the Celtic god Ogmios, god of
poetry, whom the Gauls, he informs us, identify with Heracles?
Does it not suggest that the Hellenized Gauls learnt the
association of Heracles with poetry from the Greeks?

Eumenius has much to tell us, both directly and indirectly,
about this great school, where his grandfather had settled as a
Greek rhetorician, and where he himself was a professor, and,
later in life, tutor to the son of the Emperor Constantius. His
love and respect, even reverence, for its ancient tradition, its
ancient and historic buildings, and for the noble calling of
teacher of the young students within its walls, has nothing of
perfunctory oratory, but rings with the sincerity of a passionate
devotion. It is tempting to linger over his great speech, with its
dignified appeal for imperial financial aid for the work of reconstruction and maintenance. One special detail claims our attention before we pass on to a period nearer to the subject of this
book. I refer to the interesting account which Eumenius gives
us of the great maps of the regions of the world which adorned
the walls of the porticos of the university. These, Eumenius tells
us (caps. 20, 21), the students study each day, and these the
governor of the province has himself recently seen in the course of

[1] Galletier, p. 108.

his tour of inspection of the buildings. Here, declares Eumenius, the students can look upon all the countries of the world, all the seas, all the cities, races, nations, now subjected to the Empire through the valour of the Roman conquerors. Here, in order to make more effective the teaching of the students, who can apprehend more readily what they see than what they are told, the position of all the countries has been depicted, together with their names, their size, and their relative positions, and the courses of all the rivers from source to mouth, all the indentations of the coasts, and wherever the ocean surrounds the land or forces its way into the interior. This map, adds Eumenius, enables the students to follow intelligently the imperial campaigns; and when a sweating envoy arrives with a dispatch, they can immediately ascertain the exact spot where victory has been won – 'the twin rivers of Persia, the parched Libyan deserts, the bend of the arm of the Rhine, the multiple mouths of the Nile . . . , or where, under your dominion, Emperor Constantius, Britain raises her squalid head above forests and waves'.

In the following century, one of the most interesting of the panegyrists is Latinus Pacatus Drepanius, who was a friend of the poet Ausonius, and who is believed to have been an Aquitanian by origin. His surviving speech[1] was delivered in 389 before the whole Roman senate immediately after the death of the usurper Maximus at Aquileia, on the accession of his conqueror and successor Theodosius. It is one of our chief sources of information for the final fate of the Priscillianists, condemned at Trier by Maximus in 386,[2] a subject to which I shall return towards the close of the present chapter. Pacatus, as the official panegyrist of Maximus's enemy Theodosius, naturally stresses the tortures which the Priscillianists were made to suffer, and seeks to discredit Maximus still further by suggesting cupidity as a motive for his action; for the Priscillianists were known to be wealthy, and their estates were perhaps confiscated on the condemnation of the leaders (cf. p. 44). It is a striking fact that immediately after delivering this panegyric on Theodosius, Pacatus was made proconsul of Africa[3] – a most honour-

---

[1] Baehrens, op. cit., p. 89 ff.; Migne, P.L., Vol. XII, 25, 68, col. 504 f.
[2] For this date, usually given as 385, see p. 34, n. 5.
[3] See G. Rauschen, *Jahrbücher der Christlichen Kirche* (Freiburg, 1897), p. 299. Pacatus was proconsul of Africa in 389–390.

able post. I know of no clearer testimony to the enormous value of the panegyrics as propaganda and to the frank recognition of this by the emperors.

It would, of course, be absurd to suppose that poetry, eloquence, and rhetoric were degraded among the Gauls to mere technique or academic accomplishment. In the panegyric of Eumenius referred to above the art and intellect of the speaker have created within the conventional framework a moving and picturesque expression of gratitude and appreciation, accompanied by a passionate, tactful, carefully reasoned appeal. We have to remember also that some of the chief poets of the closing years of classical Latin literature were Gauls by birth. The poet Claudius Rutilius Namatianus, who flourished early in the fifth century, and who has been called the last poet of the Silver Age of classical Latin literature, was a native of southern Gaul. A generation earlier the poet Ausonius, the friend of Symmachus, and tutor to the Emperor Gratian, was born at Bordeaux. His love for his native country breathes through his whole work – in the local allusions of the verses which he composed on his own family; in the series of poems in which he celebrates his teachers and colleagues in the university of Bordeaux; and above all in the itinerary and scene-painting contained in his poem on the river Moselle. And it was to his native land of Gaul that he thankfully returned in old age to pass a contented and dignified retirement on his paternal estate. We shall make a closer study of both these poets in later chapters of the present book.

In the meantime I should like to say something more of the university life in Gaul at a period later than that for which Eumenius furnishes information, and in a different area. I have already mentioned that the centre of intellectual life in Gaul shifted in the fourth century from Autun and Marseilles to Trier and Bordeaux, and that in the time of Ausonius, Bordeaux was the most important seat of learning in the Empire. Himself a Professor of Rhetoric there, Ausonius has left us a series of vignettes of some twenty-five of his colleagues which form a unique personal register and record of the kind of men who constituted the staff of a great fourth-century university.

Among these professors there is one family in particular which is of special interest, both because we are introduced to its members through several generations; and because it is said to trace its origin from a family of Druids in Armorica. The statement is made by Ausonius in more than one passage. It is difficult to know exactly how much weight to attach to the evidence, since Ausonius was no antiquary. But there can be no doubt that the supremacy of rhetoric among the Gauls, especially those of Aquitaine, and their natural aptitude for poetry and eloquence, had been fostered in the past by training such as that which Caesar attributes to the Druids. Moreover the testimony of Ausonius in regard to this family is sober and convincing, and it receives interesting corroboration from other contemporary writers, notably St Jerome, Pacatus the panegyrist, and Sidonius Apollinaris. .

The family in question is first brought before us by Ausonius in connection with the temple of Belenus[1] in the neighbourhood of Bordeaux, in which 'old Phoebicius', the first member of the family of whom we hear, held the position of *aedituus*, or temple priest. Belenus, a native Gaulish god, is associated with warm springs, and he is generally equated with Apollo,[2] especially in his healing capacity. Was he an Æsculapian deity? The number of inscriptions in which he is commemorated would lead us to suppose that his cult was more wide-spread than that of any other Gaulish god.[3] The poet Ausonius, whose youth had been largely spent at Bordeaux, where his father had practised as a doctor, and who was in close touch with the family of this last heathen priest of the local temple to Belenus, has left us some interesting notes on the old priest himself, his descendants, and the nature of their careers and reputations.

In the catalogue or series of brief poems referred to above, the fourth, fifth and sixth are devoted to the descendants of Phoebicius. The first of these poems is addressed to Attius Patera the elder, a famous rhetorician, whom Ausonius saw in his youth when Patera was already an old man. Ausonius refers to Patera's father as 'the old man Phoebicius, who, though the keeper (*aedituus*) of the temple of Belenus, got no profit from

---

[1] The best account of Belenus is that of Ihm in Pauly-Wissowa, *Real-Encyclopädie der Classischen Altertumswissenschaft*, Vol. III, col. 199 ff.

[2] See G. Dottin, *Manuel pour servir à l'Étude de l'Antiquité celtique* (Paris, 1915), p. 314; C. Jullian, *Histoire de la Gaule*, Vol. II (Paris, 1908), p. 124, cf., footnote 2. See also P. Lamprechts, *Contributions à l'Étude des Divinités Celtiques* (Brugge, 1942).

[3] See M.-L. Sjœstedt, *Dieux et Héros des Celtes* (Paris, 1940), p. 22.

it'.[1] Yet he was descended, according to tradition, from the stock of the Druids of Armorica, and obtained a Chair at Bordeaux through his son's help[2]. Perhaps Ausonius is referring here to Attius Patera.

Further, Ausonius also compliments Patera himself, the famous rhetorician and son of Phoebicius, as a man outstanding for his eloquence (*fandi nobilis*), and as a teacher of able rhetoricians (*doctor potentium rhetorum*); and he refers to him as descended from the line of the Druids of Bayeux, and as tracing his ancestry from a family consecrated to the temple of Belenus, hence the names and titles borne by himself and his family, reminiscent of the shrine of Apollo at Delphi:

'You are Patera, so the mystic votaries call the ministers of Apollo. Your father and your brother were named from Phoebus, and your son from Delphi', and he winds up: 'In that time there was none who had so much knowledge as you, such unhesitating and flowing eloquence. . . . You had clarity and melodious speech, and the gift of polished phrasing.'

From all this it is clear that when Phoebicius realized that Christ had superseded Apollo at Bordeaux, he placed his gifts and knowledge of poetry and eloquence at the disposal of the university, where his son, already a famous teacher of rhetoric, obtained for him a similar post as a kind of a pension.

Next, Ausonius celebrates the brilliant but luckless Delphidius, the son of Attius Patera, and himself also a heathen and a famous rhetorician. Ausonius tells us that he was a poet almost from his cradle, beginning in his youth with a Hymn to Jupiter. He composed epics faster than anyone could tell the tale in prose; and Ausonius regrets that Delphidius had not been satisfied to pursue quietly the path of poetry and learning. On the contrary his great intellectual gifts gained him early fame both at home and abroad. His eloquence and literary ability 'outran his judgment'; and his ambition, and perhaps, as Ausonius hints, his personal animus, led him to accept high legal appointments which he had not the qualifications of character and mind to fill with success. He fell under a cloud politically, and though his father's influence saved him from the worst disgrace,

---

[1] The passage recalls Bede's account (Book II, cap. 13) of the speech of the heathen priest Coifi at the Northumbrian Council of King Edwin in 627.

[2] *Commemoratio Professorum Burdigalensium*, 'Poems commemorating the Professors of Bordeaux'. Poem X.

he was forced to earn a living in comparative obscurity as a teacher of rhetoric at Bordeaux. Even here, so Ausonius tells us candidly, his lack of zeal as a teacher was a source of disappointment to the parents of his pupils, till death carried him off in middle age.

It is particularly for his gifts of poetry, his eloquence, and polished facility in language, that Delphidius won universal praise, and for which he was long remembered. Ausonius addresses him as 'facunde, docte, lingua et ingenio celer.'[1]

Pacatus, himself a famous rhetor, and well qualified to judge a distinguished contemporary, speaks of his wife Euchrotia as 'Clari vatis matrona.'[2]

Even in the following century Sidonius Apollinaris refers to the polished literary gifts of Delphidius in the highest terms.[3]

The high intellectual gifts of Attius Patera and Delphidius were fully recognized by no less learned and exacting a critic than St Jerome. In his *Chronica* s.a. 339 we read: 'Patera rhetor Romae gloriosissime docet'; and again in 358: 'Alcimus et Delphidius rhetores in Aquitania florentissime docent.' In St Jerome's letter to the lady Hedibia, who was a younger member of the same family, he refers to both men in terms of the greatest admiration on intellectual grounds. (See p. 35).

The picture of the mercurial and brilliant Delphidius, as we see him through the eyes of his friend and contemporary, Ausonius, can be verified and supplemented from other sources. In 359 he conducted the impeachment of Numerianus, the governor of Gallia Narbonensis, accused of embezzlement before the Emperor Julian. The scene, vividly described by Ammianus Marcellinus, testifies to the vigour of Gaulish eloquence, and illustrates both the impetuous nature of the man, and his lack of judgment – traits which are perhaps in part those of his nation, in part characteristic of his family.

'When he defended himself by denying the charge, and could not be confuted on any particular point, Delphidius, a very vehement speaker (*orator acerrimus*), attacking him vigorously and being exasperated by the lack of evidence (*documentorum inopia percitus*), cried: " ' Where will there be a guilty person to

---

[1] *Prof.* V.
[2] *Panegyric on Theodosius* (cap. 29) ed. Baehrens, p. 114.
[3] *Ep.* V, 10.

C

be found, most Glorious Caesar, if it is enough to deny the charge?" To which Julian wisely made instant reply, "Where will there be an innocent person to be found if accusation alone is needed?"[1]

Ausonius in his youth had known Delphidius at Bordeaux, and had probably been taught by him. The final poem devoted in the *Professores* to this ancient and cultivated family celebrates a man of Ausonius's own generation, Alethius Minervius, the son of Delphidius, whose name still keeps alive the ancient family tradition of Greek culture and the echo of Belenus-Apollo. Alethius, like his forefathers, was a brilliant rhetorician and teacher at Bordeaux, equal in gifts, so we are told, to Delphidius and Patera, but, unlike them, content to teach the youth of his native town. He is said to have made a brilliant marriage, against the wishes of his father,[2] while he himself died untimely without heir.

There is a tone of great sadness in Ausonius's references to Delphidius and his family. He is acutely conscious of the failings of a brilliant man; but he is even more conscious of his great possibilities and the deep tragedy which befell his house. 'It was by God's mercy', he concludes his poem on Delphidius, 'that you were carried off in middle age,[3] spared the pain of your daughter's heresy and the execution of your wife'. The concluding words are a reference to the death of Euchrotia, Delphidius's wife,[4] who, together with their daughter Procula, became involved in the Priscillianist controversy and suffered along with Priscillian himself and his followers. Euchrotia was beheaded in 386[5] and perhaps Procula with her.

It would seem that there were members of the family of Delphidius who did not share in the views, or at least in the fate, of the Priscillianists. I have already referred above to the

---

[1] Ammianus Marcellinus, XVIII, 1.

[2] *Connubium nobile soceris sine pace patris.*

[3] E. C. Babut, who identifies Delphidius with the Helpidius referred to by Sulpicius Severus and St Jerome as jointly responsible, with his wife Agape, for the spread of the Priscillianist heresy in southern Gaul, concludes that Delphidius was born c. 330 and died c. 380 (*Priscillien et le Priscillienisme*, Paris, 1909, p. 87, note 2); but the whole question of both the identity and the dates bristles with difficulties (cf. p. 40, n. 3).

[4] The identity is certain. See Sulpicius Severus, *Chron.* II, 48, 51; and Prosper of Aquitaine, *Chron.*, s.a. 388; Pacatus, *Panegyr. Theod.* (ed. Baehrens), 29.

[5] The date usually given is 385; but cf. Adhémar d'Alès, *Priscillien et l'Espagne Chrétienne à la Fin du IVe Siècle* (Paris, 1936), Appendix II, p. 167 ff., 'La Date de l'Exécution de Trèves'.

lady Hedibia, who was closely related to Attius Patera and probably a daughter of Delphidius. Her education and the quality of her mind were of a high order. She was a valued correspondent of St Jerome on serious subjects of scriptural interpretation and practical morality, both in relation to herself and to her friends. Among other matters, she consulted him as to the right way of life for a childless widow; and c. A.D. 405 or 406 she put down in writing twelve questions on these lines which she confided to a priest called Apodemius, who was about to depart for the Holy Land (cf. p. 15), bidding him deliver them to St Jerome, and bring back to her the answers in either oral or written form. Jerome replied with pleasure, for her family was well known to him, possibly from his sojourn in Gaul during his youth:

'Your ancestors, Patera and Delphidius, one of whom was a teacher of rhetoric at Rome before I was born, while the other in my youth was delighting all the Gauls with his skill in prose and verse – your ancestors, now silently sleeping in the grave, will reproach me justly for having dared to mutter thus to one of their family.[1] Although I concede to them mastery in eloquence and in knowledge of secular learning, deservedly I shall deny them knowledge of the Law of God.'[2]

The family history of the old Gaulish priest which we have been tracing is a strange and enthralling one. A few generations could hardly show more startling changes of faith and of intellectual and spiritual activity on the part of both men and women. Yet nothing could illustrate more convincingly the continuity of provincial life in Gaul, from the heathen temple official of Belenus, turned university teacher in Bordeaux, through three generations of brilliant rhetoricians, to the lady who lost her life for her ideals and her loyalties with a little group of religious intellectuals at Trier. And nothing could demonstrate more convincingly the vitality of Gaulish culture from heathen Druidism and oral poetry, through polished and highly trained Roman rhetorical eloquence, to the quiet literary Biblical learning of the lady Hedibia.

The Priscillianist movement, in which Euchrotia and Procula lost their lives, is perhaps the most interesting phase of thought

[1] *Quod audeam ad stirpem generis sui quippiam mussitare.*
[2] St Jerome, *Ep.* 120 (to Hedibia), Preface.

in western Europe in the late fourth century, and is closely bound up with the lives and activities of some of the leading intellectual personalities of the time. The movement belongs primarily to Spain, and Priscillian himself was consecrated Bishop of Avila; but some important supporters of Priscillian were Gauls, and the final tragedy took place at the court of Maximus at Trier. The origin of the movement, the outline of events, and the exact nature of the tenets of the 'People of Christ', as the Priscillianists called themselves, are still far from clear, and a whole literature has grown up around the subject. Even the exact nature of the charges brought against the sect, and the order in which they were preferred, are still uncertain. They seem to have involved chiefly heresy and magical practices; but it is uncertain how far the charges were proved. St Ambrose exerted himself in an attempt to avert the tragedy, and we shall see in a later chapter that Sulpicius Severus represents St Martin of Tours as pleading their cause before the Emperor Maximus.

Our information about the views attributed to the Priscillianists comes largely from late fourth- and fifth-century allusions in the works of their opponents. From these allusions[1] we are able to trace in some measure the history of the sect after the death of Priscillian, and also the development of its members' views from its early days to its final extinction at the council of Braga in 563. It is believed that the Priscillianists are designated under the name *abstinentes* in ch. 84 of a catalogue of heresies compiled by Philastrius of Brescia in the latter part of the fourth century, and here they are associated with Manicheeans and Gnostics, and described as keeping strange fasts, and holding views derogatory to the physical body and marriage. Sulpicius Severus also accuses them of holding Gnostic views, and by 415 St Jerome is coupling the name of Priscillian with that of Manes.

Our chief sources of contemporary information, however, come from the Spanish priest Orosius, who in 415 presented a

---

[1] They are traced by Adhémar d'Alès, in a series of articles on Priscillian and Priscillianism in *Recherches de Science Religieuse*, Vol. XXIII, p. 5 ff, where the author gives full references and a valuable résumé of the contents of the relevant passages. In 1936 he published the articles with some corrections and three valuable Appendices in book form: *Priscillien et l'Espagne Chrétienne à la Fin du IVe Siècle* (Paris, 1936). My references in the following pages are to this book.

memoir on Priscillianism to St Augustine, which, together with Augustine's reply and his allusions to the sect elsewhere, enables us to form some idea of what was currently reported of the teaching of the sect at this time. We must, however, be on our guard against accepting the views there discussed as necessarily those held by Priscillian and his colleagues in their own day. Their own views seem to have been little known outside their immediate circle, and the secretiveness ascribed to them must have made it still more difficult for a succeeding generation to represent them correctly. Orosius was writing from a hostile camp thirty years later, and Augustine assures us that the order of the sect was *Jura, perjura; secretum prodere noli*: 'Swear, forswear; but do not reveal your mystery.'

Orosius[1] attributes to Priscillian the view that the Trinity is merely a name devoid of personal individuality, for in describing divine unity he declares that 'the Father – Son – Holy Spirit is a single Christ'. The human soul is a part of the divine substance[2] which has been captured by the power of evil and imprisoned in the body. But, Orosius continues, according to the view of Priscillian even the prince of darkness is capable of redemption. Orosius reports some of the strange myths in which Priscillian embodied his teaching, and the still stranger use to which he put Old Testament history. The myths we may presume to have had a figurative significance. We may remind ourselves that Priscillian was extolled by no less a critic than Sulpicius Severus for his eloquence, and that his oratorical powers were outstanding; and he doubtless employed the figurative and symbolical traditional oratorical style of the rhetors in his own teaching. But it is not difficult to recognize certain elements which were identified by Priscillian's contemporaries with Manicheeism. It was also held against the sect that they accepted apocryphal scriptures as being no less authentic than the canon.

We are now in a position to form a more authentic and less bizarre picture of the original views of the sect. In 1885 Schepss discovered at Würzburg, eleven anonymous treatises[3] in a

---

[1] *Ad Aurelium Augustinum Commonitorium de Errore Priscillianistarum et Origenistarum*, Migne *P.L.* Vol. XXXI.
[2] This view aroused strong opposition from Augustine. See *Ep.* 166, 3 (Migne, *P.L.*, Vol. XXXIII, col. 720 ff.).
[3] Published by Georg Schepss, *Priscilliani quae supersunt opera* (Vienna, 1889).

manuscript of the fifth or sixth century, and these documents are now generally accepted as the authentic writings of the Priscillianist party. It was originally believed by Schepss and others that they were the work of Priscillian himself; but in 1913 Dom Morin[1] published an article in which he showed reasons for believing that the writer was more probably Priscillian's colleague and supporter, the Bishop Instantius; and Morin's conclusions have met with general approval.

The documents in question make it clear that the view attributed to the Priscillianists by Orosius in regard to the impersonal nature of the Trinity, and the identity of the Trinity with Christ, was actually held by the sect in the life time of Priscillian and his colleagues.[2] They also suggest a view of the Incarnation which in its attitude to both virginity and human generation is consistent with that of the sect of the *Abstinentes* denounced by Philastrius, and savours of the Manicheeism of which the sect was accused during the lifetime of its founders.[3] Yet the writer, the Bishop Instantius, is certainly not consciously aligning himself with the Manichees. He anathematizes the sect as a whole, and Manes specifically, and in many points of Christian doctrine he shows himself perfectly orthodox.[4] It may be added that the only surviving works which appear to be from the hand of Priscillian himself[5] are the collection of ninety canons in which he summarized and grouped the teaching of St Paul;[6] the prologue which he composed for it; and the fragment of a letter which Orosius has quoted in the *Commonitorium* which he drew up for St Augustine, and which has been referred to above.

Babut has rightly insisted that a distinction is to be made between the original views of the sect, as we have them in these documents, and the views which may have developed in Spain after the death of the leaders.[7] The charges brought against

---

[1] 'Pro Instantio', *Revue Bénédictine*, Vol. XXX (1913), p. 153 ff.

[2] See Adhémar d' Alès, op. cit., p. 78 ff.

[3] ibid.; see especially p. 109 ff.

[4] These points are enumerated, with references to the original documents, ibid., p. 113 f.

[5] ibid., p. 118 ff.

[6] The original text has not come down to us. Our text has been revised and corrected by Bishop Peregrinus. For references, see Adhémar d'Alès, op. cit., p. 118, n. 1.

[7] See E. C. Babut, *Priscillien et le Priscillianisme*, p. 16, note.

Priscillian and his followers during his lifetime were, in brief, heresy, more specifically Manicheeism, magical practices, and immorality; but, as Babut points out, the charges were not brought against them simultaneously. Moreover, it would appear that the charge of immorality in its literal sense was never made against them officially.[1] We will trace briefly the outline of the events, and of the charges levelled at the party until their trial and condemnation at Trier in 386.

It is unlikely that in the inception of the movement Priscillian was himself actually the leader. In the opening phase he was still a layman, and as the movement was associated principally at this time with two Spanish bishops, Instantius and Salvian, we may assume that Priscillian's rôle was originally a subordinate one. The earliest text in which reference is made to Priscillian in a way which seems to represent him as the head of the sect is that of Jerome's *De Viris Illustribus*,[2] which dates from 392; but already at the time of the first specific indictment, when, in 381 and 382, he and his immediate followers journeyed to Rome to plead their cause before Pope Damasus, Priscillian seems to have become the recognized leader. Eventually he was consecrated Bishop of Avila in Spain.

It is interesting therefore, to turn to the portrait of Priscillian left us[3] by Sulpicius Severus, a contemporary who may well have had an excellent opportunity of observing the Priscillianists during their week's sojourn in the neighbourhood of Elusa (mod. Eause), Sulpicius's own home (cf. p. 92), and who has left us our fullest contemporary information about the history of the group. He describes Priscillian as 'of noble rank, extremely wealthy, ardent, restless, eloquent, very learned and well-read, very ready in discussion and debate. He would have been happy had he not corrupted a splendid intellect with perverted activities. One could see much good in both his mind and body. He could endure long vigils, could bear hunger and thirst, was in no way desirous of possessions and most sparing of display; but deluded withal, and excessively inflated with

[1] See R. P. E. Suys, 'La Sentence contre Priscillien', *Revue d'Histoire ecclésiastique*, Vol. XXI (1925), p. 534 f. – an important article, which deals with the legal aspect of the question.

[2] St Jerome, *De. Vir. Illustr.* 122, 123.

[3] *Sulpicii Severi Libri qui supersunt*, *Chronica* II, 46, edited by C. Halm (Vienna, 1866).

secular knowledge. It was even believed that he had practised magic arts (*magicas artes*) from the time of his youth.'

Whatever the origin and true nature of the movement, the persecution of the members began by the action taken by Bishop Hyginus of Cordova, who drew the attention of his fellow Bishop, Hydacius of Emerita, or Merida, to the little Society of the 'People of Christ', as they came to call themselves. Hyginus withdrew his accusations later and remained loyal to the group to the end; but the fire had been kindled. Hydacius was inexorable, and was joined in the attack by his suffragan Bishop, Ithacius of Ossonoba, whose zeal against the party even exceeded that of Hydacius himself. The matter eventually appears to have come in some form or other before a council of bishops of Spain and Aquitaine, which was summoned at Saragossa in 380 to consider and to deprecate the extreme asceticism of the so-called *Abstinentes*, and more particularly those affected by Gnostic and Manichee views. Among the bishops who were present, we notice with interest Delphinus, the Bishop of Bordeaux and life-long friend of St Paulinus of Nola.

It is difficult to know what actually took place at this council.[1] Sulpicus Severus, our fullest contemporary authority, tells us[2] that the Priscillianists did not dare to present themselves, but that in their absence the sentence of excommunication was pronounced against two bishops, Instantius and Salvian, and two laymen, Priscillian and a certain Helpidius.[3] Ithacius, Bishop of Ossonoba in Lusitania (then a part of Hispania, but now in Portugal) was authorized to make public the notice of the sentence. On the other hand the second of the Priscillianist treatises, which bears the title *Liber ad Damasum Episcopum*, claims that no sentence of excommunication was pronounced. As this treatise is doubtless the appeal which the Priscillianists had composed to lay before Damasus in the hope of establishing their orthodoxy, it carries great weight in a matter with which Damasus himself must have been well acquainted.

---

[1] For a discussion of the proceedings of the Council, and of the conflicting accounts which have come down to us, see Adhémar d'Alès, op. cit., p. 36 ff.

[2] *Chronica* II, 47.

[3] Babut (op. cit., p. 98) seeks to identify Helpidius and his wife Agape with Delphidius, the famous orator of Bordeaux, and his wife Euchrotia (cf., p. 34). His arguments have not been regarded as convincing; but he may nevertheless be right.

Almost immediately after the Council of Saragossa, Instantius and Salvian consecrated Priscillian Bishop of Avila;[1] but an appeal was made by Hydacius and Ithacius to the Emperor Gratian, who granted a decree forbidding the Priscillianists to enter the churches or the towns. Instantius, Salvian and Priscillian set out for Rome, probably towards the close of 381, intending to lay their cause before Pope Damasus. During their passage through Aquitaine, Bishop Delphinus refused them admission to Bordeaux,[2] but at Elusa (the modern *Eause*) many joined their cause, and they were entertained by Euchrotia, the wife of the orator Delphidius, and she, together with her daughter Procula, decided to proceed with them to Italy. Euchrotia was evidently wealthy, and it would no doubt be expected that the influence of her husband's family, as one of famous orators, would be considerable at the court, whither they betook themselves on their arrival in Italy. Gratian, however, let time pass without admitting them, and the party went on to Rome, and while they were in Rome Salvian died. The *Liber ad Damasum Episcopum*, the second of the Priscillianist documents already referred to, was doubtless composed to be laid before Pope Damasus on this occasion;[3] but Damasus refused them audience and on their return journey through Milan an attempt to obtain access to Ambrose proved equally fruitless. They were, however, fortunate in procuring a favourable response at the court from Macedonius, the Master of Offices, and were restored to their sees on their return to Spain, perhaps in 382.

Meanwhile proceedings were taken against Ithacius on the technical charge of 'disturbing the peace of the churches' (*perturbatio ecclesiarum*), and he, seeing his danger, fled to Gaul and took refuge at Trier, where he was well received by Britto, the bishop of the town and the primate of the Gaulish church, as well as by Gregorius the Prefect, who ordered the arrest of the Priscillianists. The Emperor Gratian, on representations from

[1] In the *Liber ad Damasum Episcopum* no mention is made of this elevation of Priscillian to the episcopate. His ordination was perhaps irregular. (Adhémar d'Alès op. cit., p. 42, n. 1).

[2] Sulpicius Severus, *Chron.* II, 48. Cf. also Babut, *Concile de Turin* (Paris, 1904), p. 38 f. In view of Gratian's decree Delphinus had in any case no choice.

[3] For a discussion of the authorship, see Dom Morin, loc. cit.; cf. also Adhémar d'Alès, op. cit., p. 55 ff. The latter regards the actual composition as the work of Instantius, doubtless with the full co-operation of Priscillian.

Macedonius, intervened, and ordered the arrest of Ithacius; but the sudden accession to power of Maximus in 383 gave Ithacius a chance to appeal to the new emperor, himself a Spaniard by origin, to free the church in Spain from the 'Manicheeans', by which term he designated the Priscillianists.

A council was accordingly convened at Bordeaux in 384, and Instantius was forthwith deposed from his see. It is now believed that the first of the Priscillianist treatises discovered by Schepss, which bears the title *Liber Apologeticus*, and which was formerly thought to be the work of Priscillian himself, was composed by Instantius to be read before the bishops on this occasion. Priscillian, for some reason,[1] does not appear to have pleaded before this council of bishops, and appealed directly to the Emperor. Ithacius and Hydacius, anxious, no doubt, to justify themselves in the eyes of the Church for arraigning two of their fellow bishops before a civil court, succeeded in getting a double charge of magical practices and immorality[2] preferred against them, and Priscillian and his companions were summoned to Trier to stand their trial in a civil court before the Prefect Evodius in the winter of 384 to 385. The party were condemned. In a letter from Maximus to Pope Siricius the usurping emperor claims that the Priscillianists were charged

---

[1] See Adhémar d'Alès, op. cit., p. 49 ff.

[2] Cf., however, p. 39, n. 1. The immorality with which they were charged was that they held nocturnal gatherings with immoral women in a state of nudity for the purpose of prayer. The expression used by Sulpicius, *nudum orare solitum*, means that Priscillian prayed in a state of nudity. This, as Dom Leclercq observes, (*L'Espagne Chrétienne*, Paris, 1906, p. 183) is to be regarded as 'une bizarrerie répréhensible', but, he adds quaintly, 'on n'avait qu'à le laisser seul'. Babut (op. cit., p. 179, n. 2) considers that the words in question can only be understood as having reference to those immediately preceding in Severus' text – *nocturnos feminarum conventus* – and he refers to Jerome, *Ep.* 123 (3) where the Priscillianists are represented as shutting themselves up with women, and as justifying their sinful embraces by quoting Virgil, *Georgics* ii, 325–7. Babut refers also to Ithacius as having stated in regard to their conventicles that their prayers ended *inter coitum amplexusque*. Finally he refers to a passage in St Augustine (*De Natura Boni* XLVII) written after 400, which doubtless contains a reference to this charge of immorality preferred against Priscillian. Duchesne regards the practices here referred to as certain forms of *ascesis*. In this connection the important contribution of Suys to the legal aspect of the charges against Priscillian is relevant. Suys claims (loc. cit., p. 534 f.) that the charges made at the trial were not against the morals of the Priscillianists, and that the *doctrinae obscenae*, which appears as the first of these charges, is simply a rhetorical term for 'magic'. Sulpicius Severus (*Chron.* II, 48) mentions a scandal current at the time when the party passed through Aquitaine, to the effect that Priscillian had been guilty of undue intimacy with Procula, the daughter of Euchrotia and Delphidius; but no charge was ever made officially against Priscillian to this effect, even by his enemies, and I think we may safely dismiss it as a vulgar rumour.

and condemned as *Manichaei* and *malefici*, that is to say on both ecclesiastical and civil charges.

The members of the Priscillianist party condemned at the trial were Priscillian himself, and the Bishop Instantius, the lady Euchrotia, the poet Latronian, and two clerks, Armenius and Felicissimus.[1] Despite the intervention of St Ambrose, who was present at Trier early in 385 on an embassy from the Emperor Theodosius, Instantius was banished to the Scilly Isles, and the rest of the Priscillianists were decapitated. Others were also accused and condemned later, some to death, others to confiscation and deportation. One of these, the literary man Tiberian, was banished, like Instantius, to the Scilly Isles; but St Jerome tells us that after the death of his friends Tiberian was overcome by the 'tedium of exile' (*taedio victus exsilii*). The orator Latinus Pacatus Drepanius, in his panegyric on Theodosius,[2] pronounced before the Roman senate in 389, makes detailed reference to the indignities and horrible execution of the victims in a moving passage which is the requiem of the little group.

There can be no doubt that the animus against the Priscillianists was inspired in part by a genuine conviction among the ecclesiastics of the time that the rising tide of asceticism, of which this movement was only one facet, was a threat to the unity of the Church, as being too individualistic and free from ecclesiastical control. Latinus Pacatus Drepanius, to whom Ausonius dedicates three poems,[3] and who may very well have known the Priscillianists personally, hints that their fault was that 'they were too religious, and tended to carry their religious exercises too far'.[4] But there are other factors in the Priscillianist tragedy. It is generally agreed that the usurping Emperor Maximus was extremely anxious to stand well with the Church, and to this end he had had himself baptized before he assumed the purple. His anxiety to commend to the Church his zeal for the Faith is shown very clearly in his letter to Pope Siricius[5] on the occasion of the trial and condemnation of the Priscillianists.

---

[1] St Jerome (*De Vir. Illustr.* 122) also mentions one Julianus as having been executed with them.
[2] G. Baehrens *XII Panegyrici Latini*, p. 89 ff.
[3] Viz. the *Eclogues*, the *Technopaegnion*, and the *Ludus Septem Sapientum*.
[4] *Nimia religio et diligentius culta divinitas*. Baehrens, *XII Panegyrici Latini*, p. 114.
[5] Migne, *P.L.*, Vol. XIII, col. 592.

Perhaps an even more important element in the situation was Maximus's serious need of funds. The Priscillianists were known to be wealthy. The cupidity of both Maximus and Hydacius and his party is stressed by the orator Pacatus. Sulpicius Severus also hints at cupidity as an element in the animus of the accusations.[1] We are still very much in the dark about the facts.

The outcome of the attack has shocked and distressed all who have followed the fortunes of the little group down to our own day. In order to understand the atmosphere in which the tragedy took place, and the background of conflicting convictions and emotions in fourth-century thought, we have to recall the crisis through which Christianity was passing. The persecutions of the Church were only recently over. Manicheeism was still flourishing, to say nothing of other heresies. Many of the most intellectual members of society were still heathen. The future hope for the Church lay in purity of doctrine and unity. Both were threatened on every side, and zeal for the purity of doctrine is an important element in the animus of Priscillian's enemies.

Perhaps the most serious threat of all to Christianity came from those emperors who, while supporting the Christian Church, sought to extend their influence by interfering in ecclesiastical affairs. It is to be suspected that this was the chief danger which Ambrose saw in the appeal of the bishop Ithacius to Maximus for a sentence of death against Priscillian, and which shocked him[2] even more profoundly than the merciless attitude of one bishop towards another, and induced him to attempt intervention. Ambrose had come to Trier on a royal embassy, and he was dismissed by Maximus for his attitude to the Priscillianist trial. As the most responsible and statesman-like ecclesiastic in the Church, Ambrose would hardly have risked the rebuff of the new emperor either from motives of disapprobation of Ithacius, or even from an outraged sense of justice on behalf of the accused, had he not realized that the situation threatened danger to the integrity of ecclesiastical liberty and prerogative.

The Priscillianists were the first people to suffer 'martyrdom'

---

[1] *Chronica* II, 46.
[2] *Ep.* 126 (3) (Migne, *P.L.*, Vol. XVI, col. 1042 f.).

at the hands of the Church, and the proceedings against them have been somewhat loosely styled the 'First Inquisition'. The persecution and final sentence seem to have had the effect of spreading rather than allaying the Priscillianist cause. After the downfall of Maximus in 388 a reaction set in, and the matter was widely discussed.[1] Ithacius was deprived of his see and Hydacius was exiled. There can be no doubt that at least in the Iberian Peninsula the numbers of adherents increased very considerably. I have followed the cause only during the crucial period of the rise and fall of Priscillian himself, hardly more than five short years, from c. 380–386. But the movement continued to spread in the Iberian Peninsula, and lasted till well into the second half of the following century, only finally fading out after the Synod of Braga in 563.

Whatever the origin and precise views of the Priscillianists, there can be no doubt that they were a devoted and ascetic group of intellectual people – a little *intelligentsia*. Priscillian himself was, by the general agreement of his contemporaries, a very intelligent and learned man, of great oratorical powers, and one cannot fail to be impressed by the number of educated men – bishops, clerks, orators and poets – among the small number of Priscillianist names which have come down to us. The poet Latronian is described by St Jerome as of great learning, and in his skill in metre comparable to the ancients.[2] Tiberian also was a literary man of some distinction, though his inflated literary style is referred to in disparaging terms by St Jerome.[3] The panegyric poet Pacatus, who belonged to southern Gaul, did not hesitate, as we have just seen, to use a state occasion to sing the praises of the little group before the new emperor. Urbica of Bordeaux, said to have been stoned outside the city, was almost certainly a daughter or near relative of the poet and orator Urbicus, celebrated by Ausonius among the professors of his university. Euchrotia herself is referred to by the orator Pacatus as the wife of a famous poet; and she and her daughter Procula link the group still more closely with Euchrotia's husband, the celebrated orator and poet Delphidius, and the ancient Druidical family of the temple

---

[1] *Vehementior facta est*, i.e. *quaestio* (Ambrose, *Ep.* 26, Migne, XVI, col. 1042).

[2] *Valde eruditus et in metrico opere veteribus comparandus* (*De Vir. Illustr.* 122).

[3] St Jerome speaks of the style of an *Apologia* which he wrote as *tumenti compositoque sermone*. Op. cit. 123.

of Belenus. It is surely rare in any period of history to meet so many poets, orators, and highly educated and literary men carrying their ideals to such extremities – enduring confiscations, exile, and death – and facing the end with such gallant courage. Poetry and eloquence in Gaul and Spain produced great idealists.

CHAPTER II

Ausonius and his Circle

In the first chapter attention was focused on a particular family in Bordeaux, who claimed to be descended from the Druids of Armorica, and who provided some of the most brilliant teachers of rhetoric at Bordeaux. The present chapter deals with the poet Ausonius, the friend and contemporary of these rhetoricians, and himself a 'schoolmaster to royalty'. He is the most significant figure in the intellectual life of the close of the Roman era in Gaul, and as we study his work we shall be able to trace the important place held by rhetoric in the Roman educational system generally, and the extent to which it permeates all that Ausonius wrote.[1]

The poet has given us a brief autobiography in the little poem (*Ausonius Lectori Salutem*) which usually stands first among his *Opuscula* in the printed editions of his works;[2] and much personal matter is contained in the two series of brief poems on his family entitled the *Parentalia*, and the *Domestica*, which together constitute a little family history and genealogy.

He was born c. 310 at Bordeaux, where his father practised as a doctor, and where his early education seems to have begun. But from about the age of ten he was educated under the supervision of his maternal uncle, Aemilius Magnus Arborius, a professor of Toulouse, of whom I shall have more to say later. About the year 328 he returned to Bordeaux, and continued his studies there under various professors of rhetoric, one of whom was probably the Delphidius whose family history has

---

[1] Sir Samuel Dill has an admirable general account of Ausonius and his circle in *Roman Society in the Last Century of the Western Empire* (second edition, reprinted, London, 1933). Dill's work is free from the patronizing tone which disfigures many studies of Ausonius.

[2] The chief edition of the works of Ausonius is that of K. Schenkl (Berlin, 1883), which contains a valuable introduction on the manuscript tradition, and some biographical information. R. Peiper's edition (Leipzig, 1886) is also valuable. A useful and handy edition, with an English translation, is that of H. G. Evelyn White (Loeb Classical Library, 1929), two volumes. For the convenience of the reader I have given references to White's edition; but I have consulted Peiper's text and also that of Schenkl throughout.

already been traced. Ausonius himself became a teacher of grammar in Bordeaux, and later a professor of rhetoric, and for about thirty years he lived on in his native place, where he married the daughter of one of the leading citizens.

About 364 he was appointed a tutor to the young Gratian, the future emperor, a post which he held for some ten years. In 368–9 he and his royal pupil accompanied Valentinian I in his expedition against the Germans. It was at the court of Valentinian on the Rhine that he formed his long friendship with the great Roman senator Symmachus – a friendship to which we owe some of the most interesting letters of the period. When in 375 Gratian ascended the throne, the advance of Ausonius and his family was rapid, and in 378 he was made prefect of the Gauls. Finally in 379 he attained to the consulship. At the close of the same year he retired to his family estate near Bordeaux, the 'nest of his old age' as he calls it, where the closing years of his life were passed in serene happiness and amid great wealth as a country gentleman, busy with his estate and his literary work, and in entertaining his friends. He probably died in 393 or 394,[1] since we have no literary works from him which can safely be dated later than this. He had raised the status of his own family from that of the professional class and the bourgeoisie to that of a grand seigneur,[2] and his immediate relatives and descendants filled some of the most important posts in the Empire.

Ausonius loved to write of his own relatives, and in his *Parentalia* he has recalled by his title the ancient festival appointed to commemorate departed relatives with offerings. The poem is our most intimate and delightful picture of a Gallo-Roman family of the close of the Empire. Of his father's parents he has left us no names, but we know that the poet inherited the family estate from his paternal great-grandfather, and that it was situated in the country at some little distance from Bordeaux, with the River Garonne hard by, so that the poet could

[1] See Peiper's edition, p. CXIII; cf. O. Seeck, *Symmachus* (Berlin, 1883), Introduction, p. LXXX, where valuable information relating to Ausonius is given.
[2] He is said to have had at least three extensive estates. See C. Jullian, *Histoire de Bordeaux* (Bordeaux, 1895), p. 59; and for other properties, including Saintes, see ibid., 'Ausone et son Temps', *Revue Historique*, Vol. XLVIII (1892), p. 29; cf. also ibid., Vol. XLVII, p. 263. According to the same author the whole of Bordeaux was owned by a very small number of people. One of these was probably Paulinus of Nola, from whom the hill Puy-Paulin in the city takes its name.

visit the town in his boat. His father, who had been born at
Bazas, some distance up the same river, had settled in Bordeaux,
where he held the position of a senator. There his skill as a
physician and his kindness to the poor earned him the respect
and love of all, and not least of Ausonius himself, who composed
verses full of warm affection and regard on his death. He speaks
also with deep respect of his father's sister, Julia Cataphronia,
who was vowed to virginity. Of his father's brother, Clemens
Contemtus, or more probably Contentus, he gives us the interesting note that he had been a man of wealth who had died at
Richborough (*Rutupiae*) in Britain.

His mother's family is more fully portrayed, and of great
interest. His own mother, Aemilia Aeonia, was a native of
Aquae Tarbellicae, the modern Dax, on the Adour, near the
Spanish border. The place-name suggests medicinal springs.
Her father, Caecilius Argicius[1] Arborius, was originally from
the territory of the Aedui, deriving his name from his Aeduan
ancestors, and his blood from noble families of the Aedui and of
the provinces of Lyons and of Vienne. He came from the town
of Autun, both he and his father, Argicius, having been pro-
scribed after the insurrection of the Aedui under Victorinus
and the two Tetrici; and it was during his exile in the neighbourhood of Dax that Arborius married the poet's grandmother, Aemilia Corinthia Maura, a high-born lady without
fortune. The nick-name Maura (a 'Moor') is said to have been
given to her by her girl friends because of her dark colour.

We are told something of the intellectual pursuits of old
Arborius (*Parentalia IV*). He was knowledgeable in the measures
of the heavens (*caeli numeros*) and the stars which govern human
destiny; but he pursued his studies surreptitiously (*dissimulan-
ter*). The old man is said to have been aware of the outline
(*formula*) of the fate of his grandson Ausonius, which he kept
hidden in sealed tablets. He seems to have been something of
an astrologer and scientist according to old-world Gaulish
lights; but indeed astrology, though prohibited by law, was
practised by many important people of the time, for example,
the orator Claudius Mamertinus, and Macrobius.

The early youth of Ausonius seems to have been spent, not in

---

[1] The form is not quite certain. See A. Dauzat, *La Toponymie française* (Paris,
1939), p. 131 ff.

D

the house of his parents, but in that of his maternal grandmother, the lady Aemilia Maura. The household consisted
largely of women of strong character and intelligence, and
some measure of independence. Ausonius ascribes the major
part of his upbringing to his aunt, Aemilia Hilaria. 'She', he
says, 'was to me in the position of a mother' (*vice matris*), and he
recalls her 'with a son's affection', while her own sister Aemilia
Dryadia, who had been left a widow young, is also spoken of as
almost a mother to him.

Aemilia Hilaria is a particularly interesting person. She is
said to have always hated being a woman, and, like his father's
sister, Julia Cataphronia, she had vowed herself to perpetual
virginity[1] and occupied herself in science like a man.[2] Even in
her cradle she was so like a gay little boy that instead of being
called by her true name, Hilaria, she was nick-named Hilarius.
Her devotion to medicine, taken together with that of
Ausonius's father and of his own brother Avitianus (*Par.*
XIII), suggests that it was perhaps the common tradition of
medicine which first brought the two families together.

The uncle, Aemilius Magnus Arborius, to whom Ausonius
attributes 'in infancy, boyhood, youth, and manhood' his
whole education, was the brother of his boyish aunt Hilaria. He
is spoken of as in close sympathy with the poet's father, and as
having been to Ausonius almost a father and mother combined.
He wore the academic robe of Toulouse, and in addition to his
excellence as a rhetorician he must have been a fine teacher,
for he was made tutor to one of the sons of the Emperor Constantine at Constantinople c. 328, and Ausonius is proud to
reflect that this learned and eloquent[3] uncle had looked upon
him as an apt pupil. The portrait of Arborius illustrates the
extent to which the eloquence and intellectual gifts of the educated Gauls were appreciated in the highest circles in the
Empire.

It will have been noticed that the family nomenclature is
unusual and interesting. The name *Ausonius* has been thought
to be of Gaulish origin,[4] though Greek has also been suggested.[5]

---

[1] *Feminei sexus odium tibi semper* (*Par.* VI).
[2] *More virum medicis artibus experiens* (ibid.).
[3] *Doctus, facundus, tu celer* (ibid. III).
[4] See Jullian, 'Ausone et son Temps', *Revue Historique*, Vol. XLVIII, p. 244.
[5] Holder, *Sprachschatz*, s.v.

Argicius, and *Megentira*[1] would seem to be Gaulish, and perhaps also *Aeonia*. *Maura* is doubtless a 'Moor'. The name *Arborius*, which recurs repeatedly in the family, is extremely rare elsewhere. It has been suggested that the choice of names betokens a bourgeois milieu.[2]

The poem by which Ausonius is best known today is the *Mosella*, composed about the year 370 or 371. It is a little masterpiece of descriptive poetry, in which the poet enumerates with charming intimacy the various features of the river and its occupants, the exact appearance, behaviour, and habits of each fish, and its qualities as food; the details of the under-water world in motion, and its flora; the play of light and shade revealing the varied character of its bed. We see the villas on its banks, the countryside through which it flows, and the daily life of nobles and peasants, of men and boys and children on its banks. The whole conveys an idyllic picture which undoubtedly owes something to the Alexandrines,[3] but is predominantly Gaulish in its setting and its local colour. Even the principal rivers of Gaul are enumerated. There can be little doubt that the poem was composed as a compliment to Valentinian, to be read primarily by the people of Gaul, whose frontiers he had made safer in the war against the Germans. The purpose of the poem was to inspire the Gauls with confidence in the renewed peace and security.[4]

There is a more personal poem, the *Ephemeris*, 'The Daily Round', which is nevertheless still something of a catalogue. Unfortunately it is incomplete, though the beginning and the end have been preserved. We hear the poet rousing the sleepy slave boy, calling for his sandals and his clothes, and for water to wash, and ordering the chapel to be made ready for morning prayers. His own prayer follows – a devout and dignified, indeed a beautiful little poem in hexameters – after which he briskly begins another little poem with the words: 'Now God has been prayed to enough'[5], and after

---

[1] 'From *Maginti*' (Holder).   [2] On this subject, see Seeck, *Symmachus*, p. clxxiv.
[3] For further references to literary itineraries, see Hosius, 'Die literarische Stellung von Ausons Mosellied', *Philologus*, Bd. LXXXI (1925–6), p. 193. Hosius emphasises the scarcity of strictly local features in the *Mosella*, and the literary debt of Ausonius to classical writers. Cf. also for this debt F. Marx, 'Ausonius und die Mosella', *Bonner Jahrbücher*, CXX (1911), p. 9 f.
[4] See F. Marx, *Rheinisches Museum*, Vol. LXXX (1931), p. 368 f.
[5] *Satis precum datum deo* (*Ephemeris* IV: *Egressio*).

adding apologetically the words 'though in fact we can never pray enough', he calls for his morning coat with the intention of going forth to invite friends for lunch, first giving careful orders to his cook to ensure that the dishes shall be well seasoned and savoury:

'Shake your simmering pots and turn them about in your hands and make a quick dip with your fingers into the hot broth, and then give them a few licks with your wet tongue.'[1]

Unfortunately the break comes at this point, and we gather that his literary work is relegated to the evening, for when the text is resumed, the poet is addressing a highly complimentary speech to his stenographer who is writing with great efficiency to his dictation on folding tablets spread with wax. The poem closes with a complete repertoire of the nightmares to which he claims to be subject, some at least of which are of literary origin.

Ausonius had a strong leaning towards catalogue poetry, of which he has left us a considerable quantity in a great variety of metres. Work of this kind is essentially educational in purpose, and a typical example is the *Technopaegnion*, appropriately addressed to the rhetor Pacatus (cf. p. 33 ff.) and consisting of a series of mnemonic verses on such subjects as lists of gods, lists of rhetorical tags in the form of monosyllabic line endings, lists of articles of food, of the parts of the body – each with its appropriate characteristic or function attached. Many of these brief definitive or descriptive tags might appropriately serve as answers to hypothetical riddles, and indeed one group entitled *Per Interrogationem et Responsionem* is virtually a riddle sequence. The work is typical of a wide-spread class of descriptive and semi-didactic poetry which is well known to students of Celtic and Teutonic poetry from the Dark Ages, and which has survived to the present day in Russia in the oral ritual poetry associated with weddings and other popular ceremonial occasions.

Of more intrinsic interest are the catalogue sequences entitled *Domestica* and *Parentalia*, which have already been discussed, and the *Commemoratio Professorum Burdigalensium* ('Poems commemorating the Professors of Bordeaux'), a kind of residents' list of the university staff, with testimonials appended to each entry. All his catalogue poems consist like these of a series of

[1] ibid., VI.

brief interrelated verses on interrelated subjects. His themes are *Epitaphs* on the heroes who took part in the Trojan War and on other heroes of more immediate and ephemeral interest; little poems on the *Seven Sages*; *Eclogues* on various subjects of antiquarian learning, such as the *Toils of Hercules* – a singular little poem in which each poem is devoted to a 'toil'.

A particularly interesting little series is the *Ordo Urbium Nobilium*, which gives us glimpses into the cities of Ausonius's own time. We see Carthage, 'hardly a step lower than Constantinople'; Trier, then a royal residence, which 'feeds, clothes, and arms the forces of the Empire'; Milan, so furnished with stately Roman buildings that even her close association with Rome cannot put her in the shade. Arles is now 'the little Rome of Gaul'; Toulouse, his 'foster mother', has a great cordon of walls, yet a population too numerous to be contained within their limits; Narbonne has a population whose mixed speech and dress show it to be largely composed of foreign merchants. Finally there is his own city of Bordeaux, with her pleasant climate and smiling plains, her Roman lay-out,[1] her deep marble fountain, with its gushing water and sacred Gaulish dedication.

The prosaic nature of many of Ausonius's themes, and his love of catalogues and classification, have often been made a subject of raillery, and no doubt rightly, by those who demand inspired themes. But his work should perhaps be judged, not so much by the absence of lofty subjects as by the way in which he brings his poetical talent to what is essentially educational matter. His is the poetry of the life-long teacher, tutor, and professor. The little vignettes which he gives us of the famous cities are derived from the kind of catalogues which were doubtless in vogue as oral geography lessons; and the *Eclogues* and the little poem on the *Labours of Hercules* are a type with which we are all familiar from the schoolroom. It is easy to see the value of such mnemonics for educational purposes at a time when books were relatively rare, and it is to the credit of Ausonius as a teacher that he makes them so engaging. The tutor to an emperor must learn to make knowledge attractive.

Catalogue poetry was, of course, not new. It is as old as Hesiod. Many Latin poets had made use of it, and it continued

[1] See C. Jullian, *Histoire de Bordeaux*, p. 49.

to form an important element in Roman education till the Roman schools were finally closed. Moreover, knowledge of the metrical art, and skill in metrical technique, in classical diction, allusion, and figures of speech, were among the most important subjects of Roman education, and proficiency in these subjects constituted the most essential qualifications for a professor of rhetoric. What strikes us as new and individual in the work of Ausonius is the extent to which he made use of technique as an actual subject of poetry. It is as if a wood carver were to cover the surface of his object with beautifully carved representations of his mallet and chisels, his bench, his clamp, and even himself and his companions, clad in aprons, and making the chips fly. It is only the compass and quantity of the catalogue poetry of Ausonius which causes surprise.

We have seen that in the time of Ausonius the art of oratory and the teaching of rhetoric were mainly in the hands of the Gauls, and that it was because of the proficiency of the Gauls in rhetoric that the education of the young Roman nobility was largely in their hands. Of these Gaulish teachers of rhetoric Ausonius is the most illustrious example, and it would seem probable that in this, as in so much else, he owed much to his Gaulish upbringing, in addition to what he would have derived from the universal Roman system of education. His poetry marks a new phase in its love of his native district and his home, his devotion to, and passionate interest in, his own parents and older relatives, and his native Gaulish countryside. It is not impossible that the ancient traditional Gaulish oral poetry, once so highly cultivated by the Druids, has left some traces on the poetry of Ausonius, more especially in its general tendency to classification, and the nature of his subjects. The *Parentalia* reflects the interest in genealogy and brief personal reminiscence characteristic of people with an advanced oral tradition, but with little, or only recent knowledge of letters. We have seen that the *Mosella*, behind its charm of imagery and serene love of quiet cultivated nature, shows this same habit of classification. Indeed it has much in common with medieval Irish and Welsh descriptive catalogue poetry and prose, and especially the later Irish bardic poems on the River Shannon.[1] The

[1] See the translations by O. Bergin, 'Bardic Poetry', *Journal of the Ivernian Society*, Vol. V (1912–13), p. 210 ff.

Irish, like the Gauls, regarded the springs from which their
great rivers derive their sources as sanctuaries, and their
medieval poems celebrate the ancient rivalry of the springs at
the sources of the Shannon and the Boyne, each personified as
a goddess.

There is a certain element of provincialism, almost of paro-
chialism, in the work of Ausonius. It shows itself, not so much
—in his choice of subject and his love of his own home and
countryside, as in his excessive appreciation of the second-rate
literary work of his own friends. And combined with this
provincial complacency, and perhaps springing directly from
it, there breathes throughout his work an unruffled serenity,
untroubled by memories of the disastrous barbarian raids on
Gaul hardly a generation before his own lifetime, or of apprehension of the fate impending for his own family and friends at
their hands a few years hence. Undisturbed by any such mis-
givings he writes of his quiet life on his country estate near
Bordeaux, his journeys in his little boat on the Garonne, and no
hint obtrudes itself[1] that soon his vineyards and his woodlands
will have passed into alien hands, and his own grandson, the
heir to his smiling acres, will be a fugitive, forced to cultivate
a little patch of land with his own hands to keep himself from
starvation.

These lovable but homely qualities are especially characteristic of Ausonius's letters, of which some twenty-five or so are
extant. When the writer speaks of literary matters, as he does to
Symmachus, to his own son Hesperius, or to the grammarian
Ursulus, the reader nods at once. Not so when he writes to his
friends among the Gaulish squirearchy, even when they happen
to be rhetoricians by the way, like Axius Paulus, to whom we
owe six of Ausonius's most charming letters. He writes, in *Ep.* 4,
from a farm near the town of Saintes not far from Bordeaux,
and near the sea, where he has gone to escape from the bustle
and noise of Bordeaux, till the approaching Easter celebrations
make it incumbent on him to return to the city. He urges his
friend to come and join him in a mule-drawn *petorritum*, the
Gaulish 'four-wheeler', or in a three-in-hand, or else on horse-

---

[1] The allusions to freebooters of Bas-Médoc (*Ep.* 14), and to food shortage (*Ep.*
26 and elsewhere) do not necessarily imply any greater irregularities than would
be incidental to country life in south-west Gaul at any time in the ancient world.

back. A further letter (*Ep.* 5) follows which might aptly be called the romance of the oyster, for in it the various types of oysters and their habitat are gravely enumerated and described with the loving care of an old professor, who is yet not too old to poke about among the rocky holes and seaweed and the sandy oyster beds of Médoc within easy reach of his home. But at the request of Axius Paulus he catalogues all other known oyster haunts, even oysters from far Byzantium, or those which the Picts and Caledonians collect along their shores, or those which he has tasted here and there when dining with his friends.

Paulus must still have delayed, for the invitation is repeated (*Ep.* 6), urging him to come quickly by river or road, either by the Garonne, or on 'the beaten gravel of the newly-covered road'.

'For in the first days after holy Easter I long for the sight of my country seat. For I feel a loathing at the sight of the crowds of people, and the sordid jostling at the cross-roads, the narrow lanes swarming, and the broad streets not worth the name because of the dense rabble. A confused noise re-echoes the din of voices: "Stop!" – "Strike!" – "Lead!" – "Look out!" Here is a filthy sow in flight, there a mad dog rushes to attack, there oxen struggling to pull the wagon. It does not help if I take cover in the innermost recesses and shelter of my house. The shouts penetrate through the building. These, and everything else which can vex a man of quiet habits, force me to leave the walled city and seek again quiet rest in the heart of the country and the delights of trifling in earnest; and there you may dispose of your own time as you will, and you have the right to do nothing or whatever you like.'

How modern it all sounds! – and the closing touch of the following letter (*Ep.* 7):

'As soon as I shall get wine carried to Saintes by a two-horse cart, get your ostrich-egg cup, which your steward says was left on your distant farm in your native Bigorre.'[1]

From a later letter (Ep. 10) we gather that Paulus must have interpreted too literally Ausonius's request for a speedy visit, for he seems to have come to grief on the way, and is now invited in more measured terms to join his friend in Saintes:

'Do not make more haste than suits your strength and your

---

[1] In the Department of Hautes-Pyrénées.

age; I shall see you soon enough, provided I see you safe. If you have regained your strength after that unfortunate drive, and if the stiffness has left your limbs . . . be careful, and travel by some light vehicle or leisurely post-horse. Do not be tempted by a chariot[1] or a spirited horse. I warn you to avoid the notorious four-wheeled car with its geldings, and do not drive swift mules.'

One wonders if the friendship with Paulus could have survived this cruel sally. Anyhow there are no more letters.

Ausonius's humour at the expense of his friends is most marked in letters to his strange correspondent 'rustic Theon of Médoc', a 'poetic tiller of the sands'. These letters are the cream of the collection, and give us our only full-length portrait of an unspoilt Gaulish squire of the old school. We may suspect that Ausonius could have given us an even more vivid and telling portrait gallery of the squirearchy than of the Bordeaux professors had he chosen. *Ep.* 14 is a kind of *Ephemeris* – a 'Daily Round' – of his friend Theon, and addresses him as 'ploughing the shore', living in a mean yokel's hovel thatched with reeds, in which his eyes water with the sooty smoke. His occupations are enumerated – trading with clipped coin in tallow and wax, candles, torches, and other means of lighting; rounding up the roving brigands of the countryside, and to such purpose that they are driven to compounding with money to save their lives; stag and boar hunting with his brother – his brother who is not too refined to be above pulling back his breeches unduly far to display the wounds of previous boar hunts. Again he pictures Theon as fishing with net and line, till the whole house is 'crammed with the spoils of the sea-shore' – and again follows a catalogue of the sea-fish which furnish the table at Médoc. But Theon is also a poet, and albeit an indifferent one, this is perhaps the bond between them; for Ausonius concludes playfully:

'You will no longer be able to learn, Theon, and it is not fitting for me, a royal tutor, to teach metres to the common folk.'

The next letter (*Ep.* 15) thanks Theon for a present of thirty oysters, and in a later letter (*Ep.* 16) he offers to forgive him a debt if he visits him at his country house at Lucaniacus:

---

[1] The word used is *petorritum*, the Gaulish four-wheeled carriage, but evidently looked upon by Ausonius as dangerous.

'The south wind of Médoc will send you as you lie under an awning, so that the bulk of so large a body may not be tossed about . . .   You shall find a carriage ready with a team of mules, and soon reach the villa Lucaniacus.'

The last letter (*Ep.* 17) of this whimsical correspondence thanks the imperturbable Theon for a present of apples of gold, but verses of lead.

One wonders if it can have been the oyster trade that took Ausonius's wealthy uncle to Richborough in Kent, where he died. Oysters play a surprisingly large part in Ausonius's correspondence, and Richborough was the place most famous for them in Britain. It is probably from his uncle that he obtained the impression of the Caledonian shore which he gives us in the *Mosella* (lines 68 ff.).

'As the whole shore extends before the Britons of Caledonia, when the tide lays bare green seaweeds and red corals and whitening pearls, the seed of shells – the delights of mankind – and under the rich waves mimic necklaces shadow our elegance; even so beneath the joyous waters of gentle Mosella weeds of varied hue disclose the pebbles scattered among them.'

We owe to this habit of sending little presents of food, accompanied by a gracious letter, some of our freshest natural descriptions in this century. In a letter (*Ep.* 18) to his son Hesperius, Ausonius mentions that he is sending him twenty birds, caught along the wintry hedges, when 'in the dawning light they flew headlong into the net'; and he compares the way in which the thrushes, after growing fat on olives, or grapes, hang entangled in the nets which had floated loosely in the evening like clouds, but had become taut with dew at dawn. He adds to his present some wild duck caught on the neighbouring meres, praising as he does so their lovely crimson legs and the beauty of their plumage.

It is not without reluctance that we leave these glimpses into the life of farmer and peasant in the fishing villages and the hedgerows of southern Aquitaine and return to the schoolroom where a couple of letters (21, 22) introduce us to the poet's little grandson, Ausonius, while the child is still at school. The old man opens tactfully with a reference to the value of holidays, as a respite from the 'sour schoolmaster's sharp voice' – a pleasant touch from one who owed his career to his success in school-mastering. And he urges little Ausonius not to be scared though his master be grim with age, harsh of voice, and given to frowning and outbursts. After all Achilles was not afraid of Chiron who was quite half a horse; so 'You also must have no fear though the school resound with many a flogging.' He is to mock at fear, and not to let the cries of the victims or the whacking of the birch make him afraid to go to school in the morning.

'Your father and mother[1] went through all this, and have soothed with gentle touch my quiet and serene old age.'

He proceeds to give some advice as to the kind of man his grandson should aim at becoming—in short, a literary man, a poet, and a consul like himself; and he concludes with a brief survey of his own school-mastering days, his care for his boys, his methods of dealing with their difficulties and his own, his growing experience, and final triumph. The letter is an intimate little picture of fourth-century school life, not like that which St Augustine gives us, from the point of view of one of the boys, but from that of the master.

Ausonius is perhaps the most representative author of the overlap from the old order to the new in Gaul whose work has survived. The household of his mother's family seems to have been a conservative home of the native Gaulish type, under the management of vigorous and independent women, unmarried, married, and widows, at least one of whom had a professional career of her own. The Druids were still remembered and the poet himself was evidently intimate with a family who claimed to be their immediate descendants. He was perhaps even taught by one of them. His pride in his genealogy and his love of his ancestral home, and of the natural features of his native land, belong rather to the Gaulish country squire than to the Roman citizen.

Ausonius viewed political success and wealth in their true proportions and perspective, and combined with them a deep love of natural ties and the more intimate things of life. Not the least valuable aspect of his poetry is the self-revelation in the wider sense which it offers – the revelation, not only of a genial and noble personality, but also of a family and a milieu. Ausonius has shown us in his poems how the humbler virtues and

---

[1] An interesting ray of light on the education of girls in Roman Gaul.

sterling qualities of the middle classes can produce a great gentleman. His ideals are virtually the same in essence as those of the old Gaulish nobility, to which a classical education has added a love of good literature and a taste for writing, perhaps, we may add, the new knowledge of how to spend one's indoor leisure in the country.

On the other hand Ausonius had definitely crossed the border line into the new world. He is a Christian,[1] and although, in contrast to his more devoted and ascetic pupil, Paulinus, his religion may seem to lack fervour,[2] we have no reason to doubt his sincerity. On the contrary, the religion of Ausonius is much nearer to that of most modern Englishmen in its balance and reserve of emotion than is that of the adherents of the new ascetic movement with whom he has nothing in common and whom he did not understand. Indeed he hardly seems to realize their existence. The religion of Ausonius is perhaps the most attractive feature of this old professor, in its simplicity and its naturalness. His harmonious blend of Christianity and literary culture leaves us speculating as to what might have been the history of the Christian religion in the West if the new wave of asceticism and monasticism from the East had not swept like a tidal wave over the little churches of Gaul in which this cultured old Roman layman quietly attended morning prayers as the simple and obvious opening of the 'daily routine', until, as he quaintly puts it, 'God has been prayed to enough'.

It is, of course, not only the laity who struggled to maintain the ancient Roman balance between culture and religion in

---

[1] We do not know the date of the introduction of Christianity into Bordeaux, or, indeed, into Gaul. The first bishop of Bordeaux known from historical record is Orientalis, in the time of Constantine. It is thought to have been probably in his day that the first Christian church was built, and consecrated to St Étienne outside the south-west angle of the recently constructed town wall (Jullian, *Hist. de Bordeaux*, p. 63).

[2] On the Christianity of Ausonius, see T. R. Glover, *Life and Letters in the Fourth Century* (Cambridge, 1901), p. 109 f., where its perfunctory character is insisted on. Sir Samuel Dill speaks of Ausonius as 'paying a cold and conventional deference to the Christian faith', and refers to his 'doubts about personal immortality' (*Roman Society in the Western Empire*, p. 168). Similar strictures are made by Teuffel, *Hist. Rom. Lit.*, trans. by Warr (London, 1900), Vol. II, p. 369 f. I confess I see no ground for this view. The prayer incorporated in the *Ephemeris* is a strong argument to the contrary, despite its conventional imagery. It is true that Ausonius took no interest in theology or technical religious thought and he may have been far from clear on points of essential doctrine, like many other sincere Christians. They did not happen to interest him. It must still have been much easier to procure editions of classical authors than copies of the Scriptures or Christian writers in the days of Ausonius.

Gaul and Spain. Despite the pioneer work in democracy and
asceticism which is best represented in Gaul by St Martin, and
in the literature of the day by Sulpicius Severus and St Paulinus,
and which was probably inaugurated by St Athanasius during
his sojourn at Trier, the church in Gaul and Spain was still
largely governed by bishops representative of the Roman
tradition. Hosius of Cordova, the confidential adviser and
reputed converter of the Emperor Constantine, must have been
a man of this type. Delphinus, the Bishop of Bordeaux, and
many of his contemporaries in Gaul, were opposed to a movement which seemed to them to be leading away from the
traditional established order and marching towards ecclesiastical anarchy. We shall see that even in the late fifth century
the great Bishop of Auvergne, Sidonius Apollinaris, was more
of a Roman territorial aristocrat than an ascetic or a thinker.
Like Ausonius he was untroubled by the religious movements
of his day, and gave more care to the temporal safety of his
immediate flock and his wider territorial dependents in
Auvergne than to the Pelagian controversy which was still
raging in the Christian Mediterranean world. It was only as a
result of the impact of the Barbarian Invasions that the old
classical habits of thought finally gave way and broke up,
leaving an easy victory for the new movements of thought
from the Greek world, and the East.

Nothing in the work of Ausonius would lead us to suspect
the restless seas of ideas in which the more venturesome
spirits of his day were voyaging. Of the tragedy of the Priscillianists, which was taking place in his immediate circle, we
have a bare mention. He must have been a boy of about
fifteen when the Council of Nicaea was held, but one of the
greatest events in the history of Christianity made no impression on him. His lifetime is exactly contemporary with those of
St Martin of Tours and St Hilary of Poitiers; but neither the
pioneer monastic movement nor the struggle against the state
for ecclesiastical independence seem even to have penetrated
his consciousness. In his lifetime the British Church is becoming
prominent in the Councils and Synods of the Continent, and
Ausonius's contemporary and near neighbour, Sulpicius
Severus, a busy church builder of Aquitaine, is well informed
and keenly interested in the new advent of the Britons into the

continental world of thought. But the tutor to the emperor, the consul and pro-consul, the travelled man of affairs who has held the highest offices in this changing and restless Roman world, remains to the end a quiet scholar, withdrawn from movements of thought and politics, devoted to his ancestral Gaulish estates and his home and to classical literature, and to the culture which he has known and loved all his life.

CHAPTER III

St Paulinus of Nola[1]

MEROPIUS PONTIUS PAULINUS, better known as St Paulinus of Nola, was the younger contemporary and beloved pupil of Ausonius, and in early life his close friend. He belonged by birth, by education, and by his whole social and intellectual background, to Aquitaine, where he spent his life till he was close on forty years of age. About this time he married a Spanish wife Therasia, and there was a brief period, perhaps about four years, during which they lived in Spain. After that they passed together to Nola in Italy where the remainder of their lives was spent. On their way to Italy they seem to have passed through Aquitaine. The link with Aquitaine remained a close one for many years, and Paulinus continued to correspond with his old friends in Bordeaux and Eause till the Barbarian Invasions rendered communication no longer possible.

St Paulinus seems to have been born at Bordeaux,[2] perhaps about 353 or 354 — possibly even earlier.[3] Hebromagus or Eburomagus, the modern Bram near the foot of the northern slope of the eastern Pyrenees, was his customary residence in early life,[4] and here his brother had estates; but Sidonius Apollinaris associates the family chiefly with Burgus in the Pyrenees. Paulinus's own estates, apart from his possessions in

[1] My references to the works of Paulinus are to the edition of G. de Hartel in two volumes: Sancti Pontii Meropii Paulini Nolani, Part I, *Epistulae*; Part II, *Carmina* (Vienna, 1894). I have also given references to Migne, *P.L.*, Vol. LXI. References are given also to Helm, referring to his article on *Paulinus* (9) in Pauly-Wissowa, *Real-Encyclopädie der Classischen Altertumswissenschaft*, col. 233 ff., which contains a recent scholarly account of the saint, and a full bibliography. An important recent work, apparently never completed, but containing valuable information, is that by R. C. Goldschmidt, *Paulinus' Churches at Nola* (Amsterdam, 1940). Among useful general works may be mentioned A. Buse, *Paulin, Bischof von Nola und zeine Zeit* (Regensburg, 1856); F. Lagrange, *History of St Paulinus of Nola*, (Engl. transl., Mainz, 1882); A. Baudrillart, *Saint Paulin, Évèque de Nole* (Paris, 1928).

[2] So Uranius, *Epistola de Obitu S. Paulini ad Pacatum* (Migne, *P.L.* Vol. LIII, col. 860).

[3] For the date see the evidence discussed by Helm in the article cited above.

[4] Ausonius, *Ep.* 25; cf. 26.

Italy – both in Latium and at Nola in Campania – were among the richest and most extensive in Gaul, and were augmented by his marriage to the rich and noble Spanish lady Therasia. Ausonius speaks of them as *regna*.[1] Paulinus himself belonged to one of the most aristocratic Roman families. St Ambrose declares (cf. p. 75) that no family surpassed it in splendour. It may have formed a branch of the great family of the Anicii, to which belonged his contemporary and friend, the famous saint Melania.[2]

Paulinus had been educated at Bordeaux, where he became a favourite pupil of Ausonius, and where he acquired a reputation for the kind of classical learning and facility in composition which was fashionable at that time – truly *rhetoricis litteris eruditus*, as Gregory of Tours describes him.[3] St Jerome is unstinted in his praise of both his natural gifts and his literary style, and also his early literary achievements. He praises Paulinus's *Defence of Theodosius*, both for the arrangement of the subject matter and for the style, which he says is terse and neat, and as pure as that of Tully.[4] After leaving Bordeaux Paulinus held honourable offices in Italy, perhaps as consul and as governor of Campania.[5] But he returned to Gaul as soon as he was free of his official obligations and we hear of him shortly afterwards (c. 390) in Spain with his wife Therasia.

As was not unusual in the fourth century, he was baptized in middle age, and it is possible that this, like the baptism of Paulinus of Pella later, may have been the result of political disturbances, such as that in which his brother was slain, and in which his own life seems to have been endangered.[6] He received baptism at the hands of Bishop Delphinus of Bordeaux[7] to whom we shall have frequent occasion to refer later; but Paulinus himself tells us that the personality of St Felix had

[1] *Ep.* 27, §116.
[2] See *Ep.* 29; and cf. Lagrange, *History of St Paulinus of Nola* (ed. cit.), p. 4 ff. Helm regards this as merely a supposition, though he appears to favour it.
[3] *De Gloria Confess.*, CX.
[4] Jerome, *Ep.* 58.
[5] There appears to be some uncertainty as to the exact offices held by Paulinus. See Dill, *Roman Society in the Last Century of the Western Empire*, p. 396, and the references there cited; and cf. Helm; see also C. Bigg, *Wayside Sketches in Ecclesiatical History* (London, 1906), p. 29 – a delicate and sympathetic little study, to which I am much indebted. Cf. earlier, Lagránge, op. cit., p. 28 ff.
[6] *Carmen* XXI (Birthday Ode XIII), 416; *Ep.* 35 (Migne, *P.L.*, LXI, col 350); Hartel I, p. 312.
[7] *Epp.* 10, 20.

had a strong attraction for him from his childhood,[1] while as a young man he had come into personal contact at Vienne both with St Martin of Tours[2] and with Victricius, the Bishop of Rouen.[3] Perhaps also the loss of his only son in infancy,[4] and, as Ausonius hints, the spiritual inclinations of his wife, may have strengthened his early love of spiritual things. But it is probable that the family to which he belonged was already Christian.[5] There can be no doubt, however, that as a young man he looked forward to a quiet family life in the country, with a beloved and obedient wife and children. These are the blessings for which he prays to God.[6]

Up to this point Paulinus had been an ambitious narrative poet and man of letters, a lover of the classics, with a delicate and genuine gift of poetry. His chief correspondent on literary matters was his old master, Ausonius, the professor of Bordeaux. Most of the letters which passed between them are in the form of poems; but after his baptism the literary output of Paulinus gradually lessened. Some new influence was at work, perhaps that of his wife Therasia; perhaps that of the saintly Bishop Delphinus;[7] or again some reminiscence of his meeting with St Martin at Vienne, at the time of his life when he was not only 'in the darkness of his sins . . . but also full of the cares of the world'.[8]

Of the exact circumstances which led to his final decision to withdraw himself from his old milieu we know nothing. But gradually it becomes clear that Paulinus is making his final renunciation of the world and of his great estates in Aquitaine. For four years he does not seem to have written to Ausonius, who wrote four letters to him, apparently at yearly intervals.

---

[1] *Carmen* XXI, 365 ff.

[2] Paulinus, *Ep.* 18, § 9. See also Sulpicius Severus, *Life of St Martin*, translated by A. Roberts (Oxford, 1894), ch. XIX. Gregory of Tours, *De Gloria Confess.*, cap. CX.

[3] Paulinus, loc. cit.

[4] Cf. St Ambrose, *Ep.* 58 (quoted on p. 75).

[5] See Lagrange, op. cit., p. 10 f. Cf. Paulinus, *Ep.* 12, § 10.

[6] *Carmen* XXIII.

[7] In the Birthday Ode XI, 154 to St Felix, St Paulinus coupled Delphinus with St Martin '*Gallia Martinum, Delphinum Aquitania sumpsit*' (*Carmen* XIX, l. 154).

[8] *Ep.* 18, § 9. It was on this same occasion that he also met Victricius, later to become the apostle of Normandy and bishop of Rouen. In *Ep.* 18 Paulinus undoubtedly refers to the days before his spiritual eyes were opened. Sulpicius Severus, referring to this meeting, tells us (*Life of St Martin*, ch. XIX) that Paulinus was suffering at that time from a clouded vision (*pupillam eius crassior nubes superducta texisset*) which St Martin healed.

E

Actually it would seem[1] that the first letter never reached Paulinus, while the second, third, and fourth letters reached him simultaneously, and he replied to all together on receiving them, when he had been four years in Spain. To another letter of Ausonius (*Ep.* 27) he also replies later. From the letters of Paulinus written after the long silence, it is clear that the moving appeals of his old friend and tutor can never succeed in winning him back to the little classical world of Bordeaux. This correspondence, in which the old professor, now over eighty, expresses in classical imagery his yearning for a visit or letters from his brilliant and beloved pupil, who is gently withdrawing from the early intimate relationship, and passing to a new world of emotions and transports undreamed of in the schools of Bordeaux, forms one of the most poignant passages in the literature of the period. We feel in the beauty and dignity of these two men, so different in outlook, so incompatible in ideals, the eternal gulf which separates each generation from its predecessor and which no affection or education can bridge.

The letter in which Paulinus declares his resolution to leave the world of his own day, and at the same time to renounce the world of classical thought and classical tradition, is the more impressive and beautiful in its tone of exaltation and simplicity, because of the love which it breathes for the beauty and value of all that the writer is giving up. Dill justly remarks that 'the solemn farewell which the monk of Nola bade to the studies of his youth and the great world reveals alike the force of the new ascetic ideal, and the enthralling influence of pagan culture'.[2] The passage has been quoted very often, but a repetition needs no apology:

Carmen X, line 20 ff.

'Why, my father, do you bid the Muses whom I have disowned return to my affection? Hearts vowed to Christ are closed to the muses and cannot receive Apollo. There was a time when I could join with you, not with the same gifts, but

---

[1] For a discussion of the difficult chronology of the letters see P. de Labriolle, 'Note sur la Chronologie' in *La Correspondance d'Ausone et de Paulin de Nole* (Paris, 1910), p. 51 f. The correspondence is published, with an English translation, by H. G. Evelyn White, *Ausonius*, Vol. II (London, 1921), p. 80 ff., *Epistles*, No. 23 ff. See also Helm's reference to P. Reinelt (*Studien über d. Briefe d. hl. P. v. Nola*).
[2] Dill, *Roman Society in the Last Century of the Western Empire*, p. 399.

with like eagerness, in invoking the divine Muses, and deaf Phoebus in his cave at Delphi, and in calling upon groves and mountains to bestow the favour of eloquence, the gift of the god. Now another power impels my soul, a mightier God imposes new ideals upon me . . . . He forbids me to fill my time with idle ploys, whether business or pleasure, or with the literature of myth and legend, that I may obey His precepts and that I may have the vision of his light, which is obscured by the casuistries of the sophists, and the eloquence of the orators, and the vain imaginings of the seers, who fill our hearts with fictions and illusions. . . .'

Carmen X, line 304 ff.

'In the knowledge of His coming my heart trembles and is shaken to its depths; my soul is full of longing, even now full of apprehension for the future, for fear lest, being fettered by painful cares about my body and burdened with the weight of worldly things, when the Heavens open and the fearful trumpet resounds, it may be unable to rise to the skies on light pinions to the assembly of our King, to fly to Heaven among the glorious thousands of the saints who raise to the sublime stars their winged feet freed from earth's fetters. Borne by the light clouds, they will pass through the constellations in the airy spaces, to pay homage to the King of Heaven, and join their bright ranks to the adored Christ. This is my fear, this my agony, lest the last day may come upon me slumbering in thick darkness . . . and wasting my time in futile activities and submerged in empty cares. For what would become of me if I should be dozing in dilatory homage and the Christ should reveal himself to me, flashing in glory from his citadel in the skies; and if, blinded by the sudden radiance of the Lord approaching when the Heavens open, I must seek to hide myself, dazzled by the violence of the light, in the darkness and the joyless night?'

The picture is classical—a sentinel waiting at his post, his great fear being lest he should doze and miss the moment for which he is watching, when Christ should appear in glory to hold His great review, and the spirits of the saints should gather in the ethereal regions and form themselves into ranks like a Roman army before the divine emperor.

If we accept the chronology of the correspondence between Paulinus and Ausonius suggested by de Labriolle[1] we must suppose that yet another letter[2] passed from the pupil to his old master before the correspondence finally closed – a letter full of tender affection, and of generous sympathy, opening with a gentle but dignified reproach to Ausonius for his insinuation that Therasia had come between them.

'You complain', he says, 'of the obstinate silence of my tongue while your own is never mute. And you reproach me with enjoying an idle retreat; you accuse me moreover of neglecting our friendship, and you charge me with being afraid of my wife, thereby wounding me in the depths of my being. Cease, I beg you, from wounding your friend with these reproaches, and do not mingle bitterness with your fatherly words, like wormwood with honey. I have always loved, and I still love to pay you honour with every attention, and to cherish you with unwavering devotion. My tenderness for you has never been marred by even the smallest blemish. I have always been anxious to avoid causing you pain, even by a careless frown . . . My household has always been devoted to you, and holds you in honour for ever, and we are as united in our love for you as in adoring Christ with our undivided hearts.'

There are difficulties in the chronology of the life and the correspondence of Ausonius about this time; but the letters in which he chides Paulinus repeatedly for neglecting to write to him or to visit him are full of references to Spanish localities[3] and are clearly addressed to Paulinus during his sojourn at Barcelona. Here he was ordained presbyter by force – apparently a common occurrence in his day.[4] The date usually given for this event is 393.[5] It was probably about this time, or shortly after, that he wrote to his friend Sulpicius Severus who

---

[1] Op. cit., p. 51.

[2] *Carmen* XI. In the edition of *Ausonius* published by Evelyn White this letter (No. 30 in his edition) is placed before the letter which we have just discussed, and which he numbers as 31.

[3] See Ausonius, *Ep.* 27, 29.

[4] St Jerome was practically ordained by force, stipulating, like St Paulinus, that he should not be attached to any particular church. Jerome's own brother, Paulinian, was forcibly ordained, first a deacon, and next day a priest. St Athanasius, St Ambrose, and St Augustine had all been 'forcibly' consecrated to the episcopate. An unsuccessful attempt was made by the people of Hippo to force St Augustine to ordain Pinianus, the husband of the younger Melania, as priest, while he was on a visit to the town (cf. p. 99).

[5] Cf., however, J. Duff, *The Letters of St Jerome* (Dublin, 1942), p. 217.

was living at Eause in Aquitaine, inviting him to visit him in
Spain. He begs him to come for the Easter festival, or at least
afterwards; but preferably before, so that they may celebrate
it together. He urges that the Pyrenees are not impassable.
Their name is the most alarming thing about them, and he adds
that the messenger who had brought him Sulpicius's letter, and
who will convey the answer, will tell him that he only needed
eight days to get from Eause to Barcelona.[1]

The connection with Ausonius and the cultivated life of
Bordeaux comes to an end at this time; but the correspondence
with Sulpicius Severus continued for many years, and the
invitation to visit Paulinus was frequently repeated after he
had moved from Spain to Italy.

There are grounds for believing that the migration of Paulinus into Spain was necessitated by his private affairs which
were in jeopardy, perhaps even his life. One of his brothers had
perished in some political crisis, and it is possible that Paulinus
had been implicated. Could it have been Priscillianism? This
influential sect had drawn some of its most influential adherents
from Aquitaine. The reference of Sulpicius to the cure worked
by St Martin on the clouded vision of St Paulinus would be
more appropriate to heresy than to paganism, which would
more probably have been described as total blindness. We are
very much in the dark about Paulinus's spiritual life till he
reached the age of forty. On the other hand it is probable that
if any stigma of heresy had rested on him we should have had
some hint of it from other writers.[2] Speculative theology seems
to have been alien to his whole cast of thought.

Meanwhile powerful influences were at work to induce him
to adopt the ascetic life. Already before the sale of his estates in
Gaul and Spain he had received letters[3] from St Jerome at
Bethlehem which deprecated delay and urged him to a speedy
sale of all his goods and an early and final dedication of himself to a humble and holy life, and his great literary gifts to the
cause of Christianity. 'I shall not be satisfied', he writes, 'with
any mediocrity in you; I shall look for complete perfection'.[4]

[1] Paulinus, *Ep.* 1, § 11.
[2] Notably Gennadius, who devotes to him a short notice (cap. 49) in which he
emphasizes his piety.
[3] Jerome, *Epp.* 53, 58 (Migne, *P.L.*, Vol. XXII).
[4] Jerome, *Ep.* 58 (Migne, *P.L.*, Vol. XXII, col. 579).

This letter in particular is written with a vigour and a pressure of white-hot eloquence which could not fail to act as a final and irresistible stimulus to anyone who had already set his heart on perfection of life and spirit.

In 387 Paulinus had met St Ambrose at Milan during his earlier sojourn in Italy, at the time when the great bishop was preparing St Augustine of Hippo and Alypius, later Bishop of Tagaste in Numidia, for baptism.[1] Now, on their way to Nola, Paulinus and Therasia again visited him in Florence. Ambrose received them with great joy. He even sought to attach Paulinus to his own church; but the democratic form of Christianity represented by the humble St Felix was more in accord with the new monastic movement, of which Paulinus was a pioneer, than the cathedral of the Imperial See. Paulinus accordingly pursued his way first to Rome, which he had left some ten years earlier, and then to Nola, near Naples, where formerly, during his official life in Italy, he had made a road to the little shrine of St Felix, the humble saint to whom it was dedicated.

He had also built an adjoining hospice for the sick and poor, and it is not impossible that already at this early date he had dreamed of settling here.[2] Now, on his return to Italy, perhaps c. 395,[3] he and his wife established themselves in Nola, where they added an upper storey to the hospice. Despite Paulinus's modest references to it, the whole building seems to have been fairly extensive, since it housed not only the saint and his immediate household, but also distinguished visitors such as St Melania and her train. There was also a little garden and an orchard through which Paulinus could pass from the hospice to the basilica, untroubled by the crowd. The aristocrat still valued his privacy. His letters contain many charming references – some of them figurative – to gardens and garden lore. In *Ep.* 11 (§ 14) to Severus he playfully parries his friend's accusation that he has left Hebromagus for the sake of this little garden.

There was also a group of churches round the shrine, and Paulinus himself built another great basilica[4] to accommodate

---

[1] See Paulinus, *Ep.* 3 (to Alypius).

[2] A passage in *Carmen* XXI (l. 404) would seem to strengthen this probability. '*Ex illo quamvis alio mihi tramite vito curreret*', etc.   [3] See Helm, loc. cit.

[4] For some account of the buildings and the difficult archaeological and architectural problems to which they give rise, see R. C. Goldschmidt, op. cit., ch. IV, and refs. Goldschmidt also reproduces a valuable but very difficult 'map' or plan of the excavations which were begun on the site in 1933 and published in 1939.

the throngs of pilgrims who crowded to the spot with their sick relatives and friends and even their sick cattle. He said that the bigger basilica was needed because the existing church was so small that there was not room enough for the congregation to extend their hands in prayer. The accommodation for pilgrims included an outer courtyard. A water-supply was brought from the neighbouring town of Abella to feed the fountains, and Paulinus decorated the porticos with frescoes depicting scenes from Scripture history, and with little explanatory captions to edify the pilgrims.

Here he and his wife lived as brother and sister[1] for the rest of their lives in a *familia* in the hospice with a few relatives and friends, devoted Christians like themselves. At one time the community consisted of some ten persons, four women and four men in addition to his wife and himself. All were members of the high Roman aristocracy, and most were related to one another, several being married couples. One couple also had their two children living with them, a practice not unknown in Egyptian communities at this period.

Nola was no isolated example of early community life in Italy (cf. p. 20). In his youth, during his sojourn in Aquileia, St Jerome had been in the habit of frequenting a similar domestic monastery in the dwelling of a certain Chromatius,[2] where he used to meet Rufinus, and which he describes as 'a choir of the blessed.'[3] In the year 412 he wrote from Bethlehem that Italy was full of nunneries (*virginum monasteria*).[4] St Augustine tells us of a community (*monasterium*) outside the walls of Milan, with St Ambrose at its head, and another at Trier – in the latter he had found a book containing a *Life of St Antony*.[5] Augustine's own household at Tagaste may have been not wholly dissimilar. It was to Tagaste that members of the family of St Melania withdrew after spending some time at Nola with St Paulinus after the sack of Rome, and it was here that they lived

---

[1] See Helm, and the references there cited. St Jerome refers to Therasia in a letter to Paulinus as *sancta soror tua* (Jerome, *Ep.* 58, § 6). For this ascetic practice cf. p. 152.

[2] For a description of this community, see P. Monceaux, *St Jerome: The Early Years* (translated by F. J. Sheed, London, 1933), p. 70.

[3] *Chronicle*, s.a. 379.

[4] Jerome's letter (*Ep.* 127, to Principia, Migne, Vol. XXII, col. 1087) contains an account of Marcella's life, and some interesting details of the sack of Rome by the Goths under Alaric in 410.

[5] *Confessions*, VIII, vi.

in a retreat after the fashion of Nola. We may perhaps compare the community described by St Victricius of Rouen in the *De Laude Sanctorum*.[1]

It has been remarked that 'the monasticism of Nola bears that idyllic impress of freedom and simplicity which preceded the era of organization and of rules'.[2] Paulinus himself calls it a *monasterium*[3] and its occupants *fraternitas monacha*;[4] but there were no vows and no rule[5] and no rigid organization, so far as we can tell—just a little group of relatives and friends, withdrawn from society, living and working together in mutual goodwill, devoting their lives and their wealth to the service of God and to the help of the sick and suffering. We see the community most intimately in the thirteen letters which Paulinus wrote to his life-long friend Sulpicius Severus, and in them we can follow the quiet daily devotions, the work for the sick and poor, the entertainment of travellers of all ranks, the building and beautifying of the churches. The two friends followed with the keenest interest the life and daily round of one another, their plans for building bigger and more splendid churches, and for developing their sanctuaries. We can appreciate how great must have been Paulinus's disappointment when his repeated invitations[6] to Sulpicius to visit Nola passed unheeded. 'Come to us', writes Paulinus on one occasion; 'and if you can, fly to us'.[7]

The community of Paulinus and Therasia was perhaps austere rather than ascetic. Much time was devoted to church services and to the building and decorating of the basilica.[8] Paulinus and his family fasted till 3 p.m.; but their food and dress seem to have been simple rather than coarse. Wheaten bread was in use, but the platters and vessels were of boxwood and earthenware.[9] A certain disciple of St Martin, a monk Victor, who carried letters annually[10] between Paulinus and his

[1] Migne, *P.L.* XX, col. 445.
[2] F. J. E. Raby, *A History of Christian Latin Poetry* [2] (Oxford, 1953), p. 102.
[3] *Ep.* 5, § 15.   [4] *Ep.* 23, § 8.
[5] In *Ep.* 22 (to Sulpicius Severus), Paulinus mentions briefly some standards which he considers should be observed by a household of monks.
[6] See Paulinus, *Epp.* 1, 5, 11, 17.
[7] *Ep.* 11, § 14.
[8] See p. 69, and the references cited below, p. 85 f. See further *Ep.* 32, §§ 10–17.
[9] Cf. *Ep.* 5, § 21.
[10] Owing to the difficulties of the roads (*vias duras*, cf. Paulinus, *Ep.* 28, § 1), travel was rare in winter.

old friend Sulpicius Severus in Aquitaine, professed himself scandalized at the wheaten fare, and insisted on making them dishes of beans and pulse and cooking the porridge of barley or millet according to the recipe in *Ezek.* iv. 9. One of the most charming of Paulinus's letters to Severus is that in which he describes[1] with gentle humour the rigour with which Victor prosecuted his reforms at Nola and the horrible smells which permeated the entire establishment as the result of his ascetic cuisine. He tells us that Victor's concoction was so horrible that the very pot in which it was boiled cracked – it was the mixture of things cooking together which was fighting. However, adds Paulinus lightly, it was wholly to the taste of a poor old country-man who had joined them, partly because he had never known anything better and partly because he had no teeth.

Victor was a useful man in many other ways. He used to cut Paulinus's hair and shave him, wash his feet and massage him. His activities constitute something of a reform on the model of Sulpicius's *familia* in Aquitaine or St Martin's community at Tours. The association of Paulinus with St Martin was very close, for Paulinus's letters to Sulpicius are full of devotion to the saint, and Sulpicius represents St Martin in his turn as extolling Paulinus in the highest terms, holding him up to his followers as the best Christian example of the Age.

'His whole discourse', says Sulpicius, speaking of St Martin, 'was how we must leave the snares of this world, and the burdens of life, and follow the Lord Jesus with no impediments. And he would put forward as the supreme example of the present day Paulinus, that eminent man whom I have mentioned above, who had abandoned his enormous wealth to follow Christ, and who was the only man of our times who fulfilled the precepts of the Gospel. "He was the man we must follow", he would say; "he was the man we must imitate. Blessed", he would add, "was the present Age in having such an example of faith and virtue".'[2]

One of the many delightful aspects of the correspondence between Paulinus and Sulpicius is their habit of 'puffing' one another. This adroit compliment of Sulpicius to his friend may not have been wholly without its effect on the efforts made by

[1] *Ep.* 23, §§ 7 and 9.
[2] Sulpicius Severus, *De Vita Beati Martini*, cap. XXV.

Paulinus in publicizing Sulpicius's *Life of St Martin*, to which I shall refer in the following chapter.

This raises the natural question as to why Paulinus chose as his patron an obscure saint like St Felix rather than St Martin. From references in the letters and poems of Paulinus[1] it is clear that the stories of St Felix are highly popular in character, stories of simple peasant life, full of naïve miracles. Paulinus seems to have been guided by a strong democratic sense. Felix was a Syrian, Martin an Illyrian, and both saints were *peregrini*, having left their homes in early life and become local saints in other lands. Their traditions were remembered among the people of their adoption, and the miracles ascribed to them were of a kind likely to satisfy the peasantry. As such they were good propaganda. Sulpicius and Paulinus could not afford to dispense with them, still less to abolish them. Felix was already the centre of a popular local cult, and his annual festival brought the peasantry together to his shrine in a common ideal. Paulinus encouraged and developed it, allowing the peasants to amuse themselves in their own way, and painting frescoes of Bible scenes on the porticos where the crowds were entertained, at the same time offering them hospitality and composing birthday odes for the saint.

It is clear that Paulinus was under something of a shadow in Rome during the early days of his life in Nola, especially under Pope Siricius.[2] The cause is not known, but it may possibly have been connected with the trouble which disrupted the family life and caused the death of his brother in Aquitaine, possibly, as suggested above, precipitating his own departure into Spain. Whatever the cause[3] it seems to have been of a transitory nature, for he speaks with appreciation[4] of the sympathetic attitude of Siricius's successor Anastasius, and he seems to have spent ten days or a fortnight every year in Rome at the time of the festival of St Peter and St Paul.[5]

Paulinus tells us how his days were passed during these visits. In the mornings he visited the basilicas and the tombs of the

---

[1] For some account of St Felix, see *Carmen* XV, XVI.

[2] *Ep.* 5, § 13.

[3] Buse attributes Siricius's disapproval to the nature of Paulinus's enforced ordination; but this seems to be hardly likely.

[4] *Ep.* 20, § 2.

[5] *Ep.* 20. In the year 408 his visit probably took place, not at the great festival, but after Easter.

martyrs. The afternoons were devoted to the full social life incidental to his wide circle of acquaintances in the capital. He also kept a close scrutiny on the book-stalls and acted as a kind of informal publicity agent to his friend Sulpicius Severus (see pp. 79, 109).

Owing to his great wealth and prestige, coupled with his intellectual attainments, his renunciation of worldly life made a profound impression on his Age.[1] This is clearly illustrated in a letter of St Ambrose to Bishop Sabinus of Placentia:

'I have ascertained from reliable sources that Paulinus, whose high rank is second to none in Aquitaine, has sold both his own properties and those of his wife . . . to endow the poor with what he has converted into money. And he who was rich has made himself poor, as if he were unloading himself of a heavy burden, and has bidden farewell to home, country, and kindred so as to serve God more zealously. And he is stated to have chosen a retreat in the city of Nola where he may pass his life in seclusion from the tumult of the world.'

His wife also is only second to him in virtue and zeal, and does not dissociate herself from her husband's course. She has transferred her estates to other owners and followed her husband, contenting herself with his little plot and compensating herself with wealth in religion and charity. They have no offspring, and so they hope to be the parents of good deeds.

What will our leading men say when they hear of these things? That a man of such a family, such ancestry, such natural gifts, and endowed with such eloquence, should have withdrawn from the Senate and have cut off the succession of a noble line – such a thing cannot be endured! And although they themselves shave their heads and their eyebrows whenever they perform the rites of Isis, yet if a Christian who shows greater devotion to a religion which is really holy should take the habit of a monk they denounce it as a shameful deed.'[2]

We realize Therasia's whole-hearted co-operation with, and influence on Paulinus more from references in the letters of others than from any direct statement by Paulinus himself. This is in keeping with the personal reserve and delicate good taste which characterize all that Paulinus says and does. It

---

[1] See St Augustine, *Ep.* 31; St Jerome, *Ep.* 118; Sulpicius Severus, *Dial.* III, 17.
[2] St Ambrose, *Ep.* 58 (Migne, *P.L.*, Vol. XVI, col. 1178).

would have been unthinkable that he should exploit the virtues of Therasia, or enlarge on the strength of their mutual affection. Once only, in the exquisite lines which he sent to Severus to be inscribed at the tomb of Clarus, Martin's favourite disciple, in the basilica which Severus had enlarged and reconstructed at Primuliacum, Paulinus gives permanent expression to the strength of their attachment which, he declares, unites them in this life, and which death itself will be powerless to sever.

'O Clarus . . . accept of your goodness these vows of the sinners beseeching you that you be mindful of Paulinus and Therasia. Care for them, as they have been consigned to your care by the intercession of Severus, even though you know them not in the body, undeserving as they are. . . . You cannot part them, for they are inseparable. If you take one, he will bear with him the other wherever he is carried. Cherish us equally, therefore, since we are united. . . . Thus has God called us together; thus has Martin loved us; as we are one, do you also, O Clarus, esteem us one, alike in affection, though not in virtue. You, O saint, will have power by your prayers to make us equal in virtue also – if you strive with piety allied to that of Martin – that your prayers will be stronger than our sins, that at the same time we have part in you with your Severus, we shall for ever be protected by the shadow of your wings.'[1]

Therasia was a remarkable woman. It is clear that she shared her husband's life and work whole-heartedly, and her death in 408 must have been a cruel blow to Paulinus. She does not play a prominent part, and we hear little of her personally after they had settled at Nola. Nevertheless, ten[2] of the letters in the fifty-two of the collection of Paulinus are signed jointly: 'Paulinus et Therasia, peccatores' – the common formula of the period. It is remarkable that none of the letters signed by Therasia are addressed to her husband's old friends, Ausonius and Sulpicius Severus. In the case of Ausonius we may probably account for this by the fact that the correspondence was almost all in verse. Moreover there is no evidence that Therasia had ever met her husband's old master. It is surprising, how-

---

[1] *Ep.* 32, § 6.
[2] G. Boissier (*La Fin du Paganisme*, Vol. II (Paris, 1894), p. 95) is mistaken in saying that Therasia's name is joined with that of her husband in all his letters.

ever, that she should never have signed the numerous invitations, or any of the thirteen letters sent by her husband to Sulpicius Severus. On the other hand she joins her husband in signing letters to ecclesiastics, including letters to St Augustine, as well as one to the Bishop Alypius of Tagaste;[1] another to Romanianus of Hippo, Augustine's friend and benefactor; others again to Amandus, first a priest of Bordeaux under Delphinus and later his successor (cf. p. 112), and to the presbyter Aper and his wife Amanda whom we shall meet again as neighbours of Sulpicius Severus in Aquitaine. The association of Therasia with her husband in these letters to ecclesiastics strengthens our suspicion that the shrewd old Ausonius was right in his hint that Therasia was the influence that led Paulinus to renounce the world.

The geographical position of Nola was peculiarly favourable to wide communications by letters and to the visits of friends and strangers. The urbanity and gentleness of Paulinus enabled him to carry on a correspondence with the most strongly opposed personalities, while himself holding aloof from all controversies. It was perhaps natural that he should be in touch with Rufinus, the translator and champion of Origen, since Rufinus probably visited Nola in the train of St Melania on her visit from the Holy Land where she had settled. But it is surely surprising to find Paulinus also in friendly communication with St Jerome.

Paulinus was a voluminous letter writer, and the range of both his correspondence and his personal contacts is very wide and included St Pammachius of Ostia; St Victricius of Normandy; St Niketas of Dacia; St Eucherius who became Bishop of Lyons; St Honoratus, the founder of the famous monastery of Lérins. Many of the letters contain long passages relating to Scripture, for copies of the Scriptures were comparatively scarce and Christianity was still something of an enthralling novelty. But Paulinus also gives much engaging and intimate information and much picturesque personal detail about himself and his visitors. The picture of a life lived in simplicity and holiness, yet in intimate contact with the most eminent thinkers of his time in Europe and in the whole Mediterranean world, gives unique value to his letters.

[1] Alypius was consecrated bishop in 394; St Augustine in 395.

These letters are the only prose writings of Paulinus which have survived.[1] It was an Age when letter writing was not only much cultivated, but when letters were also carefully collected and preserved. Sometimes we shall see the authors collecting and publishing their own letters. Paulinus expresses himself astonished when an old friend of his early life, a certain Sanctus, informs him that he has made a collection of his letters, and sends him a list of them. Paulinus declares he himself had forgotten all about them.[2] Many of them nevertheless show traces of having been written for publication.

The style of the letters is careful and polished. Despite the Biblical nature of much of their content, and the wealth of homely detail of life at Nola which relieves this somewhat sombre basis of his correspondence, his prose, moulded by the great masterpieces of the past, retained its classical purity. The letter in which he expressed to Ausonius his renunciation of the haunting beauty of classical mythology is proof of the hold which it retained on him and the extent to which it permeated his intellect. Like St Jerome he remained a classic at heart to the end. A letter written to his Gaulish kinsman, Jovius,[3] is a remarkable paradox. He entreats Jovius to abandon classical philosophy and read only the Scriptures; but he writes with all the artifices of contemporary rhetoric and a vocabulary saturated with Vergil and Cicero.

'Seek Christ', he writes, 'the touchwood of true light . . . You are redolent of the flowers of all the poets; you flow with the streams of all the orators; you are refreshed by the springs of philosophy,[4] and, being rich with foreign literature, you fill Roman lips with Attic honey. What value is there, I ask you, in poring over Tully and Demosthenes . . . in wading through Xenophon, Plato, Cato, Varro? . . . Be a Peripatetic to God, a Pythagorean towards the World, a preacher[5] of true wisdom in Christ, and, keeping silence about vain matters, eschew this perilous charm of empty learning, as you would those lotus-eaters who make one forget one's native land by the sweet

[1] Gennadius (*De Viris Illustribus*, cap. 49) also mentions among the prose works written by Paulinus the *De Poenitentia*, and the *De Laude Generali Omnium Martyrum*; but neither of these is extant. For a reference to the edition and English translation of Gennadius by Richardson, see p. 206 below.
[2] Paulinus, *Ep.* 41, § 1.   [3] *Ep.* 16.
[4] The irrigation metaphor is a favourite one with Paulinus. Cf. *Ep.* 19.
[5] *Praedicator*, a favourite word of Cicero's.

flavour of their fruit – eschew also the strains of harmful fascination as if they were the songs of the sirens.'

This struggle between love of classical learning and Christian zeal for the Scriptures recurs constantly throughout the period.

Both letters and books were readily carried between friends, and references in the letters of the period give the impression of the Christian world at this time as something like a circulating library. We shall see Paulinus busying himself in publicizing the *Life of St Martin* by his friend Sulpicius Severus. St Augustine sends copies of his own works to St Paulinus by his letter carrier;[1] and Paulinus writes to Augustine[2] about his five books against the Manichees which he has received from Bishop Alypius. To Alypius himself Paulinus sends St Jerome's version of the *Chronicle* of Eusebius, which Alypius had asked him to obtain for him in Rome.[3] To Sulpicius Severus he sends his own work, *Defensio Theodosii*.[4] The letters of St Jerome himself from the Syrian desert are full of references to books which he was borrowing or returning. Later in the century we shall find Sidonius Apollinaris and his friends seeking new books with the same zeal.

The contents of the mail-bags were not confined to letters and books. St Paulinus sends to St Jerome a present of a cap with which Jerome expresses himself delighted—'just the very thing to keep an old man's head warm.'[5] Severus sends to Paulinus a cloak of camel hair,[6] while Paulinus sends to Severus and others little presents of loaves (*eulogia, panis*), and to Severus also a boxwood platter,[7] and a woollen tunic, which St Melania has brought for him from the Holy Land, and which he naïvely tells his friend will no doubt be all the more acceptable through its having been already worn a little by himself.[8] He also sends a portrait of himself[9] for which Severus has begged in order that he may place it beside the portrait of St Martin at the sacred font in the new baptistery which he has built at his home in Primuliacum,[10] between the two basilicas likewise erected or reconstructed by him; and for the dedication of the

---

[1] St Augustine, *Ep.* 27 (to Paulinus).
[2] Paulinus, *Ep.* 4.
[4] ibid., *Ep.* 28.
[6] Paulinus, *Epp.* 23, 29, § 1.
[7] *Ep.* 5, § 21.
[9] *Ep.* 30, § 2.
[3] ibid., *Ep.* 3.
[5] Jerome, *Ep.* 85.
[8] *Ep.* 29, § 5.
[10] *Ep.* 32, § 1 f.

'Great Basilica' Paulinus sends his friend a fragment of the Cross which St Melania had brought to him from Jerusalem.[1] He also sends verses for all these edifices, and accompanies his own portrait by more verses to be inscribed below it in the baptistery.[2] Their humility and gentleness, and the excellent taste justify his acquiescence in Severus's request:

'Whoever you be who purify your souls and bathe your limbs in these sacred fonts, observe the two ways leading to the good life: Martin offers you the "rule" of the perfect life: Paulinus teaches you how you may obtain pardon. Look on me, ye sinners; on him, ye blessed. Let him be the exemplar for the holy, and me for the sinners.'[3]

This touching interchange of mutual esteem is the last that we hear of Severus. His home was in the area shortly to be devastated by the Barbarian inroads, and after the year 406 we have no more letters to him.

Letters and parcels were conveyed to their destinations by a very varied assortment of people,[4] and an interesting book might be written about the mail-bags and mail carriers of the period. Naturally even distinguished travellers would sometimes convey letters between friends. St Paulinus receives a letter from St Augustine by the hand of his friend Romanianus.[5] Later in the century we shall see Sidonius Apollinaris employing petty traders to carry letters between himself and the Bishop of Bordeaux. We rarely hear of letters miscarrying (cf. p. 314 ff).

Priests and monks were not infrequently employed in the

---

[1] *Ep.* 31, § 1.

[2] The inscribing of verses on the walls of buildings, both religious and secular, especially below a portrait, was particularly in favour at this time. We may compare Ausonius's *Epicedion* or 'Epitaph' on his father, 'verses which', so he tells us, 'were written under his portrait' (*Domestica* IV). Sidonius Apollinaris, at the request of Bishop Perpetuus – 'a worthy successor of his great predecessor . . . the saintly pontiff and confessor Martin' – composed an inscription for the walls of the basilica built by Perpetuus to take the place of the 'modest chapel' erected by Martin's successor, Brice, over the tomb of the saint. The verses are quoted in the letter (Book IV, letter 18) written c. 470 by Sidonius himself to his friend Lucontius. Again in another letter (Book II, letter 2), Sidonius mentions verses which are inscribed on the walls of the *frigidarium* of his own bath-house at Avitacum (cf. *Ep.* II, 2).

[3] *Ep.* 32, § 3.

[4] See C. Bigg, *Wayside Sketches in Ecclesiastical History*, p. 40.

[5] Augustine, *Ep.* 27 (to Paulinus), English translation by J. G. Cunningham, *Letters of St Augustine* (Edinburgh, 1872). An interesting account of the bearers of St Augustine's letters will be found in the Introduction to J. H. Baxter's edition of *Select Letters of St Augustine* (London, 1930), p. 36.

capacity of letter carriers, perhaps because their calling and habit protected them from interference. Two early letters and a reply passed between Sulpicius Severus and Paulinus by the hand of a certain Vigilantius, who probably began life as the son of a *caupo*, or keeper of a place of refreshment, on the Roman road from Aquitaine to Spain, but who later became a priest, first in Aquitaine, then later in Barcelona. In 394 Paulinus sent him with a letter of high commendation to St Jerome at Bethlehem;[1] but he soon became dissatisfied with what he saw in the East, and returned home, bearing with him a letter from Jerome to Paulinus. Ultimately Vigilantius expressed adverse criticism of extreme asceticism and superstitious practices in a work written c. 403. The work is lost, and we know it chiefly from the treatise, *Contra Vigilantium*, which Jerome wrote to combat it.

In 397 Paulinus received a letter from Sulpicius by a messenger of a very different type, a red-faced, hard-drinking fellow in military boots and a red coat – probably an ex-soldier, by name Marracinus. Paulinus was not a little dismayed at the appearance and bearing of his guest. This did not prevent Sulpicius from employing Marracinus a second time, though charging him to assume more sober clothes. Marracinus, however, preferred to pass on the letter to another acquaintance of Sulpicius, a certain Sorianus, who was anxious to make Paulinus's acquaintance. Paulinus found these light-hearted Aquitanian messengers an inconvenience to his quiet household, and sent back a note to Sulpicius begging him to send him in future no one except true monks who wore the monastic habit instead of an elegant cloak, and a rope girdle instead of a military belt, and a shaven head instead of a great mop of hair.

'Just as our fast', he writes, 'displeases them, so their drunkenness displeases us . . . my parched frugality hurts them, their overloaded stomachs us . . . and so let them see us, not drunk in the morning, but still fasting at evening, not flown with the wine of yesterday, but even abstaining from that of today; not maudlin and unsteady from a drunken orgy, but reeling though sober from our decent vigils.'[2]

As a result of this gentle reproof Sulpicius sent to Paulinus as his messenger in future the monk Victor, whose stern reforms

---

[1] Jerome, *Ep.* 61.   [2] *Ep.* 22, § 2.

F

at Nola we have already witnessed. This 'post-horse on two feet', as Paulinus humorously.calls him,[1] carried letters also from many of Sulpicius's friends in Gaul, notably from Florentius, Bishop of Cahors; from Alethius, his brother and successor; from the priest Desiderius, to whom Sulpicius dedicated his *Life of St Martin*. The contrast between Victor and the ex-soldier Marracinus, illustrates the varied types whose coming and going to the hospice at Nola can hardly have left it either secluded or ignorant of the life of the time, however greatly the little *familia* longed for a quiet retreat.

The pointed request of Paulinus to Severus that his friend should send his letters by such only as are true monks suggests that Sorianus, perhaps even Marracinus, were toying with the monastic life. At this time, before the establishment of the cenobitic life and uniform Rule, this type of 'part-time' monk must have presented a serious problem to men like Severus and Paulinus. In particular it must have been difficult to discriminate between the duty of hospitality and the necessity of excluding undesirable and undisciplined characters. And in making the difficult decision, the hope of being able to convert and reclaim must have been an important element. Marracinus, though greedy and drunken, it would seem, perhaps aroused such hopes in Severus, though not in Paulinus. Yet Paulinus could take a generous view of such failings, as the case of Cardamas will show.

Cardamas[2] was the letter carrier from Delphinus and Amandus of the episcopal household of Bordeaux. He is an even more striking figure than Marracinus. He had been some kind of a comic actor,[3] and much given to gluttony and drunkenness; but under the kindly and wise influences of the households of Bordeaux and Nola, he had changed his calling of actor for that of exorcist, and had become, as Paulinus puts it humorously, 'a cleric as we can see, and sober, as we believe',[4] no longer gorging himself at the midday meal, 'even with husks', but fasting till evening, and even than 'indulging rather in the drops from the wine-cups than in deep potations.'[5]

'He has become so abstemious that he has not held back

[1] *Ep.* 28, § 1.
[2] *Ep.* 19, § 4.
[5] *Ep.* 21, § 6; cf. 15, § 4.

[2] For Cardamas, see *Epp.* 15, 19, 21.
[4] *Ep.* 15, § 4.

from being our guest almost every day, and when he has sipped an occasional and tiny cup, which scarcely passes his lips, he makes no complaint of the wrongs suffered by his empty belly or his dry gullet.'[1]

In short, he is in a fair way to becoming, as Paulinus observes, 'a cleric acceptable to men, and an exorcist terrifying to demons'.[2] The tone of Paulinus is humorous and indulgent whenever he speaks of Cardamas, whose reform he pictures elsewhere in significant phrases as 'inebriated to sobriety, no longer with a full measure of wine, but with a small quantity, by which his belly is not distended, but his heart gladdened'; and he describes him as 'belching forth in spiritual drunkenness a hymn to God'.[3] He adds that his reform is proved by the attenuation of his body and the pallor of his face.[4] Poor Cardamas! We shall see when we read the letters of Sidonius Apollinaris that Cardamas is not the only mail carrier who stands in need of reform.

Meanwhile St Paulinus never abandoned his love of composing poetry.[5] Some thirty-three poems have been preserved, including narrative historical poems; personal letters in verse; a charmingly sympathetic elegy on a dead child; an epithalamium; the inscriptions for the wall of Sulpicius Severus's new church and baptistery already mentioned; above all, the annual birthday odes which he composed for St Felix. The odes contain simple stories of peasant life and miracles, and matter of edification, all touched in with the lightest brushwork, and adapted to the ready comprehension of the peasants who flocked to the shrine at the annual festival of the saint. Paulinus's love of his patron saint, and Felix's intimate relations with the simple people of Nola, are never lost sight of. The odes give us glimpses of the festivals themselves, of the country people thronging to the shrine, the brightly lighted church, the flowers and perfumes, the frescoes, the assembled crowd in holiday mood, the atmosphere of gaiety and relaxation, of joy and religious exaltation.

The odes were intended to be read aloud at these popular

---

[1] Loc. cit.
[2] Ep. 21, § 6; cf. 19, § 4.
[3] Ep. 15, § 4.
[4] Ep. 19, § 4.
[5] For a detailed account of the poetry of Paulinus, and his metres and style, see Helm, loc. cit. and the references there cited. See also Raby, Christian Latin Poetry,[2] p. 101 ff., and the references there cited.

festivals; but they were not composed haphazard. The first two form a lyrical prelude to the narrative of the life of the saint and his miracles, the latter very rustic in tone. These poems, like the letters, are often verbose and diffuse, and in the earlier work the imagery is still largely drawn from classical mythology, not always with the happiest results, as when the myth of Danae is introduced to illustrate the Virgin Birth of Christ. The style and diction still bear the impress of Latin classical poetry and contemporary rhetoric. Paulinus has, nevertheless, a delicacy and quiet lyrical gift which claim comparison with Prudentius.

Two of the odes are of especial interest for their close association with St Niketas, the Bishop of Remesiana, the modern Palanka, in the Roman province of Dacia.[1] St Niketas twice visited St Paulinus at Nola, first in 398 and again in 402.[2] Paulinus wrote with pleasure to Sulpicius of these visits, speaking of his guest with reverence. In more than one passage he expresses his admiration of him for his encouragement of hymn singing, notably among the Barbarians on the Danube. In Carmen XVII, a *Propemptikon*, or Ode on the departure of Niketas who has come from Dacia to take part in the birthday celebrations of St Felix in 398, Paulinus makes charming reference to the sailors on the return voyage singing hymns instead of sea shanties to the rhythm of the oars. He traces the return journey of the bishop to his own country with interesting precision, first from Apulia through Calabria, then by way of Epirus, through the Aegean to Salonica.[3] The details of this journey, the allusions to the Bessi – the tribes of Niketas's episcopal see – and to the Goths whom he counts among his converts,[4] give us some of the most interesting information which we possess about this important but little-known bishop.

Niketas was perhaps the most intellectual influence in the life of Paulinus. At least one passage seems to suggest that he

[1] The best account of St Niketas is that of A. E. Burn, *Niceta of Remesiana* (Cambridge, 1905). Burn regarded him as the author of the hymn *Te Deum*; so also Duchesne, and Dom Morin (see *Rev. Bénéd.*, Vol. XI, 1894, p. 48 ff.); but the evidence is far from conclusive.

[2] The date is fixed by *Carmen* XXVII, 333: 'Venisti tandem, quarto mihi redditus anno', for this poem was composed for the ninth annual festival kept by St Paulinus for St Felix, i.e. in 402.

[3] See especially the opening strophes.

[4] The Goths would presumably be converts from Arianism.

himself was also responsible for building improvements, [1] and this may have been the chief bond between them. *Carmen* XXVII, in which Paulinus takes his friend on a conducted tour (p. 360 ff.) round the buildings at Nola, certainly assumes that the interest and enthusiasm of Niketas will be equal to his own; and the new basilica was Paulinus's greatest pride. Here Paulinus once more welcomes Niketas to Nola to witness the birthday celebrations of St Felix. He points out to him all the improvements in architecture and general lay-out[2] which he has made since Niketas was last in Nola, and though the poem is perhaps reminiscent of Statius's description of villas, [3] the descriptions are delightfully fresh and concrete, and it is clear that Paulinus is speaking at first-hand of things which are very near his heart, and of which he is extremely proud.

'Come then, Father, and let us walk together while I take you round and show you what we have done in detail. You see this portico, where you enter by the first door? It used to be overshadowed by a dark roof, but now a new roof has been erected, higher, with fresh colours. But where the cloistered entrance court spreads its open centre to the sky, there used to be a little garden, poorly cultivated, a poor plot which produced only a few vegetables and those quite useless. And meanwhile we felt an increasing wish to erect this building in its place, . . . so that when the doors were opened a brighter lustre from the opposite façade, should illuminate the venerable church of the Martyr.'

He points out the addition of a new storey to the adjacent buildings, apparently as a dormitory for strangers. He has much to tell us of the courtyard:

'Perhaps as you look at all this you may ask how this court, furnished with so many fountains, is to be fed, because the town is a long way off, and the water, which is brought from there by a small aqueduct, is no more than a little trickle.'

Well, says Paulinus with engaging candour, we don't rely on our own resources at all, but hope for wells from Heaven.

---

[1] *Carmen* XXVII, 221 ff. Sir Arthur Evans relates the finding of a marble slab in Remesiana on which the Latin lettering seems to be of fourth- or fifth-century date, 'evidently relating to the dedication of a church, which may well have been the church of St Nicetas'. *Archaeologia*, XLIX (1885), p. 154 f.

[2] For a critical account of the evidence relating to the architecture and lay-out, see the work of Goldschmidt already cited.

[3] So Helm, who refers to *Silvae* I, 3; II, 2.

So we have built cisterns everywhere against the houses to collect rainwater.

'However', he continues, 'if, all the same, a lack of water should sometimes occur, the court will be a beautiful sight, even when the basins are dry, because the basins are adorned with sculpture and are charming with their conch-shells and coloured bases. After all, you know how beautiful the dry sea in Solomon's great temple was held to be.'

He adds naïvely that it is always the same water, issuing from various orifices.

In *Carmen* XXVIII he confesses that this little inner court is a bit cluttered up with his improvements.

'The court is connected with the three basilicas, and from one centre opens on to them all ... and ... allows exit from all three, with its spacious paved area in the midst of them. Nevertheless, on account of the arrangement of the series of five rows of gleaming basins, this close-set collection of marble offers a marvel to the eyes, but makes walking a delicate matter.'

However, he adds that there is ample opportunity for walking in the surrounding colonnades.

Paulinus's improvements were not carried out without some difficulties, and even a certain measure of opposition. In the middle of the open space opposite the entrance to the old church stood two wretched hovels, which were so close to the door that when it was open the church could not get proper light. Moreover they completely spoilt the view. They were, in fact, extremely ugly, and very much in the way. Demolition was desirable; but, strange to say, the occupants refused to budge. They liked their hovels.

'On our wanting to pull down these obstructions, the people living in them made a protest to us, and swore they would die rather than let themselves be evicted. It looked as if we should have to waive this protest; but I confess that this went against the grain with me, for even victory is distasteful if it is the result of wrangling.'

It is interesting to get this little glimpse of the peasants and their housing rights in Italy at this time. The little huts were evidently flimsy structures, because to the relief of Paulinus one of them was burnt down almost immediately, and the peasant, evidently the owner of both huts, pulled down the other in dudgeon, leaving two heaps, one of ashes, the other of rubble.

In 408 Paulinus lost his wife Therasia, who had shared his life and his ideals so loyally. In 409 or 410[1] he was consecrated Bishop of Nola, and in the latter year Campania was ravaged by the army of Alaric. Paulinus was taken prisoner. We know that he was soon released and allowed to return to Nola, and that he continued to officiate as bishop until his death. But from the time of the sack of Nola almost all detailed information of its routine and communications ceases.

There is, however, one important letter[2] addressed by Paulinus to Eucherius, afterwards Bishop of Lyons, and his wife Galla, which was almost certainly written some time after 410,[3] since it refers to the island monastery on the Lérins, founded by St Honoratus probably about this time, and also to the religious settlement on the neighbouring island of Léro, to which Eucherius and Galla had attached themselves. It is clear from what Paulinus says here that shortly after the settlement of Eucherius and Galla on Léro they had sent some of their companions to Nola with greetings. At the same time the messengers acquainted Paulinus with Honoratus's establishment of the monastery of Lérins. The following year Honoratus had himself sent three of his monks, Gelasius, Augendus, and Tigridius, to Nola; but Eucherius had been unaware of their departure and had sent no further letter by them. In the letter which Paulinus now entrusts to the returning monks he makes reference to Honoratus as a man praiseworthy and illustrious in Jesus Christ, 'our brother and my co-presbyter Honoratus' and also to his 'three young and fervent companions' whom he has sent to him; and he expresses himself delighted thus to receive news of the well-being of his friends on Léro, and begs for further letters. It is evident, therefore, that communication was still taking place between the newly founded monastic settlements on the Lérins group and the earlier settlement at Nola.

Paulinus died in 431.[4] His disciple Uranius has left us an

[1] Buse, op. cit., II, p. 333.

[2] *Ep.* 51. A French translation of this letter is given by Alliez, *Histoire du Monastère de Lérins*, Vol. I (Paris, 1862), p. 75 f.

[3] Lagrange (op. cit., *ad fin.*) dates *Ep.* 51 shortly after 410; but de Labriolle and others between 423 and 426, probably in 423 or 424.

[4] The evidence is to be found in Uranius, cap. 12 (*Epistola de Obitu S. Paulini ad Pacatum*), Migne, *P.L.*, Vol. LIII, col. 861. Uranius, in his account of the saint's death, has left us the names of the consuls then in office.

account of his last hours, which he wrote at the request of a
Gaulish poet, Pacatus, grandson of the celebrated orator of the
same name (cf. p. 43). Pacatus intended to compose a poem on
the life of the saint; but if it was ever written it has not survived.
We possess, however, the letter of Uranius, who tells us that
Paulinus on his death-bed called, not upon St Felix, but upon
St Martin of Tours, and St Januarius of Naples, both of whom
had promised to be with him in that hour.[1]

A beautiful, but unconfirmed tradition, given by Gregory
the Great,[2] relates that after the return of Paulinus to Nola
from his brief absence following upon the sack of the place, he
had voluntarily sold himself into slavery among the Vandals in
Africa in order to raise money to ransom the only son of a widow
whom they had carried off. Here he worked as a gardener,
declaring that this was the only work he could do – a touch
which recalls Sulpicius's playful taunt that the little garden at
Nola was the chief attraction of the place to Paulinus. Eventually, according to Gregory's story, Paulinus had to admit
who he was, and was then allowed to return to Nola. The story
is precisely the kind of tradition to which his gentle character
would give rise.

The pioneer work of Paulinus and Therasia in religious community life is to be regarded not as contempt for the world, but
as a constructive renunciation. Theirs was a spiritual ideal fulfilled in daily life. Paulinus, the Christian devotee, with his
background of classical culture, is typical of all that is best in
the early Church in the West. Fanaticism is entirely absent,
superstition as yet little developed. Persecution, force, quarrel-
ling are utterly distasteful to this gentle spirit. In his tolerance
and his close sympathy and observation of nature he fore-
shadows the Celtic Christian anchorites. His quiet dignity and
reserve, and perhaps most of all his humour, still link him to
the ancient world, and at the same time make him peculiarly
modern and congenial to us today. He is perhaps the most
beautiful personality among the great figures of the transition
from the ancient world to the Christian world which was rapidly
taking its place in the late fourth and early fifth centuries.

[1] Gregory of Tours refers to St Martin's promise as a vision. (*De Gloria Confess.*
CX.)
[2] Gregory the Great, *Dialogues*, III, i (Migne, *P.L.*, Vol. LXXVII, col. 215. Cf.
Buse, II, p. 196). On the value of the tradition, see Helm.

CHAPTER IV

Sulpicius Severus and St Martin of Tours

IN the preceding chapter we made a study of St Paulinus of Nola, a member of the high Gallo-Roman aristocracy, educated in the classical traditions of Bordeaux. We have seen that by his dedication of himself and his wealth to the service of the Church and the poor, he made a great impression on his own day. At the same time his central position in Campania kept him in personal communication with the choicest spirits throughout the entire Mediterranean world and beyond. The many letters and poems which have survived from his pen allow us to see him as his contemporaries saw him; but owing to the fact that we have no contemporary biography of the saint, his memory has not been worthily preserved.

In the present chapter the position is reversed. We are now studying St Martin, both the saint himself, and his biographer and contemporary, Sulpicius Severus,[1] Paulinus's greatest friend. There is a personal relationship between the three; but St Martin is a great contrast to Paulinus. Unlike the latter, Martin has left no writings. His family was comparatively obscure, and he was not even a native of Gaul. He was not widely known in his own day, and he is never mentioned by any of his own immediate contemporaries except Sulpicius Severus and St Paulinus. His very existence has been questioned.

The St Martin whom the world knows is the humble and democratic saint of Tours. He is traditionally held to have been simple, unlearned, and almost wholly occupied in converting the heathen of Gaul, and in contemplation and prayer. This picture of the saint is the creation of his great biographer, Sulpicius, the most delightful writer in Gaul in his day. I propose in this chapter to suggest some modifications of this con-

[1] For an account of the evidence relating to Sulpicius Severus, see the article s.v. by Kappelmacher, in Pauly-Wissowa's *Real-Encyclopädie der Classischen Altertumswissenschaft*, and the references there cited. I have referred throughout to this article simply as *Kappelmacher*. The works of Sulpicius Severus have been edited by C. Helm, *Sulpicii Severi Libri qui Supersunt* (Vienna, 1866). My references are to Helm's edition throughout.

ception of St Martin, and to study the saint and his biographer simultaneously, as indeed one must.

It is in the pages of Sulpicius Severus that we can best study the atmosphere of Gaul at this period. He was a friend of the eminent panegyric poet, Pacatus, and a contemporary of the Priscillianists, about whom he furnishes us with some important information. He gives us our only detailed contemporary picture of the overlap of heathenism and Christianity in Gaul, of the destruction of the heathen monuments, of the foundation and organization of mission churches, and of the management of a diocese. As our only contemporary authority for the life and work of St Martin he gives us our earliest picture of the rise and spread of monasticism in Gaul, and an interesting contrast between the earliest monastic foundation in western Europe and the discipline which prevailed among the Desert Fathers in Lower Egypt.

Sulpicius also introduces us to the conflicting currents of thought among the Christians of his day in Gaul, and more particularly in Aquitaine. We see travellers returning from the East and listen to their reports of the ecclesiastical quarrels in Carthage and Alexandria, the nature of the life and personality of St Jerome at Bethlehem, the wonders and miracles of the Desert Fathers of Egypt. We can watch the bitter hostility with which the ascetic movement had to contend in its early days in Gaul. We can watch the revival of national consciousness and national pride among the Gaulish people, and at the same time we become aware of the rise of an active and practical democracy, and of sympathy with the poor, backed by ascetic and monastic sympathy and capital.

Sulpicius Severus is a man whose name and fame were widespread throughout Gaul even in his own day. St Jerome refers to him in his commentary on the 36th chapter of *Ezekiel* as 'our friend Severus', and St Augustine alludes to him in *Ep.* 205 as 'a man who excels in learning and in wisdom'. We have already made his acquaintance as the life-long friend of St Paulinus, to whom thirteen of the saint's surviving letters are addressed. Sulpicius appears never to have left Gaul, and he was probably known in his own day chiefly through his letters, most of which seem to have perished. We possess only three certainly authentic from his hand. His fame rests chiefly on his books.

Gennadius,[1] the presbyter of Marseilles (A.D. 496) already alluded to, writes of him as follows:

'The presbyter Severus, whose cognomen was Sulpicius, who belonged to the province of Aquitania, was a man distinguished on account of both his family and his education, and was outstanding for his devotion to poverty and humility. He was also intimate with some holy men, such as Martin, Bishop of Tours, and Paulinus, Bishop of Nola; and his works are by no means to be neglected.'

A list and brief account of his works follow, and the entry concludes with the statement that 'In his old age he was led astray by the Pelagians, and recognizing the guilt of much speaking, kept silence till his death, in order that by penitent silence he might atone for the sin which he had contracted by speaking.'

Sulpicius is thought to have been born c. 363 and, as Gennadius tells us, of a good family. It is generally assumed that he was educated at Bordeaux. Ausonius was absent, acting as tutor to the youthful Gratian about the time when Severus would have been at the university, and this may account for the lack of evidence that Ausonius and Sulpicius ever met. It is clear, however, that he received an excellent classical education, and he seems to have adopted a profession as a solicitor or pleader. He married into a wealthy family, at least one member of which held the rank of consul; but his wife died early,—while his father was still alive.[2] No children are mentioned, and it is fairly certain that he had none. His closest personal tie throughout his life was undoubtedly that with his mother-in-law, Bassula, who lived at Trier. Sulpicius addresses her in terms of the warmest affection, and with a playfulness which manifests the delightful relationship existing between them (cf. p. 93 f.).

At this point, possibly c. 392, by the advice of St Martin, Sulpicius renounced the world, despite the opposition of his father,[3] selling most of his property,[4] and becoming a presbyter.

---

[1] *Liber de Viris Illustribus*, cap. 19. For fuller details of the work of Gennadius, and for the edition and translation of his work by Richardson, see p. 206, n. 3 below. In general I have referred to this work simply under the name Gennadius.

[2] For these details, see Paulinus, *Ep.* 5.

[3] Paulinus, *Ep.* 5.

[4] Paulinus, *Ep.* 24.

He settled as a monk, first at Elusa (the modern Eause) in the valley of the Adour, near the Pyrenees, and later in Primulia-cum.[1] He seems to have had secretaries for whom he was in-debted to the generosity of Bassula.[2] He could also employ *pueri*, as members of his household,[3] and as letter carriers.[4] These may have been the domestic freemen. His chief letter carrier was, as we have seen, the monk Victor, a zealous disciple of St Martin.

The picture which Sulpicius gives us of his monastic retreat has little resemblance to the ordered community at Nola, and the term 'community' is too restricted a term to describe the little independent Christian society among whom Sulpicius lived. He himself speaks of a *turba monachorum*[5] who were assoc-iated with him either at Elusa or at his favourite estate at Primuliacum. In contrast to this society he also gives us in quieter colours a glimpse of himself sitting alone in his little cell, ruminating on spiritual things,[6] just as he pictures St Martin seated outside his cell in the courtyard of his monastic settlement.[7]

Many of Sulpicius's associates, the *turba monachorum*, are known to us from other sources, especially from letters. They include Refrigerius, Evagrius, Aetherius, and Aurelius, all priests.[8] Probably the latter is the Aurelius to whom Sulpicius addresses the second of his three letters. There were also Calu-pio, a deacon, and Amator, a sub-deacon, besides Aper, Sab-batius, and Agricola, all monks.[9]

Sabbatius was probably the anchorite Sebastian, an acquaint-ance of our old friend Victor. Victor tells Paulinus that Sebas-tian was living as a religious hermit on the bank of a stream, subsisting on the bare necessities of life, which were provided for him by his brother, himself a deacon serving a neighbouring

---

[1] Paulinus, *Epp.* 1, 31, 32. The place has never been satisfactorily identified. M. F. Mouret places it near Vendres in the Biterrais (*Sulpice Sévère à Primuliac*, (Paris, 1907). M. R. Ricaud rejects all previous identifications in favour of Saint-Sever-de-Rustan in the Bigorre (*Sulpice Sévère et sa Villa de Primuliac à Saint-Sever-de-Rustan* (Tarbes, 1913).

[2] Sulpicius Severus, *Ep.* 3.

[3] *Dialogues* I (II) 14.

[4] Paulinus, *Ep.* 5.

[5] ibid., II (III), 1.

[6] Sulpicius Severus, *Ep.* 2.

[7] *Dialogues*, II (III), 15.

[8] Aurelius, here a *presbyter*, is referred to in *Ep.* 2 as *diaconus*.

[9] For this list, see *Dialogues*, II (III), 1.

church. Paulinus, charmed with what he has heard, sends a letter of greeting to Sebastian by Victor from himself and Therasia.[1] Aper and his wife Amanda seem to have been inspired by the example of Paulinus and Therasia, and like them, to have withdrawn from the world when already advanced in life, and the parents of a number of children. Aper himself became a priest, and one of the most interesting letters from Paulinus and Therasia is no. 44, in which the duties of a priest's wife of the period are brought before us with some fullness.

Probably the most important personal and literary influence in the life of Sulpicius was that of Bassula. Only one letter to her has been preserved; but we can hardly doubt that she is the 'sister', in a spiritual sense, to whom, as Gennadius tells us, he wrote many letters which were not published because they contained personal or family matters. Even the extant letter is enough to show that she was a forceful and highly intellectual woman, on whose sympathy and understanding he could count, and to whose kindness he was indebted for the most ample secretarial help and speedy postal service. Paulinus refers to her in a letter to his friend as 'your blessed mother-in-law, more generous than any parent'.[2] She seems to have played something of the same part in his life and work that St Paula played in that of St Jerome, stimulating and encouraging his production, and furnishing all the assistance in her power. She lived, at any rate for a time, at Trier, then the capital of the West, and seems to have acted as his literary and publishing agent, not even scrupling – so he laughingly accuses her – of pirating his work before he has had time to correct or revise it.

'If it were legally possible', he writes to Bassula, 'to bring an action against one's relatives, I should have a clear case for bringing a charge of piracy and theft against you in the courts with a fair grievance. For why should I not lodge a complaint of the damage which I suffer from you? You have not left in my house one scrap of paper, one small book, or one letter; for you steal them all and publish the lot. If I write a personal letter to a friend; if I happen, in a lighter moment, to dictate something which I would like, nevertheless, to keep secret, everything reaches you almost before it is written or dictated. I am certain

---

[1] *Ep.* 26.
[2] *Ep.* 5 (*socrum sanctam omni liberaliorem parente*).

you have my secretaries in bondage to you, and they enable you to publish my trifles. And then again I cannot be angry with them for obeying you, because it is only by your generosity that I have them at my command, and they are aware that they are still yours rather than mine. It is you only whom I accuse, you alone are guilty of setting traps for me, and cheating them into handing over to you indiscriminately all my personal correspondence and my casual drafts completely unelaborated and unpolished. Now to say nothing of the rest, I wonder how the letter which I wrote a little while ago to the deacon Aurelius reached you so quickly? for I am at Toulouse, and you are in Trier . . . so how have you managed to steal this private letter?'

And what follows is very interesting as revealing the influence which is stimulating him in his writings on St Martin:

'I have received your letter in which you write that in the same epistle in which I made mention of the death of St Martin I ought to have written a full account of the passing of the Blessed One, as if I had actually intended that letter to be read by anyone except the person to whom it was addressed . . . I have decided to write nothing to you for fear you should publish me everywhere. Still, if you promise not to read it to anyone, I will satisfy your wish in a few words and share with you such information as I have.'

The letters of Paulinus to his friend enable us to follow the quiet routine at Elusa and Primuliacum during a number of years. We hear of Sulpicius, like Paulinus himself, busy with the building and decoration of his churches, a baptistery, and at least one new basilica at Primuliacum in 402.[1] He seems to have formerly paid an annual visit – perhaps even more – to his friend St Martin of Tours.[2] In this way of life he continued till his death, which is thought to have been connected with the invasion of the Vandals and Visigoths, and to have taken place between 410 and 420. The latter date would seem to be the more probable (cf. p. 96).

As we study the works of Sulpicius, especially the *Dialogues*,

---

[1] See Paulinus, *Epp.* 31, 32. Kappelmacher (op. cit., col. 864) understands the second letter to refer to only one (a parish) church, and a baptistery.
[2] See Paulinus, *Ep.* 17. The letter is dated 398, less than a year after St Martin's death. See P. Reinelt, *Studien über die Briefe des hl. Paulinus von Nola* (Breslau, 1903), p. 59.

with their gentle charm and quiet atmosphere, the impression which they convey is that of an idyllic existence. This tone of serenity and blitheness is a measure of his own graceful literary style. In reality the atmosphere of Gaul was a troubled one for those who sought to devote themselves to the life of a recluse, or to the practice of austerities. The Church for the most part, especially many of the bishops, viewed the growth of monasticism with deep distrust. Their views were emphatically voiced early in the following century by Pope Celestine, who expressed their point of view unequivocally in his famous letter, *Cuperemus quidem*, dated July 26th, 428, and addressed to the bishops of Narbonne and Vienne.

'It is not surprising that they who have not grown up in the Church act contrary to the Church's usages, and that, coming from other customs, they have brought their traditional ways with them into our Church. Clad in a pallium, and with a girdle round the loins, they consider that they will be fulfilling the letter rather than the spirit of the Scriptures . . . Such a course may perhaps be followed as a matter of custom rather than reason by those who dwell in remote places and pass their lives far from their fellow men. But why should they dress in this way in the churches of Gaul, changing the usage of so many years, of such great prelates, for another habit?'[1]

It is not unnatural that Sulpicius's hero, St Martin, should have been an unpopular figure with those holding such views. Himself a bishop, and a pioneer of the monastic movement in Gaul, he was not even of great family, not even a Gaul by birth. His teaching and way of life were dictated in a considerable measure by personal initiative rather than by ecclesiastical tradition. His appearance and habits were, in the eyes of the episcopal party, so Sulpicius assures us, unbecoming in a bishop.

This hostility of the Gaulish bishops towards the new ascetic and monastic movement was widely known in Italy and the East. In A.D. 392 St Ambrose makes the episcopal quarrels his excuse for not going to Gaul.[2] Again in 406, Jerome, in his treatise against Vigilantius (cf. p. 81) refers, with bitter abuse,

---

[1] Mansi III, p. 264; Migne, *P.L.*, Vol. L, col. 430.
[2] *Gallorum episcoporum, propter quorum frequentes dissensiones cerebro me excusaveram.* (*De Obitu Valentiniani Consolatio.*)

to the opposition to asceticism in Gaul. But it was not confined to Gaul. In Rome hostile demonstrations had taken place against the monks at the funeral of St Paula's eldest daughter, whose death was believed to have been the result of her excessive austerities. In Alexandria feeling against the monks ran even higher (cf. p. 110).

On the other hand this attitude was by no means universal, even in Gaul. In itself it is not enough to account for Sulpicius's undoubted unpopularity, which is clear throughout his own writings, and also from a letter of invitation from Paulinus,[1] in which he urges Sulpicius that a visit to Nola would allow time for the hostility of the Gaulish bishops to abate. What the exact charge against Sulpicius was we do not know; but his own attitude was anything but conciliatory. Indeed, he never loses an opportunity of pressing home a thrust against the bishops and clergy.

Although Sulpicius's home was in the part of Aquitaine which had given support to the Priscillianist cause, we have no hint that he was ever suspected of sympathizing with their party, and he repudiates their views unequivocally. On the other hand we have seen that Gennadius records a tradition that in his old age he was led astray by the Pelagians,[2] and he adds that as a penance Sulpicius imposed silence on himself until his death. The two statements are often regarded as apocryphal;[3] but Gennadius was a careful writer who possessed much precise information. He wrote only about seventy years after the death of Sulpicius. Moreover Gennadius himself wrote a refutation of Pelagianism which is lost. He would hardly be likely therefore to make a mistake in a matter of this kind.

It will be noticed that Gennadius says that Sulpicius was led astray, not by Pelagius himself, but by the Pelagians (*a Pelagianis*). It is relevant to the question of the date of Sulpicius's death that the statement, true or false, could hardly have been made at all if Sulpicius had died c. 410, as some assert. The later date, 420, when the Vandals and Visigoths settled in the south, is much more likely, for by this time Pelagianism was widely known and well established. By this time also the

---

[1] Paulinus, *Ep.* 5 (*zeli fuga, qui maxime conspectu aut vicinia aemulae conversationis accenditur*). .
[2] *In senectute sua a Pelagianis deceptus.*
[3] See e.g. T. R. Glover, *Life and Letters in the Fourth Century*, p. 300 f.

monastery of Lérins, to the south of the Gulf of Lyons, had been established for at least ten years, probably more. The monastery of St Victor in or near Marseilles is believed to have been founded between 411 and 420.[1] Both these monastic institutions regarded with sympathy certain views also held by the Pelagians, though they disclaimed adherence to their heretical opinions. It would seem in no way unlikely that Sulpicius himself, after the death of St Martin, had come under influences either acting upon or emanating from Lérins or Marseilles; and that he afterwards came to regard their views as heresy, and decided to lay down his pen for life. We need not take the statement about his self-imposed silence in any save a figurative sense.[2] And it seems to be a fact that after the *Dialogues*, which appeared in 404, he wrote nothing else.

We have seen that Sulpicius had made a promise to Paulinus and Therasia to visit them in Nola, and that Paulinus repeatedly invited him in the most pressing terms; but Sulpicius never went. A comparison of the chronology of his own writings with the letters of Paulinus suggests that the reason was pressure of work. Sulpicius's time must have been too fully occupied to allow of foreign travel; and indeed he never shows any inclination for it. He was busily engaged at this time in writing the *Life of St Martin*, of which at least the first draft seems to have been finished at the time of the saint's death, probably in 397, and to have been shown to St Paulinus in the same year,[3] though it is thought to have been revised about 400.[4] In the intervening period appeared his three letters, or at least two of them.[5] His *Chronica*, or 'Sacred History', was composed during the consulship of Stilicho in 400,[6] and enlarged and revised later in 403.[7] In 404 appeared his *Dialogues*. His literary work was therefore compressed into a very short period.

---

[1] See O. Chadwick, *John Cassian* (Cambridge, 1950), p. 189.

[2] Gennadius's statement is accepted by Kappelmacher (see Pauly-Wissowa, s.v. Sulpicius Severus).

[3] Paulinus, *Ep.* 11; Sulp. Sever., *Dial.*, I, 23; II (III), 17.

[4] P. Monceaux, *St Martin of Tours* (translated by M. C. Watt, London, 1928), p. 2. See also T. R. Glover, *Life and Letters in the Fourth Century* (Cambridge, 1901), p. 294, n. 2. Kappelmacher suggests the date 393 (? a misprint for 398). For a résumé of views on the death of St Martin, see Delehaye, 'Saint Martin et Sulpice Sévère', *Analecta Bollandiana*, Vol. XXXVIII (1920), p. 19.

[5] So Kappelmacher.

[6] *Chronica* II, 9.

[7] See Kappelmacher.

St Martin had perhaps been Bishop of Tours for some twenty years before Sulpicius knew of his work. It would seem therefore that the period of contact and the writing of the *Life* extended between the years 391 and 397. We shall see that the concluding portion of the *Chronica* or 'Sacred History' is devoted to an account of the part played by St Martin in the Priscillianist controversy. The last work of Sulpicius, the *Dialogues*, is also composed with the same object of glorifying the saint. The three extant letters of Sulpicius are devoted to the same subject. He had, moreover, modelled his own ideals on those of Martin, and had placed his portrait in the church at Primuliacum. It is abundantly clear that from the time when he first heard of the saint, c. 391, Sulpicius had devoted himself exclusively to the furtherance of the cult of St Martin as the pioneer of asceticism and the monastic life in Gaul.

The narrative of the life of St Martin which Sulpicius has left us is made up of two elements, biography[1] and miracles.[2] The biography is admirably conducted. Sulpicius relates the birth of the saint[3] from pagan parents of some standing[4] in Sabaria[5] in Pannonia, his boyhood in Pavia in Italy, his early life in the army, his retirement from the world, and his first visit to St Hilary of Poitiers, by whom he was ordained an exorcist. We are then told of his return to Illyria with the object of converting his parents; his sufferings at the hands of Arian persecutors; and his subsequent withdrawal to Milan, where he dwelt in a retreat, perhaps alone.[6] Next comes his banishment from Milan, again owing to the persecution of the Arian governor, and his further withdrawal to the island of Gallinaria off the coast of north-western Italy,[7] with only one disciple. (Was this his beloved disciple, Clarus?). On Hilary's recall, Martin is said to have followed him to Poitiers, where he

---

[1] I have confined myself here to a narrative treatment of the *Vita*. For a discussion of the historicity of the biography, see Delehaye, op. cit., p. 5 ff. See more especially p. 86 ff.

[2] For a discussion of the miraculous element in the *Life*, see Delehaye, op. cit., p. 73 ff.

[3] St Martin's birth is thought to have probably taken place c. 315.

[4] '*parentibus . . . non infimis* (*Vita*, 2).

[5] Identified with the modern Szombathély in Hungary, some twenty miles south of Vienna.

[6] We may remind ourselves of the little community under the walls of Milan referred to by St Augustine.

[7] The islands off the north-west coast of Italy were favourite retreats of hermits, as we may gather from the work of Rutilius Namatianus (cf. p. 132).

was warmly welcomed by the saint, and where he settled in a *monasterium* near the city. Sulpicius does not mention the name of the site, but from Gregory of Tours we gather that it was *Locotigiacense monasterium*, known in later times as *Ligugé*.[1]

We hear little of Martin's life at Ligugé except that he restored to life a catechumen who had died while Martin was absent on a journey, and also a slave who had hanged himself. But shortly afterwards, Martin – we are following Sulpicius's narrative throughout – was forcibly consecrated Bishop of Tours,[2] apparently in accordance with the common custom – perhaps even a convention – of the time (cf. p. 68, n. 4). Finding his life seriously interrupted by visitors to his cell near the church[3] at Tours, he moved to a secluded site some two leagues from the city, where he settled with some eighty monks in cells and caves. The monastic settlement came to be known later as *magnum monasterium*, or in modern French *Marmoutier*.

Here Sulpicius pauses to give us an interesting account of the routine of the inmates of the settlement of Marmoutier – our earliest picture of a monastic community on a considerable scale in Europe, and probably the earliest in western Europe. The bishop and many of the monks lived in wooden cells, but the majority excavated caves for themselves in the overhanging rock. No one possessed personal property, and all trading was forbidden. The younger monks occupied themselves in some measure with copying MSS., but the older ones were wholly given up to prayer. They ate their evening meal together and met together for common worship, but otherwise remained most of the time in their cells. No wine was drunk save in sickness, and they wore garments of camel-hair. Many of the monks were of noble birth, and several of them became bishops.

Immediately after this the account of Martin's miracles is inserted into the *Life* in a solid block. We shall see a similar device adopted later by Constantius in his *Life of St Germanus*. Martin's miracles are unusually interesting, and, as Sulpicius himself points out, eminently useful; and partly owing to Sulpicius's brilliant narrative powers, even a critical Protestant is

---

[1] *Virtutes S. Martini* IV, 30; cf. *Vita S. Hilarii*, XII (*in vico Locoteiaco*).

[2] Martin's episcopal consecration seems to have taken place in 371 or 370 (Delehaye, op. cit., p. 31).

[3] Sulpicius, *Vita S. Martini*, 10. *Aliquamdiu ergo adhaerente ad ecclesiam cellula usus est.*

almost convinced against his judgment of the truth of the marvels.[1] When, for instance, the dead catechumen of Ligugé relates the experiences which he underwent in the spirit world while he was dead, we are struck, not only by the similarity of the narrative to such ancient Greek stories as that of Plato's story of Er, Son of Armenius, but to many other experiences of people in a condition of mental dissociation; and we are inclined to ask whether there is indeed any miracle involved, but rather a natural cure. Again, when the slave who had hanged himself – also at Ligugé – responds to the saint's treatment by 'a quivering in the face', after which 'the heavy eyes fix themselves on Martin's face', we are tempted to wonder if death had really taken place at all – the whole incident is so life-like. Sulpicius would have made a good teller of ghost-stories.

Sulpicius avoids the jejune type of miracle by the most skilful artistry. When the saint suspects a false cult at an ancient tomb, reported to be that of martyrs, he is represented as employing the methods of the most scientific research worker to ascertain the truth. He interviews the church authorities on the spot, both priests and clerks, enquiring as to the name of the martyr and the occasion of the martyrdom, for he feels gravely dubious, owing to the vague nature of the tradition. He keeps away for a long time, being unwilling to countenance the popular devotion, and equally unwilling to discourage it on suspicion. After much circumspection, he visits the place, and, standing on the tomb, begs the Lord to reveal the name and merits of the dead man, whereupon a fearful and hideous spectre rises on his left, and declares his name and former life of crime; for he had been a brigand, and had been executed for his crimes. Must we dismiss the whole story as a hagiographical commonplace? Or has some vague tradition of Martin's sagacious procedure in regard to a local cult been approximated by Sulpicius to a widespread type of story?

The atmosphere of verisimilitude in the miracle is greatly increased by the frequent touches of local colour introduced by Sulpicius. We hear of sacred trees,[2] and, accordingly, of the

---

[1] Cf., however, Delehaye, op. cit., p. 73 ff. Delehaye regards Sulpicius as not, in general, inclined to give any very serious credence to the miracles himself. Cf. especially p. 78. For a summary of various opinions on this matter, including those of Babut, see P. de Labriolle, *Latin Christianity*, p. 383 f.

[2] We shall meet the veneration of trees later in the *Life of St Germanus*, p. 246.

burning of ancient sanctuaries – the sanctuaries of rustic folk. We are also in a country of ancient Roman splendour, and we hear of a rich temple with altars and statues, which even the saint cannot raze to the ground without the help of two heavenly angels. Even the disguises assumed by the devil in order to deceive the saint are those of the Roman gods Mercury, Jupiter, even Venus and Minerva; but Mercury most of all. Elsewhere also we are again told that Mercury frequently worried him, but that Jupiter, being a heavy, stupid fellow, gave little trouble! It is easy to exaggerate the anthropomorphic element here. Except in the large towns Gaul was as yet largely pagan, and there must have been many Roman religious statues and temples which may have been a source of sore difficulty and temptation to any saint, who would no doubt feel it his duty as a Christian to destroy them, but who, like Paulinus and Sulpicius, might well feel an involuntary appreciation of classical art or literature. To this subject I shall return later.

When we hear of the saint on a missionary tour among the Aedui, destroying temples and idols; when we learn of fierce attacks against him with sword and knife, miraculously frustrated, we shall do well, before we lightly dismiss such stories, to remember that this had been a stronghold of Druidism. We must give a liberal interpretation to the miraculous elements, remembering on the one hand that hagiographical writings may have already tended to conform to a pattern; and on the other, that Sulpicius himself tells us, after relating the miraculous destruction of many temples and sanctuaries, that usually it was, in actual fact, the pagans themselves who destroyed their own temples after hearing the preaching of the saint. If we recall the incident of the saint's cure of the affection of Paulinus's eye – a cure which, according to Sulpicius, was miraculous – we shall allow something for the growth of the miraculous element by a literal interpretation of figurative and hyperbolical diction in the interpretation of tradition. And it is well to recall that hyperbolical and figurative speech was characteristic of Gaulish eloquence, which was extremely flourishing at this period, and of which the standard was kept up by many professional panegyric poets and orators.

This brings me to the chapter which relates Martin's visit to the table of the Emperor Maximus, then ruling in Trier. Sulpicius touches more fully on the relations between Martin and Maximus in his later work, in regard to the Priscillianist controversy, where we shall see that he utilizes the occasion of Martin's visit to the capital to inveigh against the episcopal party, especially that in Trier. It is in the light of these later passages that we must interpret the opening words of the present chapter, in which he declares that the times are so corrupt that it is little short of a miracle to find a bishop such as Martin, who, unlike his fellow bishops, would not stoop to flatter Maximus. He proceeds to relate the great difficulty which Maximus has in persuading Martin to come to his table as a guest; and he tells how, when the saint finally yields to the imperial persuasion, he upholds the dignity of the Church by honouring the priest who has accompanied him, even above the emperor himself. Sulpicius adds that the courageous and dignified bearing of Martin in this matter won for him the admiration of all present, not excluding the emperor.

The final chapters bring us into more personal touch with the saint, for they relate among other matters the first visit of Sulpicius to his patron. Having, as he tells us, for long heard tales of Martin's life and works, and feeling a burning desire to write an account of both, he determined to undertake the long journey. He tells us of the welcome which he received, and of the saint's discourse, and he here introduces Martin's panegyric on Paulinus of Nola quoted above – an adroit compliment to one who was about to circulate the *Life* throughout Italy and Illyria.

Sulpicius has left us a life-like and consistent portrait of the saint, whom we see in his pages as a dignified and austere person, ascetic in habit and appearance, with the peculiarly happy and unruffled countenance of one whose inner life is attuned to a lofty ideal. He never laughed we are told, never showed anger or excitement. Though he might spend time in reading, in travelling on missionary enterprise, or in attending to the churches of his diocese, yet his main attention was given to prayer and contemplation. Without malice, without desire of vengeance, he was, Sulpicius enthusiastically assures us, a man such as not Homer himself, should he return from Hades, would be able to describe as he deserved.

The enthusiasm is genuine; but it is double edged. Martin, Sulpicius adds, was so full of Christian charity that, bishop though he was, he allowed himself to be insulted by clerics, though he wept over the sins of those who decried him. Many there were who were jealous of his power, and of the virtues of the ascetic, and the majority of his persecutors were bishops. Here Sulpicius touches on the feud in the Church and the growing prestige of monasticism, and he does not hesitate to throw down the gauntlet as a challenge to the episcopal party. 'I shall not shrink from the censure of such people as these, if only I am hated along with a man such as Martin.'[1] There can be no doubt that these aggressive attacks on the bishops had the effect of fanning the flame against asceticism, and arousing hostility against Sulpicius himself.

The three letters, which are all that remain to us of undoubted authenticity from the correspondence of Sulpicius, may be regarded as supplementary to the *Life*. The first, which is addressed to the priest Eusebius against a detractor of St Martin, makes clear that, while the *Life* had been in general well received, there were some bad 'reviews'. In particular, scepticism in regard to the miracles had already made itself felt. It was to answer this objection that Sulpicius relates in this letter an incident[2] which occurred to St Martin while visiting one of his parishes, 'as it was his annual custom, and that of bishops to visit their churches'. The saint was lodged in the sacristy of the church,[3] and as it was winter, a fire had been lighted in the hypocaust below; but the surface of the pavement was cracked and very thin,[4] and the flames made their way through the *tesserae* and ignited the straw which he had flung aside, preferring to sleep on the bare ground. The point of Sulpicius's story is that when the saint attempted to unlock the door he failed until he sought help by prayer, when the fire was powerless to harm him, and the saint was rescued by his disciples from outside. For us, perhaps, the chief interest in the story lies in the picture of the conditions of life among Church dignitaries in the fourth century – the annual tour around their parishes; the lodging in the sacristy; the ascetic habit and its

---

[1] *Vita S. Martini*, 27.
[2] Cf. also *Dialogues* I (II), 9.
[3] *Mansionem ei in secretario ecclesiae cleri paraverunt.*
[4] *Multum ignem scabro jam et pertenui pavimento subdiderunt.*

rigours; and the somewhat derelict condition of the Roman basilica.

The second letter, addressed to the deacon Aurelius, opens with a charming picture of Sulpicius himself, seated, after the deacon's visit, alone in his little cell, plunged in meditation, till, wearied with penitential reflections, he lies down on his bed and falls into a light sleep. In a dream or vision St Martin appears to him, holding the *Life* in his hand, and after blessing its author he disappears into the open Heavens, followed by his disciple, the presbyter Clarus. Before Sulpicius has fully aroused himself a slave arrives with tidings of Martin's death. It is noteworthy that in the panegyric on the saint which follows we are again reminded of the reproaches of enemies, the railings of the rabble. It is clear from both this letter and the last that even during Martin's lifetime his good name and his prestige by no means passed unchallenged. The naïve devices by which Sulpicius sought to spread his cult, such as that of the vision of the dying saint with the *Life* in his hand, were undoubtedly inspired by a strong body of opposition already making itself felt. The third letter, which is addressed to Bassula, and which gives a detailed account of the saint's death, and of the vast concourse which formed the funeral procession – 'the whole population of the city, all the people of the countryside and the villages, and many others from the neighbouring towns also were present' – is undoubtedly dictated by the same motives as the preceding works.

The letters and the *Life* alike afford invaluable testimony to the extent and nature of the obstacles which the new element in Christianity, ascetic monasticism, had to overcome in Gaul, and the part played by the local saints, such as Martin – perhaps even more by their literary exponents – in forwarding the new movement. Sulpicius was an admirable Boswell, and also an excellent writer of propaganda. The letters, in particular the first letter, are written throughout in a pamphleteering spirit, and with the avowed object of replying to adverse criticism. From the first letter (to Eusebius) we infer that the *Life* had been written, not to fulfil the purpose of an exhaustive biography, or a library tome, but as something suited for general use. He says (par. 1) that he is glad that his book is being eagerly read by many; and later in the same letter (par. 8) he says that he had no intention of writing a completely exhaustive *Life* of Martin, since this would have made his book too long for his readers. The opening passage of the *Letter to Bassula*, and the picture presented to us in the *Dialogues*, to be discussed later, of the newly arrived traveller, Postumianus, producing the little volume out of the fold of his garment, repeat the same idea. Sulpicius, doubtless following St Athanasius's *Life of St Antony*, aimed at producing a popular handbook which might serve, like the latter, as a guide to new communities seeking to follow the ascetic way of life.

There is, however, another object which Sulpicius seems to have in view, and which will become clearer as we consider his later works, especially the *Dialogues*. This object is the establishment of a local, or rather a national cult. Martin, bishop of Tours, though born in Pannonia and brought up in Italy, was certainly Gaulish by adoption.[1] Sulpicius's later work, the *Dialogues*, are so strongly coloured by the author's representation of Martin's hatred of the episcopal party that one is tempted at times to suspect that the main object of Sulpicius in writing of Martin was to 'show them up'; and perhaps the impulse in this direction was, indeed, his strongest emotion. Yet it is an undoubted fact that the avowed object of the *Dialogues* was to prove that the Saint of Gaul excelled by his piety and spiritual grace all the monks of the East; and we shall see that the framework of the composition is carefully constructed to emphasize this argument and to carry conviction.

About this time chronicle writing became fashionable among Christian writers, who, educated in the classical tradition of such writers as Tacitus, carried on the work with a new zest and a new bias under the inspiration of the Bible and Christian teaching. In 303, Eusebius, the Bishop of Caesarea, had published a Chronicle in two Books, the first containing a universal history, the second a series of chronological tables. In 324 or 325 the same author had published his *History of the Christian Church*, in which, while narrating the history of the Church, he

---

[1] It was a characteristic feature of the new monasticism that the monks abandoned all association with their native land, literally 'giving up' home and country, and becoming a *peregrinus* 'a pilgrim (to God)'. An outstanding example is that of St Severinus († 482), the apostle in Pannonia and Noricum on the Danube, who would never reveal his place of origin. (See his *Life* by his disciple Eugippius, translated by G. W. Robinson (Cambridge, Mass., 1914)).

sought to convince his readers of its divine origin. About a century later, Orosius, a Spanish monk, wrote (417 or 418) his 'History of the World', *Historiae adversus Paganos*, expressly to show that the evils which had befallen mankind had not become worse owing to the adoption of the Christian religion, despite the contrary statements of its traducers.

Among works of this kind, the *Chronica*[1] or 'Sacred History' of Sulpicius is one of the most interesting and attractive. It consists of an epitome of sacred history in two Books. The narrative is clear and bright, and thoroughly readable, with little trace of the scrappiness which generally characterizes epitomes. The author points out that he has made use of profane historians to fix both his absolute and his relative chronology, and to supplement sacred Scriptures. At the same time he is careful to add that he does not wish his book to be read to the neglect of the original authorities, but in order to supplement and synthesize the material contained in various sources.

The first part opens, as we should expect, with the Creation, and concludes with the Captivity. The second part takes up the narrative from this point. The later chapters are extremely interesting, not so much for their clear and bright epitome of Biblical history, readable though this is, as for the historical supplement which carries the narrative down to the writer's own day. After an enumeration of the ten persecutions of the Church, a brief account of the Arian controversy follows, and the *Chronica* ends with the Priscillianist movement, for which Sulpicius is a valuable contemporary authority. At this point his narrative becomes fuller and more detailed. His personal views on the points at issue undoubtedly colour his presentation of the facts in his accounts of both the Council of Rimini and of the Priscillianist trial. Here, as elsewhere, his profound disapproval of the bishops of Gaul is abundantly clear; but we must admire the restraint and artistic sense with which the expression of his burning convictions is in general kept subordinate to his respect for historical truth.

The Council of Rimini had been convened by the Emperor in 359, and according to the usual custom the expenses of the

---

[1] For a valuable general study of this work and its sources, see J. Bernays, *Gesammelte Abhandlungen* (edited by Usener, and published in Berlin, 1885), Vol. II, p. 81 (cap. XXIX, 'Über die Chronik des Sulpicius Severus', 1861).

delegates were to be paid at the public cost. Sulpicius tells us that the Aquitanians, the Gauls, and most of the Britons refused to accept their expenses, though three of the British bishops, being without private means, and unwilling to accept the contributions offered by their fellow bishops, accepted the public bounty. Sulpicius adds that 'our bishop Gavidius' used to speak of the action of the three British bishops with disapproval; but that he himself held quite the opposite view:

'I hold it to be a matter of praise that the bishops were so poor as to possess nothing of their own . . . They offer us an outstanding example.'[1]

Sulpicius here allows us to see the ill-will of the bishops of Aquitaine towards asceticism and voluntary poverty. Moreover he leaves us in no doubt as to his own attitude in the matter. He is flatly opposed to 'our bishop Gavidius', and upholds the three censured British ascetics. This uncompromising attitude towards the Gaulish bishops he maintains throughout his writings. It is hardly surprising that he should have incurred their hostility.

The account of the Priscillianist 'heresy' which closes the *Chronica* is marked by what appears to be a measure of fair-mindedness and moderation. Sulpicius sketches the rise and spread of the heresy, and declares that in his view it was right that the upholders should have been condemned; but it would have been enough, he maintains, to deprive them of their offices in the Church without depriving them of their lives. Moreover, it was abominable that they should be tried, and in particular the Bishops Priscillian and Instantius, in a civil court. His special censure falls on the Bishop Ithacius, who had even accused Martin himself of heresy because he had denied the right of the civil court to condemn the 'heretics', and had extracted a promise from the emperor that no cruel measures should be taken against them – a promise which was, of course, not kept.

With Sulpicius, however, the root of the struggle lay deeper. It was a struggle of the 'bishops', of whom he regarded Ithacius as a typical representative, against the monastic and ascetic innovator Martin. It is the success of this episcopal party, and more especially Ithacius, which arouses his bitterness. He

[1] *Chronica*, II, 41.

emphasizes the fact that the execution of the Priscillianist leaders only served to strengthen their party and to prolong and spread the 'heresy', and he rejoices that Ithacius himself was ultimately deprived of his episcopate. He concludes with bitter accusations against the episcopal party whose stupidity and avarice have triumphed over the wiser councils of the minority, to the lasting detriment of the Church in Gaul. As we read these last chapters of the *Chronica* we hardly feel any doubt that the struggle of the rising monastic movement in Gaul against the opposition of the established episcopal party was the most serious concern of Sulpicius's intellectual endeavours.

We now come to the most charming of all the works of Sulpicius, his three *Dialogues*. In the perfection of their style the author has combined the freshness and brightness which we like to associate with native Gaulish culture; the polish and restraint of the classical training and the classical tradition; and the vigour and seriousness, and the intellectual and spiritual quickening from the Christian East. The framework is probably derived ultimately from the works, more especially the Dialogues of Plato, with which Sulpicius was familiar, as he shows by his references both to Plato himself, and to the death of Socrates.[1] The actual model followed, with a leader in charge of the Dialogue, and one speaker carrying on the main discourse, interrupted by longer or shorter observations from the other speakers, perhaps owes something to Cicero.

The scene is laid in the seclusion of Sulpicius's cell, where they are at leisure and undisturbed.[2] In the first two *Dialogues* only three persons are present, namely, his friend Postumianus, who has just returned from a three years' sojourn in the East; Gallus, a Gaul, who is an intimate friend of Sulpicius and also a disciple of St Martin; and Sulpicius himself, who is there in the capacity of question-master. Gallus is a man well educated in the rhetorical training of the day, in which, as we have seen, the Gauls excelled. He is addressed as *scholasticus*,[3] and he refers to himself as having joined Martin as a disciple after leaving the 'schools' (*relictis scholis*). He is probably one of the number of high rank and gentle nurture among Martin's dis-

---

[1] See *Dialogues* II (III), 17.
[2] Cf. *Dialogues* I, 2 (*Quia secreti inter nos nec occupati sumus*); cf. ibid., I, 1.
[3] *Cum sis scholasticus, Dialogues* I, 27. .

ciples already referred to. Postumianus figures in the letters of Paulinus[1] as a member of his own household, and as bringing letters from Sulpicius on his return to Nola. It was Postumianus who carried the *Life of St Martin* to St Paulinus immediately on its completion, and at the close of the *Dialogues* Sulpicius especially enjoins on him to go straight to Campania and relate to Paulinus all that he has heard from the lips of Martin's disciple Gallus.

In this first *Dialogue* Postumianus is warmly welcomed by Sulpicius after his long absence, and at once introduced to Gallus. The discourse takes place in a 'retired spot', evidently in or near Sulpicius's own home. Sulpicius begs Postumianus to relate his experiences. Postumianus consents, but first enquires whether those whom he left as priests continue as they were, to which Sulpicius replies that they are no better than when he left, and one in particular, who used to be a dear friend, has shown himself less kind than he ought to have been. The subject is dismissed as too painful to be dwelt on, and the three friends seat themselves on their rolls of sackcloth on the ground and the talk begins in earnest.

The travels of Postumianus have taken him to Rome and North Africa and to the Holy Land. He has visited Carthage, Alexandria, Bethlehem, and the North African desert, as well as the ascetics in Lower Egypt. This is, in fact, the climax of his story, and it is on the marvels of the ascetic lives and the miracles of the monks that he dwells most fully. He tells us that Sulpicius's *Life of St Martin* was selling rapidly in Italy,[2] and at a high price, and that it had preceded him to Carthage, while in Alexandria they knew it even better than the author himself. It was read in Egypt, Nitria, Thebes, and Memphis. Even in the heart of the North African desert he had found an old anchorite reading it, and begging him to urge Sulpicius to add a sequel.

Postumianus narrates his experiences with much freshness and detail. The opening scene relates how his vessel, which was bound for Alexandria, was forced by contrary winds to anchor

[1] Paulinus, *Epp.* 16, 27, 28.
[2] Paulinus speaks of having read it to St Melania and others (*Ep.* 29). He also read it to St Niketas of Remesiana during his visit to Nola (cf. p. 84 f.). The latter was delighted with it, and Paulinus had copies made for Niketas to take with him beyond the Adriatic.

off the coast of Cyrenaica. He gives us a delightful glimpse of a little scattered desert community which he found there, and of the old presbyter in his little hut half-buried in the sand, with whom he spent a week before resuming his voyage. In Alexandria the controversy about the writings of Origen was at its hottest, and he was glad to leave the city from which many monks had been banished. In Bethlehem he spent six months with St Jerome, for whom he seems to have entertained great respect, though the Gaul interrupts him at this point to say that St Jerome's strictures on monks have not been well received in some quarters among his own friends. Later in the discourse, however, Postumianus himself draws so trenchant a picture of the degeneracy of clerics that Gallus declares he can have left little for St Jerome to add.

The greater part of the *First Dialogue*, devoted to an exposition and panegyric of the ascetics of Egypt, is intended to lead up to the subject of the *Second Dialogue*, which is devoted to St Martin, to whom the miracles and austerities of the Egyptian monks serve as a foil. In this *Second Dialogue* the chief speaker is Gallus, who, as already stated, is a disciple of St Martin, in whose monastery he has received his training. It is interesting to note that the speaker here is not a Roman, or even a cultured Aquitanian, but a provincial Celt, who, though well educated in the 'schools', has a touch of rusticity in his idiom, and speaks before Sulpicius and Postumianus with a modesty which is repeatedly emphasized.[1] He hesitates, even blushes, and is very diffident; but though Sulpicius and Postumianus tease him good-naturedly about his Gaulish appetite and love of good cooking and plentiful meals, the Gaul is careful to explain away the charge on rational grounds. Postumianus, he says, after tossing at sea, may well have found the sparse ration of the desert sufficient. Again, the climate of Greece is less rigorous than that of Gaul, where asceticism cannot go to extreme lengths; and he adds with a touch of conscious pride: 'As I have

---

[1] See *Dialogues* I, 4, 27. This preliminary deprecation was a commonplace of contemporary oratory, hence the reply of Postumianus: 'As you are an orator (*scholasticus*), you carefully, after the fashion of an orator, begin by begging us to excuse your unskilfulness because you really excel in eloquence.' So the rhetor Pacatus, the friend of Ausonius (cf. p. 43), speaking before the Roman senate, expresses his diffidence as a provincial from remote Gaul for fear lest his 'transalpine eloquence' may seem somewhat rustic and unpolished to these heirs of pure Roman speech (*Panegyric* XII, 1, 2).

often told you, Sulpicius, we are, in a word, Gauls.' He is, in fact, proud of his nation, and it would seem that for some reason Sulpicius is anxious to demonstrate that it is among the native Gaulish element that Martin's chief supporters are to be found. And perhaps the chief object of the *Dialogues* – certainly one of the main objects – is the theme that the ascetics of Gaul are not behind those of Egypt in holiness and austerities. The *Dialogues* breathe a spirit of self-conscious nationalism.

This interesting aspect of the *Dialogues* – the sympathy of the cultured Aquitanian scholar with the native Celts of Gaul – is closely bound up with the new spirit of democracy which Sulpicius is primarily concerned to forward. This may be seen in the emphasis laid on Martin's missionary activities[1] – his conversion of large numbers of the country people after the felling of a pine tree sacred to the heathen,[2] and the demolition of the heathen temple at Leprosum near Chartres;[3] in the account of Martin's travels to his more distant parishes;[4] his destruction of Roman monuments; his energy and hard work, and his simplicity of life, 'resembling that of the Gaulish peasants', though himself a bishop; his constant sympathy for and interest in the poor, more especially the agricultural peasantry. We see him proud only on behalf of the Church, proud only before bishops, high officials, and emperors. He refuses to allow the Prefect Vincentius to lodge in his monastery, though frequently importuned by him for hospitality;[5] but he forces Valentinian to receive him against his will.[6] He never humbles himself to Maximus or his court, but firmly upholds the precedence of the Church, even at Maximus's own table.[7]

There can be little doubt that the object of Sulpicius in all this is to represent Martin, not only as a national Gaulish saint, but as a popular hero also, the saint of the Gaulish peasantry. If we were only told of his rough and unkempt appearance and his simplicity of life in general terms, we might suppose that Sulpicius was merely making his patron conform to the models of Gospel history or of the Eastern saints; but this is by no means all. While Martin goes on foot or on a

---

[1] For a résumé of Martin's activities, as distinct from his contemplative vocation, see Delehaye, op. cit., p. 101 f.
[2] *Life*, 13.
[3] ibid., 14.
[4] *Dialogues* I (II), 4.
[5] *Dialogues* I, 25.
[6] *Dialogues* II, 5.
[7] *Life*, 20; cf. *Dialogues* II, 6.

donkey,[1] the bishops and clerics have fine horses, and Brictio even keeps slaves.[2] While Martin himself is content to occupy a little cell, a cleric, when he becomes puffed up, erects elaborate structures with many rooms, fretted ceilings, carved doors.[3] While Martin sits on a little stool – 'such as our Gaulish peasants use and call a *tripeccia*' – a certain bishop is stated to have been seen seated high in the air on so lofty a seat that it resembled an emperor's throne.[4]

There can be no doubt that Martin's holy and voluntary poverty is intended by his biographer to reflect as much odium on the bishops as credit on Martin. This anti-episcopal feeling is a smouldering passion which breaks into flame constantly throughout the *Dialogues*. It is a passion wholly independent of the cult of Martin, which nevertheless bears some close relationship to it.

It is not easy for us to understand the strength and bitterness of Sulpicius's attacks on the ecclesiastics, and more especially on the bishops of his day. Even making allowance for the part that bishops, like Ithacius, had taken in the Priscillianist controversy, it would seem to us impossible to condemn the Gaulish bishops as a class.[5] Many of them are among the finest men of the time. St Ambrose,[6] Bishop of Milan, had been born and brought up at Trier. St Paulinus, Bishop of Nola, was an Aquitanian by birth and education. We call to mind figures like Delphinus,[7] Bishop of Bordeaux, and his successor, Amandus; Victricius, apostle to Normandy, and afterwards Bishop of Rouen; Honoratus, founder of the monastery of Lérins, and afterwards Bishop of Arles; and Eucherius, the great Bishop of

---

[1] *Dialogues* I (II), 3.

[2] *Dialogues* II (III), 15.

[3] *Dialogues* I, 21.

[4] *Dialogues* I (II), 4. At this period the bishop used a throne higher than the seats of the priests. See Beck, *Pastoral Care of Souls*, p. 31.

[5] It is somewhat surprising to find how readily learned Catholic scholars animadvert against the bishops of Gaul as a class of men 'lax', and 'luxurious', even degenerate. Delehaye speaks (op. cit., p. 103) of the 'clergé relâché de la Gaule' at this period. Doubtless the stricture is just in some individual cases; but one is inclined to suspect that the opinion is based rather on the generalizations of such writers as Salvian than on a categorical survey of the leading ecclesiastics of Gaul at this period.

[6] Ambrose, as we have seen, had refused to receive Priscillian and his adherents, Instantius and Salvian (see Sulpicius, *Chronica* II, 48), though he had opposed their trial in a civil court.

[7] Delphinus, it will be remembered, had refused to admit Priscillian and his adherents to Bordeaux.

Lyons, and his two sons, both bishops (cf. p. 152), all trained in this same monastery of Lérins, as was also Hilary, the successor of Honoratus in the see of Arles. And in the following chapters we shall find this fine tradition continued by the bishops of the next generation – Exuperius, Bishop of Toulouse, who is believed to have inspired the successful resistance of the city against the Visigoths; and Patiens of Lyons, whose private granaries and wealth were devoted to the needs of the Gauls in the famine consequent on the Barbarian Invasions. Sidonius Apollinaris was typical of his class – a man of the local hereditary aristocracy, known all his life to his flock and sharing their interest and their fate to the uttermost.

It was, in general, from such a class that the bishops were drawn, a class which combined the interests and the responsibilities of the locality which they served with the experience and political education of the Roman official class from which, in origin, their office sprang. They had every reason to keep up a certain traditional pomp and splendour in their equipment. Why was this so offensive to Sulpicius? For we note that it is not so much the personal characters of the bishops that Sulpicius attacks as the pomp and splendour of their way of life.

The reason lay in the fact that Sulpicius's ideals represented a strong reaction from the accepted and the traditional forms of Christianity. As a pioneer of the new monastic movement, he represented a new element in Gaulish society, essentially popular and democratic. His own renunciation of his wealth and the world, no less than the renunciation by Paulinus, testifies to the strength of these new ideals. The attitude was undoubtedly Christian and inspired by the Gospel; but it was strengthened by the very force which was making Christianity strong – a widespread growth of self-conscious democracy. Sulpicius was in touch with all this, as we can see from the *Dialogues*, in which Postumianus is pictured to us as bringing all the latest news from Alexandria. Sulpicius in Gaul had caught something of the spirit which made St Athanasius the idol of the Egyptian peasants, and the cynosure of the popular movement among the Copts, who hated the Greek Church and the Greek officials.

The struggle between the conservative elements in the Church and the new ascetic ideal must have been a source of

H

serious discord in St Martin's own monastery. Towards the close of the *Dialogues* Sulpicius depicts an interesting scene which takes place between St Martin and his disciple, Brictio.[1] One day, while Martin was seated outside his cell on his customary little stool, two demons were seen on a rock above calling: 'Heia te, Brictio! Heia te Brictio'![2] and shortly afterwards Brictio himself appeared and proceeded to revile Martin, by whom he had been reprimanded the day before. Sulpicius tells us that before Brictio became a priest he had possessed nothing of his own, and had been maintained in the monastery by Martin's charity. Now, despite this, he was keeping horses and purchased slaves, both foreign youths and also young and pretty girls; and this was doubtless the cause of the reprimand. Brictio declared himself to be a more holy man than Martin, having been brought up from his earliest years by Martin himself in the monastery in the sacred precincts of the Church, while Martin, he declared, had been subjected in youth to all the irregularities incidental to the military life, and was now in his old age, so declared Brictio, becoming the prey of vain superstitions and the absurd phantasms of visions.

Sulpicius is at pains to tell us that Brictio repented and apologized shortly afterwards; but the incident is doubtless indicative of the strong spirit of opposition to asceticism with which Martin had to contend.[3] It was just about this time (396) that St John Chrysostom wrote his *Apology for the Christian Life*, and a strong body of opinion was making itself felt against austerities and the monastic life. It would seem that even among Martin's own followers a reaction had already set in during his lifetime. This Brictio is most probably the Brice who eventually[4] succeeded Martin as Bishop of Tours. He is probably one of the clerics referred to elsewhere in the *Dialogues* as given to fine horses, splendid buildings, and fine clothes.[5] It is not the luxury of episcopal life which is new in Gaul, but its condemnation, the superimposition of the ascetic ideal. And in his condemnation of luxury, in his insistence on holy poverty,

[1] The modern form of the name is *Brice*.
[2] *Dialogues* II (III), 15.
[3] Cf., e.g. *Dialogue* III, 9.
[4] The see seems to have been filled for a brief space after the death of Martin, first by Justinianus, and then by Armentius. See Duchesne, *Fastes Épiscopaux de l'ancienne Gaule*, Vol. II, p. 299 f.
[5] *Dialogues* I, 21.

Sulpicius is unsparing. We may hope that Sulpicius in his picture of the two devils seated on the rock above the monastery and urging Brictio to the attack, does not mean to imply that Brictio is incited by two bishops; but it is to be feared appearances are against him.

Two further points come in for consideration here. The first is this: If the picture of the Gaulish ecclesiastics presented to us by Sulpicius is partly biassed, to what extent may this be true also of his picture of St Martin himself? The other question is closely connected with it: what does the biography tell us of the chief influences affecting the saint in early life, and what kind of a saint would they have been likely to produce? Our idea of St Martin is based on the picture which Sulpicius has carefully presented to us – that of a simple and earnest ascetic, with energy of purpose and a compelling and magnetic personality, but unpolished, unlearned, and with very little education. To what extent is this picture borne out by the actual facts related in the biography?

Let us consider the second question first. Sulpicius tells us how readily and easily St Martin solved problems of the Scriptures, and how full he was of knowledge, though he adds that there were many who would deny this.[1] We have seen that his disciple, Gallus, is a rhetorician (*scholasticus*), trained in the schools, and that the young men in Marmoutier occupied a part of their time in copying manuscripts. In the *Chronica* (II, 50) Martin is classed with those who, because they are fond of fasting and also reading, are accused of being tainted with the heresy of Priscillian, a highly intellectual man. Is it possible that, in calling Martin unlearned, Sulpicius meant more especially that Martin did not cultivate classical studies? If Martin were, as Sulpicius tells us, a soldier in early years, he would not, although knowing the Greek language, have been deeply versed in the classics; and I am tempted to interpret on these lines the curiously persistent assertion of Sulpicius that the devil tempted Martin in the guise of pagan gods – Jupiter, Mercury, even Venus and Minerva.[2] Is this a figurative way of saying that the devil tempted Martin, as he had tempted Paulinus, by the poetry of Homer and Virgil, and Jerome by

---

[1] *Life*, 25.
[2] *Life*, 22; *Dialogues* I (II), 13.

the prose of Cicero? Both Sulpicius and Paulinus reproach themselves for their leaning to classical letters. Theirs was, indeed, the commonest self-reproach of the intellectual Christians of the day. Love of classical authors was opposed to the ascetic ideal.

Now the most significant factor in regard to St Martin's intellectual training is his relationship to St Hilary, Bishop of Poitiers. Hilary was in his own time the greatest churchman in the West. He was not only the most courageous, as well as the most intellectual of the anti-Arians – the 'Athanasius of the West', as he has been called; he was also the most vigorous opponent of state intervention in ecclesiastical matters. His strength of character and far-sighted policy were backed by great learning in Greek as well as Latin and, after his exile in Asia Minor, by an unusually wide acquaintance with the Eastern Churches and their views.

The facts as related in the narrative of Sulpicius suggest that Martin was not only Hilary's disciple; he was virtually his creation. It was Hilary who, at the outset of Martin's career, sought to 'associate him with himself in the diaconate at Poitiers'; and who, on Martin's refusal on the grounds of his own unworthiness, appointed him an exorcist, still at Poitiers. Again, on Martin's departure for his mission to his own home in Illyria, we are told that Hilary parted from him with tears, making him promise to return. In Illyria Martin fought 'almost single-handed' against Arianism within the Church, as a result of which he was publicly scourged, and obliged to leave his city (*civitas*). It is significant that the time of Martin's absence in Illyria coincided with Hilary's exile in Phrygia for his anti-Arian policy, following on the Council of Biterrae (Béziers) in 356. There can be little doubt that we are to understand the main motive of Martin's journey to Illyria to have been an anti-Arian campaign; and the campaign itself to have been inspired by Hilary, with whom he was already associated as a valued colleague. Let us see what follows. We continue to follow Sulpicius.

On being driven from Illyria by the Arians, and hearing that Hilary was in exile, Martin settled at Milan in some form of retreat; but again he was persistently persecuted and finally driven from the city by Auxentius, the leader of the Arian party. After a further period of retreat in Gallinaria, hearing that Hilary was about to return to Gaul, Martin set out to Rome, hoping to meet him there; but as Hilary had already left, he followed him to Poitiers, and was joyously welcomed by Hilary, and established his first monastic retreat at Ligugé not far from the city. In 364 Hilary impeached Auxentius of Milan for heterodoxy. We can hardly doubt that there is a close connection between Hilary's action and the previous persecution and banishment of Martin by Auxentius as related by Sulpicius.

Some years later, in 371 or 372, Martin was called upon to fill the episcopate at Tours; but only by guile and force was he prevailed upon to leave his *monasterium* near Poitiers. The prolonged and close union of interests between Hilary and Martin, as related by Sulpicius, taken together with Martin's part in the Arian troubles, suggest that the saint may have taken an active part in the intellectual ferment of his time as a close colleague of Hilary. Moreover he can hardly have been ignorant of Greek. Indeed it may well have been more familiar to him than Latin in his early home in Pannonia. His home was not far from Remesiana, the home of St Niketas, which was politically in Greek territory. It was possibly Martin's Greek background, and perhaps his knowledge of the Greek language, which in the beginning of their acquaintance would commend him to Hilary as a useful colleague.

At Tours also, despite the assurances of Sulpicius that Martin lived a secluded life, Sulpicius represents the political questions of the day as having occupied his earnest attention. He interests himself on behalf of the political prisoners of Count Avitianus of Tours;[1] and he makes a journey to the court at Trier for the purpose of interceding with Maximus on behalf of two of Gratian's officers.[2] Above all he takes an active and courageous part in the Priscillianist controversy. While mercy and justice weigh heavily with him in the Priscillianist trials; his dominant motive as a disciple of Hilary would be a desire to prevent state intervention in ecclesiastical affairs. In this, as in other matters, Martin appears to adhere closely to the policy of his master, Hilary.

The question has often been asked whence Martin obtained

[1] *Dialogues* II (III), 4.   [2] *Dialogues* II (III), 11.

the original impetus towards his monastic activities, and under what influences he created his monastic communities, first at Ligugé and afterwards at Tours. Such communities can hardly have developed directly from the little *monasterium* at Milan, or the retreat with a single disciple in Gallinaria. The collection of cells in the caves at Ligugé suggests rather the caves of the hermits in the Syrian desert, with whom St Jerome sojourned for a space of six years, or the cells occupied by the monks of Egypt. Ligugé was in the immediate vicinity of Hilary, and it is permissible to raise the question whether the idea of founding the community was not in the first instance suggested or inspired by Hilary on his return from Asia Minor.

In the pages of Sulpicius, Martin made a strong impression in his own day, especially in regard to the contest for control in Church government. He is represented as the strongest force with which the accusers of the Priscillianists had to contend. For such controversies he would have already had a rigorous training in Illyria and in Milan. However we view the anti-episcopal prejudices of Sulpicius, the part which he assigns to Martin in the religious struggles of the time is impressive, perhaps even more impressive than the part which he assigns to him in the internal life of the Church itself.

Perhaps the most persuasive passages in the *Life* as a whole are those in which the saint is brought into connection with leading political figures of his day. The contacts of Martin with Maximus may well be genuine; and his conditional surrender, and communion with the Bishop Ithacius on Maximus's promise to spare the Priscillianists is consistent with the whole policy and character of the man. He preferred to communicate with fellow-churchmen who were unacceptable to him, rather than allow a civil court to start a religious inquisition for which it was unqualified. Yet the picture which Sulpicius draws of Martin after he had communicated is equally impressive. He left the court, we are told, and never again attended a synod, keeping himself aloof from all assemblies of bishops for the rest of his life.[1] It is not impossible, as Babut claims,[2] that he left under a cloud, and that his future absence from episcopal gatherings was not wholly voluntary.

[1] *Dialogues* II (III), 13.
[2] E. C. Babut, *Saint Martin de Tours* (Paris, 1920), p. 150 ff.

The picture which Sulpicius gives us of the saint as he left the court of Maximus is deeply moving. He shows us Martin plunged in deep grief and hurrying away from the court on the following day. Then, while seated alone in solitary woods, 'reflecting on the cause of his grief and of what had happened, alternately accusing and defending himself in his mind', he receives comfort from an angel, who urges him to renew his virtue and take fresh courage. Sulpicius does not fail to arouse our sympathy with his hero in his struggle for spiritual perfection and in his distress at falling short of his own lofty ideal, the warfare within his spirit. Again the apparent candour with which the author tells us that Martin felt a diminution of his power over demons from the moment of his communion with the party of Ithacius does credit to the saint's humility and sense of perfection unattained. Nevertheless Sulpicius in reporting this is undoubtedly influenced in the main by the serious reflection which it implies on Ithacius and his party.

The portrait of St Martin presented to us by Sulpicius is in no respect that of a rustic. Though he is unassuming and modest, making no claims on his own behalf, he comes forward judicially and without hesitation in public affairs when his conscience bids him; but there is nothing aggressive in his bearing. The same quiet dignity characterizes his religious devotions. His deep religious fervour and unworldliness is without trace of fanaticism. His is the simplicity of the best educated classes, rather than of the backward and rustic elements among the people.

This impression of quiet dignity and unassuming modesty, combined with self-possession and self-command, probably owes something to the *Life of St Antony*, now generally attributed to St Athanasius, and believed to have been written between 356 and 362. This fine literary portrait became the model for all future biographies of saints; and in seeking to represent Martin as a saint of the people, it would be natural for Sulpicius to emphasize in Martin those traits which had made St Antony a popular hero. In accordance both with this literary model, and with his own democratic ideal, Sulpicius naturally seeks to minimize Martin's education and acquired culture, and lays weight on his visionary and miraculous powers.

In other respects also the *Life of St Martin* is indebted to literary sources, and this is a factor which we must constantly bear in mind in regard to the difficult question of the historicity of St Martin. Sulpicius follows the custom of all early hagiographers in drawing material from earlier writers to build up his narrative. The biographers of the early saints were engaged, not upon historical research, but upon the creation of an impressive and an edifying portrait.[1] The technique is that of the historical novelist rather than of the scholarly biographer. We may suspect that the paramount importance which Sulpicius attaches to Martin in his lifetime is in a very large measure the creation of the biographer himself.[2]

The question of the miracles still remains a problem. Did Sulpicius really believe them himself? It is difficult to feel any confidence that he did, despite his repeated and grave assurance of their genuineness. We have seen that he could hardly have hoped for the success and wide circulation of his *Life* of the saint without a liberal introduction of the marvels which were the literary fashion of the day, and rapidly growing in popularity under the stimulus of fresh influences from the East. They were already becoming a 'compulsory subject' in Christian biography.

The most important question of all still remains unanswered. How far is the *Life of St Martin* worthy of credence?[3] Unfortunately this problem cannot be isolated from a similar problem relating to other saints known to us from literary rather than from primary historical sources, especially during this period. The question is essentially one for experts, and it cannot be said that agreement has been reached, or even that a final conclusion is in sight. In general, students of hagiography are in disagreement only as to exactly how far credence is to be given to the facts as presented to us in the earliest biographies; the question is generally confined to the details, not to the authenticity of the saint himself.

Whatever conclusion we may feel inclined to favour on this difficult subject as a whole, we must not allow either the miracles or the materials derived from literary sources to discredit

[1] For a full-length study of the aim and methods of the early biographers, see Delehaye, *Les Légendes hagiographiques* (Brussels, 1927).

[2] Strangely enough Delehaye, in the book cited above, places Sulpicius Severus, together with a small number of others, in a class apart, as having aimed at writing as genuine historians (p. 57).

[3] For a brief but well-balanced discussion of this important matter, see P. de Labriolle, *Latin Christianity*, p. 383 ff.

Sulpicius's narrative in its essential features. He assures us of his personal intercourse with the saint, and furnishes us with much matter of wide political bearing in regard to Martin's life and work. His narrative was accepted in good faith by both Paulinus and Gennadius, and would seem to be further tacitly supported by the person of his disciple Victor. Moreover, Sulpicius was writing as a contemporary of his hero. There were not lacking in Gaul many ecclesiastics unfavourable towards Sulpicius, and we may be assured that any attempt at fraud on his part would have been instantly exposed and derided. With a full recognition of the difficulties of the case, there is at least a presumption in favour of the general truth of the core of the narrative. Such an acceptance of its general fidelity, however, does not preclude us from holding that Sulpicius, in accordance with the object for which the *Life* was written, has thrown specially high lights on certain aspects of Martin's character, while modifying others which he held as of less importance, or as calculated to diminish the impression which it was his purpose to create.

Probably no-one has ever reached the final page of Sulpicius Severus without regret. His Latin style was praised by Scaliger for its purity,[1] and his versatility and charm make him the most delightful prose writer of his Age. His 'Life of St Martin' is agreed by all to be a perfect literary work. His *Chronica* became a standard work on ancient history, and was evidently read down to the Renaissance, as the number of surviving manuscripts shows. His letters, and still more his *Dialogues*, offer a delightful and informal narrative of really important matter. And what brilliant vignettes he brings before us, what intimate and restful discourses we take part in, what refreshing and gay meetings we are privileged to attend with Martin at Marmoutier, and with Gallus and Postumianus at Primuliacum! As a literary artist Sulpicius has no rival in our period, and for long afterwards. It is hardly surprising that we still find difficulty in gauging just how much the beautiful and magnetic personality of St Martin owes to the literary genius of his biographer.

---

[1] *Ecclesiasticorum purissimus scriptor.* For an account of the Latin classical authors whose influence can be traced in the work of Sulpicius Severus, see Kappelmacher, op. cit., p. 867.

CHAPTER V

The Last of the Classics

IN the preceding chapters we have had some glimpses of the
effects of the Barbarian Invasion of Italy, and of the evacuation
of the high Roman nobility to North Africa and Palestine. In
Rome the sufferings of the religious households were terrible.
We have seen the fugitives seeking asylum in North Africa and
the Holy Land. We have seen Nola in Campania sacked, and
Paulinus forced for a time to leave his establishment. In Gaul
the Barbarian occupation was no less heavy a burden. The
occupation of Aquitaine, the 'pearl of Gaul', by the Visigoths,
and the repeated devastation of Trier by the Franks, brought
about a widespread displacement of ownership among the
aristocracy, and a general lowering of civilization. The more
cultured elements tended to move into Provence, now the only
truly Roman area, and the centres of literary activity shifted
from Trier and Bordeaux to the kingdom of Toulouse and the
Valley of the Rhône. Marseilles became what we should now
call a 'reception area'.

The sufferings of the refugees seeking shelter before the in-
vading armies form the subject of two poems formerly ascribed
to Prosper of Aquitaine, the author of the famous *Chronicon*, and
the chief supporter of St Augustine in the Pelagian controversy.
His authorship of the first of the two poems in question, the
Carmen de Providentia Divina,[1] has been disputed,[2] on the grounds
that the views expressed are contrary to those of Prosper in
regard to Pelagianism. Against this, however, it has been
pointed out[3] that the style and versification of the poem re-
semble those of Prosper closely, and that it was already cited
under his name by Hincmar of Rheims in the ninth century.

The *Carmen de Providentia Divina* ('Song of the Divine Provid-

[1] Migne, *P.L.*, Vol. LI, col. 617 ff.
[2] Ebert, *Gesch. der christ-latein. Lit.* (Leipzig, 1874), p. 305 ff.); Bardenhewer,
Patrology, p. 514; de Labriolle, op. cit., p. 432, n. 1.
[3] Manitius, *Gesch. der Christ. – Lat. Poesie* (Stuttgart, 1891), p. 171 ff.; L. Valentin,
S. Prosper d'Aquitaine (Toulouse, 1900); cf. T. Scott Holmes, op. cit., p. 383.

ence') gives a lively picture at first-hand of the way in which the barbarians provisioned themselves by driving off the cattle from the farms, and emptying the barns of their seed corn; and of the burning of the farmsteads and the destruction of the vineyards. The poet himself, we learn, was compelled to march, covered with sweat, as a captive behind the chariots of the conquerors. In the second poem, the *Poema Conjugis ad Uxorem*, ('Poem of a Husband to his Wife'),[1] written in southern Gaul, c. 414, the author is again a rich farmer. He had owned extensive ploughlands, yet it is only with difficulty that he has managed to keep two oxen for himself. But his grief is chiefly for his wife, and he urges her to join with him in devoting the rest of her life to God. The poems, whatever their authorship, are interesting contemporary pictures of the disruption of settled life in these harrassing times, and the second of the two poems gives us a significant hint of the part which monasticism was beginning to play in helping to solve the problem of housing and providing for the refugees.

One of the most interesting of the refugees living in Marseilles about the middle of the fifth century was Paulinus of Pella.[2] Though born at Pella in Macedonia, where his father was viceregent, Paulinus was moved as an infant 'in his nurse's arms', as he tells us, together with the rest of the family, first to Carthage, his father being proconsul in Africa, and shortly afterwards to Rome and Bordeaux. Here he arrived in his third year, and here he was brought up in the household of his grandfather, who is almost certainly to be identified with the poet Ausonius. In 459, in his eighty-third year, Paulinus composed his autobiography[3] in a poem of 616 hexameters, the ostensible motive of which, as its name – the *Eucharistikon*[4] – implies, was a thanksgiving to God for ordering and directing his life. The poem is of great interest for the picture which it

---

[1] Migne, *P.L.* LI, col. 611 ff. Manitius (op. cit., p. 212) is, on the whole, in favour of assigning this poem to Prosper. So also Scott Holmes and Valentin. See the *Catholic Encyclopedia*, s.v. Prosper. Contrast, however, Bardenhewer (loc. cit.).

[2] For a recent account of Paulinus, see the article s.v., in Pauly-Wissowa, *Real-Encyclopädie*, and the references there cited. The notes on Paulinus's family, and his relationship to Ausonius are especially helpful.

[3] The author's name does not appear on the only MS. now available, Berneus 317, but was probably included in the MS., now lost, from which the *editio princeps* was published in 1579.

[4] Paulinus refers to the poem in his prose introduction under the title *Eucharistikon, Opusculum sub Ephemeridis meae Relatione*.

gives of the contemporary life of the gentry of Aquitaine at the time of the invasions of the Visigoths and Alani, and it enables us to see at close range the disintegrating effect on family and individual lives; the burning and pillaging of the great estates; the great landowners, driven from one country mansion to another, with their families and slaves in their train; the social disruption; the progressive impoverishment; the gradual draining away of life and substance, and finally of hope.

Even more interesting than these things are personal details – the candour and brightness of the biography, and its completeness. The account of the early travels over, the poet dwells in happy mood on his early education. His lessons in Homer and the philosophy of Socrates were easy because he had been used to talking Greek with the servants; his Vergil not so easy. He tells of an early illness which took him from his studies, and gave his parents an excuse to pamper him with fine horses and hawks, splendid harness and tall grooms to encourage outdoor sport, in which his father was more a friend and companion to him than a parent. Then came the love adventures of an over-indulged young aristocrat with as much common sense and as little idealism as the conditions would lead one to expect, but with a happy ending, or fairly happy, in marriage. He lingers lovingly on his grand house, or rather his wife's, with its fine rooms to suit the seasons, its tasteful plate, and the fine horses and carriages. All this is what we should expect in one of Ausonius's family, at least in one of its less distinguished members. There is the same love of home, the same close ties with the family, the same unquestioning devotion to parents. And when, c. 406, the poet's father dies, the lines which are virtually his epitaph, though perhaps not attaining the dignity of Ausonius's lines on his father, are as tender and loving and intimate as ever a son wrote of a parent. The blow came just at the time of the Visigothic Invasion:

'But for me the damage to my home as a result of devastation by the enemy, however great in itself, was very slight in comparison with the grief beyond all measure for my dead father, who had made both my country and my home itself dear to me. For we showed such kindness and genuine affection to one another, notwithstanding the disparity in our ages, that our friendship was even better than that of contemporaries.

But that dear companion and true counsellor was withdrawn from me in my early youth.'[1]

After this point all the brightness and colour fades from the little biography. The family house is sacked and burnt, owing to its not having a Gothic guest in residence – 'For I know that some of the Goths showed themselves most humane in their eagerness to be of use to their hosts by their protection'. The poet, despite his sufferings, pays homage to the chivalry of the Goths, who offered no wrong to the honour of any of the companions and handmaidens who had been attached to Paulinus's household. He tells us that he would have preferred to make peace with the Goths rather than fulfil the office of *Comes Largitionum* with which the 'tyrant' Attalus, the puppet emperor set up by the Goths in Rome, had invested him.

After the loss of his home in Bordeaux, Paulinus and his household, robbed/of everything, fled to Bazas in the country south-east of Bordeaux, to the estates of the poet's grandfather, only to find themselves besieged within the city by an allied army of Visigoths and Alani. The social disintegration within the city can be seen in the poet's narrow escape from a plot made by some slaves under the leadership of a few free men to massacre the aristocracy. Goaded to desperation, Paulinus made his way out to the heart of the Alan camp, and managed to relieve the city by detaching the Alani from their allies and attaching them to the Roman cause. Yet poverty haunted him, and at this point he seems to have thought of becoming a monk (l. 451 ff.), but was deterred by the advice of holy men (*consilio sanctorum*). After 421 he gradually lost all his family, and finally we find him in Marseilles, 'a city in which there were many saints, my friends' (l. 521), where he managed to cultivate a smallholding of land still left to him. Finally with failing strength he returned to Bordeaux, where he existed on the sum paid by a Goth for his estate in Marseilles.

It can surely be no accident that this unique biography in verse of a private individual is the work of a Gaul of Bordeaux, and almost certainly a descendant of Ausonius.[2] We must grant that the tone of Paulinus's poem is on a humbler plane

---

[1] *Eucharistikon*, l. 239 ff. I have used the text by H. G. Evelyn White, included in his edition of the works of *Ausonius*, Vol. II (London, 1921), p. 295 ff.

[2] This is now generally regarded as a certainty. See the article on Paulinus in Pauly-Wissowa, *Real-Encyclopädie*, and the references there cited.

than that of Ausonius, as is to be expected of a man who was little in public life. It would seem indeed that both in early youth, and again after his disastrous losses, Paulinus had thoughts of devoting himself to a religious life, but was deterred, first by his parents, and later by wise monks, who realized the absence of a religious vocation, though his devotion was simple and sincere. But what links Paulinus so closely with Ausonius is the love of his environment and of putting it into poetry, and the gift of drawing us into the circle of his home and his life; his noble and tender devotion to his parents; his feeling for the importance and value of the cultivation of the land; his love of the Garonne, with its tidal port and water gate; his selection of the concrete details which bring the whole scene home to us with such apparent casual artlessness. And again, as with Ausonius, we can only surmise the source of this rise of a new and most original type of provincial poetry[1]. Was it something of native Gaulish origin, born of strong family ties and genealogical lore? Or was it the outcome of classical culture, entering with first hesitant steps upon the modern world? The Alan and the Visigoth withheld from us the answer, and none of Paulinus's family or descendants seem to have survived him to carry on the tradition.

The free exercise of the poetic imagination within a restricted personal environment was not confined to the family of Ausonius. It is the most striking feature of the work of a Gaulish poet of the early fifth century, Rutilius Namatianus, who, about 416 composed a poem in elegiac verse, which is generally known by the title *De Reditu Suo* ('On his Return').[2] The poem was planned in at least two Books; but of the second only sixty-nine lines have survived. Rutilius was certainly a Gaul, possibly of Poitiers, but more probably of Narbonne or Toulouse,[3] who had lived long in Italy. Here his father

---

[1] On the strictly literary features of the poem, see the article referred to above.

[2] Edited by L. Mueller (Leipzig, 1870). The best modern edition, with French translation, is by Vaissereau and Prechac, *Rutilius Namatianus. Sur son Retour* (Paris, 1933). The most considerable recent book on Rutilius is that of Vaissereau himself, *Cl. Rutilius Namatianus* (Paris, 1904). See also the penetrating criticism in the chapter on Rutilius by R. Pichon, *Les Derniers Écrivains Profanes* (Paris, 1906), p. 243 ff.

[3] For various opinions and references, see ed. cit., Introduction, p. VI. See also P. Courcelle, *Les Lettres Grecques en Occident*[2] (Paris, 1948), p. 210, footnote 2, and the references there cited. For a general account of the poet and references, see Vollmer in Pauly-Wissowa, *Real-Encyclopädie*, s.v., Rutilius Claudius Namatianus.

Lachanius had held high offices, and here Rutilius boasts that his own position as *magister officium*[1] and governor of the capital[2] has been no less distinguished. His poem, however, celebrates, not his career as a grand functionary in Italy, but his return to his ruined home in Gaul. Gaul is in distress, torn and riven by protracted wars, the invasions of Vandals, Burgundians, Franks, and Visigoths, and he must mourn on the site the destruction of the houses of his ancestors. He can no longer ignore the vast numbers of ruins which are increasing by neglect; and on his estates, burnt out by cruel fire, he must set about some temporary building scheme, some plan of setting up at least huts fit for shepherds (I, 19 ff.).

The description of his homeward voyage forms the subject of his poem, which opens as he lies in port at the mouth of the Tiber, listening to the echo of the games in the circus and the acclamations of the crowds in the theatre. Did Salvian read the *De Reditu Suo*? Rutilius traces his route closely, mentioning by name the ports and harbours and the places passed on the voyage, with notes, archaeological, mythological, or practical, on their origin or present condition, and the condition of routes, roads and bridges, too often ruinous or disused since the incursions of Alaric. Indeed it is for this reason that the sea route has been chosen. And Rutilius relates, after the manner of a log-book or diary, when and where they land, what interesting places they pass on their course, and how they spend their time.

The poet has little care for natural beauty, though he gives us a fine picture of the marble of Carrara, its gleaming walls whiter than the lilies, offering a superb challenge to the untrodden snow (II, 63 ff.). His general habit of mind is more official, and he has an eye for the commercial, or still more the strategic possibilities of a site, how it could be developed by skilled engineering and industry, how its natural advantages have been allowed to suffer neglect. Passing the mouth of the Umbro he remarks on its navigable channel, and on the excellence of its estuary as a safe retreat for ships in distress (I, 1. 337 ff.). As they pass the island of Ilva (modern Elba) he reflects on its wealth in iron, and on iron as the source of all modern wealth and civilization, much like a modern Minister of Mines in

[1] I, 563 f.   [2] I, 157–60 (cf. 467).

holiday mood; while in his ears drone the notes, half heard, of the rhythm of some sailors' shanty (I, 351 ff.). Off Populonia the ruined pharos arouses reflections on the splendid use made of the site in the past, both as a defence for the land and as light in the night (I, 401 ff.). There are halts and landings, and lighter hours of rustic pleasure on the voyage, and rural scenes, charming with the studied charm of Theocritus, the delight in country pursuits which is not rare among educated townsmen in all periods and countries. At night he camps on the seashore north of the Umbro, beside a bonfire of myrtle branches, in a little tent improvised of oars, with a boathook for a cross-beam (I, 343 ff.). In Falerii he finds the local peasants celebrating a rustic festival which, he declares, is in honour of Osiris (I, 371 ff.). He takes refreshment in an hostelry kept by a Jew who gave them poor entertainment, and Rutilius is not at all pleased about it (I, 377 ff.). At Triturrita, near Portus Pisanus at the mouth of the Arno, they hunt the wild boar with dogs lent by a local farmer who acts as their host (I, l. 615 ff.), and Rutilius shows himself a true Gaul in his appreciation of the chase. The circumstantial details of the voyage, and the seemingly artless narrative of consecutive scenes, as day follows day, have led serious critics to the view that the poem was literally composed on the journey 'au jour le jour, on pourrait presque dire heure par heure';[1] but the studied form and style, the rhetorical devices, the gnomic observations and clichés, above all the pleasing contrast and variety of experiences, seem perhaps to suggest rather an art which succeeds in disguising itself, 'un poème écrit après coup sur les souvenirs encore récents'.[2] The vicissitudes of the voyage, with its natural variations of wind and weather, form an excellent literary framework for his kaleidoscopic theme.

The poem abounds in little personal sketches as vivid and as varied as the scenes of the voyage. For, like Ausonius and Paulinus of Pella, Rutilius held his relatives and friends in the same honour which earlier poets of the classical Age accorded to the heroes of old, and his poetry is his record of his environment, both in the narrower personal sense, and in the wider

---

[1] So Vaissereau, quoted by R. Pichon, *Les Derniers Écrivains Profanes* (Paris, 1906), p. 245.
[2] Pichon, loc. cit.

sense that it reflects the Roman world he knew best, the milieu of the more enlightened and cultured of the high civil officials of the Empire, with their lofty ideals of their functions and civic duty. It reflects also the unrest with which the Empire had to cope. The refugee and housing problems are prominent. We see Gaulish officials, who had retired to their paternal estates, forced by the Visigoths and the Franks to flee to Italy; those who had previously settled in Italy, forced by the incursions of the Goths to take refuge in the islands off the coast; Rutilius himself, an official in active service, returning home to Gaul to set about building temporary houses. There are indications of the break-down of public services; but there is never a shadow of the possibility of the fall of the Empire.

The picture which Rutilius presents to us is the more valuable because, while it combines an unquestioning devotion to Rome with strong local Gaulish patriotism, it does not idealize its subject, and it does not exaggerate. It has the value of actuality. Rutilius's work is often contrasted with the more elevated tone and loftier themes of Claudian's poetry, and though his Latin is pure and his technique excellent, he is not a professional poet. His poem is the work of a cultured and manly official, with scholarly, or at least bookish interests and refined taste, writing for other Roman and Gaulish functionaries who occupy their leisure with similar intellectual work. This comes out very clearly from a survey of the individuals whom he addresses in the poem, and of those to whom he refers as personally known to him, all men of a similar walk in life, and of similar literary interests.

And here it may be mentioned in passing that there is a striking general resemblance between the range of portraits in the poem of Rutilius and those which we have already found in the work of Ausonius. First, there is the tribute to his father, Lachanius (I, 575 ff.), whom he reveres and loves with a filial devotion equal to that shown by Ausonius and Paulinus of Pella. Then there is another relative, Exuperantius (11. 213–16), who is pictured as having quelled the rebellion in Armorica,[1]

---

[1] Cf. p. 264. Jullian includes under this term the whole coast of Gaul from Rouen to Bayonne. See 'Ausone et son Temps', *Revue Historique*, Vol. XLVIII (1892), p. 14; and cf. the *Notitia Dignitatum* (ed. Otto Seeck, Berlin, 1876), *Occidentis* 37. Some modern writers include the whole coast of Gaul as far as the Pyrenees. See *Rutilius Namatianus*, ed. cit., p. 40, note to 1. 216.

I

and who has succeeded in re-establishing peace and law and
order, 'no longer allowing servants to make their masters
slaves'.[1] From other sources we learn that Exuperantius was
probably a native of Poitiers, and that he was assassinated at
Arles in 424 while acting as prefect of the Gauls. His son,
Palladius, who excels in eloquence (*facundus iuvenis*), is indulg-
ently described by Rutilius as 'the hope of my family'. He has
just left Gaul to study law in Rome, and Rutilius speaks in
terms of deep affection of the bond which unites them. Palladius, indeed, not only accompanied him to the port, but
waited a whole fortnight there till a favourable breeze enabled
Rutilius to take his departure (207 ff.).

Again like Ausonius, Rutilius introduces us to a number of
his friends and colleagues, with glimpses also of his more casual
acquaintances. Among a number of others is Rufius (I, 168 ff.,
421 ff.), 'the living glory of his father Albinus', who accompanies Rutilius to the port on his departure. The eloquence of
Rufius has won him high office, and it is curious to learn that
already, when quite a youth, he had governed Carthage as proconsul, as the orator Pacatus had done before him (cf. p. 29 f.).
Rutilius adds that he fully expects to hear of him as consul, and
he does not forget to tell us (1. 415 ff.) that when, in the course
of his voyage, he arrived at Populonia, he learned that Rufius
had already been made prefect of Rome. Nothing is said of
Albinus, at this point, but in c. 466 we hear of him as prefect of
the city.

Among other contemporaries referred to in his poem are
Messala (I, 267 ff.), a member of the high Roman aristocracy,
prefect of Italy between the end of the fourth and the beginning
of the fifth centuries, and a friend of Symmachus, who addresses
twelve letters to him.[2] He is praised by both Symmachus and
Rutilius for his literary excellence, for the quality of his thought,
and for his eloquence, as well as for his competence as prefect.
He it is whose command was obeyed by the praetorians (I, l.
273). At the time when Rutilius meets him as he lands to make
a brief visit to *Thermae Tauri*, Messala has composed a poem on
the locality (267 ff.). Another of these literary magistrates is

---

[1] The reference is probably to the *Bagaudae* (cf. p. 166 f.). We may compare the
plot of the slaves against their masters to which Paulinus of Pella refers (*Eucharistikon*, 1. 328 ff. (cf. p. 125.)
[2] *Symmachus* (ed. O. Seeck), VII, lxxxi ff. (p. 199 ff.).

Decius, son of Lucillus (I, l. 597 ff.), an excellent administrator in Tuscany and Umbria in 417; and Lucillus himself, whose onerous duties of protecting the finances of the state against robbery are lightened by the composition of biting satirical verse.

Among the names which must be included in this little roll of honour of notable magistrates who formed the literary and administrative circle in which Rutilius moved, two of the most interesting are certainly Gauls.

Protadius (I, 542 ff.), like his two brothers, was a friend of Symmachus, who addresses eighteen letters to him.[1] He was a distinguished orator,[2] and among his other literary works he hoped to write a history of Gaul. Towards the close of the fourth century he had been Prefect of Rome, in which office he was succeeded by his brother Florentinus; but he was driven from Trier by the Franks in 413, and in 417 he had retired to an estate which he owned in Umbria, where, as we learn from Rutilius, he lived with some contentment owing to his gift for 'valuing little things as if they were great, and treating as trifles what were commonly regarded as important'. He had two sons whom he sent to Rome to be educated. Protadius in fact 'represents one of those old Gaulish families in which the cultivation of letters was perpetuated from father to son, and from whom Rome recruited her best magistrates'.[3]

Another Gaulish friend celebrated in the poem is Victorinus (I, 493 ff.). He has a special interest for us in that he had been Vicar of Britain, doubtless before 408. He had retired to Toulouse, but on the capture of the city by Ataulf in 413 he had been obliged to flee with his household to Tuscany. Rutilius has a special admiration for him because he had won the lasting affection of the Britons during his firm administration. His rule extended apparently over sea as well as land, 'in Thule and the whole country ploughed by the haughty Briton'. Rutilius adds, for the information of his readers, that this country is situated on the extremity of the habitable globe (cf. p. 16), yet Vic-

[1] *Symmachus*, IV, xvii ff. (p. 103 ff.).
[2] According to Vaissereau and Préchac, Protadius was the son of the Minervius who was celebrated by Ausonius as chief of the professors of rhetoric at Bordeaux his native place, but who had also taught rhetoric at Constantinople and at Rome (ed. cit., p. viii); but Ausonius says that Minervius died without heir (*quamquam heredis egens, Prof.* I, 37).
[3] *Rutilius*, ed. Vaissereau and Préchac, Introduction, p. viii.

torinus had governed it as if it had been at the heart of things; and the poet gravely assures us that Victorinus deserves all the more credit for having won the affection of people whose hatred would, he considers, have done him no discredit. This fine old Gaul had refused to hold office at the imperial court because of his love of country life, and when Rutilius meets him in Tuscany he feels that already he has begun to enjoy a bit of his native land.

On religious matters in general Rutilius says so little that there is still some difference of opinion as to whether he was a Christian or a pagan. His conservative attitude to Roman institutions might account for the lip service which he pays to the old Roman gods. His fanatical hatred of Jews, which expresses itself in a remarkable passage (383 ff.), has been thought to be inspired by the fact that Christ belonged to their nation, though financial considerations are more likely to account for his attitude. It is indeed not really certain that Rutilius was anti-Christian. Pichon, who does not doubt that he is a pagan, suggests that his reserve on this subject may be due to his good feeling and good manners towards his fellow officials, many of whom were, of course, Christians.[1] Of his detestation of monks he leaves us in no possible doubt; but these views were shared by a great many of the people of Rome, where riots against monks and ascetics had broken out on the death of the eldest daughter of St Paula, who was believed to have died from too much devotion to ascetic practice. Even later Salvian tells us that in Carthage the monks were subject to every sort of persecution, and that they could scarcely appear in the streets without being reviled and cursed.[2]

The feeling of Rutilius against the monks is so bitter that one is tempted to seek some more immediate cause, such as might be supplied by the foundations of the great monastic establishments at Marseilles and on the Lérins. As the ship approaches the island of Capraria (l. 439 ff.) he speaks of its occupants, as a handful of monks, men who 'flee the light', suggesting that their object is that they may live alone (*monachus*) in order that their lives may be without witness. As he passes the rocky island

---

[1] De Labriolle also argues for the heathenism of Rutilius. See the *Revue des Études romains*, Vol. VI (1928), p. 30 ff.
[2] *De Gubernatione Dei*, VIII, v.

of Gorgon (l. 515 ff.) he remarks, with a resentment which is perhaps less unnatural, that there one of his fellow citizens has recently shut himself up 'alive', and, what makes it more bitter, he was a young man of high rank who had made a splendid marriage, and now 'he lives as an exile, poor deluded creature, in a disgraceful retreat'. It is strange to see Rutilius who is habitually so urbane and humane, thus moved beyond his usual reserve and respect, indeed we might add, his good manners.

The *De Reditu Suo* is a kind of catalogue poem, a narrative of a journey, like the *Mosella*. Its nearest affinities are with the works of Ausonius, though travel poems had preceded it, to which, in superficial features, the poem of Rutilius may have approached more nearly; and it may have been influenced also by the works of Horace and Ovid. But in particular he may have known the works of Rufus Festus Avienus, who flourished during the second half of the fourth century A.D. Avienus wrote descriptive geographical poems, modelled in part on earlier works. Among them are the *Descriptio Orbis Terrarum*, a paraphrase of the Περιήγησις τῆς γῆς of Dionysius, and another work describing the coasts of the Mediterranean, the Caspian, and the Black Sea. Only a fragment of the first of these remains, but such poems may possibly have suggested the form to Rutilius. Certain it is that the Gaulish poets of the time could hardly refrain from including an itinerary whenever opportunity offered. We have already seen (p. 84) that when Niketas, Bishop of Naissus in Remesiana in Dacia,[1] visited St Paulinus at Nola on the occasion of the birthday celebrations of St Felix in 398, Paulinus addressed a poem of welcome to him, in which he sketches his visitor's return route to the 'Dacians of the far North'.

Rutilius's poem resembles the work of Ausonius even more in its point of view than in its superficial geographical form. This resemblance lies partly in the fondness for the personal portrait, or rather the series of personal portraits, resulting in a picture gallery of a little society of cultured and literary officials such as do not often appear in poetry. It might well bear the title of *A Mirror for Magistrates*. Moreover it resembles

---

[1] See A. E. Burn, *Niceta of Remesiana* (Cambridge, 1905), especially Introduction, p. xlix ff.

the work of Ausonius in other features, such as the dignity and humanity with which the author invests duty and justice and love of family, and friendship. To him, as to Ausonius, those officials who live devoted and valuable lives, manly in character, intellectual and unworldly, are worthy of a place in poetry. We shall find all these features in the verses of Sidonius later. They belong to the provincial poetical school of Gaul.

We have just seen Rutilius setting out from the port of Rome with the applause of the spectators in the theatre ringing in his ears. And we have seen from the writings of Salvian the great hold which the theatre had on the people everywhere. Even when Trier was burnt, and the dead were lying unburied in the streets, the people clamoured for the circus and the theatre (cf. p. 166). The Barbarian Invasions, with the consequent disorders, famine, ruin and homeless misery, were powerless to kill the love of stage-plays, and may even have given them a fresh impetus, as affording some distraction from the intolerable reality. Even in his poem addressed to Consentius, Sidonius describes the *pantomimi* as still flourishing and possessing a wide repertoire.[1] The gladiatorial combats, so much prized as a social function by Symmachus, had come to an end in 404; but the circus and the theatre continued to exert their fascination.[2]

We are able to take part with Gaul in the comedy of the closing years of the Empire, for we possess a complete text of an anonymous Latin comedy, the *Querolus*, or, to give it its alternative title, the *Aulularia*, 'The Pot of Gold',[3] which was almost certainly composed in southern Gaul,[4] probably between 420 and 430 or thereabouts.[5] It is the only complete Latin comedy

[1] *Carmen* XXIII, 263 ff.
[2] On this subject in general, see S. Dill, *Roman Society in the Last Century of the Western Empire*[2] (London, 1933), p. 56 ff.
[3] A list of the early editions of the play is given by G. Ranstrand, *Querolus sive Aulularia* (Göteborg, 1951), p. ix. This is also the most recent critical text. Other editions of recent times are those by R. Peiper, *Aulularia sive Querolus* (Leipzig, 1875); by L. Havet, *Le Querolus* (Paris, 1880); by L. Hermann, *Querolus* (Brussels, 1937).
[4] Wernsdorf (see below), points to the phrase (Havet, Act I, Sc. 2; Ranstrand, p. 17, l. 18) *sic nostra loquitur Graecia*, which suggests that the native country of the author is Gaul. See further the local allusions cited below.
[5] Havet *Le Querolus*, p. 5 f. Pichon dates it cautiously: 'très certainement du quatrième ou du cinquième siècle.' (*Les Derniers Écrivains Profanes*, ch. IV, 'Une Comédie de Société Gallo-Romaine', p. 218). Raby places its composition in the fourth century, but does not state his reasons (*A History of Secular Latin Poetry in the Middle Ages*, Vol. II, Oxford, 1934, p. 59, footnote 2).

which has survived apart from those of Plautus or Terence. M. Havet leans to Lyons or Autun as the place of its origin;[1] more recent critics, such as Pichon,[2] assign it to somewhere in southern Gaul without closer specification. Thus it would seem likely that comedy was still flourishing[3] in the very heart of the country which had just given birth to a great monastic life; but the actors are on the stage for the last time, while the monasteries are looking to the future. The play is dedicated to a certain Rutilius, who is described as *venerandus* and *illustris*, and who is evidently a man of some pretension to letters and philosophy. The author says that he has composed the play to thank him for his generosity, and to amuse his guests as they converse after dinner. Evidently Rutilius is the author's patron, and all that we learn about him makes it probable that he is Rutilius Namatianus, Prefect of Rome in 416 and the author of the *De Reditu Suo*.[4] Wernsdorf reminds us[5] that responsibility for the shows and theatres was the special function of the office of the Prefect of Rome which Rutilius held in 416, and that more than one passage in his poem shows Rutilius taking great pleasure in such things, and cultivating the poets of his day and delighting in their songs.[6]

Certain allusions in the play, such as those to the *solidus* and to the *Bagaudae*,[7] and the whole internal evidence, favour such a date, while the play is clearly written for an aristocratic and educated, perhaps even a learned audience, such as we should expect to find at Rutilius's country house. The play, in fact, as Pichon observes, enables us to see how Gallo-Roman society amused itself. It has, indeed, been suggested that the *Querolus* was composed by the rhetor Axius Paulus, Ausonius's friend;[8]

[1] Havet, *Querolus*, p. 4.

[2] Op. cit., p. 217.

[3] For a brief discussion of the question of survival, and of the composition of new comedies in the fourth or fifth century, see G. W. Johnston, *The Querolus, A Syntactical and Stylistic Study* (Toronto, 1900), p. ix f.

[4] Cavallin ('Bemerkungen zu Querolus', *Eranos*, Vol. XLIX (1951), p. 139 f.) points to some interesting cases of verbal correspondence between the *Querolus* and the poem of Rutilius, e.g. the references to Circe and the Harpies; and he regards these as echoes deliberately introduced by the author of the *Querolus* from the work of his patron. He regards this as additional evidence for the circle in which the *Querolus* was composed.

[5] See the extract from Wernsdorf's *Proem* published in Peiper's edition of the *Querolus*, p. xxx.

[6] Lines 201 ff.; 267; 603 ff.

[7] For the *Bagaudae*, see p. 166 f.

[8] M. Dezeimeris, *Études sur le Querolus* (Bordeaux, 1881).

but though *Querolus* may well have been composed by a rhetor, he was probably of a later date than that of Ausonius.

The play is generally printed as prose, and it is so regarded by most early critics, notably those of the sixteenth and seventeenth centuries.[1] Some recent scholars, however, hold that the original version, which has not been preserved, was composed in verse, and that our MS. tradition is derived from a paraphrase made before the ninth century. The scholars who believe that the play was composed in verse are not in agreement however as to the metre of the original. Havet urged that the play was originally composed in trochaic tetrameters, a favourite metre of Plautus. He reconstructed the play in this form, and printed it in the same volume as his prose text. His results have been accepted by so discriminating a critic as Pichon, but have been disputed by Ranstrand and others. Ranstrand regards the medium as rhythmical prose,[2] and prints it as prose in his edition. The medium of the play has been re-examined recently by Cavallin, who comes to the conclusion that it is certainly metrical, and based, as Havet suggested, on the metre of Plautus.[3] The author, says Cavallin, has succeeded in some measure in introducing something of the old Latin speech-verse into his comedy, notably the characteristic independence of the two halves of the Roman long line; and such metrical irregularities as his work shows would seem to be deliberate.[4] The question is one which we must leave to specialists, but of the rhythmical nature of much of the original there can be no doubt. The play is probably dependent, in part at least, on some lost Greek original, since the author promises to give his audience 'Greek philosophy spoken by barbarian lips',[5] and some of the names, such as Euclio and Mandrogerus, are manifestly of Greek origin. The author, however, claims to be basing himself on Plautus, and the alternative title of the play, the *Aulularia*, as well as the motif of the pot of gold and the character and name of its owner, the old miser Euclio, are clearly derived from the *Aulularia* of Plautus. In the play of

[1] For a useful summary of the views expressed on the medium of the *Querolus* see G. W. Johnston, op. cit., p. xii f.

[2] See S. Cavallin, '*Bemerkungen zu Querolus*', loc. cit., p. 138, n. 1.

[3] ibid., pp. 138, n. 1; 147 f.; cf. also the reference to the study by Wilhelm Meyer (of Speyer) there cited.

[4] ibid., p. 150.

[5] *Prologue.*

Plautus also, as in the *Querolus*, the miser hides his gold in the shrine of his domestic *Lar*; and in that play, also as in the *Querolus*, it is stolen. But here it is ultimately returned to Euclio himself. Apart from these features the plays have little in common, and a comparison of the *Querolus* with the *Aulularia* of Plautus serves to bring out with striking emphasis the individuality and independence of the former.

The plot is simple, very amusing, and highly moral. The hero, Querolus, is, as his name implies, a discontented person, one out of harmony with his surroundings, not because he has any serious grievance, but because he has a carping habit, and is therefore, according to fifth-century standards, not a very good member of society. He is fortunate, however, in that his destiny is guided by the domestic *Lar* who is a prominent 'character' of the play. The father of Querolus, an old miser Euclio, has died while on a journey before the play opens, first, however, confiding to a parasite Mandrogerus that he has buried his treasure at home in front of the *Lar's* altar. He bequeathes to him in writing half his wealth on his promising to deliver up the remaining half to Querolus. Mandrogerus, disguised as a magician, gains admittance to the house of Querolus and, with the help of two accomplices, gets possession of the chest which he believes contains the treasure; but on opening it he finds only a funerary urn, and in his anger he and his two friends fling the urn back into the house of Querolus. It breaks; but instead of the ashes of a dead man, the gold pours out at the feet of the astonished heir. Such, reduced to its simplest terms, is the bare outline of the plot.

But, as in all good comedy, the essence and flavour vanish when the plot is set down in outline. The play depends for its success on other elements. The use made of quibble, both in the plot and the dialogue, is extensive, and produces constant surprise, constant unexpected turns of phrase, amusing reversals. Mandrogerus has promised Euclio to give half the gold to Querolus; but when Querolus accuses him of being a thief, he points out that he has discovered the treasure and handed it all to Querolus without touching it. The impudence of Mandrogerus is unbelievable. He is an artist in it, and he so manages matters, in the scene where he appears before Querolus to answer for his crime, that at the crisis it is not easy to know whether he or Querolus is the plaintiff. Arbiter, a friend and neighbour of Querolus, begs him to pardon the thief and take him to live with him, and when Querolus replies 'Him? The thief? I should be afraid to!' Arbiter has his answer ready: 'What have you to be afraid of? He has already robbed you of everything you possess.' And when finally Querolus grants the thief his life, at once comes the ready request: 'You have given me my life, give me something to live by.' Mandrogerus's only real penitence is that he, who has learnt astrology, should allow himself to be duped by a dead man – an allusion to the funerary urn which contained the gold.

The play is highly diverting and full of wit. Perhaps the gayest and brightest thing about the whole is the imperturbable impudence of everyone in it, not excepting the domestic *Lar*, Querolus's tutelary deity, who, to say the truth, is not quite our ideal of a divinity. But the supreme instance is the slave Pantomalus, who, in a monologue which is really superb, puts with supreme impudence the point of view of all slaves as opposed to that of their masters. There is neither hatred nor rancour, hardly even vexation; but as Pantomalus sees the situation, his master is unreasonable, and this he proceeds to explain in somewhat excessive detail. Yet when a neighbour, Arbiter, accuses Querolus of habitual ill humour, Pantomalus hastily comes forward to defend his master's good name: 'Well, what of it? Is the sky always bright? Even the sun doesn't shine the whole time.' And the curses that Pantomalus calls down on his master are more humorous than venomous: 'May he greet with over confidence those who disdain him; may he run to welcome those who don't come; and may he pass the summer in tight new boots.' After all, why should he be bitter? He knows that he is really much better off than his master – he has safety, peace, a good living, no anxieties, and a full life of surreptitious pleasure denied to his master, who is exposed to all eyes. Perhaps the sunniest thing about this gay little play is that no-one has any real grievance against any one else, though they all like to grumble. Even Querolus would never have found his treasure if the thief had not revealed it to him, albeit involuntarily. As Arbiter points out to Querolus, Mandrogerus's only fault is that he doesn't know how to steal.

It will have been noticed that in contrast to the plays of

Plautus, and to the *Aulularia* in particular, there are no women characters in the *Querolus*, and no intrigue. At the same time there is an almost total absence of coarseness of word or allusion. With the exception of one or two slight expressions, *Querolus* could be played in a modern drawing-room, and, as Pichon observes, no comic work of antiquity has less need of expurgation. Despite the author's claim to model himself on Plautus, his own work is wittier and more sparkling, and there is a refinement and elegance, and an irony in *Querolus* which are absent from the more robust humour, and coarser, possibly more telling jokes of the earlier dramatist. The characters of *Querolus*, too, are less boldly conceived, less crude, and drawn with greater restraint and reserve. The author and his characters alike avoid extremes of statement, and show a lively capacity for seeing both sides of an argument, a situation, or a character. This is, of course, the source of the quibbling which forms so important an element in the humour. The play is essentially intellectual, and in its cast of thought approaches more closely to the spirit of Terence than to that of Plautus.

Querolus was certainly composed for an aristocratic audience. This would have been abundantly evident, even if we had not been told so by the author in his dedication to Rutilius. It is clear from the tone of the play, the absence of women, and of impropriety, the politeness and refinement, both of allusion and of general style. The author knows well how to amuse without violating the canons of good taste. Querolus is not a 'sympathetic character', he is rather a fool; but he is a gentleman. Even Mandrogerus pays him the compliment of recognizing this. When the latter stands convicted of theft and perfidy before Querolus, he still has no hesitation in placing in his hands the piece of paper on which Euclio has made him co-heir. 'Here, take it and read it – I know that I can rely on your good faith.'

The audience is not only aristocratic, it is also highly educated, a trifle scholarly. Its members could appreciate allusions to early Latin poetry; they were acquainted with the procedure of the tribunals; they were familiar with the jargon of the schools. Above all they must have been keenly interested in the philosophical and theological questions of the day. The author declares that he bases his theme on a *sermo philosophicus* of Rutilius, and the implications of the play are an acceptance of the Stoic and pagan conception of Fate. The work contains no reference to Christianity, and this silence, which is shared by most of the pagan writers of the time, notably Symmachus, Martianus Capella and Macrobius, has been ascribed to Roman etiquette.[1] We have found this silence also in the poem of Rutilius.

At the same time it must be pointed out that Fate, or Destiny, is here seriously called in question. One feels that the choice of theme was not wholly independent of the great question of Predestination which was ringing in the air. The questions which especially interest Querolus himself are those which were interesting all the educated minds of the time, philosophers, theologians, and educated laymen, the burning questions of Destiny (? or Pre-destiny) and why the innocent suffer. As Pichon points out, there is no consistent answer given to the complaints of Querolus against Destiny; but ought we to look for a consistent philosophical solution? Is it only a question of Stoicism? We seem to be amidst the varied questions and answers which were in the air of southern Gaul in the fifth century; and as one reads the sermons of the age, especially those of St Valerian of Cémélé,[2] with their reiterated insistence on the necessity for charity and on the sin of avarice, one realizes that the alternative title of the play, *Aulularia*, and the choice of subject, the troubles which arise from the avarice of old Euclio, are not fortuitous. We seem now and then to hear not only the voice of the Stoic, but almost the voice of Salvian, speaking with the lips of the *Lar* who complains to Querolus that people are more concerned about the welfare of their bodies than of their souls, and who declares that if a man is unhappy it is his own fault; that the good things given by God cannot be taken away; that one can neither obtain nor lose anything without the will of Him who is all powerful. The *Lar* is surely not only a pagan and a philosophical conception; not only a kind of Chorus. He is also something like an external conscience. He is a protean figure.

The play is of especial value for us, not so much for what it actually expresses as for the nature of the audience which it

---

[1] See H. F. Stewart, *Cambridge Medieval History*, Vol. I (Cambridge, 1911), p. 572.

[2] Migne, *P.L.*, LII, col. 691 ff. See further, p. 164 below.

implies. This audience is a gay, pleasure-loving, intellectual company who even in their amusements like to be reminded of their reading, to be complimented by learned allusions, to be treated as serious thinkers, even as gentlemen-philosophers, who occasionally lend an ear to talk of Predestination, and the value of renunciation, but who do not allow themselves to be too deeply committed to any party, or to have their emotions very deeply engaged. They are, as we infer from the dedication, the guests of one of the great country houses in Gaul, who are thus entertained, while chatting after dinner, by one who is at least intellectually their equal, probably their superior, and who, by the favour of his patron, is enabled to associate on terms of social equality with his audience. A happy chance has thus preserved for us an evening with a Gallo-Roman house-party; and to quote the words of Havet:

'In the midst of invasions, brigandage, civil war and famine, while manners were growing hard and the human spirit weak, when the West had already entered upon its great decline of a thousand years, this unknown author was writing for us the last gay work of the ancient world.'[1]

[1] Op. cit., p. 20.

CHAPTER VI

Foundations of Western Monasticism
The Monastery of Lérins

SOUTHERN PROVENCE must always have had an active intellectual life owing first to its history as a Greek colony, and later
to its active intercourse with North Africa and Rome. The life
and writings of St Irenaeus,[1] Bishop of Lyons in the latter part
of the second century, and the letter from the Gallican Churches
preserved by Eusebius,[2] who flourished during the later third
and the first half of the fourth centuries, afford valuable testimony to the continuity of this intellectual life among the earliest
Christian communities. It is possibly because of the strength of
the classical tradition, and the effectiveness of Church life in
this area, that monasticism was relatively late in obtaining an
important position. We have no clear evidence of organized
monasticism in southern Gaul before the fifth century.

Before this time, however, we hear, more or less incidentally,
of individuals who had withdrawn themselves from social life
to live as religious recluses, whether temporarily or permanently.
Caprasius, who is referred to by Hilary of Arles among the
community of Lérins as an old man (senex), and who had been
the spiritual guide of Honoratus and his brother in their youth,
had previously spent some time as a Christian recluse. And a
disciple of Honoratus himself, Theodore, who became Bishop
of Fréjus about 432, is said to have previously established some
form of monastic retreat on the Stoechades (modern Hyères)[3]

---

[1] A detailed and valuable account of St Irenaeus is that of F. Vernet in the
Dictionnaire de Théologie Catholique, Vol. VII (1922), cols. 2394–2533. For a useful
account of Irenaeus in English, and a translation of some important passages, see
F. R. M. Hitchcock, St Irenaeus' Treatise against the Heresies (London, 1916).

[2] The epistle was extracted by Eusebius from a document which contained a
number of accounts of Gallican martyrdoms and letters. The whole Epistle was
incorporated in his Collection of Martyrdoms, which is lost; but in his Ecclesiastical
History (V, 1–3) he gives fragments of it, which, it is thought, probably represent
the most important portions (Migne, P.G. Vol. XX, col. 407 ff.). For an English
translation, see T. H. Bindley, The Epistle of the Gallican Churches (London, 1900).

[3] For others living in retreat on the Stoechades, see L. Duchesne, Histoire
ancienne de l'Église, Vol. III (Paris, 1910), p. 273.

between Nice and Marseilles. The islands off the north-western coast of Italy were also a favourite resort of the early anchorites. We have seen St Martin sojourning temporarily with a single disciple on the island of *Gallinaria* (modern *Gallinara*) off the coast of the Riviera. Rutilius Namatianus speaks with disapproval of monks whom he knows to be in retreat on the islands of Gorgon and Capraria off the north-western coast of Italy.[1] These retreats, however, were probably not permanent in character.

The inrush of population from the north and west into Southern Provence must have had an overwhelming effect on these little retreats; and in fact we hear little of them after the early years of the century. An idyllic community such as that of Paulinus at Nola, or the little eremitical retreats of Sulpicius Severus and his fellow anchorites, could neither meet effectively the important practical needs of the time, nor enable the 'religious' to fulfil their vocation. A way of life had to be found which would be better suited to larger numbers and to less contemplative vocations, and which at the same time would enable the intellectual and spiritual life of the community to go forward. The same problem had already been faced by Pachomius in the desert of Tabenna in Upper Egypt in the preceding century, and had been solved by the creation of institutions involving a closer community life, organized on a self-supporting basis, and disciplined with a rigour which may have owed much to the early military career traditionally assigned to their founder.

Nothing on the same scale developed in these early days in western Europe. The earliest recorded monasticism in Gaul under St Martin gives no impression of an elaborate organized economy, or regular discipline, and his monastery left no permanent monastic tradition.

About the beginning of the fifth century, however, cenobitic monasticism sprang up in Southern Provence. Both the date and the exact circumstances are somewhat obscure. The earliest foundations planned for community life on a considerable scale were in the neighbourhood of the mouth of the Rhône and on the islands to the south. Towards the close of the century the

[1] The island of Palmaria, off the coast of Naples, was similarly used as a religious retreat. See also Ambrose, *Hexaem.* iii, 5 (*insulas velut monilia*).

movement spread northward up the river, and c. 512 Caesarius founded his monastery for men at Arles, and a nunnery under his sister – the first nunnery in the West of which we have record – on an island in the Rhône.

The question of the immediate influences which inspired this impetus to cenobitic monasticism is a difficult one. They are commonly attributed to the system flourishing in Upper Egypt in the fourth century. But other monastic influences were also at work, and it is very possible that the stimulus to Gaul from Upper Egypt has been over-estimated, owing to the fact that our information about the cenobitic monastic system of Upper Egypt is relatively full. We have a number of sources, of which the most reliable are the Greek and Coptic 'Lives' of Pachomius, the founder of the system, and of Theodore, who held office in the monastery of Tabenna under him, and who ultimately succeeded to the abbacy. The source of information for the system most widely known in the West, however, is that of the monk Palladius, who claims to have visited the Egyptian communities towards the close of the fourth century, and who has left us a detailed and lively account which is commonly known as the *Lausiac History*, owing to its dedication to one Lausus, a chamberlain at the court of Theodosius II (cf. further p. 216 below). Of almost equal importance is another work known as the *Historia Monachorum in Aegypto*, which is generally attributed to Rufinus.[1] A brief contemporary picture is given by St Jerome in his letter (*Ep.* 22) to Eustochium.

The history of asceticism in Egypt is itself obscure. There can be no doubt that in origin it is pre-Christian. During the early centuries of the Christian era, however, great numbers had retreated to the desert, perhaps in part to evade the exactions of the Roman tax-collector, perhaps still more to escape the

---

[1] The fullest general account of the *Lausiac History*, and of the questions which have arisen regarding the value and authenticity of this work and of the *Historia Monachorum*, is that of Dom. Cuthbert Butler, *The Lausiac History of Palladius* (Cambridge, 1898). The Greek text was also edited, with introduction and notes, under the same title and by the same author, and published at Cambridge, 1904. A text with a French translation was published by A. Lucot, *Palladius Histoire Lausiaque* (Paris, 1912); and an English translation by W. K. Lowther Clarke, *The Lausiac History of Palladius* (London, 1918). For the debt of the writer of the *Lausiac History* to Evagrius, see R. Draguet, 'L'Histoire Lausiaque', *Revue d'Histoire ecclésiastique*, Vols. XLI and XLII (1946–7). A readable, but not a very sympathetic, general study of Egyptian Monasticism will be found in *Pilgrims Were They All*, by Dorothy Brooke (London, 1937), pp. 1–88.

persecutions; and finally the numbers were recruited by refugees fleeing from the Barbarian Invasions. In Lower Egypt the
settlements of the monks do not appear to have been closely
organized from any central nucleus, though scattered communities of anchorites, living more or less independently, tended to
concentrate in special areas, such as the desert of Nitria to the
north-west of Cairo; and beyond them the more remote group
of isolated cells known as *Cellae*; the settlement of Scete still
further west in the desert; and the waterless Climax, most
distant of them all. In Upper Egypt, about fifty miles north of
Luxor, in the district known as the Thebaïd, a further scattered
community of monks lived more remote from the usual pilgrim
route, and consequently less visited, though Palladius appears
to have direct knowledge of it. Here at Tabenna, at an uncertain date in the fourth century – possibly as early as 305 –
Pachomius, a disciple of the hermit Palaemon, is believed to
have organized the monks into closer communities than the
scattered northern groups.

This new institution was known as the *coenobium*, and its
members lived together as a community under a superior. The
ordered life of the *coenobium* seems to have partaken of the rigour
and discipline, even of something of the organization of barrack
life. The community was self-supporting and hard-working,
with its own bakery and work-shops, each staffed by separate
groups of monks. The brethren met daily for common prayers,
and all owed obedience to a single superior. The nucleus of the
system, and its most important element, was the institution of a
common way of life for all members living within the community. The system spread rapidly, other monasteries and nunneries sprang up, and in Cassian's day the whole population
living under the Pachomian system in the neighbourhood of
Tabenna is said to have numbered seven thousand.

There is another form of monasticism which is less familiar to
us than that of Egypt, but of which we must not lose sight in
attempting to trace the foundations of the cenobitic ideal in the
West. This is the monasticism of St Basil,[1] who was born in 329
or 330 and died in 379, and whose monasticism, which began

---

[1] An important recent book on St Basil is that of D. Amand, *L'Ascèse Monastique de Saint Basile* (Maredsous, 1948). For brief accounts of the institutions of St Basil, see also Butler, op. cit. (1898), p. 243 f.; and N. H. Baynes and H. St L. B. Moss, *Byzantium* (Oxford, 1948), p. 141 f.

K

near Neocaesarea in Pontus, rapidly became the principal form of coenobitic life in the Greek and Russian Churches. He left no 'Rule' in the technical sense, but the traditional ideal of his monasteries is well preserved. He seems to have received his original inspiration from the ascetic Armenian Bishop Eustathius, under whom there is reason to believe that cenobitic monasticism was already well established before the work of Basil began; but Basil had received his own education at Athens, and had travelled in Egypt, both among the ascetics of Lower Egypt and in the Pachomian institutions of the Thebaïd. It is not surprising therefore that his own system, while closely resembling that of Pachomius in many respects, differs in others, and is thought to approximate in its ascetic ideals to that of Eustathius.[1] He is known, moreover, to have favoured a much closer cenobitic life than that of the Pachomian monasteries of Egypt. The monks in his institutions lived a full community life which almost excluded eremitism. Meals, work, and prayers were in common, and austerities were strictly subject to obedience to a superior. Personal initiative is practically excluded.

It is generally held that the monasticism of Southern Provence in the fifth century was directly inspired by the newly developed system of Pachomius. This is, however, by no means clear. Of the two earliest monasteries in this area of which we have detailed knowledge, that of the island of Lérina or St Honorat in the Mediterranean, to the south of Marseilles, probably drew its original inspiration from Greece or the eastern Mediterranean rather than from Egypt; while the other, the monastery of St Victor in the neighbourhood of Marseilles, appears to be indebted rather to the more independent communities of Lower Egypt, the anchorites and recluses, than to the cenobitic institutions of Pachomius. And again, John Cassian, the chief monk associated with the latter monastery in its initial stages, claims to have had his original training in a monastery in Bethlehem. Doubtless both these south Gaulish monasteries had something in common with the Pachomian institutions; but it is not impossible that the good fortune which has preserved our relatively full and intimate knowledge of the communities of Upper Egypt has led us to over-

[1] See Amand, op. cit., p. 51 ff.

emphasize, and perhaps slightly to distort the extent of the relationship of the communities of southern Gaul to the Pachomian foundations. The debt may be at most indirect.

The monastery of Lérins, or St Honorat, as it is called from the name of its founder, St Honoratus, stands on the island of Lérina, which, like its neighbour, Léro, belongs to the Lérins Group in the Bay of Cannes to the south of Marseilles. The exact date of the foundation is uncertain, but it was most probably in the first decade of the fifth century, possibly even a few years earlier.[1] The foundation of the monastery of St Victor at Marseilles was probably a few years later, perhaps between 410 and 420. I will postpone discussion of this latter monastery till a later chapter. Here I will endeavour to trace the early history of Lérins.

In order to understand the nature of this monastery in its earliest period, a word must be said on the life of the founder himself. In the absence of any writings from his hand, we are dependent for our knowledge on the reports of his contemporaries, most of all on the commemorative oration or sermon composed for his anniversary by St Hilary,[2] who had been a monk under him at Lérins and who became his successor, first as abbot of this monastery, and later as Bishop of Arles.[3] From these sources we learn that Honoratus probably belonged by origin to Gallia Belgica, whence he and his brother set out under the tutelage of an elderly anchorite, Caprasius by name,[4] to prepare themselves for the monastic life. Leaving Marseilles

---

[1] J. E. L. Oulton gives the date as 'c. 397' (see his chapter on 'The Church of Gaul' in the *History of the Church of Ireland*, edited by W. A. Phillips, Vol. I (Oxford, 1933), p. 23, n. 7) and as authority for his view refers to Scott Holmes (*The Christian Church in Gaul*, p. 284 (for 281 ff.). In the passage in question, however Scott Holmes is basing his date on a visit which he states that St Honoratus paid to St Paulinus of Nola. Scott Holmes gives no authority for his own statement, however, and I can find no evidence for such a visit, unless Scott Holmes is referring to a passage in Hilary of Arles (*Sermo de Vita Honorati*; for fuller reference, see p. 160, n. 3), cap. 15, according to which Honoratus visited the priests of Tuscia (modern Tuscany) on his way home from Greece to Gaul. St Paulinus is not specifically mentioned, however. No argument for the date of the foundation of Lérins ought to be based on what seems at best a doubtful conjecture. It is perhaps worth remarking that had such a visit taken place, it would seem strange that Paulinus should make no reference to it in his letter to Eucherius and Galla, sent by monks returning from Nola to Lérins (cf. p. 87).

[2] *Sermo de Vita Honorati*, in *Vitae Sanctorum, Honorati et Hilarii*, edited by S. Cavallin (Lund, 1952); Migne, *P.L.*, Vol. L, col. 1249.

[3] Gennadius, ch. 22.

[4] Eucherius refers to him (*De Laude Eremi*) in these terms: *Haec (insula) nunc possidet venerabilem gravitate Caprasium veteribus sanctis parem.*

c. 380 Honoratus sailed for Greece, together with his brother and Caprasius. We do not know how long they were in Greece, but at Methone Honoratus's brother died, and Honoratus and Caprasius returned to Gaul, staying some time in Italy with the priests of Tuscia.[1]

On their arrival in Gaul, they took up their abode on the smaller of the two islands of the Lérins Group. Here Honoratus founded the monastery which still bears his name, and here Caprasius lived as a presbyter till his death in 430. Honoratus probably ruled as abbot till c. 428, when the death of Euladius, who seems to have succeeded Patroclus in the episcopate of Arles, left the see vacant, and Honoratus, by the invitation of the people of Arles, succeeded him, and occupied the see till his death, which probably took place about the beginning of 430.[2]

The relationship of Honoratus and his foundation on Lérina to Leontius, the Bishop of Fréjus, seems to be analogous to that of St Martin and his early foundation or settlement at Ligugé to St Hilary of Poitiers. St Hilary of Arles, in his account of St Honoratus, speaks of the saint occupying the island, not only on account of its favourable position and character, but also for the privilege of being near to Leontius.

'Vacantem itaque insulam ob nimietatem squaloris, et inaccessam venenatorum animalium metu, Alpino haud longe jugo subdit(a)m, petit, praeter secreti opportunitatem sancti ac beatissimi in Christo viri Leontii episcopi oblectatus vicinia et charitate constrictus, plurimis a tam novo ausu retrahere conantibus. Nam circumiecti accolae terribilem illam vastitatem ferebant, et suis illum occupare finibus fidei ambitione certabant,' etc.[3]

At a somewhat later date the relationship of the abbey to the Bishop of Fréjus, in whose See it was situated, became a matter of important dispute. It would seem that certain rights or privileges, accorded either deliberately[4] or tacitly[5] to Honoratus by Leontius, were called in question by Leontius's successor Theodore; and a council was called at Arles, perhaps about

---

[1] Hilary, *Sermo*, 14, 15.
[2] For the succession at Arles, and the chronology as outlined above, see O. Chadwick, 'Euladius of Arles', *Journal of Theological Studies*, Vol. XLVI (1945), p. 200 ff.; ibid., *John Cassian* (Cambridge, 1950), p. 188.
[3] *Sermo S. Hilarii de Vita S. Honorati*, 15 (Cavallin); Migne, *P.L.*, Vol. L, col. 1257.
[4] See Scott Holmes, op. cit., p. 283.
[5] So A. Malnory, *Saint Césaire* (Paris, 1894), p. 272.

455,[1] by Ravennius, bishop of that city, assisted by Rusticus,[2] Bishop of Narbonne, and the bishops of the province, to settle the dispute. Indeed,there is reason to suspect that the foundation of Lérins may be due in a considerable measure to the efforts, or at least the inspiration, of Leontius.

It would be interesting to know more of Leontius.[3] He was already Bishop of Fréjus in 419, and it is generally assumed that he is the Leontius to whom, together with a certain Helladius, Cassian dedicates Parts I and III of the *Conferences* (cf. p. 224). Leontius is said to have been the brother of Castor,[4] the Bishop of Apta Julia, to whom Cassian dedicates the *Institutes*, and by whom he had been urged to write the *Conferences*, and who was himself intending to introduce the system into his own diocese. It would seem probable, therefore, that, if this identification of Cassian's Leontius is correct, a close sympathy existed between the monastic institutions of Lérins and Marseilles from the start, through their common interest in the Bishop of Fréjus. Indeed such good feeling between the two monasteries must in any case have existed, since we also find Cassian dedicating the Second Part of his *Conferences* to Honoratus and Eucherius of Lérins, while Eucherius himself made an *Epitome* of Cassian's *Institutes*,[5] modifying the statements which suggest a Pelagian tendency.

From what has been said it would seem that the earliest influence on the founder of Lérins was not that of Egyptian or Eastern monasticism, but was rather Greek. Why, we may ask, did Honoratus choose to visit Greece? It will be remembered that it was in Athens that St Basil (†379) first turned his thoughts seriously to religion, and it is possible that Honoratus may himself have had Athens as his goal; or again that he hoped to put himself under the discipline of some Greek institution where St Basil's rule had been adopted. It is tempting to see in early Greek influence on Lérins the shaping force which gave to the monastery its 'Golden Age', the phase which was primarily intellectual. The intellectual florescence of the first

[1] See Duchesne, *Fastes Épiscopaux*, Vol. I, p. 124, footnote 5.
[2] For an interesting account of Rusticus, see Duchesne, loc. cit.
[3] For details, see Duchesne, *Fastes*, I, p. 276.
[4] It would seem from this that he was occupying his see in 419, and that he was already dead by 426. See Duchesne, *Fastes* I, p. 273.
[5] Migne, *P.L.*, Vol. L, col. 867.

two generations is very marked. It produced some of the best thinkers and the most brilliant writers of the day, and there can be little doubt that the personality and intellectual training of Honoratus must have been the inspiration of this splendid monastic flowering. Hilary reports Eucherius as saying in praise of the eloquence of a letter from Honoratus inscribed on wax: 'You have restored to the wax its honey.'[1] Hilary himself remarks that 'If Charity desired to have her portrait painted, she would borrow the features of Honoratus.'[2] These brief words of praise are significant of the rhetorical literary style cultivated at Lérins, and colouring the writings of the ecclesiastics trained there. We shall see this style highly developed in the writings of Eucherius, and also in the *Commonitorium* of Vincent, himself a monk of Lérins. Lérins, indeed, owing partly, no doubt, to the intellectual quality of its foundation, partly perhaps to its proximity to Marseilles, rapidly became a famous literary centre, and almost from the beginning developed as the principal school of religious thought and spiritual activity in the west of Europe.

The praise which Eucherius bestows on Honoratus in that he calls him 'a master of bishops' was indeed well deserved. The same phrase is used later by Gennadius of Salvian, the presbyter of Marseilles, who had probably been a monk of Lérins, and who for a time held there the office of novice-master. Lérins itself has been, with equal justice, styled 'a nursery of bishops,' for here for more than a century the principal bishops and most distinguished thinkers of Gaul received their spiritual education.[3]

It was in Lérins that Hilary of Arles received his early training; and here he afterwards became abbot in succession to Honoratus its founder, before proceeding to the See of Arles. Here Eucherius found his most congenial retreat before entering upon his long episcopacy of Lyons. Here St Lupus, Bishop of Troyes, who is reported to have accompanied St Germanus to Britain (cf. p. 251 ff.), spent a year before his election to his bishopric. Here a brother of Sidonius Apollinaris, Bishop of Clermont – Ferrand in Auvergne, received his early discip-

---

[1] *Sermo*, 22. [2] ibid., 26.

[3] They are cited by A. Cooper-Marsdin, *The History of the Islands of the Lérins* (Cambridge, 1913), *passim*. Cf. Alliez, *Histoire du Monastère de Lérins*, Vol. I (Paris, 1862), *passim*.

line.[1] Here Faustus 'the Briton', or perhaps 'Breton', was educated, to become later abbot of the same monastery, and ultimately Bishop of Riez. Here belonged the theologian, Vincent, author of the *Commonitorium* to be discussed later. Here, towards the close of the century, came the great Caesarius, to live as a monk in strict asceticism in preparation for his work as founder of the famous monastery and nunnery of St John at Arles, and as head of its episcopal see. And here a later age not unnaturally pictured St Patrick as sojourning for a time while in exile in Gaul. For the sojourn of Patrick there is no contemporary authority; but during the following century, when St Augustine and his party were sent by Pope Gregory on their missionary journey to England, commendatory letters, intended no doubt to secure hospitality and assistance, were forwarded by Gregory to Stephen, Abbot of Lérins. And it was Vergilius, Archbishop of Arles, and formerly Abbot of Lérins, who was appointed by Pope Gregory to consecrate St Augustine as Bishop of the English in 597.[2] The high esteem in which Vergilius was held by the See of Rome may be gathered from references in the letters of Pope Gregory.

Perhaps the most eminent among the contemporaries of Honoratus is Eucherius, a layman of the high Gaulish nobility, who became a monk of Lérins under Honoratus, and ultimately Bishop of Lyons. He was perhaps related to Priscus Valerian, the Prefect of Gaul, and through him to the Emperor Avitus.[3] We have already (p. 87) met Eucherius and his wife Galla in the correspondence of Paulinus of Nola, at a time (c. 412) when they were living in solitary retreat on the island of Léro.[4] Their ascetic relationship is typical of the time, for again and again

[1] Sidonius, *Carmen* XVI, 70.
[2] See Bede, *Hist. Eccles.*, Book I, cap. 27. Bede erroneously gives the name of the Bishop of Arles as Etherius, whereas it was, in reality, Vergilius, and it was Vergilius who consecrated St Augustine. In cap. 24 Bede has made the converse error of giving the title of Bishop of Arles to Aetherius, the bishop who entertained Gregory and his followers as they were on their way to Britain. Aetherius was, in fact, not Bishop of Arles, but of Lyons c. 586–602. Bede seeks to correct his error at the beginning of cap. 28 by stating that Vergilius succeeded Aetherius as Bishop of Arles. On these passages see the valuable notes by Plummer, *Baedae Opera Historica*, Vol. II (Oxford, 1896) ad loc. (pp. 39, 45, 55).
[3] L. Alliez (*Histoire du Monastère de Lérins*; Vol. I, p. 422 f.), suggests that the 'perfect Attic' style of Eucherius, even more than his name, would suggest that he was of Greek origin; and reminds us that many noble families of Greece and Asia Minor had followed Constantine the Great to Arles.
[4] So Tillemont (XV, pp. 120, 124 f.; cf. XVI, p. 206).

we find this devotion between husband and wife, which makes a total parting unacceptable to either, despite the inclination of both towards an ascetic life. So it is with Paulinus and his wife Therasia; with Salvian and his wife Palladia. We shall meet with it again between Amator and his wife Martha; between Lupus of Troyes and his wife Pimeniola. The latter pair, like Salvian and Palladia, are stated to have first lived together for seven years (cf. p. 278). Many other cases could be cited.[1] Eucherius placed his sons, Salonius and Veranus, in the monastery of Lérins when Salonius was scarcely ten years old.[2] Here they were tutored by Honoratus and Hilary of Arles, at this time still a presbyter in Lérins. Later they were taught by Vincent of Lérins and by Salvian.[3] Both Salonius and Veranus became bishops.[4]

In his dedication of the Second Part of the *Conferences*, Cassian tells us that Eucherius had always longed to leave 'the cold of Gaul' and visit Egypt and see the brotherhoods there; and he adds that it is partly in order to 'remove the necessity for so risky a journey' that he has composed the *Conferences*, the second part of which, as we have seen, he dedicated to Honoratus and Eucherius. The chronology of Eucherius's early life is not very clear. At some period – possibly after the death of his wife – he became a monk of Lérins, as we learn both from a poem of Sidonius Apollinaris addressed to Bishop Faustus of Riez, and as we should infer from the words of Eucherius himself in praise of Lérins, towards the close of his work *De Laude Eremi*, 'In praise of the Desert' (§ 42). The exact date at which he retired from the world is uncertain. He was living in Léro

---

[1] Cf. also pp. 71, 253. The same practice is traditionally associated with the British Church of the period. Thus we read of St Woollo of Newport in Monmouthshire and his wife St Gwladus, believed to have been induced to adopt such an ascetic mode of life by their son, St Cadoc, c. 500 (*Life of St Gwynllyw*, ch. 6 ff., edited and translated by Wade-Evans, *Vitae Sanctorum Britanniae et Genealogiae*, Cardiff, 1944).

[2] Eucherius, *Instructionum Praefatio ad Salonium* in the works of Eucherius, edited by C. Wotke (*Sancti Eucherii Lugdunensis*, Vienna, 1894), p. 63. The age of Veranus is not known; but he was probably the younger of the two, for in the *Dialogues* composed by Salonius, Veranus is represented as taking the part of questioner. Cf. also Tillemont, Vol. XV, p. 122.

[3] Eucherius, loc. cit.

[4] Salonius was Bishop of Geneva; Veranus, probably of Vence. The insertion of their names as successors to Eucherius in the lists of the Bishops of Lyons is probably due to interpolation, though accepted as genuine by Schaenemann (Migne, *P.L.*, Vol. L, col. 685).

apparently in 412, as we learn from the letter from St Paulinus of Nola to Eucherius and his wife (cf. p. 87); and St Hilary seems to refer to his sojourn on Léro when, in his commemorative sermon on St Honoratus referred to above, he speaks of Eucherius as having received a letter from Honoratus written on wax tablets 'ab eremo . . . in proxima insula'.[1]

Tillemont considers[2] that Eucherius retired first to Lérins, for in his *De Laude Eremi* he declares that, while he must honour all places which serve as retreat for the saints, he has a very special devotion for the Isle of Lérina, which, with kindly arms, welcomes the sailors cast up from the shipwrecks of the world – 'What congregations, what families of holy men I have seen there!'[3] Certain it is that after passing some time in retreat, perhaps on Lérina, he retired to Léro, where he was living ascetically in 412 with his wife Galla when St Paulinus wrote to them; but it is with Lérina that he is especially associated, both in his own work already cited, and in the poem of Sidonius Apollinaris addressed to Faustus (cf. p. 193).

It was perhaps about the year 424[4] that Eucherius was elected Bishop of Lyons, and for perhaps some twenty years he held the see with great honour. He died, according to Gennadius (cap. 63), between 450 and 455, the date favoured by Duchesne being 449.[5]

Tillemont[6] regarded Eucherius as the most distinguished Bishop of Lyons, both for learning and piety, since Irenaeus. He stood equally high in the opinion of his contemporaries. Cassian, in his Dedication of the Second Part of the *Conferences*, speaks of Eucherius and Honoratus as 'shining like great luminaries with marvellous brightness'. Claudianus Mamertus speaks of him[7] as 'by far the greatest of the great bishops of the Age'. Sidonius Apollinaris, in a poem addressed to Faustus, Bishop of Riez, concludes his account of the great men of Lérins

---

[1] Hilary, *Sermo de Vita S. Honorati* (ed. cit.), ch. 20; Migne, *P.L.*, Vol. L, col. 1261.

[2] Tillemont understands Eucherius to have passed from Lérins to Léro (XV, p. 121). Bardenhewer places his first visit to Lérins c. 410, and also believes that he moved to Léro at a later date (see *Patrology*, p. 518).

[3] Ed. Wotke, cap. 42; Migne, *P.L.*, L., col. 710 f.

[4] So Bardenhewer (loc. cit.); but there seems to be considerable doubt about the date.

[5] Duchesne, *Fastes Épiscopaux*, Vol. II, p. 163.

[6] Vol. XV, p. 120.

[7] *De Statu Animae* II, § 9 (Engelbrecht's ed., p. 135; Migne, *P.L.* LIII, col. 752).

who are brought to the memory of the brethren in the discourses of Faustus, with the words: 'And thou dost acclaim in these praises the coming of Eucherius and the return of Hilarius.'[1]

Hilary of Arles himself speaks of him as rivalling St Honoratus in virtue, and as 'shining most brilliantly in the world, still more gloriously in Christ'.[2] He seems to have enjoyed the friendship of all the most important people of his age – of St Paulinus, St Honoratus, Hilary of Arles, Salvian, John Cassian, and a number of others.

Like Paulinus of Nola, Eucherius while still young exchanged wealth, aristocratic connections, and a brilliant career for the ascetic ideal. These renunciations were in the air. Yet it is clear from his writings that his spiritual discipline and asceticism in no way weakened his affection for his family. To his kinsman, Valerian,[3] he dedicated what is probably his earliest work, written before 430, and perhaps therefore the earliest work[4] issued from Lérins. This is a treatise composed in the form of a letter, the *De Contemptu Mundi et Saecularis Philosophiae* ('On Contempt of the World and of Secular Philosophy').[5] To Veranus, one of his sons, he dedicated his *Formulae Spiritalis Intelligentiae* ('Principles of Spiritual Knowledge'); to Salonius, his other son, two books of 'Instructions' (*Instructionum libri duo*), in both of which he frequently addresses them in terms of affection; and Salvian, who had received and read his books with appreciation, found them 'beautiful' and 'useful' works for the instruction of his 'holy and blessed children'.[6] Later, in

[1] Sidonius, *Poems and Letters*, I (ed. W. B. Anderson, London, 1936), *Carmen* XVII, l. 114 f.

[2] 'pulcherrime splendidus mundo, splendidior in Christo', *Sermo de Vita Honorati*, ch. 22; Migne, *P.L.*, Vol. L, col. 1261.

[3] As stated above, Tillemont regarded this Valerian as identical with Priscus Valerian, who, he says, was not a Christian. Alliez (op. cit., Vol. I, p. 79), however, regards the Valerian of the 'Letter' as distinct from Priscus Valerian, 'qui resta dans la siècle'. It would seem that Alliez probably identifies the 'relative', the recipient of the 'Letter', with Bishop Valerian of Cémélé, who, according to Tillemont (XVI, p. 17), was still living in 455.

[4] The complete works of Eucherius are published by Migne, *P.L.*, Vol. L, col. 685 f. The best edition of a selection of the works is that of C. Wotke, published at Vienna, 1884. My references are to Wotke's edition where possible.

[5] This work was translated into English by Henry Vaughan, under the title of *The World contemned* in his book *Flores Solitudinis* (London, 1654); and again by Robert Reade, *The Spiritual Combat* (Paris, 1656), following p. 271 ff.

[6] *Ep.* VIII from Salvian to Eucherius, Wotke, op cit., p. 197. A French translation of most of this letter is given by Alliez, *Histoire du Monastère de Lérins*, Vol. I, p. 195 ff.

the same letter, Salvian again refers to Eucherius's 'admirable children'. Salonius in particular was a favourite pupil of Salvian, who dedicated to him his two treatises, one 'On Avarice', which has survived, and another 'On Providence', which is lost. He also dedicated to him his great work 'On the Government of God'; and when Salonius wrote to ask him for some explanations, Salvian addresses him as 'Master and most blessed pupil, father, and son, pupil by instruction, son by affection, and father by reason of your status'.[1]

The affection between the brothers is naïvely charming. Salonius wrote two treatises, one on the *Book of Proverbs*, here ascribed to Solomon;[2] and another on *Ecclesiastes*.[3] Both are composed in the framework of a dialogue between Salonius and Veranus, in which Veranus propounds difficulties in the form of simple questions, and Salonius in a tone of grave authority gives brief explanations by way of answer. For example, the first dialogue opens with a question from Veranus:

'To what language does the word "Parable" belong?' ('*Parabolae*' *qua lingua dicuntur?*)
and the answer from his brother:

'Greek; in Latin it would be translated by "Simile".' (*Graeca*; *Latina vero interpretantur* '*similitudines*'.)

Apart from these works the two brothers are associated, together with a certain Ceretius, as *episcopi Gallorum*, in the signatures appended to a letter indited to Pope Leo the Great, in which they thank him for a letter which they have received, and submit to him for his approval a copy which they propose to publish throughout the Christian communities of Gaul.[4] It is gratifying to find the mutual respect and good breeding, which characterized the family relationships of Ausonius and Sulpicius Severus in the fourth century, still untarnished in this little family of saints and bishops in the fifth.

The surviving literary works from the pen of Eucherius him-

---

[1] Salvian, *Opera Omnia*, edited by F. Pauly (Vienna, 1883), *Ep.* IX; Migne, Vol. LIII, col. 168.
[2] *In Parabolas Salomonis Expositio Mystica*, Migne, *P.L.*, Vol. LIII, col. 967 ff.
[3] *In Ecclesiasten Expositio Mystica*, ibid., col. 993 ff.
[4] Migne, *P.L.*, Vol. LIV, col. 887. A French translation of the latter part of it is given by Alliez, op. cit., Vol. I, p. 220 f. The word used for 'communities' is *conventicula*; but the letter is to be read, not only by the *sancti episcopi*, but also by *multi ex laicis filii vestri*.

self are very varied. They include[1] communications on the *Books of Genesis* and *Kings*, a number of sermons, and some collections of 'Instructions' to monks and nuns. The latter has an interest as indicating the growing recognition of monastic women. The least known of his works are in some ways the most interesting. It is clear that he and his sons, who still belonged to the classical world, realized the importance of knowledge as the first requisite for sound theology and intelligent worship, and they set themselves to provide explanatory commentaries on the Scriptures which could serve as reference books for those seeking to comprehend and expound them. These works are composed on the traditional models of the old school books. The dialogue – the traditional form of the schools – utilized by Salonius to elucidate the *Books of Proverbs* and *Ecclesiastes*, was used by Eucherius also in his *Formulae*, which he composed to elucidate figurative and symbolical expressions of the Bible not readily understood, at least in their metaphorical sense, by the congregation.

The *Instructionum Libri Duo* are also composed as a dialogue. This work is more interesting than the *Formulae*, and perhaps even less known. Book I aims at interpreting difficult or significant passages in the Books of the Old and New Testaments, generally endowing them with a figurative sense by way of addition. Book II consists of a compendium of brief explanations of proper names and technical terms, and also of little-known animals and birds of the Bible – as we should say, a brief 'Biblical Encyclopedia'. The explanations are not arranged alphabetically, but under subject headings, as *De Nominibus Hebraicis, De Variis Vocabulis, De Expositione Diversarum Rerum, De Gentibus, De Locis, De Fluminibus vel Aquis,* etc. The book must have been useful to the untravelled Gaulish pastor with little learning and few books of his own, and no maps of Biblical lands. Thus he would learn that Mesopotamia is the land embraced by the rivers Euphrates and Tigris; that the mandragora is a kind of fruit resembling a small pumpkin in character and

---

[1] Among the works of Eucherius, the *Patrologia Latina* (Vol. L, col .867 ff.) includes the *Epitome Operum Cassiani,* under the impression that this is the work attributed to Eucherius by Gennadius, ch. 64. It has, however, been conclusively shown by Fr. Diekamp that the text printed by Migne is not the work of Eucherius, but dates from the seventeenth century. (See Diekamp's article in *Römische Quartalschrift für christliche Altertumskunde,* Vol. XIV, Rome, 1900, p. 342 ff.)

smell; and that 'the Scythians think that Magog was a Goth; some people think that Gog and Magog were Goths'. It will be seen that some of Eucherius's explanations are perhaps open to question.

The Semitic names of the months are carefully translated, and names of festivals, vestments, and idols explained. *Syrenae* in Esaia are glossed as 'demons or great flying crested dragons'; but here even Eucherius seems to have doubts, for he adds with scholarly caution: 'or so some suppose'. And again: '*Lamina* in Esaia, 'a kind of monster, as some say'. Rare animals are not forgotten, especially the horned varieties. *Rhinoceron*: 'a terrible beast carrying two horns in its nose'; *monoceron*: 'in the Psalms is called a unicorn'. Local Gaulish touches are all too rare, but we find: *Framea:* 'very long swords, so-called by the Armoricans who still use them. Some claim that the *gladius* is also meant'. The book ends with a useful glossary of Greek words.

These somewhat trifling works of scholarship help us to form an idea of the intellectual range and preoccupations of an episcopal family of Gaul in the fifth century. The learning is neither extensive nor profound. It belongs to the twilight of the classical age; but it still bears traces of the rhetorical schools in which Eucherius was trained in youth, and is an early effort to supply information to the Christian of Gaul which might help him to feel more at home in his religion. It is an aim which was shared by the whole of this united family, and not the least interesting side of their work is the respect accorded to learning as distinct from theology.

At the same time we cannot close our eyes to the fact that notwithstanding the respect of Eucherius and his sons for classical learning, their knowledge of Greek was very slight. Though Eucherius knew certain well-worn passages of Greek philosophy, or perhaps rather a collection of *placita*,[1] there is nothing to prove that he had any first-hand acquaintance with Greek Christian literature; and he knew the works of Clement of Rome only through the intermediary of a fanciful biography translated by Rufinus. Neither the *Formulae* nor the *Instructiones* shows any serious knowledge of Greek beyond the etymologies of the Greek terms which had passed into the ecclesiastical language. The only Greek writer whose work exercised a profound influence on him seems to have been Evagrius of Pontus, whose

---

[1] See P. Courcelle, *Les Lettres grecques en Occident*[2] (Paris, 1948), p. 216 ff.

doctrine is known to him through Cassian. Already Rufinus is almost the sole intermediary through whom the great Greek writers of the preceding age are known to many of the most intellectual ecclesiastics in Gaul. The decline of classical culture was already far advanced.

The best known work of Eucherius is the much praised *De Laude Eremi* ('In Praise of the Desert'), composed in the form of a letter addressed to Hilary, who, as yet still a presbyter, had just returned to Lérins from Arles, whither he had accompanied Honoratus. This work, and the *De Contemptu Mundi* ('On Contempt of the World'), are really supplementary. The latter, written first, is an earnest appeal to a certain Valerian to abandon temporal wealth and honours and worldly philosophy.

'Repudiate the gnomic wisdom of the philosophers, to the reading of which you devote your time and your genius, and apply your mind to drinking in what Christianity teaches.'[1]

Despite the admirable advice, we seem to feel throughout the work the dead hand of the rhetorical training lying heavily on the words of Eucherius himself. The sincerity and earnestness are beyond doubt, but the style is too studied and artificial, the reasoning is too balanced and too abstract to be compelling – the arguments are too logical, the thought too academic, too ecclesiastical. It is not known whether Valerian was moved by these arguments to abandon the learning of the world, but we might hazard a guess that he was not.

An incidental interest in the work is the list of eminent men whose example Eucherius commends to Valerian – Clement of Rome, Gregory Nazianzen, Basil, Ambrose; and here also we get a glimpse of the contemporary estimate in which Paulinus of Nola was held:

'Paulinus, Bishop of Nola, Gaul's own blessed exemplum, a person formerly of vast wealth, and a veritable fountain of eloquence, turned to our Christian way of thinking and profession, so that he has sprinkled absolutely the whole world with his eloquence and works.'[2]

While the *Contempt of the World* focuses on the ephemeral glory and splendour of earthly rulers, and of the order of things which Eucherius and Valerian could watch daily crumbling

[1] *De Contemptu Mundi* (Migne, *P.L.*, Vol. L, col. 724).
[2] Migne, *P.L.*, Vol. L, col. 718.

before their eyes, the *Praise of the Desert*, with quiet and measured dignity of style, dwells on the large and blessed part which the desert has played in Biblical history, and on its silence and freedom from worldly distractions. Yet here again, despite the lofty thought which inspires the work, the modern reader is chilled by a kind of abstract quality in the style. Its atmosphere is academic, the product of the schools turned theological; and while the writer seeks to be compelling, the rhetoric gives a semblance of artificiality even to the genuine emotion which inspires it.[1]

Yet under the device of rhetorical question and repetition one can see that the writer had experienced the silence and spaciousness of a life which had cut itself off from worldly affairs, and had learnt the gain which renunciation brings. As a modern writer aptly puts it, 'To Eucherius solitude is like a halting place in the march towards the true homeland; in order to contemplate the gifts of God in the world of this life one must have lived in the desert'.[2]

The work is a little gem of eremitical literary exercise, and it ends on a welcome note of reality in the panegyric on his beloved Lérins, 'who, in her motherly arms, welcomes the sailors cast up from the shipwrecks of the world'. The figure is a favourite one with this island saint, himself a fugitive from the troubled age. Already in the *De Contemptu* he had written:

'Look around you, and lift your gaze from the sea of your affairs to the harbour of our Christian profession, and turn your barque to our shores. This is the only port in which we can take shelter from all the buffeting and vicissitudes of this Age – a port which we may seek when we are wearied in the midst of the vortex of this world. Here is the refuge for all who are distressed by the raging hurricane of our world. Here is a safe anchorage and a calm which is secure. Here is a placid harbour far removed from the breakers.'[3]

---

[1] See, e.g. the use made of a series of rhetorical questions, *De Laude Eremi* (ed. Wotke, § 43, p. 193; ed. Migne, *P.L.*, Vol. L, col. 711). A similar series occurs in *De Contemptu Mundi* (ibid., col. 720).

A very similar rhetorical device of the cumulative effect of a series of questions and answers is used by Vincent of Lérins in his disquisition on Origen, *Commonitorium*, cap. xvii; Migne, Vol. L, col. 660 ff.; translated by C. A. Heurtley, in *Nicene and Post-Nicene Fathers*, Vol. XI, p. 144, § 43.

[2] Alliez, *Histoire du Monastère de Lérins*, Vol. I, p. 435.

[3] *De Contemptu Mundi* (Migne, *P.L.*, Vol. L, col. 726).

Perhaps after all we have underrated his eloquence.

How far was the great impetus which was given at this time to monasticism in Gaul stimulated by the Barbarian inroads which Eucherius has in mind? He has just confessed that they constituted a strong incentive. His contemporary, Rusticus, Bishop of Narbonne, scared and discouraged by the terrors of the age, besought Pope Leo for permission to retire into solitude; and we have an eloquent letter in which Leo seeks to uphold and strengthen his faltering courage,[1] bidding him bethink him who will guide the ship on the waves if the captain abandons it? Who will protect the sheep from the wolves if the shepherd does not keep anxious watch? We shall find Bishop Faustus of Riez using very similar arguments in his sermons to the monks of Lérins,[2] and reminding them that they have not come to the island in order to rest and loiter in a disgraceful safety, but in order 'to fight and combat vigorously' – to fight, that is to say, in the ranks of a spiritual army. We have already seen that there were many besides Eucherius whom the disintegration of the Empire impelled to seek a temporal refuge, as well as a spiritual life which could not be destroyed by the enemies closing in on them. We need not wonder that Lérins is described in the *Life of Hilary of Arles* as an 'Earthly Paradise'.[3]

Among those who sought shelter in the comparative peace and security of Marseilles and in close contact with her rising monastic centres was Salvian, fleeing from the blazing ruins of Trier. In the little intellectual aristocracy at the mouth of the Rhône, and in close association with the brethren of Lérins, he passed the remainder of his life as a priest and writer. The horrors of the Barbarian Occupation of the north had inspired him with a burning message to the Christians of Gaul; and the active intellectual life around him at Marseilles, combined with the relatively settled conditions in which he found himself, provided a congenial atmosphere for his constructive literary work. At the same time, his own services to the community of Lérins

[1] Migne, *P.L.*, Vol. LIV, col. 1199 ff.

[2] See, e.g. especially *Sermons* XXIII, XXIV (*Ad Monachos* I, II). Cf. Alliez, Vol. I, p. 182 ff.

[3] *Vita S. Hilarii Arelatensis*, cap. 5, § 7 (Migne, *P.L.*, Vol. L, col. 1226; more recently edited by S. Cavallin, *Vitae Sanctorum Honorati et Hilarii Episcoporum Arelatensium* (Lund, 1952), p. 86.

enable us to trace the direct contribution which the educated elements among the refugees in Marseilles were able to offer to the newly formed monastic bodies.

The known facts of Salvian's life are not numerous. He was probably born c. 390.[1] The internal evidence of his most important work,[2] *De Gubernatione Dei*, ('On the Government of God') makes it almost certain that his parents belonged to the Gallo-Roman aristocracy in or near Cologne or Trier, and that his up-bringing was that of a cultured and well-to-do home. He was already a Christian when he married Palladia, the daughter of pagan parents, Hypatius and Quieta. His conversion came when he was still young, and despite the fact that the young couple had a daughter, Auspiciola, they resolved by mutual agreement to embrace the ascetic life. Palladia's parents resented their decision and for seven years there was an estrangement between them; but during this interval Hypatius was converted, and we have a delightful joint-letter (*Ep.* 4) from the young Salvian family seeking a reconciliation. Unfortunately we do not know the answer, and we never hear of Palladia or Auspiciola again. I shall refer to this letter again later.

Gennadius (cap. 68), who is our most important contemporary authority, speaks of Salvian as 'a presbyter of Marseilles, well informed both in secular and in sacred literature,[3] and a master of bishops (*episcoporum magister*).'[4] Gennadius adds that Salvian wrote many things in a scholastic and clear style, and gives a list of those which he himself has read, but which are now all lost with the exception of the *De Gubernatione Dei* and a work in four books to which Gennadius gives the title *Adversus Avaritiam*, ('Against Avarice') but which is called *Ad Ecclesiam* in the manuscripts and by Salvian himself.[5] This work is referred

[1] So Tillemont, XVI, p. 182.
[2] The complete works of Salvian are to be found in many editions, notably Migne, *P.L.*, Vol. LIII; Halm, Berlin, 1877; Pauly, Vienna, 1883. An English translation of his chief work, *De Gubernatione Dei*, has been published by E. M. Sanford, *On the Government of God* (New York, 1930). My references are to Pauly's text throughout except where otherwise stated.
[3] There are no sufficient grounds, however, for supposing that Salvian had any first-hand acquaintance with Greek, and his knowledge of Greek philosophy is thought to be derived from some Latin *Compendium*, perhaps the same as that used by Eucherius. See P. Courcelle, *Les Lettres Grecques en Occident*, p. 220.
[4] Some MSS. read *magister episcoporum sanctorum Salonii et Verani* (see Migne, *P.L.*, Vol. LVIII, col. 1099, footnote f.), and this in any case is possibly the correct explanation of the expression. Eucherius applies the same phrase to St Honoratus (cf. p. 150).   [5] *Ep.* 9.

L

to in the *De Gubernatione Dei*, and is therefore earlier than the latter. Gennadius, who wrote about 470, closes his notice with the words 'He is still living at a good old age.'

It was probably shortly after the third sack of Trier, between 416 and 420,[1] and most probably as a direct consequence of the devastation, that Salvian and his wife moved southwards.[2] His description of the destruction of the city claims to be that of an eye-witness. It has been thought that he must also have spent some time in North Africa. The conjecture is based on the familiarity which his work shows with African affairs.[3] The conditions in North Africa occupy his attention at least as much as those of Gaul, and he is even more severe on the vices and frivolities which he attributes to its inhabitants. The Christian writers who influence his work, with the exception of his friends at Lérins and Marseilles, are all those of the African Church.

Soon after 429, Hilary of Arles, in his sermon on the life of St Honoratus, speaks of 'Salvian the presbyter, a man of distinction not unmerited, and most blessed in Christ, one of Honoratus's dear associates (*carorum suorum unus*).'[4] Presumably, therefore, the ordination of Salvian must have taken place before that date, probably at Marseilles. The passage from Hilary suggests that he was a member of the community of Lérins, and there are other arguments in favour of this supposition. We have found him acting jointly with Vincent, and in succession to Honoratus and Hilary, as tutor to the two young sons of Eucherius, whose initial education at least is known to have been given at Lérins. We shall see him later writing to a community of monks to commend to their care a young relative of his own, and this has been thought to suggest that he belonged to the monstery himself, and that this monastery was Lérins. On the other hand the wording of the letter in question suggests that he was asking a favour of friends rather

---

[1] Trier seems to have been four times sacked (*D.G.D.* VI, viii). Most recent editors regard the Franks as the authors of the destruction in all four cases, and hold that the attacks were fairly close together (cf. *ter continuatis eversionibus*, ibid. VI, xv), and took place between 411 and 428. Haemmerle regards the first destruction of the city as that by the Vandals in 406, and the three successive ones as Frankish, and as taking place in 411–13, 418, 438–9 (the latter possibly earlier). See E. M. Sanford, op. cit., p. 170, footnote 29.
[2] So Tillemont, Vol. XVI, p. 183.
[3] *D.G.D.*, V, XVI, LXX.
[4] *Sermo* 19, ed. cit.; also Migne, *P.L.*, Vol. L, col. 1260.

than of a community to which he actually belonged; and Hilary's reference is not incompatible with such a relationship. Salvian may perhaps have made a more or less temporary sojourn in Lérins without being actually a member of the brotherhood. Tillemont expresses himself with caution on the subject,[1] and Salvian's name does not occur in the list of distinguished members of this community mentioned by Eucherius,[2] nor in that of Sidonius Apollinaris in his poem *Euchariston* addressed to Bishop Faustus of Riez (*Carmen* XVI; cf. p. 193).

Salvian's writings, both the letters and the more sustained works, make it clear that he had witnessed many of the horrors of the time, and that his own relatives had been among those taken captive and reduced to penury and forced labour. It is undoubtedly acute consciousness of suffering born of personal knowledge which inspires the earliest of his two surviving works, the *Ad Ecclesiam*, written between 435 and 439. The object of the work is to urge on all men the importance of giving alms and bestowing money on the Church during their lifetime, and of making the Church their heir after death. This duty is urged even on those who have families. The writer insists that the most precious heritage a man can hand down to them is faith, the fear of God, modesty and homeliness, goods which cannot perish; and he continues, burning with indignation as he thinks of the hungry and shivering poor:

'Where are those who claim that our Lord Jesus Christ has no need of our wealth for his service? . . . I declare . . . that not only is Christ in need like others, but that He is far more in need than others . . . Christ is absolutely the only One to whom everything is lacking which others have. None of His servants suffers exile or cold or is sent naked away but He shivers with him . . . And this being the case, what have you, O man, to say who call yourself a Christian?'[3]

Salvian speaks as one who has seen the wounded and the dead lie untended and unburied about the streets of Trier, and the sick and the aged driven from the smoking ruins of their homes, wealthy and noble women brought to penury and slavery, the poor to starvation; and he proceeds 'You see Christ in need,

---

[1] XVI, p. 187; cf. p. 184.
[2] *De Laude Eremi*, Migne, *P.L.*, Vol. L, col. 711.
[3] *Ad Ecclesiam* (ed. F. Pauly, Vienna, 1883), Book IV, 21 f.

and you leave your property to people who are not poor . . .
Christ is hungry and you prepare delicacies for those who are
already well supplied. Christ complains that He has not even
water, and you fill with wine the cellar of those who are
drunk.'[1]

The thoughts are not new; but they are rarely spoken with
the burning indignation and irony of Salvian, to whom avarice
or lack of charity is not merely a sin; it is spiritual death and
eternal damnation. To him the only rightful recipients of
wealth are the Church and the poor. But the Church has identified herself with the poor, for the Church is the only body responsible for the care of the poor, and poverty is increasing with
terrible rapidity. In Salvian's day, when most of the public
services must have completely broken down, the Church is the
only organized body to whom the poor can turn. We shall see
in a later chapter that Sidonius praises Bishop Faustus of Riez
for attending to the burial of paupers, the feeding of prisoners,
and the care of the sick. Critics of the nineteenth century, and
of the period between the two Great Wars of 1914 and 1939 had
scant appreciation for *Ad Ecclesiam*, and a ready sneer for its
message; but it is possible that a generation which has witnessed
the horrors of forced labour, the displacement of populations,
and the devastation of vast areas of Europe may take a more
sympathetic view of a work which must have been written as a
charitable appeal for the suffering masses at a time of un-
precedented misery.

Nor indeed was Salvian by any means singular in the
supreme importance which he attached to charity and generosity towards the Church. The sermons of St Valerian, Bishop of
Céméle,[2] another of the great ecclesiastics who was probably
trained at Lérins, ring from end to end with this same appeal.
If you have a number of sons and you are dividing your inheritance among them, he says, count one extra, and give his share
to Christ; thus you will enrich them, for they will have their
patrimony not in one land only. St Valerian emphasizes that to
give to Christ is to give to the poor, and he urges his congre-

---

[1] *Ad Ecclesiam*, IV, 23.

[2] For the known works of Valerianus of Céméle, see Migne, *P.L.*, Vol. LII, col.
691 ff.; See also Tillemont, XV, p. 125. Céméle was a town of considerable size on
the hills near Nice.

gation never to put off with false promises, and never to delay –
never put off till tomorrow the good that you can do today; and
do it continually, day by day, not year by year.[1] The same
theme recurs again and again,[2] urged, not with the ornate style
of the rhetorician, but in the direct practical language of a
serious, reasoned appeal, backed by simple illustrations from
daily life. He urges his 'congregation' – his *dilectissimi* – to
practise the life of a Christian as a *rudis miles*, 'an inexperienced
soldier', before going into battle 'practises his strength against
the stump of a tree'.[3]

Salvian's greatest work is referred to by Gennadius as the *De
Praesenti Judicio*, but is usually called in the manuscripts *De
Gubernatione Dei* ('On the Government of God'). This work was
probably completed after 439, because it mentions (VII, x)
the defeat of Litorius in 439 at Toulouse; and before 451, since
it makes no allusion to the defeat of Attila by the Romans and
Visigoths, an event which Salvian would surely not have passed
over in silence. For though the first three books are largely
built up on quotations from the Bible, the last five books (of
which VII and VIII are incomplete) are largely concerned
with contemporary disasters, and the political and social disruption which was taking place in Gaul and North Africa. The
purpose of the book is to answer the question which was exercising the minds of all thinking men, pagans and Christians
alike, at that time: Why does God allow such terrible calamities
to befall the world? – above all the Christian world? And Salvian has no hesitation about the answer, for he writes as a fifth-
century theologian and moralist: it is for our sins.

The first three books are practically a sermon, which draws
its illustrations from Scripture, a habit widespread in contemporary writings, even in letters (cf. p. 78). For us the great
interest of the work lies in the picture of the time presented in
the remaining books. Here we see the desperate state of the
civilized world of the West, in sharp contrast to the vigour and
virility of the Barbarian Conquerors.[4] To Salvian the whole

[1] *Homily* IV, § 6, 7, *De Promissis et Non Redditis*. (Migne, *P.L.*, Vol. LII, col.
705.)
[2] e.g. *Homily* VII, § 4; VIII, § 4; and most impressive of all, IX, § 3.
[3] *Homily* XVI, § 5. (Migne, *P.L.*, Vol. LII, col. 743.)
[4] We may compare the similar contrast drawn by Tacitus in the *Germania* between the Romans and the Barbarians of the late first century A.D.

secret of the Roman disintegration lies in their vice and luxury, their insensate frivolity, above all in their callousness to human suffering.

He complains that the Gallo-Romans love the circuses and theatres more than the churches of God, which are abandoned in a rush for the theatre;[1] and though he admits that these shows are now lacking in many cities of Spain and Gaul such as Mainz, Cologne, and Trier, where before they used to flourish, this is only because these places have been devastated by the enemy.[2] In North Africa, while the Barbarians were fighting outside the walls of Cirta and Carthage, the Christians within the city were attending the circus and the theatre.[3] When Trier had been three times captured, and the whole city had been burned to the ground, and the population reduced to the last extremity of misery and lingering death, while the corpses still lay about unburied, breeding pestilence, the few men of rank who had survived destruction demanded circuses.[4]

'I have seen – I have endured the sight of corpses of both sexes lying about everywhere, naked, torn . . . rent to pieces by the dogs and birds of prey. The deadly stench of the dead bodies wrought a plague among the living. Death breathed out from death. What happened after? I ask you what happened after all this? The handful of the nobility who had escaped death demanded circuses of the emperors as a supreme remedy for the destruction of the city. You Treveri', he cries, 'you want circuses, do you? – and this, too, when you have been ravaged and stormed!' And he continues, 'Where, I ask, will they be held? On the mounds and the ashes, on the bones and blood of your dead? . . . Your city is blackened with fire, and you assume a holiday face.'[5]

He describes vividly the wretched condition of the poor under the serf system, which made them glad to give themselves and their estates to the Barbarians to escape the Roman tax-collector. We have from him our fullest description of the *Bagaudae*, those mysterious peasant armies which, from the latter part of the third to the middle of the fifth century, rose in various parts of Gaul and even Spain, taking the law into their own hands

[1] *De Gubernatione Dei*, VI, vii.
[2] ibid., VI, viii.
[3] ibid., VI, xii.
[4] ibid., VI, xv.
[5] ibid., VI, xv.

and living as robbers and freebooters.[1] With fine scorn he pictures the corruptions and vices of Roman society, and, in even more bitter terms of the society of North Africa. In contrast he holds the Barbarians far nobler – more chaste, honourable, hospitable. He is not blind to their faults; he knows that they are unjust, avaricious, faithless, greedy; but, he asks:

'Is the immodesty of the Huns as criminal as ours? or the perfidy of the Franks as blameworthy, the drunkenness of the Alamanni as deserving of censure as the drunkenness of the Christians? Is the greed of the Alani as damnable as the greed of the Christians?'[2] And elsewhere he adds, 'What hope . . . can there be for the Roman state when Barbarians are more chaste and pure than Romans?'

For Salvian the fall of the Roman Empire is not due to God's injustice but to the sins of His people, and as a preacher he closes the seventh book with a thundering accusation worthy of Gildas:

'If my human frailty would suffer me, I wish I could shout out even beyond the limits of my strength and make my voice echo throughout the world: shame on you, ye Roman people everywhere, shame on the lives you lead . . . Do not let anyone persuade himself to any other conclusion. It is our vicious lives alone that have conquered us.'[3]

Nine letters of Salvian are extant. They show the writer in a more mellowed and a gentler mood than do his sterner works written for publication, and the contrast reminds us somewhat of Dean Swift. The first letter, to which reference has already been made, was written to recommend to the hospitality and training of the monks, probably of Lérins, a young relative, a refugee who had been a captive, and whose family had been ruined by the Barbarians. Salvian describes him as 'of no small account in his own district and not obscure in family'.

---

[1] For a valuable account of the *Bagaudae*, see the article by O. Seeck in Pauly-Wissowa, *Real-Encyclopädie der Classischen Altertumswissenschaft*, Vol. II (Stuttgart, 1896), s.v. The *Bagaudae* are also referred to in the Gallo-Roman Comedy, the *Querolus* (see p. 135). See the edition of *Querolus* by L. Havet (Paris, 1880), p. 6. See further F. L. Ganshof in *Historical Essays in Honour of James Tait* (Manchester, 1933), p. 111 ff., and the references to the *Bagaudae* there cited.

[2] *De Gubernatione Dei*, IV, xiv.

[3] ibid., VII, xxiii. Sanford (op. cit., p. 223, footnote) aptly compares a passage in the Sermon by St Augustine, *De Tempore Barbarico* (Migne, *P.L.*, Vol. XL, col. 703).

His mother, 'a virtuous widow', had succeeded in getting free
of the 'chains of captivity' and now was labouring for the wives
of the conquerors. The terms of the letter are quite what we
might expect to find today, making due allowance for the stilted
rhetorical opening, from an old member of one of our colleges,
writing to the dons to recommend a young relative of his own to
their notice. The confidence, under the guise of diffidence; the
genuine delicacy; just enough detailed information given of the
status and vicissitudes of the family – all these sound very modern, and in a few words give the monks all they need to know to
recommend to their attention a youth who, it is hinted, in view
of his background, may well prove worthy of their care, and a
credit to their institution.

Of the remaining letters, two to Eucherius and one to
Eucherius's son, Bishop Salonius, the former pupil of Salvian,
show an intimate friendliness and even lightness of touch which
is in pleasant contrast to his more formal works. But the longest
and most interesting letter is the joint-appeal already referred
to, written on behalf of himself, his wife Palladia, and their little
daughter Auspiciola, to his wife's parents, Hypatius, now
become a Christian, and his wife Quieta. In the letter the three
members of this little family beg to be reinstated in the loving
regards of Palladia's parents after the years of estrangement
caused by the decision of the young people to embrace the
ascetic life. The letter, written some seven years later,[1] is particularly interesting as seeming to show that, while Salvian and
Palladia remained unshaken in their devotion to asceticism,
this did not result in any wide personal separation, either from
one another or from the child.

The writer points out, in the name of Palladia, that it was by
the will of her parents that she married her husband, and that
she is only following their commands in obeying him. Why,
therefore, do they hold aloof from her? She has acted from love
of God, and so far from feeling any guilt in her present way of
life she blushes that she did not adopt it earlier.

'I throw myself at your feet, my darling parents, I, your
Palladia, your little jackdaw (*gracula*), your little miss (*domnula*),
as in your affection you used to tease me with so many pet

---

[1] *Septimus iam ferme annus est ex quo nulla ad nos tam longe a vobis sitos scripta
misistis.*

names – now it would be "little mother", now "birdie" *(avicula)*, now "lady" *(domina)*.'

And the letter appeals also on behalf of their little girl whose simple innocence should move them. ·

Unfortunately, as I have said above, the answer to this letter has been withheld from us. The letter itself, nevertheless, forms a pleasing close to a chapter devoted to the foundation of the great monastery of Lérins and to a study of the early ascetics within and without its walls. The glimpses of the Salvian family, and of the family of Eucherius and Galla, add a grace and gentleness to our picture of early eremitism which we shall miss in the cenobitic monasticism formulated by John Cassian. These rare idylls of the ascetic life give way before the more profoundly conceived ideal of renunciation and austerity inaugurated by Evagrius, and introduced into the monasticism of western Europe from the cenobitism of St Victor at Marseilles. They are in spirit far closer to the so-called 'hermit poetry', and the traditions of the saints of the early Celtic Church, which perhaps received their original inspiration from this pre-monastic phase of Christian anchoritism. In a later chapter we shall trace the development of the cenobitic ideal and rule in the contemporary writing of John Cassian. Before doing so, however, we must pause to look into the spiritual and intellectual problems which were occupying the attention of the scholars and ascetics of Provence at this time, and to which the newly founded monasteries were the most important contributors.

CHAPTER VII

The Pelagian Controversy
and the School of Marseilles

IN the preceding chapters we have watched the monasteries of Southern Provence fanning the dying embers of the intellectual life of Gaul in the first half of the fifth century. We have seen, however, that intellectual activity was by no means confined to the monasteries. Apart from secular writers, such as Rutilius Namatianus, Paulinus of Pella, and the author of the *Querolus*, there were intellectual laymen who took an active part in religious controversies. Marseilles had always been an active intellectual centre since its origin as a Greek trading colony, and its continuous history as a trading centre ensured its wide interests and its foreign contacts with both North Africa and the east Mediterranean lands, and the vitality of its well-informed and active mental life. It is a fact of no small interest that some of the most active opponents of the Pelagian heresy in southern Gaul were laymen, chief among them being a certain Prosper and his associate Hilary, who were both active in combating Pelagianism; and to these we must add Gennadius, who flourished somewhat later – c. 480 – and to whom we are indebted for much of our most valuable information about his Gaulish contemporaries, and the so-called semi-Pelagians whom he favoured.

In the following pages we shall find Prosper of Aquitaine, whose correct name was Prosper Tiro, playing for a brief period a leading rôle in southern Gaul. For this reason it would have been interesting to know more about his early life, which is unfortunately obscure. He was born somewhere in southern Gaul,[1] perhaps c. 390;[2] but whether his youth was spent in Aquitaine, or in the neighbourhood of Marseilles, seems to be still undetermined. If we could accept him as the author of the two poems frequently attributed to him, the *Carmen de Providentia Divina* ('On the Divine Providence'), and the *Poema Conjugis ad Uxorem* ('Poem of a Husband to his Wife'), which have

---

[1] Gennadius, cap. 84.   [2] See De Labriolle, *History and Literature of Christianity from Tertullian to Boethius* (English translation by H. Wilson, London, 1927), p. 429.

already been noticed (p. 122 f.), we might assume that he remained in Aquitaine long enough to suffer all the miseries of the conquered population under the Vandals and Visigoths. It has been suggested that Prosper and his wife came to Marseilles at this point, and that the poems were written shortly afterwards;[1] but we have no evidence.

On the whole it seems probable that the early part of his life was spent in the neighbourhood of Marseilles and he may possibly have been connected with the monastery of Lérins;[2] but these questions are also obscure. Certain it is however that he spent much of his life in Marseilles, in close touch with ecclesiastical circles, and taking a leading part in the religious controversies of the day. We shall discuss his part in these controversies later. Before doing so, however, a word may be said about his historical writing in the form of a *Chronicle*, which is now the work by which Prosper is best remembered, and which has an especial importance for early British history in view of its references to Great Britain and Ireland, and for the knowledge which Prosper evidently possessed in some measure of what was taking place here. His recorded facts imply, of course, a similar interest on the part of his readers. Of Prosper it is safe to say that his own interest in these islands was wholly due to his strong feeling against Pelagianism.

Prosper's *Chronicle*[3] or, more correctly, *Epitoma Chronicon*, is a compilation based on St Jerome's *Chronicle*, to which Prosper contributed some additional matter, e.g. the consuls for each year. From this it is sometimes known as the 'Consular Chronicle', to distinguish it from another which is sometimes called the 'Imperial Chronicle'[4] because in the latter the chronology is

---

[1] So Scott Holmes, *The Christian Church in Gaul*, p. 384. See, however, De Labriolle, loc. cit.; Bardenhewer, *Patrology*, p. 514.

[2] For some account of Prosper and his work, see L. Pelland *S. Prosperi Aquitani Doctrina*, etc. (Montreal, 1936.) An important earlier work is that of L. Valentin, *Saint Prosper d'Aquitaine* (Toulouse, 1900). Valuable information will also be found in the articles s.v. Prosper (by G. Bardy) and *Semi-Pelagiens* (by Amann) in the *Dictionnaire de Théologie Catholique*.

[3] The best edition is that of Mommsen, *Prosperi Tironis Epitoma Chronicon*, in *Chronica Minora*, Vol. I (Berlin, 1892), p. 341 ff. An earlier edition will be found in Migne, *P.L.*, Vol. LI, col. 535.

[4] The 'Imperial Chronicle', which comprises the period from 379-455, is sometimes erroneously attributed to Prosper Tiro, who was, again erroneously, regarded as a different person from Prosper of Aquitaine. The 'Imperial Chronicle' is, however, anti-Augustine in sympathy. It also has been published by Mommsen, op. cit., p. 647 ff.

reckoned according to the regnal years of the emperors. Prosper's continuation of the original chronicle of Jerome's *Chronicle* extended from 378 to his own time. The sparsity of other sources makes the period from 425 to 455 especially valuable because this part is based on his personal knowledge. The form is annalistic.

Prosper seems to have added to the work from time to time, and to have brought it out in three recensions, dating from 433, 445, and 455. Bardenhewer points out[1] that Prosper's *Chronicle* differs from all previous chronicles in the prominence which it gives to the history of doctrine and heresies generally. In particular he furnishes us with our only contemporary information regarding Pelagianism in Britain, the activities of the deacon Palladius, and the mission of St Germanus to this country in 429. Of a mission of St Germanus, perhaps somewhere about the year 447, as related by Constantius in his *Life of St Germanus*, Prosper has no mention; but he refers again to the activity of Pope Celestine and of the mission of Palladius[2] against the Pelagians of Britain in 429 in the *Contra Collatorem*,[3] written against John Cassian (cf. p. 248 f.). It would be interesting to know from what source Prosper derived his information regarding Palladius and Germanus. As he was in Rome soon after the death of St Augustine in 430, and again in 431, it would seem probable that it was there that he learned the facts mentioned above. A discussion of the missions of St Germanus to Britain and a statement of the evidence which furnishes our information is reserved for a later chapter.

In his own day Prosper was chiefly known as a protagonist against what he regarded as Pelagian tendencies among some of the churchmen of southern Gaul. He first became prominent by his activities in this cause in 428 or 429, and in 431 he visited Rome as a partisan of Augustine's views on Predestination. In 440 he seems to have accompanied the newly-elected Pope, Leo I, from Gaul to Rome, and to have attained a secretarial post in the papal chancellery, for according to Gennadius (CH.

---

[1] *Patrology*, p. 513.
[2] The name of Palladius is not actually mentioned in this passage, but there can be little doubt that it is he who is referred to as sent by Celestine to be the first bishop to the Irish, and to free the British Isles from the 'plague' (of Pelagianism).
[3] Migne, *P.L.*, Vol. LI, col. 271.

84) he was looked upon as the author of the famous letters bearing the name of Pope Leo I against Eutyches, a presbyter and abbot of Constantinople.[1] He seems to have died in or shortly after 463.

In order to understand the background of events, and the motives which inspired much of the controversy and even of the literary output of southern Gaul at this time, a word must be said on Pelagius[2] and the Pelagian Controversy. Space will not permit me to do more than touch very briefly on those aspects which relate to southern Gaul. The actual Pelagian Controversy lies outside the sphere of my book, in so far as it belongs to theology. But we cannot entirely leave aside a theological question with which the Christian world was ringing, and which, in addition to the very considerable body of work springing from it directly, has also left traces on many writings of the period not primarily theological in character.

Pelagius himself was a monk, and a layman. The date of his birth is unknown, and also his place of origin, but contemporary references seem to suggest that he was of Celtic provenance, and from the British Isles.[3] The years of his life for which we have record extend from about 400 to 418, and there is reason to think that he had already reached at least middle life when his name became famous. Of his lofty intellect, his great learning, which included a knowledge of Greek, and of his high personal character, there have never been two opinions. His personal integrity is praised even by his great opponent St Augustine.

Pelagius probably reached Rome about 400. It was in Rome that he was joined by a certain Coelestius, an Irishman, or an Irish Scot, whose name is closely associated with that of Pelagius himself throughout the controversy. The course of the discussions would seem to suggest that Pelagius had possibly developed his views before he left Britain, and no doubt active

[1] The letters relating to the heresy of Eutyches are contained in Migne, *P.L.*, Vol. LIV, col. 713 ff. They have been translated almost in their entirety into English by C. L. Feltoe, in the *Library of Nicene and Post-Nicene Fathers*, Vol. XII (*Leo the Great*, etc., Oxford, 1895), p. 32 ff.
[2] The most important books which have appeared in recent years on Pelagius and Pelagianism are those of G. de Plinval, *Pélage, ses Écrits, sa Vie, et sa Réforme* (Lausanne, etc., 1943); and *Essai sur le Style et la Langue de Pélage* (Fribourg en Suisse, 1947).
[3] For a discussion of the evidence, see de Plinval, *Pélage*, etc., p. 57 ff.

philosophical and speculative thought were still flourishing in this outpost of the Roman world. Indeed it is commonly thought that Britain was the home, not only of Pelagius, but also of Pelagianism. The heresy spread like a conflagration over Europe, and the literature of the controversy, and the letters which have survived from the period,[1] throw a very interesting light on the religious thought of the time, while the heresy itself must have had the effect of bringing Britain into closer touch with Continental affairs than anything had done before.

In 410 Pelagius and Coelestius left Rome for Africa, and Pelagius himself went on to Jerusalem. Coelestius, however, remained in Carthage, where a number of his doctrines (which he represented as those of Pelagius) drew down upon him the condemnation of a Synod, and Pelagius himself was accused of heresy before the Synod of Jerusalem in 415. This impeachment failed, but a new Synod of Carthage, held in 416, condemned both Pelagius and Coelestius. Pelagius was banished from Rome in 418, and he and Coelestius were again condemned by the Council of Ephesus in 431. Pelagius disappeared from history about this time, and the date of his death is unknown. In 421 an imperial edict had declared that those holding these heretical views were to be exiled from Rome, and were not to be allowed to approach nearer than the hundredth milestone. Prosper Tiro states that Celestine, the Bishop of Rome, commanded that they were to be banished from all Italy, and adds that 'he was no less at pains to free Britain from the same plague'.[2]

The heresy of Pelagius is, in a word, the denial of Original Sin. He appears to have maintained that the sin of Adam did not in itself taint the human race,[3] and that man is enabled to avoid sin by the power of the free will alone, without the aid of Grace;[4] and he held that infants who die unbaptized are not debarred from the Beatific Vision hereafter. His views were the logical outcome of a classical education and of the classical philosophy, in part no doubt, of Stoicism with the Stoic belief

---

[1] See, e.g. the collection of documents edited by C. P. Caspari, *Briefe, Abhandlungen und Predigten* (Christiania, 1890). See further p. 15 f. above.

[2] *Contra Collatorem*, xxi (Migne, *P.L.*, Vol. LI, col. 271).

[3] More by implication, however, than by direct expression. He does not appear to have made direct reference to the question of Adam's responsibility for original sin. See de Plinval, op. cit., p. 150.

[4] See the summary of his teaching in the *Commentary on St Paul*, de Plinval, op. cit., p. 150 ff.

in the natural perfectibility of men.[1] These views were regarded by his opponents as claiming that the effort of the
human will for good is independent of special divine Grace.
The views of Pelagius are most fully expressed in his *Commentary
on St Paul's Epistles* – and in his letters; but though some new
fragments have recently come to light, most of his works have
perished, and we know his views chiefly through the works of
his opponents. It is often difficult, therefore, for us to ascertain
with any degree of certainty what precisely were the views
which he actually held.

It is hardly necessary to say that the great exponent of the
views most directly opposed to those attributed to Pelagius was
St Augustine, the great Bishop of Hippo Regius on the North
African coast. Augustine stressed man's absolute need of divine
Grace, and his powerlessness for good without divine aid. Grace
is a necessary condition of salvation and is 'irresistible'. Man's
original sin, incurred through Adam's fall, would in itself condemn all mankind eternally, but God's mercy selects many
souls whom He predestines to Grace and salvation. Since
Augustine also held that those predestined to Grace receive the
gift of perseverence, the logical conclusion might seem to be
that some souls are predestined to salvation, others to damnation. The doctrine has come to be referred to as the doctrine of
Predestination and Grace, and the controversy as a whole as
that of 'Grace and Free-Will'.

During the controversy which arose as the ideas attributed
to Pelagius became widely known, Augustine's views on man's
absolute need of divine Grace, and his powerlessness for good
without divine aid, gradually came to be looked upon by his
opponents as a doctrine of the arbitrary control of the human
will and of human action by divine power. Reduced to a
formula, Augustine's position appeared to these opponents to
attribute arbitrary powers to God, void of elementary justice,
and to deny to human beings any motive for effort towards
goodness, or any hope of mercy. And he does indeed appear to
have ignored the possibility that a man can receive the gift of
Grace and subsequently fall from it. His views are often spoken
of as 'hardening' as the controversy developed, and theologians
of all ages, Catholic and Protestant alike, have been concerned

[1] See again de Plinval, op. cit., p. 202 ff.

to explain away, justify, and even controvert his more extreme views, especially on Predestination.

It is no part of my purpose to enter into a discussion of the theological aspect of the controversy. It is not easy to put the vision of a great mystical thinker into a formula, brief and readily comprehensible for those of us who are untrained in religious thought and inexperienced in a life set apart for religious discipline; and those who state – and they are many – that Augustine's views on Predestination would never have been developed – or at least been expressed thus dogmatically – had it not been for the followers of Pelagius, are perhaps partly right, though the basis of Augustine's conviction can be seen from an early period in his life. Again, the difficulty felt by modern thinkers in regard to Augustine's views is undoubtedly, partly to be explained by the fact that the Pelagian controversy forced Augustine, by the necessity of polemics, to stress certain aspects of the question specially put forward by his adversaries, leaving aside others less relevant to his immediate purpose. For this reason his doctrine is expressed with less porportion than is the case with works written in an atmosphere free from controversy, and we find in his writings on this matter a tendency to press to the limit points on which he is determined not to give ground, lest the cause at stake be betrayed. On the other hand when Augustine is writing, not against heretics, but for the Catholic people as a whole, and when he abandons polemics to concentrate on the moral needs of his readers, the problem is no longer viewed from the same point of view, and his language becomes less dogmatic. The thought is the same, but the form of expression is modified.

Before considering the effect of St Augustine's teaching in southern Gaul, and the important literary works to which it there gave rise, let us pause to glance at the little monastery of Hadrumetum (Susa) on the south-east coast of Tunisia, some forty miles or so from Hippo Regius, and the trouble into which the monks were thrown by his doctrine. The gentle tolerance with which he received them and sought to remove their difficulties, and the ungrudging expenditure of his time in the midst of his busy episcopal and literary life, afford us a noble picture of a great gentleman which we do well to bear in mind in contrast to the rigour of his theological teaching. The episode is a wholly delightful one. It has, moreover, an intrinsic importance in that the anxieties and perplexities expressed by the inmates of this little monastery served as the immediate occasion of the composition of some of Augustine's most important works.[1]

His views on the necessity of divine Grace, human impotence, and 'Predestination' by God, had been forcibly and succinctly expressed in a letter written in 418 to the Roman priest Sixtus, afterwards Pope Sixtus III.[2] This letter chanced to come into the hands of Florus and Felix, two monks of the monastery of Hadrumetum, while they were on a visit to Uzala or Uzita, Florus's native place, not far from Hadrumetum.[3] Since Evodius, the Bishop of Uzala, was a disciple and old friend of Augustine, and had been in his *familia* at Hippo,[4] there is nothing strange in his having Augustine's writings at hand. Florus admired the letter, and having made a copy of it to the dictation of his companion Felix, he sent it to his monastery, where it was read aloud. The letter, however, raised a serious controversy among the monks, some of whom objected that the doctrine of Predestination practically annihilated free-will and divine justice. The monks were shocked and troubled by the doctrine in the letter as they understood it.

Under these circumstances the Abbot of Hadrumetum, Valentinus, not unnaturally wrote to Bishop Evodius, and also it seems to another priest, Januarius or Januarianus, asking for their views. The replies have been preserved.[5] That of Evodius affirms the existence of free-will, but maintains that its right exercise is warped by original sin, and insists on man's free choice of God by Grace; but the letter is especially insistent on

---

[1] For a detailed account of the relations between St Augustine and the monks of Hadrumetum, see Fr. M. Jacquin, 'Questions de Prédestinations aux V et VIᵉ Siècles', *Revue d'Histoire ecclésiastique*, Vol. V (1904), p. 266 ff. The letters between Augustine and the monks are edited by A. Goldbacher in the Vienna *Corpus Scriptorum Ecclesiasticorum Latinorum*, 1911, *Epp.* 214–216; and, earlier, in Migne's *P.L.*, Vol. XXXIII, *Epp.* 214, 215. I have given references below to Migne's edition as being more convenient and generally accessible; but Goldbacher's edition is excellent and should be consulted wherever possible.

[2] *Ep.* 194, Augustine to Sixtus (Migne, *P.L.*, Vol. XXXIII, col. 874).

[3] See Dom. G. Morin, 'Lettre inédite de l'évêque Evodius aux moines d'Adrumète sur la question de la grâce', *Rev. Bénéd.*, Vol. XIII (1896), p. 481 ff.

[4] Jacquin, op. cit., p. 268, footnote 4; four letters by him to St Augustine, written between 414 and 415, are extant, together with Augustine's replies. See Morin, loc. cit.

[5] See Dom. G. Morin, *Rev. Bénéd.* XVIII (1901), p. 241 ff., where the letter of Evodius was first published in a complete form from two MSS., and where the reply of Januarius is also published for the first time.

M

the practical issue, and recommends intellectual humility in view of the difficulties of such problems and the need for avoiding contention. Valentinus also wrote to a certain priest, Sabinus,[1] for his opinion on the matter; but eventually he was obliged to let certain of the monks go in person to Augustine, who received them with much kindness, and after discussing the points at issue in his letter to Sixtus, gave them a letter addressed to Valentinus to take back to Hadrumetum, in which he asks that Florus should be sent to him, and insists, as Evodius had done, on the importance of avoiding discord.[2] At this point, the monk Felix, at whose dictation the letter had been transcribed at Uzala, also arrived, and Augustine prolonged the stay of the monks in order to give them further personal instruction and some letters and other relevant documents to take back to Hadrumetum. In order still further to clear up their difficulties he composed for them a treatise on these matters entitled *De Gratia et Libero Arbitrio*, ('On Grace and Free-Will').[3] Valentinus replied in a gracious letter,[4] explaining to him how the troubles had arisen, and sent Florus to him as requested, at the same time commending the monk's doctrinal integrity. On this point Augustine quickly satisfied himself, and recommended that those who had shown themselves dissatisfied should be forgiven as they had evidently acted in ignorance.[5]

Meantime it was reported to him that one of the monks, doubtless with reference to the doctrine set forth in *De Gratia et Libero Arbitrio*, had observed that if it is God who operates our will and deed, one ought not to blame those who are culpable, but only to pray for them, so that they may obtain the grace to do well.[6] Anxious to meet their difficulties, and also to meet similar objections which others might feel, Augustine now wrote *De Correptione et Gratia* '(On Reproof and Grace'),[7] a short

[1] See Jacquin, op. cit., p. 270.
[2] Augustine's two letters to Valentinus and the monks of Hadrumetum are preserved. See the Vienna *Corpus*, loc. cit.; also Migne, *P.L.*, Vol. XXXIII, *Epp.* 214 (col. 968 f.), 215 (col. 971 f.). *Ep.* 214 is translated in full in Prof. J. H. Baxter's *St. Augustine, Select Letters* (London, 1930), p. 405 ff.
[3] Migne, *P.L.*, Vol. XLIV, col. 881 ff.
[4] *Ep.* 216, Valentinus to Augustine, Migne, *P.L.*, Vol. XXXIII, col. 974.
[5] Augustine, *De Correptione et Gratia*, I, 2. See below.
[6] *Retractiones*, Book II, cap. 67, Migne, *P.L.*, Vol. XXXII, col. 635. Cf. *De Correptione et Gratia*, I, 2 (see below).
[7] Migne, *P.L.*, Vol. XLIV, col. 915 ff.

book, published in 427, but one of the most important from the doctrinal point of view. He himself declares elsewhere[1] that he had never been able before to treat the question of perseverance exhaustively, as in this treatise. He appears to have sent it to Hadrumetum, accompanied by a friendly letter.[2] We are not told how the matter ended, or whether the monks of Hadrumetum were satisfied; but the correspondence and the troubles of Hadrumetum have an interest, apart from their place in the controversy, as admitting us into the intimacy of a little monastery of this early period, and enabling us to watch the interest taken by the community in the spiritual questions of the day, as well as their active correspondence and communications with the leading ecclesiastics of the North African Church. In addition it gives us an exceptional opportunity of watching the immediate reaction of the humbler religious of St Augustine's own time to some of the more difficult of his writings.

The *De Correptione et Gratia*, however, seems to have reached Gaul probably in 427 and to have transferred the controversy from Hadrumetum to Provence. Our evidence for the date is a letter from Prosper of Aquitaine to Augustine informing him of the theological crisis which his book had caused.[3] It seems extremely probable that Cassian's thirteenth Conference was written in 427 under the direct stimulus of the *De Correptione*,[4] the circulation of which in 428 was in all likelihood the immediate occasion of Prosper's letter. Early in 429 Helladius (or possibly Euladius)[5] of Arles made it clear that he would ask for an explanation of this work from St Augustine, and Prosper accordingly wrote to Augustine to state the difficulties which had arisen and to explain the doctrines held by the theologians of Marseilles.

The controversy had now entered upon a new phase, which was destined to have important developments in southern

---

[1] *De Dono Perseverantiae*, XXI, 55 (Migne, *P.L.*, Vol. XLV, col. 993 ff.).

[2] This letter was published by Dom. G. Morin in the *Revue Bénédictine*, Vol. XVIII (1901), p. 241 f.

[3] Already by c. 427 St Augustine wrote to a certain Vitalis, otherwise unknown, who had placed before him some objections to his doctrine of 'Grace'. See Amann, *Dictionnaire de Théologie Catholique*, Vol. XL (1939), col. 1798 f.

[4] Book II, xiii (The Third Conference of Abbot Chaeremon).

[5] He was formerly identified by Mommsen and other early scholars with Hilary, who succeeded Honoratus as Bishop of Arles in 428. See, however, O. Chadwick, 'Euladius of Arles', *Journal of Theological Studies*, Vol. XLVI (1945), p. 200 ff.; and compare also *John Cassian*, pp. 114, 118, n. 2.

Gaul, and which has been commonly known since the early seventeenth century as 'semi-Pelagianism',[1] though 'semi-Augustinianism' would be quite as true a description.[2] Indeed, the opponents of St Augustine repudiate categorically any adherence to the doctrines of Pelagius. They are, however, strongly opposed to St Augustine's view of Predestination, both in itself and also because it was regarded as a novel doctrine and contrary to traditionally accepted dogma. More recently the term 'anti-Augustinianism' has been gaining in favour. Harnack summarizes the matter very well:

' "Semi-Pelagianism" is a malicious heretical term. The literary leaders of this doctrine were in no respect influenced, so far as I see, by Pelagius, nor did they learn anything from him; on the contrary, they take their stand . . . on doctrines of Augustine, and it is impossible to understand them apart from his teaching. "Semi-Pelagianism" is popular Catholicism made more definite and profound by Augustine's doctrines.'[3]

This phase of the controversy seems to have arisen simultaneously in North Africa and in southern Gaul, though Gaul in fact became the chief area of so-called 'semi-Pelagian' thought, and the adherents of this school are commonly referred to by their opponents as the 'Massilians'. In this area it assumed serious proportions, and lasted long, being, as Chadwick observes, 'no mere clique of heresy, but a body containing leading bishops, priests and monks of Provence, united in the righteous conviction that they were representing the true Christian tradition.'[4]

Chadwick points out that the controversy is exceptional

---

[1] The *locus classicus* for the controversy is G. F. Wiggers, *Pragmatische Darstellung des Augustinismus und Pelagianismus* (Berlin, Part I, 1821; Part II, 1833). A lucid explanation, easily accessible, with references to the principal documents, will be found in the Introduction by W. Bright to his work *Anti-Pelagian Treatises of St Augustine* (Oxford, 1880), p. xlix ff. A brief account is also given by E. C. S. Gibson in the *Prolegomena* to his translation of the *Works of John Cassian* (in the Series of *Nicene and Post-Nicene Fathers*, Oxford, 1894), p. 190 f. A clear and well-documented account is that of Fr. M. Jacquin, O.P., in the series of articles cited above. A brief discussion is given by O. Chadwick, *John Cassian*, p. 109 ff. For a good recent account see the article by Amann, s.v. *Semi-Pelagiens* in the *Dictionnaire de Théologie Catholique*, Vol. XIV (1939), col. 1796 ff.

[2] So Loofs. See also J. F. Bethune-Baker, *An Introduction to the Early History of Christian Doctrine* (London, 1933), p. 321, footnote 2. The history of the term is traced more recently by Amann, loc. cit.

[3] *History of Dogma* (English translation from the third German edition by J. Millar, London, 1898), Vol. V, p. 245, n. 3.

[4] Chadwick, *John Cassian*, p. 113.

among the doctrinal quarrels of the fourth and fifth centuries
in the respect with which in general each side treated the
other.

To many of the adherents of this school of thought the arguments used by St Augustine were considered unsatisfactory. Not
only was it felt that they misrepresented God's attitude to man,
and the purpose of the Atonement; it was also held that the
doctrine was practically dangerous, as seeming to undermine
the need for Christian endeavour. In southern Gaul for some
time past opinions had been voiced which were not in accord
with those expressed by the Bishop of Hippo. In particular John
Cassian of Marseilles, and a certain Hilarius or Euladius, referred to by Prosper as Bishop of Arles (cf. p. 179, n. 3), rejected
St Augustine's views on Predestination as contrary to accepted
Christian teaching. They agreed with Augustine that all men
had been involved in the sin of Adam, and that no one could
be saved by his own efforts. But they claimed that the doctrine
held by Augustine limited the divine goodwill to a fixed number
of persons previously selected by God, and so was contrary to
the traditional teaching of the Fathers and to accepted Catholic
doctrine, and was calculated to undermine human effort and
perseverance.

They, for the most part, believed that the Kingdom of Heaven
is open to all men by the Sacrament of Regeneration, so that all
men are called to eternal salvation by this gift, and those who
will may become sons of God. They held that God, without
predetermining the fate of men, or even young children who
die unbaptized, has foreknowledge how those will or would
choose to act, and judges them accordingly. Thus it would
seem the Massilians distinguished sharply between divine Predestination and Foreknowledge. And in their view divine Grace
is bestowed according to human deserts and never independently of them. The point of view is strictly logical and strictly
ethical, and implies a system of divine equity. The association
of the name of Pelagius with their doctrine is unfortunate and
misleading, since their views were wholly independent of his
and even opposed to them.[1]

Augustine was informed of the opinions held in Gaul, first in

[1] See further A. Harnack, *History of Dogma*, loc. cit.

429 by a certain Hilary, apparently a layman, probably the same Hilary who had previously corresponded with St Augustine on Sicilian Pelagianism, and who had probably been his first disciple.[1] Hilary's first letter is lost, but a second letter followed,[2] accompanied by a letter from Prosper of Aquitaine,[3] who, as already stated above, was also a layman, and who had evidently been in correspondence with Augustine previously.[4] Both these letters have been preserved, and it is from them that we gather the opinions of the Massilians expressed above. From that of Prosper we learn that the Massilians had been disturbed, not only by St Augustine's recent writings, such as the *De Correptione et Gratia*, but also earlier by his books against Julian (*Libri contra Julianum*), which had given particular offence.[5] It is clear from the letters, and from the works already published in southern Gaul, that the position taken up there in regard to the great questions under discussion was no recent development, though their actual focusing and canalizing into a prolonged series of polemics undoubtedly owed its incentive to Hilary and Prosper, whose letters to Augustine brought the two opposing doctrines to a clash.

The writers of the letters beg for Augustine's assistance in replying to the Massilians who hold opposite views. The latter are spoken of with great respect as men both highly virtuous and influential, and they are referred to in Prosper's letter as 'servants of Christ', and as being numerous in Marseilles.[6] It is probable that the reference is primarily to the monks of Lérins and of the monastery of St Victor. No names are mentioned except that of Hilarius, or, more probably, [H]elladius or Euladius,[7] referred to in Prosper's letter as Bishop of Arles. He is described by Prosper as an admirer of Augustine's doctrines in all matters except those under discussion. For the most part

---

[1] For this and other suggestions as to Hilary's identity, see Alliez, *Histoire du Monastère de Lérins*, Vol. I (Paris, 1862), p. 214 f.

[2] Migne, *P.L.*, Vol. XXXIII, *Ep.* 226, col. 1007.

[3] Migne, *P.L.*, Vol. XXXIII, *Ep.* 225, col. 1002.

[4] ibid., § 1.

[5] *Ep.* 225 (ed. cit.), *Prosper ad August.*, § 3.

[6] 'Multi ... servorum Christi qui in Massiliensi urbe consistunt', *Ep.* 225 (ed. cit.), *Prosper ad August.*, § 2.

[7] For a full discussion of the Bishop of Arles in question, see O. Chadwick's article, 'Euladius of Arles', *Journal of Theological Studies*, Vol. XLVI (1945), p. 200 ff.; cf. ibid. *John Cassian*, pp. 114, 188. Chadwick would seem to have dissociated Hilary, Bishop of Arles, from connection with the so-called Semi-Pelagians by indicating that he is not the bishop here referred to by Prosper. .

the letters content themselves with referring vaguely to their adversaries by such phrases as 'some of them' (quidam horum) and 'some of us' (quidam nostrum).[1] But though Cassian's name is not mentioned he is obviously in the minds of the writers. Gibson has pointed out[2] that though in Cassian's work against Nestorius (caps. vii, xxvii) Cassian quotes Augustine as an authority for the Catholic doctrine of the Incarnation, it is remarkable that whereas a high encomium is passed on all the other authorities quoted – Hilary, Ambrose, Jerome, Rufinus, Gregory Nazianzen, Athanasius and Chrysostom – Augustine alone is referred to merely as priest (sacerdos) of Hippo Regius.

Augustine replied to his correspondents by a treatise now divided into two libri, De Praedestinatione Sanctorum and De Dono Perseverantiae,[3] in which he strongly maintained his previous contentions, but fully recognized the wide difference separating his opponents from the Pelagians. About 427 Prosper himself had written to a certain Rufinus – with whom he was evidently on terms of intimate friendship – a letter strongly supporting St Augustine's views,[4] and about the same time (before 430) he also wrote a poem of 1,002 hexameters embodying the material of this letter. This poem he called Carmen de Ingratis,[5] and in it he makes more direct reference to both the Pelagians and the semi-Pelagians. The death of St Augustine in this year by no means brought the controversy to an end. A number of publications ensued from both parties, and soon after the death of Augustine an open attack on him was published in Provence, apparently anonymously, in the form of fifteen Capitula Objectionum Gallorum Calumniantium, which claimed to summarize his doctrine. Prosper replied by a work which he called the Responsiones ad capitula objectionum Gallorum Calumniantium,[6] and about the same time, in 431, he and his supporter Hilary, repaired to Rome in order to denounce to Pope Celestine 'certain priests', who were no doubt the authors of the Capitula. Celestine received them, and in his turn wrote a letter to the bishops of

---

[1] Prosper ad August., loc. cit., § 4.
[2] Prolegomena to the Works of John Cassian, ed. cit., p. 191, footnote 1.
[3] Migne, P.L., Vol. XLV, col. 993 ff.
[4] Ep. ad Rufinum de Gratia et libero Arbitrio, Migne, P.L., Vol. LI, col. 77 ff.
[5] Migne, P.L., Vol. LI, col. 91 ff.
[6] Migne, P.L., Vol. LI, col. 155 ff.

Gaul,[1] recommending them to impose silence on those who were opposing Prosper, and reproving them for allowing mere priests to express their views while keeping silence themselves, and concluding by upholding the doctrine and great prestige of St Augustine. Celestine, however, is very guarded in his censure. No names are mentioned, and he confines himself to general terms. 'Deservedly are we to blame', he writes, 'if by our silence we encourage error. Therefore let those who are guilty of this be rebuked. Do not let them have unrestricted liberty of preaching.' And he continues still more guardedly, 'If the case be so, if this be true, then let novelty cease to assail antiquity', which is commonly interpreted as censuring the 'semi-Pelagians', but which Vincent of Lérins cleverly turns against their adversaries.[2]

The anti-Augustinians, by no means subdued by the episcopal letter, drew up another set of *formulae*, this time sixteen in number, known as the *Capitula Objectionum Vincentianarum*, in which they claimed to embody the principal points of doctrine held by their adversaries. The authorship is ascribed by many[3] to the famous Vincent of Lérins, of whom we shall have more to say later; and again Prosper replied with a series of *Responsiones*.[4] Finally Prosper, who had hitherto adopted a purely defensive attitude in the controversy, opened a direct attack with a treatise which in the printed editions[5] bears the title *De Gratia Dei et libero Arbitrio, Liber Contra Collatorem*, written probably in 432,[6] in which he concentrates especially on Cassian's Thirteenth *Conference* (cf. p. 233). He attacks especially the doctrine of Grace there discussed categorically, and seeks to demonstrate contradictions in the work itself, and to connect Cassian's teaching with that of Pelagius, which he condemns. Again, curiously enough, Cassian is not mentioned by name, and it is

---

[1] *Ep. S. Coelestini Papae I ad Episcopos Galliarum*, Migne, *P.L.*, Vol. L, col. 528 ff.

[2] *Commonitorium*, ch. 32 (Migne, *P.L.*, Vol. L, col. 637 ff.).

[3] See O. Chadwick, op. cit., p. 111, and the references there cited. H. Koch has shown on stylistic grounds that there is some basis for attributing the authorship of this work to Vincent of Lérins. See his article 'Vincenz von Lerin und Gennadius', *Texte und Untersuchungen zur Geschichte der Altchristlichen Literatur* (Leipzig, 1907), p. 55 f. Jacquin also regarded Vincent of Lérins as the possible author. So also Amann, s.v. *Semi-Pelagiens* in the *Dictionnaire de Théologie Catholique*, Vol. XL, col. 1820.

[4] Migne, *P.L.*, Vol. LI, col. 177 ff.

[5] Migne, *P.L.*, Vol. LI, col. 213 ff.

[6] So O. Chadwick, *John Cassian*, p. 119. See also G. Bardy, s.v. *Prosper* in the *Dictionnaire de Théologie Catholique*, Vol. XIII, col. 847.

not known that he ever replied; indeed he probably died soon afterwards.

It will be seen that Prosper played an important part in the intellectual life of southern Gaul for a short time from c. 427 to c. 432, or possibly a year or two later, and his influence must have lasted indirectly much longer. He cannot be said to have stimulated the works by which Vincent or Cassian are known, since they seem to have been written before his activities began. And the works of Augustine must have been already well known in southern Gaul before Hilary and Prosper opened the way to fresh polemics. Yet there can be no doubt that Prosper's activities quickened interest in southern Gaul in the deep questions discussed by St Augustine in his last years. 'Il fut le chevalier d'une grande cause.'[1]

The controversy itself continued till well into the sixth century, and was finally brought to a close at the second Council of Orange in 529 under the guidance of the great Bishop Caesarius of Arles and his colleagues. Caesarius himself lies beyond the limits of our period, for he did not become Bishop of Arles till 503 and is believed to have lived till 543. But he is one of the greatest men produced by the monastery of Lérins, and perhaps the greatest of the churchmen of Gaul in his day. He had ranged himself against the so-called 'semi-Pelagians' in an interesting little work entitled *Quid Dominus Caesarius senserit contra eos qui dicunt quare aliis det Deus gratiam, aliis non det;*[2] and at the Council of Orange[3] the heresy of Pelagius in whole and in part was officially condemned under his auspices, while the teaching of Augustine on Grace was for the most part accepted. The canons passed by this Council were approved by Pope Boniface II, and the controversy came to an end.

Meanwhile the School of Marseilles counted among its mem-

---

[1] Jacquin, op. cit., p. 300.

[2] The text was discovered by Dom. G. Morin, and edited for the first time by Dom U. Baltus in the *Revue Bénédictine*, Vol. XIII (1896), p. 433 ff.; also published by Morin in *Sancti Caesarii Arelatensis Opera Omnia*, Vol. II (*Opera Varia*, Maretioli, 1942), p. 159 ff. For a general account of Caesarius, see A. Malnory, *St Césaire Evêque d'Arles* (Paris, 1894); Also the more recent article s.v. *Césaire d'Arles* by P. Lejay in the *Dictionnaire de Théologie Catholique*, Vol. XII (Paris, 1923).

[3] For an interesting analysis of the growth and composition of the *Capitula* of the Council of Orange, see Lejay, loc. cit., col. 2178 f.; and Dom G. Morin, *Revue Bénédictine*, Vol. XXI (1904), p. 225 ff.

bers some of the most influential and interesting thinkers of Gaul during the fifth century. To these men the great religious questions of the day were of paramount importance, and religious controversy took a foremost place among their intellectual and spiritual activities. Questions which were ultimately to be decreed 'heresies' by ecclesiastical authority and the Councils of the Church were as yet open to attack and defence, and were still being frankly and hotly discussed by both monks and laymen. The intellectual activities of the time were focused on the need for definition.

One of the most important writers of southern Gaul in the first half of the fifth century is Vincent, a priest in the monastery of Lérins. Little is known of his life except what Gennadius tells us (CH. 65). As Gennadius himself flourished c. 495 he had good reason to know the facts. His words are as follows:

'Vincent, a Gaul by birth, a presbyter in the monastery on the island of Lérins, a man learned in the Holy Scriptures,[1] and thoroughly instructed in the knowledge of Church doctrines, composed in clear and plain style a very powerful dissertation for the purpose of suppressing heretical sects, which he wrote under the title of "Peregrinus against the Heretics". Because he lost the greater part of the Second Book of this work, which was stolen in manuscript, he compiled the substance of it in a few words, attached it to the First, and published them in one book. He died in the reign of Theodosius and Valentinian.'

His death, therefore, must have taken place before 450, in which year Theodosius died. Vincent refers to himself as *Peregrinus*, 'a pilgrim', and 'the least of all God's servants', but at this period the word 'servants of God' is the usual expression for monks, and *peregrinus* is used to denote something between a 'pilgrim' and a 'recluse', one who lives in this world as a pilgrim to God, in this case a cloistered 'pilgrim'.[2]

Vincent's chief work, generally referred to as the *Commonitorium*, was written c. 434, for the author refers (ch. 29) to the Council of Ephesus, which was held in 431, as having taken

---

[1] It would seem nevertheless that his knowledge of Greek authors was obtained through Latin intermediaries, and there is no reason to believe that he knew Greek at first-hand. See Courcelle, op. cit., p. 218 ff.

[2] *Peregrinari* in late Latin commonly meant 'withdrawing to a monastery', as the early Irish monks speak of 'seeking the place of their salvation'.

place almost three years before. He tells us in the first chapter that 'avoiding the throng and crowds of cities', he has his 'secluded dwelling on a small estate of a monastery in a very retired spot'. He adds that he had previously been long caught up in the 'various and disastrous whirlpools of worldly warfare'; but this does not necessarily refer to the military life, and may merely refer to spiritual warfare, and a period of life spent in secular occupations. Eucherius speaks of him warmly, and informs us that he had been, together with Salvian, the educator of his sons, Salonius and Veranus.[1]

The works of Vincent appear to have been few. Gennadius seems to have known only one, in two books. Two other works are now generally attributed to him. The first is the *Objectiones Vincentianae*, the text of which is lost, but of which the contents are known from Prosper's work *Pro Augustino responsiones ad capitula objectionum Vincentianarum*.[2] This work has already been referred to above, where it has been mentioned that the agreement between this work and the *Commonitorium* is so close as to make the attribution of the *Objectiones* to Vincent extremely convincing. The work probably dates from c. 430, since Prosper's refutation was composed very shortly after the death of St Augustine.

The second of these works which has been associated with the name of Vincent is a collection of *Excerpta*[3] of St Augustine's teaching on the mysteries of the Trinity and the Incarnation. It was first mentioned by an anonymous theologian in the ninth century. The text was recently discovered by Madoz in a Spanish library, and identified by him as the work of Vincent. Lebreton[4] supports the identification suggested by Madoz, and points out that both the thought and the theological formulae expressed in the Preface and the conclusion of the *Excerpta* are easily recognizable as characteristic of Vincent.

The work by which Vincent is generally known, and which is commonly referred to briefly as the *Commonitorium*, is of out-

---

[1] *Instructiones*, Part I, Preface.
[2] Migne, *P.L.*, Vol. LI, col. 177–86.
[3] The full title of the work is *Excerpta Sanctae memoriae Vincentii Lirinensis insulae presbyteri ex universo beatae recordationis Augustini episcopi in unum collecta*. For further references see G. Bardy, *Dictionnaire de Théologie Catholique*, s.v. Vincent de Lérins.
[4] 'Saint Vincent de Lérins et Saint Augustin', *Recherches de Science Religieuse*, Vol. XXX (1940), p. 368 f.; cf. further O. Chadwick, *John Cassian*, p. 119, n. 3.

standing importance.[1] Its full title as given in the manuscripts is *Tractus Peregrini pro Catholicae Fidei Antiquitate et Universitate adversus Profanas Omnium Haereticorum Novitates* ('The tract of Peregrinus for the Antiquity and Universality of the Catholic Faith against the Profane Novelties of all Heretics'); but in the treatise itself Vincent five times refers to the work as a *commonitorium*, and Gennadius alluding to it says: 'quam ... adtitulavit "Peregrini adversum haereticos".' The treatise, as already stated, is commonly referred to briefly as the *Commonitorium* ('Aid to Memory').[2]

It may be mentioned that considerable scepticism has been expressed in regard to Gennadius's statement (see above) about the 'theft' of the manuscript of the second half of the book. Koch long ago pointed out[3] that the recapitulation of the second part is so detailed that whoever wrote it must have had the original second part actually before him, and that this second part in its present form renders the 'original' unnecessary. Koch held that the actual publication, and perhaps even the editing, was not done by Vincent himself, and that the 'theft' is a conjecture of Gennadius to account for the recapitulation.

The author's principal object in writing the *Commonitorium* is to supply a criterion whereby the doctrine may be kept pure and handed on without change. This, according to Vincent, can only be effected by a close adherence to Holy Scripture as handed down by sound tradition, both written and oral. To guide the Christian to the tradition which is sound, and which can safely be adhered to, he lays down his famous axiom that 'In the Catholic Church we must take every care to adhere to that which has been believed everywhere, always, and by everybody (*quod ubique, quod semper, quod ab omnibus creditum est*). For that is what is truly and properly Catholic, as is shown by the meaning and root of the word itself, which comprehends virtually everything universally'.[4]

---

[1] A good edition of the text is that of R. S. Moxon, *The Commonitorium of Vincent of Lérins* (Cambridge, 1915); translated by C. A. Heurtley in the Series *Nicene and Post-Nicene Fathers* (Oxford, 1894), Vol. XI, p. 127 ff.; and later by T. H. Bindley, *The Commonitory of Vincent of Lérins* (London, 1914). A lucid popular account of the Commonitorium is given by A. C. Cooper-Marsdin in the chapter devoted to 'The Great Theologian Vincent', in the *History of the Islands of Lérins* (Cambridge, 1913), p. 50 ff.

[2] The technical meaning of the word is a paper of instructions, given to a person charged with a commission, to aid his memory as to its details.

[3] Op. cit. (see p. 184, n. 3), p. 39 ff.   [4] *Commonitorium*, ch. 2.

Yet Vincent is no advocate of spiritual or intellectual stagnation. He recognizes the need of growth and development, even in our interpretation of the creed, and he appositely compares organic growth and development of belief within the Church itself to the development which takes place within the human body from childhood to manhood, at the same time contrasting the radical change which heresy involves.

In order to assist the Christian to avoid falling into error and to recognize heresy, the principal heresies which have arisen in the Church are enumerated and defined. The work is a veritable handbook to heresies, a number of which the author passes in stern review. His cast of thought expresses itself in forceful and incisive definition and clear analysis, but his lack of refinement is in strong contrast to Cassian. At times his language is ungraceful to modern ears. But he gives fine full-length portraits of Tertullian (ch. 17), and Origen (ch. 18), contrasting them as they were before and after their defection. In these passages he departs from his customary simple direct style and adopts a highly rhetorical vein, which he could hardly have acquired outside the Gaulish schools, and which is at times closely similar to that of Eucherius.

In addition to the enumeration and definition of heresies, the author seeks to establish the articles of belief on firm lines. The doctrines of the Trinity and the Incarnation are carefully defined with admirable clarity and precision (ch. 13). These passages have so much in common, not only in regard to the actual ideas, but even the language and phraseology, with the so-called 'Athanasian Creed', that some have held the latter to be the work of Vincent.[1] This view has not been generally accepted; but it has been thought possible that the Creed was composed in Lérins shortly before the composition of the *Commonitorium*.[2] Finally the author of the *Commonitorium* lays it down that when a difference of opinion arises within the Church the matter should be laid before the General Council, whose opinions should carry authority: or decided by the opinion agreed by the Fathers of the Church.

It is not infrequently stated that the *Commonitorium* was com-

[1] See A. E. Burn, *An Introduction to the Creeds* (London, 1899), pp. 135 f., 147.
[2] See Burn, op. cit., p. 147 f. For some discussion and further references, see Bindley, op. cit. p. xv f.

posed as part of the 'semi-Pelagian Controversy'. Bardenhewer[1] even goes so far as to suggest that it was very probably written as a direct reply to Augustine's teaching on Predestination. This is perhaps to take the work of Vincent out of its setting, and to over-emphasize one aspect; but Harnack[2] also held that the work was directed exclusively against Augustine, and there can be no doubt that Vincent was opposed to Augustine's doctrine of Predestination, and that he expresses the views current at Lérins at this period, and in his own milieu. Like Cassian, Vincent omits the name of Augustine among those whom he mentions with honour in the Church. Indeed he nowhere mentions Augustine's name; but he is probably making allusion to him when he praises as the 'true and genuine Catholic' one who sets the Catholic Faith before all else – 'before the authority, regard, genius, eloquence or philosophy of any man whatsoever', and who will hold as not belonging to religion 'whatever new and unheard of doctrine he shall perceive to have been introduced by anyone in addition to, or contrary to, the belief of all the saints'.[3] It will be remembered that Augustine had received a training in the schools of rhetoric in early life, and had been a Manichean for seven years before his conversion to Christianity, and it is difficult to avoid a suspicion that the allusion to eloquence, and philosophy, and genius are pointed at the great doctor, against whom the accusation of novelty was commonly levelled by his enemies. There can, in any case, be no doubt that Vincent has the doctrine of Predestination in mind in the following passage:

'The heretics have indeed been accustomed to deceive incautious men in a marvellous way by the following kind of promises. For they dare to promise and to teach that in their own Church, that is, in the little society of their communion, there abides a certain great and special, and, in fact, personal Grace of God; so much so, that without any labour, without any effort, without any industry – even though they neither ask nor seek nor knock – whosoever is reckoned among their number receive such dispensation from God that, raised by angels' hands, preserved by angelic protection, they can never dash their foot against a stone, that is, be caused to stumble.'[4]

[1] *Patrology*, op. cit., p. 521.
[2] Op. cit., Vol. V, p. 247.
[3] *Common.*, ch. 20.
[4] *Common.*, ch. 26.

It can hardly be doubted that Vincent is impugning Augustine's doctrine of Grace, and, it would seem, somewhat maliciously; nor is it a fair representation of what Augustine actually thought. Vincent is undoubtedly actuated here by a polemical spirit. On the other hand we are perhaps not justified in supposing that Vincent's hostility to Augustine extended to any of his teaching except that on Grace and Predestination. If the recently discovered *Excerpta* from Augustine's teaching referred to above is really the work of Vincent of Lérins, we must suppose that he confined his opposition to Augustine to the doctrine of Grace and Predestination, while venerating his teaching on the Trinity and the Incarnation.

On the other hand the more one reads the works of Cassian and Vincent, the more one realizes the disproportionate part which the Pelagian question has come to assume in our interpretation and estimate of their work. This is, of course, largely owing to Prosper's activities. But these men had other views and other interests in addition to this burning question. Other and greater heresies claimed their attention, especially the tragic affair of Nestorius. The new monastic life of southern Gaul was now of paramount importance. The growing power of Rome and the dislike expressed by Pope Celestine for monastic bishops,[1] were creating many new problems. And the pouring of the Barbarian forces over the Empire's frontiers, the sack of Rome by the Arian Visigoths, the invasion of Spain and Africa by the Arian Vandals, the sack of Trier, and settlements of Frank and Goth in Gaul, must have given the monks of southern Gaul many grave fears and apprehensions for the future of the Church, and the safety of her sons, and the purity of the faith for which the confessors had suffered torture and death. All these weighty considerations must have had their part in stimulating the *Institutes* and *Conferences*, and the *Commonitorium*, and must be borne in mind by us in our estimate of the relationship of the work of Cassian and Vincent to the spiritual and intellectual life of the age.

Of the writers of Southern Provence who took a leading part on the side of the so-called semi-Pelagians after the deaths of Cassian and Vincent, the most interesting and the most in-

[1] See the famous *Cuperemus quidem*, dated 428; Mansi III, p. 464; Migne, *P.L.*, Vol. L, p. 430.

fluential was Faustus, who entered Lérins towards 430, and became its abbot in 433, and who was consecrated Bishop of Riez in eastern Provence shortly before 462. Faustus, 'the brilliant Bishop of Riez', as Dom Morin calls him, was the most independent thinker of his time, and in many ways the most interesting personality. There has been a tendency to associate him with our Islands, both in regard to his origin, and also in regard to some special features in the Celtic form of Christianity. It has been suggested that certain features of the early Celtic ecclesiastical ritual and organization have their closest affinities and their earliest reference in Faustus's works. This question has been discussed recently by Owen Chadwick,[1] and I shall refer to it more fully later in the present chapter. As regards the birth and nationality of Faustus, he is referred to as *Brito*, by Avitus, Bishop of Vienne,[2] and also as a Briton or Breton by his friend Sidonius Apollinaris,[3] to whom we are indebted for a vivid portrait of the man, both in prose and verse, to be discussed later. Others, such as Possessor,[4] an African bishop, call him *Gallus*, but this is probably due to his long sojourn in Gaul.[5]

The exact significance of the word *Brito* in this context is by no means certain. It has generally been interpreted as referring to Britain, and seems to have been so interpreted by Nennius, who was apparently acquainted with Sidonius's references to Faustus, perhaps through some intermediary work. But it is at least equally possible that the words *Britannis tuis* here refer, not to Britons, but to Bretons, to whom Sidonius is the first writer to apply the name *Brittones*, in succession to the older title *Armoricani*. I have discussed the question of the nationality of Faustus with some fullness elsewhere, in a note to which I may refer the reader for a fuller treatment of the problem.[6]

The date of Faustus's birth is unknown, but it probably took place some time before 410. Probably also he entered the monastery of Lérins while still young, but after being educated

---

[1] *John Cassian* (Cambridge, 1950), p. 201 ff.

[2] *Ep.* 4, to Gundobad, King of the Burgundians (Migne, *P.L.*, Vol. LIX, col. 219: *ortu Britannum, habitaculo Regiensem*).

[3] *Britannis tuis, Ep.* IX, 9.

[4] *Concil. Gall.* IV, 1520: cf. Alliez, *Histoire du Monastère de Lérins*, Vol. I, p. 67.

[5] See A. Engelbrecht, *Fausti Reiensis praeter Sermones Pseudo-Eusebianos Opera* (Vienna, 1891), p. VI. My references to the works of Faustus are to Engelbrecht's edition throughout.

[6] *Studies in Early British History* (Cambridge, 1953), p. 254 ff.

in the schools of rhetoric.[1] In 433 he succeeded Maximus as Abbot of Lérins when Maximus became Bishop of Riez,[2] where again, in 452, Faustus succeeded him as bishop. 'Thus', as Tillemont puts it, 'this famous monastery made two presents to the same church.'[3] It was during the abbacy of Faustus that the *Commonitorium* was composed by Vincent, the monk of Lérins, and though Faustus's own literary work was mostly composed later, during his episcopate, his keen intellect and literary gifts must undoubtedly have acted as a powerful stimulus to the monks of a community, which, from the start, had shown itself active in the production of literary and devotional work.

Sidonius Apollinaris has left us in his poems and letters a delightful portrait of Faustus, his friend and brother bishop. The fullest picture is given in *Carmen* XVI, composed as an address to Faustus about the time when Sidonius himself and other Gaulish bishops had assembled at Lyons for the dedication of the new church built by Bishop Patiens. The celebrations had lasted for a week, and on this occasion Faustus had preached at the invitation of his brother bishops, and his eloquence evidently made a great impression on Sidonius. Sidonius, moreover, speaks warmly of the hospitality which he had received previously from Faustus when he was his guest at Riez, so that from personal observation he was able in this poem to review him under various aspects. Faustus is pictured, apparently during his episcopacy, as passing considerable periods in ascetic retreat,[4] lingering in 'an unfriendly wilderness', in 'a marsh full of green slime', in 'deep gloomy caves', or where the 'precipitous Alps' tremble before the gloomy anchorite. He is said to be urged to the life of ascetic piety by the example of the desert fathers – the two Macarii, the great Paphnutius, Ammon, Hilarion, and the great St Antony. It is very probable that Cassian's writings, and his personal influence also, had inspired the young ascetic in his early austerities.

Sidonius, still addressing Faustus, next refers to the visits which Faustus was, it seems, in the habit of paying to his old home at Lérins, apparently as a sequel to the retreats which have just been described. And here, instead of resting from the

---

[1] See Engelbrecht, op. cit., p. vii.
[2] *Regium* or *Reii* in the Province of Aix.
[3] Vol. XVI, p. 414.
[4] So also *Vita S. Hilarii* (ed. Cavallin), cap. 9 (Migne, *P.L.*, Vol. L, col. 1230).

N

exhaustion resulting naturally from his austerities, he continues his fasts, taking little sleep or cooked food in the intervals of chanting the Psalms. Meanwhile he devotes himself to the brethren. Especially he loves to instruct them in the history of their monastery, and of the great men who have been trained there – of the holy life of old Caprasius and of young Lupus, of the grace destined for Honoratus their founder, of Maximus 'over whose city and monks thou, twice his successor,[1] were set as bishop and abbot', and finally of Eucherius and Hilary.

Of Lupus, who after a year at Lérins, was called to the See of Troyes, to become, as Sidonius calls him, 'the prince of the prelates of Gaul',[2] I shall speak more fully in the next chapter. The reference to Hilary's return to Lérins is to the period after his first sojourn in Arles, whither he had gone in company with Honoratus when Honoratus had been preferred to the see.

The most attractive picture which Sidonius gives us, how-ever, is that of Faustus on his return to his own see at Riez, where the humble people, encouraged by his presence, can boldly scorn the proud ways of the great when they have him in their midst. Sidonius emphasizes his personal care for the suffering, his attention to the welfare and food of the stranger and the sick, and the prisoner who pines in fetters 'till they slide loosely on his shrunken legs'. Faustus is also commended for his care that the pauper who dies shall not lie unburied. 'Even though the livid remains of a poor corpse are turning green, thou didst not shrink from carrying it thyself to the tomb'.

It would seem that Faustus, like Paulinus, Pammachius, Fabiola and other great Romans, realized the need of hostels in which the wayfarer could find adequate food and comfort; of hospitals for the sick poor; and of some system of burial for paupers. Sidonius stresses the personal note, and the care for detail which Faustus himself bestowed on these matters; and in his own picturesque way he conveys to us something of the magnetism of his rich and warm-hearted nature. What he describes as the personal actions of Faustus are probably largely to be interpreted as public works due to his instigation. He was doubtless an excellent organizer, and perhaps liberal and original in the social aspect of his duties as in other matters.

---

[1] Faustus succeeded Maximus, first as Abbot of Lérins, then as Bishop of Riez.
[2] Sidonius, *Ep.* VII, 13.

These things may not have been wholly new as public concerns, even in Gaul; but if any provision of this kind had existed in the past it must have broken down, especially in Gaul, owing to the unrest and disorganization consequent upon the Barbarian inroads. The reference to the unburied corpse carries with it a grim suggestion of the deficiencies in the organization for which Faustus sought a speedy practical remedy, while the reference to the poor, no longer afraid of the rich in the presence of Faustus, points once more to the strongly democratic element which we constantly find among those who had come under monastic influence. The whole passage has much to tell us of the prevalent social conditions and of the awakening consciousness of the Church to the need for practical measures of reform. Once more we are reminded that it will be well to withdraw the censure formerly bestowed on Salvian for his fierce demands of money for the Church.

Sidonius has shown us his friend in the retreat of the anchorite, in the great monastic establishment at Lérins, in the discharge of his episcopal duties among the poor and sick in his own see. The final picture, to which the preceding scenes have been leading up, is that of Faustus as a great bishop seated on his episcopal throne:

'Perchance you are about to deliver your discourse from the lofty steps of the holy altar, while the eager throng take up their stand around you, that their ears may drink in the healing exposition of the Law.'

Whatever the faults of Sidonius as a poet in general, he has managed here to convey a clear impression of the varied aspects of the spiritual activity of this great fifth-century bishop, so austere, so sensitive to human suffering, and practical in his methods of alleviating it; and withal, so intellectual and so eloquent.

The brief picture of Faustus preaching from the episcopal throne at Lyons with which the poem ends can be filled out from the letters of Sidonius. Thus in Book IX, letter 3, he recalls to his friend how, many years ago, he had himself sat and listened till he was hoarse with applauding while Faustus preached, 'now extempore, now, if occasion demanded, after careful preparation'; and he continues, with reference to the same event, how he recalls 'the week's festivities of the dedication of the church at Lyons, where you were prevailed upon by the invitation of your venerable colleagues to deliver an oration, and where you preserved in your oratory such a balance between spiritual and forensic eloquence . . . that we crowded round you, straining our ears, and with our emotions roused to the utmost'.

Sidonius is insistent that Faustus persisted in pursuing the ascetic way of life, even after his consecration to the bishopric. In the same letter he addresses him as:

'Dominus Faustus Papa . . . versed in the prayers of the Island brotherhood, which you brought from the school of the anchorite congregation and from the community of the monks of Lérins, to the city over the rites of whose Church you also preside, in no wise changed from an abbot by becoming a bishop, nor relaxing in any way the rigour of your former discipline in acquiring a new dignity.'

And again in Letter 9 of the same book he makes reference to Faustus's spiritual insight, and the soundness of his learning.

'For who can follow in your footsteps with a like stride, since you alone are gifted to speak better than you have been taught, and to conduct your life even better than your words.'

The last sentence is thought to bear reference to the active part taken by Faustus in the polemics against Predestination.

In one of his letters to Faustus, Sidonius gives a lively account of a visit which he has received from a certain monk called Riocatus, a fellow countryman of Faustus. Riocatus had made a journey to Riez to obtain books from Faustus, but on his return he had been forced to turn aside and spend 'a couple of months or more' with Sidonius at Clermont to avoid the pickets of the Gothic army stationed in the neighbourhood.

This account is contained in a letter from Sidonius[1] to Faustus, which appears to date from shortly after 478. The passage about Riocatus begins as follows:

'I had read your works which Riocatus, the priest and monk, doubly a pilgrim in this world[2], was taking back for you to your Britons' (or perhaps, more probably 'Bretons'; cf. p. 192).

Sidonius then goes on to say that Riocatus, to whom he

---

[1] *Ep.* IX, 9.

[2] *Riocatus antistes ac monachus, atque istius mundi bis peregrinus.* On the word *peregrinus*, cf. p. 186, and n. 2.

refers as 'the venerable man', had made some stay in the city – that is to say in Clermont – owing to the presence of the hostile armies which were beleaguering it. He also relates that Riocatus had produced freely all Faustus's other good gifts, but with great firmness, although with the utmost courtesy, he had withheld the chief treasure which he was carrying. After his sojourn he departed hurriedly, a rumour having spread that he and his company were secreting great treasures in their baggage. A day later, it seems, Sidonius followed in hot pursuit and caught up the caravan, and, searching the baggage, he found the volume he sought, pulled it out, devoured the contents, and made long extracts from the most important chapters. He dictated as fast as he could, for his secretaries made use of symbols for what they had not time to write out fully, and so shortened the whole process.

This passage and what follows seems to make it clear that Riocatus was a monk and presbyter who was taking with him to Britain or Brittany some of the works of Faustus for his fellow-countrymen, including a very recent one which Sidonius has not yet perused, but which he manages to extract from the baggage. It is not quite clear from our text whether Riocatus's sojourn with Faustus had been a temporary visit, or whether he was actually living with him and merely re-visiting his own country; but on the whole the former seems more likely. In any case the evidence for the interchange of books and ideas across Gaul, even at the height of the Barbarian occupation, throws a light on the cultural history of the period.

Sidonius's friendship with Faustus was primarily a literary one. The passage of letters, the mutual friendly criticisms of style, the exchange of ideas closely packed with literary allusions, metaphors, allegory, and every device of rhetoric, was both a solace and a stimulus in those troublous times, when polished and educated men of letters had to leave the study for more active diplomatic and administrative work, while the greatness and culture which they had grown up to believe everlasting were crumbling around them. Sidonius welcomed as a gift from Heaven the letters from his friend, both for their loyalty and friendliness, and for their 'mastery of diction'.[1] He begs earnestly for the benefit of Faustus's criticism of his own

[1] *Ep.* IX, 3.

Latin style. Faustus must indeed have been a learned classical scholar, as is shown by the formidable list of the names of Greek philosophers with whom Sidonius assumes him to be familiar.[1] He respects him for his knowledge of philosophy, and suggests that he represents 'the Platonic Academy of the Church of Christ'.

The more technical of Faustus's duties, first as abbot, later as bishop, are outside our main subject. Some early differences with Theodore, the Bishop of Fréjus, during his abbacy, had obliged Ravennius, the Bishop of Arles, to call a Council to settle the dispute,[2] and in 463 we find Faustus deputed by the Council of Arles, along with Bishop Auxanius, to assist Pope Hilary at a council in Rome in matters affecting the Church of Gaul.[3] Later, when they were appointed to arbitrate in Gaul, their decision was confirmed by Hilary.[4] Faustus was evidently held in some esteem as a diplomat, for in 474, during the siege of Auvergne, while Euric and his Visigoths were seeking to make their own the last stronghold of Roman culture left to Gaul, Faustus was chosen by the Emperor Nepos to enter into negotiations, along with other bishops, viz. Leontius, Bishop of Arles; Graecus, Bishop of Marseilles; and a certain Basilius. When ultimately, in 481, Euric completed his annexation of Provence, Riez probably became a Gothic see under an Arian ruler,[5] and Faustus seems to have been exiled to a distant part of Gaul, probably because of his writings against Arianism. He was received by Ruricius, Bishop of Limoges, and lodged in a kind of monastery,[6] but was allowed to return to his diocese, perhaps on the accession of Alaric.[7] Gennadius (cap. 86) speaks of him as still alive, and his death probably took place some time between 490 and 495,[8] and his body was honoured by the people as that of a saint.

In his theological writings[9] Faustus took the leading part in

[1] *Ep.* IX, 9.
[2] See Duchesne, *Fasti*, I, p. 124 f. Cf. also p. 148.
[3] S. Hilary, *Ep.* 8; Migne, *P.L.*, Vol. LVIII, col. 24 ff.
[4] ibid., *Ep.* 10.
[5] For the evidence, see Engelbrecht, op. cit., p. x f.
[6] See the opening sentences of his letter to Ruricius, Engelbrecht, op. cit., p. 383. Cf. Alliez, op. cit., I, p. 261.
[7] See the letter to Ruricius, *Ep.* 11.
[8] The latter date is given by the writer in Pauly-Wissowa.
[9] On Faustus's theological position the reader may be referred especially to Harnack, op. cit., Vol. V, p. 252; and to Koch, *Der Heilige Faustus*, p. 39 ff.

the recrudescence of anti-Augustinianism which arose in the latter half of the fifth century, following a *via media*, or, as he himself calls it, a *via regia*, between the views of Pelagius, whom he refers to as *pestifer doctor*, and the Predestination of Augustine, which he regards as a relic of his previous Manicheism. It has indeed been claimed that he is 'the most authentic representative of anti-Augustinianism', the true founder of the doctrine which we today call 'semi-Pelagianism'.[1] His system is most clearly expressed in his letters and in his work *De Gratia et Libero Arbitrio: Libri Duo* ('On Grace and Free-will, in Two Books'),[2] dedicated to Leontius, Bishop of Arles. The book was written at the request of his colleagues, who had met at a Council of Arles in or about 475[3] to consider the case of a 'Predestinarian', Presbyter Lucidius. Lucidius belonged to Faustus's own diocese; and Faustus had taken a leading part in the Council, drawing up six anathemas,[4] which were directed against both Pelagianism and its opposite extreme, and which Lucidius was induced to sign.[5] In the book written in consequence of this Council Faustus condemns the Pelagians as blasphemous and impious, declaring that their tenets deny Original Sin and the necessity for infant baptism, and that they imply the essential sinlessness of sexual life.[6] At the same time he insists on the necessity of human exertion in response to divine Grace, and attacks Predestinarianism, but without mentioning Augustine by name.

Apart from the *De Gratia*, the most important surviving theological work attributed to him[7] is the *De Spiritu Sancto*, published anonymously. This is, in fact, the title of the book which Gennadius places first in the list of works by Faustus which he

[1] Amann, *Dictionnaire de Théologie Catholique*, s.v. *Semi-Pelagiens*, Vol. XIV, col. 1833.

[2] Migne, *P.L.*, Vol. LVIII, col. 783 ff.; Engelbrecht gives the title simply as *Duo De Gratia Libri*.

[3] Mansi, VII, 1007 ff. See also Duchesne, *Fasti* I, p. 129 f.

[4] Mansi, loc. cit.; enumerated in English in Keble's *Hooker*, Vol. II, p. 582.

[5] Faustus had already sought to induce his friend to sign the anathemas before the Council was held. See Harnack, *History of Dogma*, p. 252, footnote 5.

[6] The work is severely criticized by Amann as Christianity 'sans mystère' and as puerile in its materialism. Amann is also severe on Faustus' prose style, which he regards as formless and obscure; but probably Amann's view, like that of Tillemont, is influenced by his religious standpoint.

[7] By C. P. Caspari, *Ungedruckte . . . Quellen zur Geschichte des Taufsymbols und der Glaubensregel*, Vol. II (Christiania, 1869), pp. 214–24; so also Engelbrecht, *Studien über die Schriften des Bischofs von Reii Faustus* (1889), pp. 28–46. Engelbrecht includes it in his book *Fausti Reiensis praeter Sermones Pseudo-Eusebianos Opera* (Vienne, 1891), p. 99 ff.

selects for mention. Here, as elsewhere,[1] Faustus maintains his somewhat startling view that the soul is material, his argument being that since God alone is spirit, to regard the soul as spirit is blasphemy.[2]

It is perhaps in his sermons that the fine quality of Faustus's mind is seen at its best. His earnest and sombre thoughts are expressed incisively and with force, often in simple direct sentences, varied at times by assonance, even rhyme, and above all by repetition and the liberal use of the rhetorical question. These characteristics, which he shares at times with other writers trained in the early years of Lérins, notably Vincent and Eucherius, are the gifts of Gaulish rhetoric to the Christian ecclesiastics of the period. The sermons of Valerian, Bishop of Céméle, a city formerly near Nice, but long ago disappeared, are also characterized by alliteration and other devices of the rhetoricians. The eloquence of Faustus is stressed by Gennadius, who thus refers to him: 'Viva voce egregius doctor et creditur et probatur'. Tillemont ranked him low, both for his style and matter, stressing those features in his style which he owed to his training in rhetoric, and denying him either depth or width of knowledge, pointing out that Sidonius, who gives him such high praise, is equally generous in his praises of works written in opposition to Faustus.[3] There can be no doubt, however, that this estimate is largely coloured by Tillemont's strong religious views.

The sermons[4] are not always easy to identify, as they are generally anonymous, or incorporated in the work of others.[5] In particular many of the sermons of Faustus are incorporated either wholly, or by quotation and paraphrase, in the great body of sermon literature left by Caesarius of Arles.[6] Like the

---

[1] Cf. e.g. Migne, *P.L.*, Vol. LVIII, col. 841 ff, (*Ep.* 3).

[2] For a clear exposition of Faustus's theological position, see Harnack, *History of Dogma*, Vol. V, ch. 5.

[3] Tillemont, Vol. XVI (Paris, 1712), p. 410.

[4] Engelbrecht, p. 221 ff. For a list of the writings of Faustus, see Koch, op. cit., p. 30 ff. The list is only complete so far as was known in 1890.

[5] The edition of the works of Faustus published in Migne, *P.L.*, Vol. LVII, col. 783 ff., contains only eight sermons. Engelbrecht (op. cit.) gives thirty-one.

[6] A critical collection of the sermons of Caesarius has been made by Dom G. Morin, *Sancti Caesarii Arelatensis Opera Omnia: Sermones*, 2 vols. (Maretioli, 1937). Cyprianus, in his *Vita S. Caesarii* I, v, 42 (Migne *P.L.*, Vol. LXVII, col. 1021), refers to the freedom with which Caesarius lent his own sermons to others to be preached in their churches. The aim of Caesarius in encouraging the composition and the preaching of sermons was essentially practical, and questions of literary proprietorship were of little or no importance.

sermons of Caesarius of Arles, they are very brief in the form in which they have reached us. But Malnory claims that they can easily be distinguished from the work of Caesarius on internal evidence.

'Il est presque impossible de se tromper, tant l'opposition est tranchée entre la gravité imperturbable et souvent froide et monotone de Fauste, et la parole chaude, vive, et tout en mouvement de S. Césaire.'[1]

It must be remembered, however, that Faustus's real gift lay, not in sermon writing, but in eloquent extempore preaching, and the sermons which we have from his pen are probably little more than his memoranda.

It is, perhaps, in his famous sermons to the monks of Lérins that his vigour and compelling genius as a preacher can be most readily apprehended by us today. Here in the opening lines of the first sermon in Engelbrecht's edition[2] he seems to have in his ears the tramping of the approaching Gothic armies; he feels the privileges of security enjoyed by those who have fled from the upheavals of the time, and with burning words he brands on the consciousness of his listeners the heavy responsibility undertaken by those who are blessed with the privileges of the spiritual life. Lérins, the *locus* or 'monastery' in which he is preaching, is a *castra*, 'an armed camp', and the ranks who occupy it have come, not for peace, but for the sword – the sword and the ceaseless warfare of the spirit.

'It is not for quiet and security, my dear brothers, that we have formed a community in this monastery (*locus*), but for a struggle and a conflict. We have met here for a contest, we have embarked on a war against our sins. For it is our sins which are our foes ... Our vigilance must be constantly on the alert, our efforts untiring, for this conflict will be without ending, with this foe there can be no treaty. You can be conquered by your enemy, but you can never come to terms with him. And therefore this struggle on which we are engaged is full of hardship, full of danger, for it is the struggle of man against himself, and will not end save with the end of man.

'To this end, therefore, have we gathered together to this tranquil retreat, this spiritual camp – that we may wage, day

---

[1] *Saint Césaire* (Paris, 1894), p. xvi.
[2] *Sermo* XXIII (Ad monachos I).

after day, an unwearying contest against our passions, that day after day we may subject our wills like handmaidens to our superiors, that we may cut out the sins of the heart and sheathe the sword of the tongue, that we may not only avoid doing harm to one another, but we may not even be sensible of harm done to ourselves.'

Perhaps the most famous and impressive passages in his writings are those which occur in a sermon[1] erroneously included in the collection ascribed to Caesarius of Arles,[2] but more correctly attributable to Faustus, both on the grounds of style,[3] and also because St Columbanus quotes sentences from it in the name of Faustus.

'Of what use is it to fight a battle outside the community (*civitas*) and to suffer destruction within? It is as if one should dig outside one's vineyard and round about it, and leave the interior overgrown with thorns and prickles. Of what use is the religion of the outer man unless he also attends to the reform of the spirit?'[4]

And again:

'To come to the "desert" (*eremus*) is surely the height of perfection; but not to live perfectly in the desert is the utmost damnation. Of what use is it to live in peaceful retreat (*locus quietus*) if disquiet reigns in our hearts? Of what use is silence in the house if the tumult of sin and the flames of passion are raging within those who are inside the house? — if outwardly we are serene, while a tempest rages within?'[5]

Faustus seeks to guide the monks of Lérins, not to the austerities favoured by the Eastern monks, but to the contemplative life which was the guiding spirit of Egyptian monasticism. He reminds his listeners that they have not met together to enjoy the things of the world more abundantly; but rather to have nothing. Even that is not enough — they must even desire nothing. Unless one is poor with one's whole heart and desire there is no virtue in poverty, but rather misery.

---

[1] Published among the sermons of Caesarius in Migne, *P.L.*, Vol. LXVII, col. 1056 ff.

[2] See Dom G. Morin, *S. Caesarii Opera Omnia*, Vol. I, 2, p. 936 f.

[3] A. Malnory, *Saint Césaire* (Paris, 1894), p. xvi; cf. Morin, loc. cit.

[4] *S. Columbani Sermones* (quoting Faustus), Migne, *P.L.*, Vol. LXXX, col. 234.

[5] Migne, *P.L.*, Vol. LXVII, col. 1057 (erroneously attributed to S. Caesarius).

'Of what use is it to mortify your bodies if there is no spiritual progress in your hearts?'[1]

It is typical of Faustus, who had been the abbot of the *coenobium*, that among the virtues which he ranks highest is implicit obedience. But he realized, like all great monastic thinkers, the emptiness and futility of a negative attitude in a religious, and he proceeds to sketch the positive ideal for which they are to strive:

'It is an obligation of our Profession to demand no comfort in this life, no glory; to turn away our face from the pleasures of the world; to prepare our soul for the promised rewards of eternity; to rejoice in obedience and renunciation, zealously to cultivate poverty, and not only to divest ourselves of our property, but to uproot from our hearts the very desire for property. Our obligation makes it incumbent on us to possess nothing; but it is in desiring nothing that virtue lies.'[2]

As with Eucherius, so with Faustus, the little community on the tiny island constantly suggests the metaphor of the crew of a vessel which, after tossing in the storm, has come safely into port. But it must not be supposed that it is therefore safe. It needs constant care and baling by the *situla* or else it will flounder, owing to the water seeping in through the crevices. So the brethren who have 'come to port in the monastery', must exercise constant watchfulness, constant obedience, constant humility and minute scrutiny of the soul. It is not only serious offences which must be carefully avoided. Some there are, who, because they have left the world and embraced the religious life, enjoy too great a feeling of security. To them God gives the choice, either to remain cold in the world or zealous in the monastery; but those who have withdrawn from the world and are giving way to indifference and negligence will be rejected by the Lord.

'Again and again I call upon you and I admonish you, my brothers, that you take pains to practise obedience and humility and charity, not only towards your seniors and equals, but also to your juniors ... Do not grumble ... or disparage ... or cherish anger in your hearts', and he concludes his 'Second Sermon to the Monks' with a special request that 'because God

[1] ibid., col. 1058.   [2] *Sermo* XXIII, *Ad Monachos* I (ed. Engelbrecht).

has thought fit to gather you in a place of peace and tranquillity, you will pray to God the more fervently for us who are buffeted by the tempests and endless waves of our world, so that we who have not been held worthy that this glory should be granted us, may nevertheless be granted pardon for our sins through your prayers.'[1]

These sermons were probably delivered by Faustus to the monks of Lérins on his visits from Riez, and one realizes even today how his compelling seriousness and deep concern for the welfare of his former monastery must have gripped his hearers, coming among them as he did from the busy life and afflicted world of the mainland to the peace of his old home. The fervour without fanaticism, the spiritual vigilance combined with a lively personal sense of the difficulties and temptations of monastic life, give force to his eloquence. His sermons, like those of Caesarius of Arles, keep in close touch with reality by simple, concrete illustrations from daily life, such as the farmer, displeased with the yield of his little acre; the baler who must constantly ply his *situla* lest the ship founder; the *fibula* which must be applied early to a wound, so as not to allow time for festering; the ship which after the buffeting of the storm now rides safely at anchor; the house-cleaning and decorating which takes place in the residence of a great man before his own or his son's birthday festivities.[2]

Sidonius emphasizes Faustus's mastery of philosophic thought, and a modern writer[3] has commented on his rigorous asceticism, and grave, philosophical cast of mind. His letters have not yet been fully collected and identified; but those which we possess[4] are of the highest value, not only for their lofty tone and the brilliance of the thought, but also for the light which they throw on the difficult and disturbed life of an ecclesiastic during the Visigothic Invasion and on this early obscure period of the Gaulish Church. A particularly interesting example is the letter 'To Rusticus, Bishop of Narbonne', in which Dom G. Morin recognized the hand of Faustus while still a monk of Lérins,

---

[1] *Sermo* XXIV (*ad Monachos* II).

[2] On the growing tendency to greater simplicity of diction in sermons, see H. G. J. Beck, *Pastoral Care of Souls*, p. 264.

[3] Hugh Williams, *Christianity in Early Britain* (Oxford, 1912), p. 420.

[4] See Engelbrecht, op. cit., p. 161 ff.; cf. Caspari, *Briefe, Abhandlungen und Predigten* (1891), p. 418 ff.

and before he had become abbot of the monastery.[1] The letter is
written about 427 to the young Bishop of Narbonne, newly consecrated in succession to Hilary, and is an answer to his request
for a treatise explaining the mystery of the hierarchy and other
ecclesiastical matters. It contains a striking and lofty exposition
of the high calling and rights of the presbyter, and seems to suggest that Faustus shared in some measure the feeling of Sulpicius
that the bishops arrogated too much to themselves, spiritually,
financially, and in matters of procedure.[2]

Among the interesting allusions to contemporary usages of
the Gallican Church, the letter contains a list of the seven orders
which constitute the ecclesiastical hierarchy. Dom Morin
pointed out that the list differs in some important respects[3]
from the Roman usage and from that contained in the *Statuta
Ecclesiae Antiqua*,[4] drawn up in the privilege of Arles probably in
the late fifth century[5] or about the beginning of the sixth, which
seems to correspond with the custom in use in the Roman
Church.[6] On the other hand, Faustus's list corresponds in
general to a list found in the *Chronicon antiquissimum* composed in
Great Britain,[7] which ends with the Emperor Justin in 578.[8] If,
then, the usage of the *Statuta Ecclesiae Antiqua* represents, as
Duchesne says, the 'Gallican' usage, it is evidently later than
that indicated in the letter to Rusticus and the 'British Chronicle' a consideration which suggests the early progress of
Roman influence on the more ancient ritual of southern Gaul,
of which Faustus's letter and the 'British Chronicle' furnish
early evidence.

The implications are, incidentally, important for the Celtic
Church. We find the word *fossor* used in the *Life of St Cadoc*,
which, though a text of the eleventh century, is believed on

[1] *Revue Bénédictine*, Vol. VIII (1891), p. 97 ff.
[2] op. cit., p. 101. Cf. also p. 102, where Morin suggests that this attitude of
Faustus towards bishops may well account for his clash with Bishop Theodore of
Fréjus (see Tillemont, Vol. XV, 406–8).
[3] e.g. in the inclusion of *fossarii* and *ostiarii*, and the omission of acolytes and
exorcists.
[4] Migne, *P.L.*, Vol. LVI, col. 887; Dom. G. Morin, *Sancti Caesarii Arelatensis*, Vol.
II, p. 95 f.
[5] Morin says early in the sixth century. See, however, Beck, *The Pastoral Care of
Souls*, p. 44 f.
[6] For this, see the *Documenta Juris Canonici Veteris* (Migne, *P.L.*, Vol. LVI, col.
587 f.).
[7] 'Precisely in Faustus's native land' (Morin, loc. cit.).
[8] Migne, *P.L.*, Vol. XCIV, col. 1161 ff.

other grounds to contain early material. Rusticus seems to have belonged to the Church of Marseilles, for he is associated in the famous inscription of Narbonne with both Bishop Venerius and the Church of Marseilles (*episcopi Venerii socius in monasterio; compresbyter ecclesiae Massiliensis*). Dom Morin points out[1] that it is under this same Venerius and his successor, Eustachius, that Museus, also a priest of Marseilles, drew up the liturgical collections referred to by Gennadius (ch. 80).

'Nous sommes donc', says Morin, 'dans un des principaux foyers où s'est élaborée la liturgie gallicane.'

And it would seem that the early British Church followed the usages, not of the Gallican Church of the *Statuta Ecclesiae Antiqua* of Leo the Great, but the earlier ones of the period of Rusticus, Venerius, and Faustus.

The theological writings of Faustus did not meet with much disapprobation in his own day. Indeed the most prominent writers of southern Gaul for the most part held the same views,[2] in particular the contemporary scholar Gennadius (ch. 99).[3] Little is known of Gennadius personally. He is thought to have died in 496. Of the list of his own works which he gives us, a few only have survived; but he must have been a highly educated and enlightened man, for he seems to have known Greek well, and to have translated part of the work of Evagrius of Pontus,[4] and to have retranslated the *Centum Sententiae*, correcting the old translation of Rufinus. He was equally well informed in the Greek writings of contemporary controversy. In particular his work, *De Viris Illustribus*, to which constant reference has been made above, is of great importance. It is a continuation of the work of St Jerome, and is in effect an international 'Dictionary of Christian Biography' relating to the author's own times, and so serves as an invaluable gazetteer of contemporary notable men. Many of the people and their works cited are personally known to the author, and some of them, e.g. Salvian and Faustus, were still alive while Gennadius was writing.[5]

It is clear that Gennadius himself held 'semi-Pelagian'

[1] Op. cit., p. 98, n. 6.   [2] See Harnack, op. cit., Vol. V, p. 254, footnote. 4.
[3] The text of Gennadius is edited by E. C. Richardson, *Hieronymus Liber de viris inlustribus – Gennadius Liber de viris inlustribus* (Leipzig, 1896); translated by the same scholar, *Jerome and Gennadius, Lives of Illustrious Men* (in the series 'Nicene and Post-Nicene Fathers', Vol. III, Oxford and New York, 1892, p. 349 ff.).
[4] For particulars, see Gennadius, cap. 11.
[5] Courcelle, op. cit., p. 221 f.

views. Apart from his *Liber Ecclesiasticorum Dogmatum* which was probably composed in a semi-Pelagian milieu,[1] traces of the same attitude can be seen in his articles on John Cassian, Hilary of Arles, St Augustine, Prosper of Aquitaine, and others of the period.[2] In particular we have found him speaking in terms of high praise of Faustus as 'a man very devoted to holy Scripture', and of his work 'On the Grace of God' as 'outstanding' (*egregius*). He assures us that 'this excellent teacher is believed in and approved,'[3] while at the same time he accuses Prosper of having regarded as injurious matters in the works of Cassian which the Church of God finds sound.[4]

The controversy was not yet wholly over, however, and some famous names are numbered among those who wrote against Faustus's views. Of these the most important and interesting is Claudianus Mamertus,[5] a priest of the Church of Vienne, who died 473–4. Of him Sidonius has left us one of his most illuminating pictures. He was the elder brother of St Mamertus, the Bishop of Vienne, who introduced the Rogations in a time of public adversity, which were afterwards adopted by Sidonius at Clermont when the siege was at its height. He was also a disciple of St Augustine and a friend of Salvian, who dedicated to him his work on *Ecclesiastes*. The *De Statu Animae*, the most important work[6] of Claudianus Mamertus, was written c. 470 to combat Faustus's view that the soul was corporeal. The work is dedicated to Sidonius, who held both the book and the author in high honour,[7] as we see both from his letter to Mamertus himself,[8] and from the very flattering panegyric on him after his death, contained in a letter (c. 474) addressed to Mamertus's nephew, Petreius.[9]

What Sidonius especially admired in the work of Mamertus was, of course, his wide knowledge of classical writers, and his

---

[1] See Bardenhewer, *Patrology*, p. 609.
[2] ibid.; and cf. Harnack, loc. cit.
[3] Gennadius, cap. 86. [4] ibid., ch. 85.
[5] For a brief general account see E. Amann, s.v. in the *Dictionnaire de Théologie Catholique* and the references to critical works there cited.
[6] A. Engelbrecht has published a critical edition of his works, *Claudiani Mamerti Opera* (Vienna, 1885).
[7] Tillemont points out somewhat maliciously (Vol. XVI, p. 245) that Sidonius praises Mamertus and his scholarship in this work as highly as he has praised Mamertus' adversary, Faustus. See Sidonius, *Ep.* IV, 3.
[8] Sidonius, *Ep.* IV, 11.
[9] ibid., *Ep.* IV, 3.

lucid and pure Latin style,[1] and he declared him a master alike
in classical Greek and Latin, and also in Christian learning.[2] In
a letter to his friend Nymphidius he refers to him as 'the most
accomplished of the Christian philosophers, and the most
learned among men'.[3] Of the *De Statu Animae* he exclaims in a
letter to Mamertus himself:

'Great God, what a great and wonderful work it is, abstruse
in subject matter, yet lucid in exposition.'

The work is, in fact, very learned for its time, and is regarded,
despite some defects, as fully meriting the praise of Sidonius.[4]
Gennadius, who held views opposed to those of Mamertus, calls
him 'vir ad loquendum artifex et ad disputandum subtilis (ch. 83).

The letters of Sidonius – both those written to Claudianus
Mamertus himself, and the one addressed to Mamertus's nephew
after his uncle's death – present us with a picture of Mamertus
which throws light on the more cultivated Christians of southern
Gaul at this time. He is described as a philosopher all his days
without prejudice to his Christian belief, one who was only distinguished from his friends of the Platonic school by his faith,
and by his wearing ordinary dress – 'for he did not let his hair
and beard grow long, and would sometimes make fun of the
philosopher's mantle and staff, and sometimes execrate it'.[5] He
seems to have been a leading man in the intellectual life of
Vienne, and Sidonius describes how he himself and a number of
others used to visit him for the pleasure of hearing him talk.
Mamertus used to discourse to them, nominating one of them as
spokesman, and questioning and arguing with each in turn – in
fact, as we should say today, conducting a perfect classical
seminar. With such a love of knowledge and gift for teaching it
is hardly to be wondered at that in a letter addressed to the
rhetorician Sapaudus[6] of his own city, Mamertus refers regret-
fully to the lack of intellectual curiosity among his contemporaries.[7]

---

[1] On the Latin style of Claudianus Mamertus, see A. Loyen, *Sidoine Apollinaire et
l'Esprit précieux en Gaule* (Paris, 1943), Appendix III, p. 174 ff., and the references
there cited.

[2] Sidonius, *Letters, Ep.* IV, 11.

[3] *Ep.* V, 2.

[4] See e.g. Bardenhewer, *Patrology*, p. 521; cf. de Labriolle, p. 472.

[5] Sidonius, *Ep.* IV, 11.

[6] For Sapaudus of Vienne, see Pauly-Wissowa, *Real-lexikon*, s.v.

[7] For the text of Mamertus's letter, see the *Epist. ad Sapaudum*, ed. Engelbrecht,
p. 203, n. 1; also Migne, *P.L.*, Vol. LIII, col. 783.

Yet as a teacher his success was due in no small measure to his unpretentious modesty, combined with a dignified simplicity of bearing and a quiet firmness. His gentle tolerance of those less intellectually gifted inspired even the dullest and most backward among his audience with confidence. Such kindly sympathy, combined with a powerful intellect and knowledge which was both profound and wide, make up the ideal equipment of a teacher of young men, and the passage in which Sidonius describes[1] their informal sittings – a passage clear cut and sharp in detail as a cameo or gem – gives us a delightful glimpse of a little provincial fifth-century academy in action.

But in addition to his scholarly interests Mamertus was a busy presbyter, 'poor in this world's goods', but charitable and kindly, and assiduous in his pastoral duties. He is described as a great strength and support to his brother, the Bishop of Vienne, to whom he seems to have acted in the capacity of private chaplain and secretary, and for whom he is said to have felt the deepest affection. The bishop in his turn regarded Mamertus with boundless admiration, knowing that he had in him 'a counsellor in all questions under dispute, a representative in his churches, an agent in business matters, a steward on his estates, a registrar of all dues, a colleague in his reading, an interpreter in matters of exposition, an attendant on his circuits'.[2]

He is even said to have been 'a precentor and leader of the Psalms', and to have 'taught the trained groups of singers to chant before the altar'. We cannot doubt the truth of Sidonius's claim that he eased his brother's shoulder of the bishop's burden, for while the bishop held the episcopal rank it was he, a priest in the second Order of the Church, who did the work. Mamertus was, in fact, a priest such as any period might well be proud of, but few periods could boast. Sidonius has done us a signal service in leaving us this delightful description of the relationship of the two brothers, and so instructive an inventory of the scope and activities of a bishop's presbyter. The fifth century has no finer example of the rare fusion of classical learning and Christian integrity.

Of the genuine familiarity of Mamertus himself with Greek philosophy and the Greek language there can be no doubt. This

[1] *Ep.* IV, 11.   [2] Sidonius, *Ep.* IV, 11.

o

shows itself most fully in his *De Statu Animae*, in which he makes allusion to Plato's theory of ideas, to the scepticism of the New Academy, to the atomic doctrine of Epicurus. He has studied dialectic and read the *Categories* of Aristotle – possibly, however, in a Latin version. In order to combat the theory of Faustus of Riez on the corporeal nature of the soul (cf. p. 200) he makes reference to the authority of pagan philosophers, the doctors of the Church, and Holy Scripture. Especially he makes precise reference, among pagan philosophers, to Plato and the Pythagoreans.[1] In particular in his refutation of the corporeality of the soul his debt to the *De Regressu* of Porphyry is especially heavy.[2] He makes incidental reference to Plautus, Cato, Varro, Cicero, etc. But he was also conversant with the leading Christian writers, Gregory Nazianzen, Ambrose, Augustine, and Eucherius of Lyons.

The letter written by Mamertus to Sapaudus already cited shows the prestige which Greek learning still held in Gaul. Greece, declares Mamertus, teaches all the arts and all discipline; its culture is expanded throughout the whole world.[3] Its thinkers have explored physics and metaphysics.[4] It is in Greece that Cicero received his instruction. Plato has united the Greek wisdom of Socrates to that of Egypt, the Hindus, and the Pythagoreans;[5] and he declares that the modern epoch, in which classical education is neglected, and the Romans dare no longer speak Latin, is a period of decadence. It is interesting to note that the writer attributes to Sapaudus a first-hand knowledge of the best authors, and that he credits him with having imbued the pupils in his school with Greek discipline, and having nourished them with Attic honey.[6] Even making allowance for some rhetorical element, such praise from Mamertus would have been merely mockery had Sapaudus not been outstanding among his contemporaries in his knowledge and appreciation of Greek.[7] It shows, moreover, beyond any doubt, where Mamertus's own tastes lay.

---

[1] For references, see Courcelle, op. cit., p. 224 f.

[2] ibid., p. 232 f. Cf. also A. Amann, *Dictionnaire de Théologie Catholique*, s.v. *Mamert Claudien*.

[3] *Epist. ad Sapaudum*, ed. Engelbrecht, p. 203, l. 1.

[4] ibid., p. 203, l. 7.   [5] ibid., p. 204, ll. 6–14.

[6] ibid., p. 205, l. 5 ff.

[7] Sapaudus is also warmly praised as a rhetorician in a letter addressed to him by Sidonius Apollinaris (*Ep.* V, 10).

It is probable that a number of elements have gone to the revived cultivation of Greek culture and the Greek language in southern Gaul at this late date. The town of Narbonne in particular was an active and varied intellectual centre, the most brilliant in Gaul, and dominated by poets. This is to be attributed in a large measure to its cosmopolitan society, recruited from Africa and Italy, and from countries farther to the east.[1] Again, it may well be that in southern Gaul the old Greek culture amalgamated in some measure with the newer currents of Greek learning and Greek thought introduced from the great North African cities, as well as from Alexandria and the Levant. We can hardly doubt, moreover, that the quickening of the intellectual life of Provence, as that of ancient Ireland, was indebted in some measure to the number of bishops, priests, and other learned men who poured in from all parts of Gaul occupied by the Barbarians.[2] Whatever the causes which lie behind this late flowering of Greek learning in and around Marseilles, the intellectual activity of the cities of south-eastern Gaul on the eve of the withdrawal of the Roman civil service and the completion of the Barbarian Occupation has justly been called 'the Little Renaissance'.

[1] See A. Loyen, *Sidoine Apollinaire et l'Esprit précieux en Gaule* (Paris, 1943), p. 85 f.
[2] For examples, see Scott Holmes, *The Christian Church in Gaul*, p. 292 f., and the references there cited.

CHAPTER VIII

John Cassian

WHILE the little island monastery of Lérins had been developing rapidly as a spiritual retreat which produced original thinkers, and educated great men, the mainland in and around Marseilles had also been developing as an important monastic centre, and a hive of intellectual activity and religious thought. The monastery of St Victor in the vicinity of Marseilles claims at least one writer of first importance. The exact date of the foundation and the name of its founder are not absolutely certain.[1] When the monastery first comes before our notice it was already the home of the famous monk and writer John Cassian, all of whose literary work seems to have been composed here.

The monastic ideal of Marseilles was very different from that of Lérins, if we may judge by the writings of Cassian. Here spiritual development and ascetic discipline are emphasized rather than intellectual activity. We have seen that Eucherius would have preferred to go to Egypt rather than to Lérins for a rigorous ascetic training, and it was with reluctance that he adopted the alternative plan of putting himself under the discipline of Lérins, where he and his sons were caught up by the intellectual vigour of the place. This difference of aim in the two foundations is perhaps itself enough to account for the fact that the monastery of St Victor at Marseilles produced few great writers in the fifth century except Cassian and possibly Salvian.

So far we have little information about the organization of any Western cenobitic community and no actual written monastic 'rule' has come down to us. Probably none existed in written form. We have, however, from the pen of John Cassian an ideal picture of a monastic foundation of his own day, as he conceived it. This is the subject of his earliest work,[2] known by the title of the *Twelve Books of the Institutes of the Coenobia*, com-

---

[1] But see Gennadius, cap. 52.
[2] The works of Cassian are edited in Migne, *P.L.*, Vol. XLIX, col. 53; and by M. Petschenig, *Johannes Cassiani Opera* (*Corpus Scriptorum Ecclesiasticorum Latinorum*, Vol. XVII, Vienna, 1888); English translation by E. C. S. Gibson, Oxford, 1894.

posed between 419 and 426. The work is dedicated to Bishop
Castor of Apta Julia near Marseilles, at whose request it was
composed, and it is intended to guide Castor in the foundation
of a monastic institution which he was projecting in his own
diocese, where we are expressly told none existed as yet. The
Institutes is a composite picture, based in the main, so Cassian
claims, on his first-hand experience of monastic life in Syria and
Egypt, modified, as he tells us, by what he regards as necessary
changes incidental to the different conditions of life in Gaul.
The work is therefore especially valuable as offering the closest
approximation available to us of the material conditions, the
discipline, and the general spiritual training adopted in the
formative period of the most important monastic institutions of
southern Gaul. And it has a special interest for our own islands,
which perhaps drew and reinforced their early monastic institutions to some extent from these great centres.

Cassian seems to have been peculiarly well qualified by personal experience for his task. His birth place is uncertain, but
he was probably born in one of the Roman provinces of the
Balkans,[1] very likely c. 360. He had received a good classical
education, and, like St Jerome and St Paulinus of Nola, he
seems to have been too deeply versed in ancient poetry to
free himself easily from its charm. In his second work, the
Collationes ('Conferences'),[2] he expresses himself explicitly on
this point:

'I do not doubt that a special hindrance to salvation is added

[1] Gennadius (*Catalogus*, ch. 62) refers to him as *Cassianus natione Scytha*, which has
been commonly interpreted as having reference to Scythia; but the excellence of
Cassian's education, and the freedom of his style from barbarisms, has led to some
doubt as to the correctness of Gennadius's statement, or at least to its having reference to Scythia. Gennadius himself, on the other hand, wrote at Marseilles c. 495,
and is in general a careful writer, and one must hesitate to ignore his authority.
The suggestion has been made that *Scytha* may refer, not to *Scythia*, but to the
desert of *Scete* or *Scitis* in Egypt, where Cassian seems to have spent some years.
E. C. S. Gibson, the translator of Cassian's works (ed. cit.) gives some reason for
regarding him as a native of Provence. See the *Prolegomena* to his translation, and
also the references there cited. For further specialized discussions of the problem,
see the references cited by P. Courcelle, *Les Lettres Grecques en Occident* (Paris, 1943),
p. 212, n. 4. Courcelle himself holds that *Scytha* means 'of *Scythia Minor*', and that,
while Greek was not Cassian's native tongue, he spoke it fluently. The history of the
discussion of Cassian's birthplace is related at length by O. Chadwick, *John Cassian*
(Cambridge, 1950), Appendix B, p. 190 ff. Chadwick himself concludes that we
may probably accept the statement of Gennadius, who was a fellow-citizen of
Cassian, and regard Cassian's original home as probably in a Roman province of
the Balkans.
[2] Migne, *P.L.*, Vol. XLIX, col. 477.

by that knowledge of literature which I seem to have in some slight degree attained, in which the perseverance of my teacher or my own application to continual reading has so reduced me that now my mind is corrupted with those songs of the poets, and, even at prayer time, it is dwelling on those silly fables; and the stories of battles with which it was infected in the earliest lessons of childhood; and when I am singing psalms or begging forgiveness of sins, either some unsuitable recollection of the poems obtrudes itself, or the picture of heroes in battle floats before my eyes, and a vision of such phantoms is always tricking me and will not leave my soul free to seek spiritual apprehension of things above.'[1]

This passage, and the rarity with which Cassian introduces himself personally as a speaker in the discussions, leads one to suppose that it is also Cassian who is personally referred to by Abbot Nesteros in a passage shortly before. Here, after giving a special warning to Cassian – in view of his youth – to keep a watch on his tongue, Nesteros warns him against following the example of those who 'have attained skill in dialectic and fluency in speech', and 'can discourse elegantly and at length on whatever they choose', adding that 'a facile utterance and graceful speech' are no guarantee of the power to penetrate into spiritual mysteries. There can be no doubt that the passage has reference to the current type of classical education in the schools of rhetoric, which Abbot Nesteros attributes to Cassian.

Elsewhere also in his writings he makes allusion to Latin writers, notably in his *Treatise on the Incarnation against Nestorius*, where he quotes (VI, ix) from Persius (*Satire* III, 116), and (VI, x) from Cicero (*In Verr. Act.* II, Book I, xv 40). It is, of course, easy to over-rate the significance of single quotations, which may always have been learnt by hearsay and do not necessarily imply any wide first-hand acquaintance with an author. But Cassian's work shows itself throughout to be that of a man of polite education, and well acquainted with Greek authors, both classical and contemporary.[2] Other passages show acquaintance with Greek stories.[3]

Cassian states that, as a young man, he entered a monastery

---

[1] *Conferences*, II, xiv, 12.
[2] The evidence is cited with some fullness by Courcelle, op. cit., p. 212 f.
[3] See, e.g. the stories which he cites (from an unknown source) of Socrates and Diogenes, *Conferences*, II, xiii, 5.

at Jerusalem[1] with his friend Germanus, whom he came to regard as a brother; but after some years of training the two men obtained permission to travel among the Desert Fathers of Egypt in order to improve their discipline in the perfect life. Some three years would seem, according to the narrative, to have passed thus in the monastic settlements in the neighbourhood of the Nile Delta, and after a brief return to the monastery at Bethlehem in fulfilment of a promise of 'a speedy return' – already perhaps too long delayed – the two friends returned to settle in Egypt for a protracted stay. It is probable that it was during this second period in Egypt that they visited the monasteries of Nitria and Scete. It does not appear likely that they visited the Thebaïd, for when they speak of the south it is only by hearsay.[2] The two visits to Egypt seem to have taken place between 380 and 400.

The account of this Egyptian sojourn forms the subject of Cassian's second work, the *Collationes* ('Conferences'). This work was not published till many years later, however, probably between 426 and 428,[3] when Cassian had been long settled in Marseilles and had already written the *Institutes*. In the interval, between his second sojourn in Egypt and his final settlement in Marseilles, he had, together with his friend Germanus, visited Constantinople (c. 400), where he had become acquainted with St Chrysostom,[4] who made a lasting impression on his theological views.[5]

During Cassian's sojourn in Constantinople he was ordained deacon, perhaps by St Chrysostom himself. Germanus was already a presbyter. After Cassian's sojourn in Constantinople we find him in Rome c. 405 on an embassy to enlist the support of Pope Innocent I for St Chrysostom, and he may have been ordained priest in Rome by Pope Innocent himself; but more probably by Proculus, Bishop of Marseilles.[6] The date of his settlement in Marseilles is not certainly known, but it is stated

[1] This cannot be the famous monastery of St Jerome, since Jerome only settled in Bethlehem late in 386. See Gibson, op. cit., p. 184, n. 8.

[2] On this subject the reader may refer to O. Chadwick, op. cit., p. 18, n. 1.

[3] According to de Labriolle it was finished in 429.

[4] See Jacquin, *Revue d'Histoire ecclésiastique*, Vol. V (1904), p. 279; cf. Gibson op. cit. p. 188; O. Chadwick, op. cit., p. 37 ff. Chadwick points out that Cassian can only have known St Chrysostom for three or four years.

[5] For a discussion of this subject, see O. Chadwick, loc. cit.

[6] See Chadwick, op. cit., p. 41.

by Gennadius (cap. 62) that he founded in Marseilles two monasteries, one for men and another for women.

In any case Cassian's early close association with the former is certain. His latest work, according to the testimony of Gennadius (ch. 61), was his 'Treatise on the Incarnation', composed against Nestorius in 430 at the request of Leo, who was at that time Archdeacon of Rome, but who became later Pope Leo the Great. Cassian himself probably died not long after the completion of Prosper's *Contra Nestorium*. The year of his death is believed to have been 433 or shortly afterwards.

The *Institutes*, or, to give it the title under which it is today generally known (cf. Cassian's Preface), 'The Twelve Books on the Institutes of the Monasteries and the Remedies for the eight Principal Faults', is composed in the form of injunctions delivered by the writer to monks living in a *coenobium* or organized community under an acknowledged spiritual master or abbot. It is customary to refer to Cassian's rule as approximating to that established by Pachomius c. 305–10 in the great monasteries – traditionally stated to have been the first of their kind – at Pabau, Tabennisi in the Thebaïd, and elsewhere in Upper Egypt. We have what claims to be a summary of the Pachomian rule, and a detailed picture of their organization and life in the *Lausiac History*, by the monk Palladius, in which a description of these monasteries is given.[1]

The foundations attributed to Pachomius[2] are far larger and more elaborate in their organization than anything in the West, and bear some relationship to a military system and military discipline adapted to a situation which required a way of life suited to large numbers of men – or alternatively of women – in varying stages of spiritual development and of varying vocations. It does not appear that the communities of northern Egypt had ever adopted such a system,[3] and it is un-

[1] The best English edition is *The Lausiac History of Palladius*, edited together with introductory and comparative matter by Dom Cuthbert Butler (Cambridge, 1898). The work of Palladius is translated by W. K. Lowther Clarke (London, 1918). Palladius was born in 367 and went to Alexandria in 388, and lived for about ten years in the Egyptian desert. In 420 he wrote an account of the Desert Fathers of Egypt, known as the *Lausiac History*, so-called from its dedication to Lausus, a chamberlain at the Court of Theodosius II. Cf. further p. 144 above.

[2] For a detailed picture of Pachomius and his monasteries and nunneries, see p. 112 ff. of the work by Dom Cuthbert Butler cited above.

[3] For a brief discussion of Egyptian monachism, with up-to-date references, see Chadwick, op. cit., p. 13 ff.

likely that the Pachomian system served as a direct model to Cassian.

Throughout the *Institutes* the writer claims to base his thesis on the practices and teaching of the monks of the Egyptian delta and of the deserts of Nitria and Scete, to whom he refers constantly as authorities; but he permits limited modifications to suit the climate and custom of Gaul.[1] The work is divided into *Twelve Books* of which the first lays down minute instructions as to the dress of the monks; the second and third relate to the canonical system of the prayers and psalms, and to the discipline associated with their observance, and with the order of monastic life generally; the fourth to monastic rules; while the remainder are devoted to a consideration of the principal temptations and difficulties to which the monks are subject in their spiritual life, together with advice and injunctions as to how these may be overcome. The *Institutes* is intended to offer guidance primarily for the 'outer' man, and the conduct of life for individual and community in the *coenobium*. In Book II, ch. ix Cassian expresses his intention of writing the *Conferences* later, in which he proposes to speak of 'the training of the inner man and the perfection of the heart, and the life and doctrine of the anchorites', the latter chiefly such as, having first perfected themselves in the obedience and discipline of the *coenobium*, have received the permission of their seniors to retire to solitary cells for greater quiet and privacy for the practice of the contemplative life.

In the *Conferences*, at the completion of the 'Conference of Abbot Piamun', Cassian speaks of the desire instilled into the heart of Germanus and himself by Abbot Piamun for 'promotion from the primary schools of the *coenobium* to the second standard of the anchorites' life. For it was under his tuition that we were first initiated into the life of a solitary, the fuller knowledge of which we afterwards acquired in Scete.'[2]

Further, in the *Conferences* also Cassian introduces us to a number of monks who have advanced through the *coenobium* to this stage. Such men, desiring greater solitude than community life affords, obtain permission from their Superior to withdraw farther into the desert to live as solitaries, though not independ-

[1] See, e.g. I, x; II, xi.
[2] *Conferences*, III, xviii, 16.

ently of the *coenobium*, with which they still retain their close connection, and to which they return, generally – but not invariably – twice a week, on Saturdays and Sundays, to attend divine service in the monastic church. The majority of the men who thus become anchorites appear to embrace this manner of life as a permanency; but they are under no obligation to do so, and we hear of some of the holiest who have found, after a period of life as a solitary, that life in the community is more conducive to spiritual discipline, and have returned to live in the *coenobium*. The advantages and drawbacks of both systems are discussed with admirable frankness in the *Conferences*. This part of the monastic experience has a special interest for us because a similar system undoubtedly prevailed in our own country, where the 'desert places' or 'retreats of the martyrs' have left their imprint on our maps in such terms as *Diserth, Dysart* (L. *Desertum*), and *Merthyr* (L. *Martyrium*).

The Preface to the *Institutes* is a particularly enlightened document. It shows Cassian singularly free from bigotry and superstition, and, what is more remarkable, from credulity. We cannot help suspecting that it is in some measure a protest against the popularity of stories of marvels which, first in the *Life of St Antony*, and later in that of St Martin, had brought the fashion to the West, partly as the heir, partly as the rival to the growth of fiction which had developed in the late Greek novel; partly again as the natural result of the extensive and ever increasing influence of Oriental tradition introduced into the West by Christianity. Such things, in the opinion of Cassian, are no aid to the training for the perfect life. Addressing Bishop Castor he expresses himself as follows:

'Since, then, you wish the institutions of the East, and especially of Egypt, to be established in your province, which has no cenobitic foundations . . . I will set these matters forth as for a newly founded monastery and for men genuinely athirst for instruction. Frankly I will not seek to weave a tale of God's miracles and signs, although we have not only heard of a great number of astounding ones through our elders, but have even witnessed their fulfilment before our eyes; still I shall omit all these things which bring to the readers merely wonder, and nothing more for instruction in the perfect life, and I shall do my best with God's help to set forth faithfully only their institu-

tions and the rules of their monasteries . . . since my proposal is
to say a few words, not about God's miracles, but about how to
improve our character, and the attainment of the perfect life. . .
Where I find that anything in the rule of the Egyptians is impossible, or hard or difficult in this country, because of the
severity of our climate, or owing to some obstacle or diversity
of our customs, I shall modify it in some measure with the
customs of the monasteries which are followed throughout
Pontus and Mesopotamia.'

The injunctions of the *Institutes* are characterized by moderation and good sense, and the rigours of the life are modified by
discretion in their application. Manual work and absolute
poverty are enjoined on all as the first necessity, but the rule of
daily life is adapted according to the capacity of the individual
monk. Too rigorous an asceticism is deprecated. A monk is enjoined to adhere rigidly to the prescribed meals if he hopes
to proceed and to engage in inner conflicts.[1] The same rule
cannot, it is stated, be laid down for everybody with regard
to fasting.[2] Again, we notice how carefully graded are the
steps in spiritual discipline.[3] Thus, in V, xvi, monks are enjoined how, like the Olympic athletes, they should yet refrain
from spiritual conflicts until they have first won battles over the
flesh. At the same time they are warned (V, x) that abstinence
from food is not in itself sufficient to preserve purity of heart
and body. The figure of athletes is a favourite one in this period
as applied to the monks and ascetics, and is used also by Palladius and other writers. Cassian uses it constantly.[4]

To illustrate the need of manual labour Cassian tells a story
of a certain abbot Simeon,[5] who had come to live among the
brethren, but who was ignorant of Greek, and also unable to
turn his hand to any of the occupations customary among
them. He declared that the only thing he could do of any value
was to write a good hand, should anyone in Egypt want to use
a Latin book. One of the elders, anxious to give him employ-
ment, feigned to have need of just such a book.

'This is God's doing, for I had been looking for someone to

[1] V, xx. [2] V, v.
[3] In this system of ascetic discipline we now know that Cassian is following the teaching of Evagrius. See p. 236.
[4] *Institutes*, X, v; V, xii, xvii ff., and *passim*.
[5] V, xxxix.

write out for me the *Apostolus* in Latin; for I have a brother who is doing compulsory military service, and is a good Latin scholar, and I want to send him something from the Holy Scriptures to read for his edification.'

Thereupon, as an act of charity, but under the guise of a 'matter of business' the Superior brought to Abbot Simeon everything that he could want 'for a whole year', and also 'parchment and everything requisite for writing'. Eventually Simeon received the manuscript 'which was of no use or value – since in that region they were all completely ignorant of this language – except that which was gained from this device and costly expenditure; for the one without embarrassment or confusion obtained the nourishment necessary to support life in exchange for his work and labour, and the other fulfilled his holy act of charity as if it were a debt he owed.'

The story has much to teach us – of the insistent need of occupation for the solitary, and of bread-winning for all, with no exceptions; of the copying of books in the desert,[1] and the use of parchment, etc. (*membranas et utensilea*); of 'good Latin scholars' impressed into military service, and dependent on the kindness of relatives for something to read. Perhaps, too, it helps to throw light on the tendency of the sons of Roman military families to join the ranks of the monks, as St Martin, and his disciple Victor, St Januarius of Naples, St Victricius of Rouen, Pachomius himself, and many another had done.

It is a noticeable feature of the *Institutes* that the value of community life and discipline is stressed far more than that of the eremitical, and we hear relatively little praise for the cultivation of extreme austerities. Simple utility is the aim in dress, whereas a cloak of goat's hair is 'utterly disapproved of' as being too conspicuous and calculated to call attention to itself, and so minister to vanity and pride.[2] It is probably the recent development in organized monasticism in Egypt, and its democratic adaptation to the capacities of a large number of people, which caused Cassian to prefer it to the discipline of the Syrian monasteries, where individualism and extreme asceticism had always

---

[1] This anecdote, and the postal system which brought letters to the monks, as well as much in the actual discourse of the monks themselves, must force us to qualify the phrase 'des moines illettrés du désert' used by Courcelle, op. cit., p. 216.

[2] *Institutes*, I, ii.

been more developed. The contrast is implied in Book II, ch. iii, where the author lays it down that:

'Everywhere throughout Egypt and the Thebaïd, where monasteries are not founded haphazard according to the whims of each individual who renounces the world, but through the succession and traditions of the fathers . . . no one is allowed to assume authority over the assembly of the brethren, or even over himself, before he has . . . come to recognize that he is not even his own master and has no authority over himself. For one who renounces the world . . . must seek a dwelling place in a *coenobium*.'

And a little before this:

'Whatever is claimed by one or a few in a community of religious, and is not held in common by the whole body of the brethren, is either superfluous or vain, and therefore to be considered harmful.'[1]

It will be seen that Cassian has the balanced and realistic outlook which a classical education seldom fails to give. To the same source we may also trace his attitude towards the burning religious questions of the day, perhaps the most important being the Pelagian controversy discussed more fully in the preceding chapter. Cassian shared with other writers of southern Gaul, notably those of Lérins, an independent attitude towards both the great protagonists in this controversy, rejecting the extreme views of St Augustine with regard to the divine predestination of the human soul, but at the same time deprecating the claim attributed to Pelagius by his enemies, that man was capable of living a sinless life without divine aid.

Cassian's views on the questions of (divine) 'Grace' and (human) 'Free-Will' are developed more frankly in the *Conferences*, one important chapter of which is generally cited as embodying Cassian's view on this question. We shall discuss this subject presently. But there can be no doubt that a deeply serious preoccupation with the controversy between Augustine and the Pelagians on the subject of the necessity of divine Grace for all human endeavour towards perfection underlies the whole of the *Institutes* also, and may well have been the principal incentive to the composition of this work. The author throughout stresses the value of discipline and effort, and of the cenobitic

[1] *Institutes*, I, ii.

as against the eremitical life. The virtues most praised are not holiness or spiritual achievement, but obedience and humility – humility towards God and man. The two sins of which Cassian gives us the most brilliant and incisive analysis are *accidie* and pride. *Accidie*[1] is especially the temptation of the solitary, and Cassian paints with swift and telling strokes the restlessness and sense of futility, of frustration and doubt which assail the anchorite alone in his cell, and which every scholar will recognize as a true portrait of the less fruitful and happy hours of one who has withdrawn from the crowd for the life of the spirit.

'When this has taken possession of some wretched soul, it produces horror of the place, distaste for his cell, and disdain and contempt of the brethren . . . It does not allow him to stay in his cell, or to devote himself to reading, and he keeps groaning that he can make no progress so long as he remains in that community.'

After describing the complaints which a man thus afflicted makes against his surroundings, the writer continues:

'He praises other monasteries and those which are remote, and represents those settlements as more profitable for spiritual advancement and more conducive to salvation; and besides this he paints the intercourse of the brethren there as agreeable and full of spiritual life. On the other hand he says that all around him is harsh, and . . . that there is nothing edifying among the brethren who dwell in that monastery.'

The malcontent then passes to complaints of the food, from which the transition to melancholia is easy:

'He fancies that he will never be saved while he stays in that monastery, unless he leaves his cell (he is doomed if he continues in it) and takes himself off from there as quickly as possible . . . Besides this he gazes about uneasily this way and that, and sighs that none of the brethren come to see him, and keeps going in and out of his cell, and gazes up at the sun very often as if it did not set quickly enough, and so a kind of irrational confusion comes over his mind . . . and so he supposes that no remedy can be found for such an attack except in visiting one or other of the brethren . . . Then the same malady suggests that visits are honourable and necessary duties, and should be paid to the brethren, etc.'

[1] *Institutes*, X, ii.

These moods of restlessness and doubt Cassian attributes, not without some truth, to absence of humility. But the last and crowning sin against which the monks are warned is pride – its only remedy is humility:

'We may first show to our brethren true humility from the very bottom of our heart, assenting to nothing which will sadden or hurt them. . . . Then the yoke of obedience and subjection must be taken up in simplicity of heart without any pretence . . . and when men are steadfast in this condition, this unruffled and unalterable state of humility will follow without any doubt, so that, regarding ourselves as inferior to everyone else, we shall bear very patiently everything laid upon us, even though it may be hurtful, and saddening, and injurious . . . For this attitude of mind is destructive, not only to pride, but indeed to all kinds of sin.'[1]

And in the closing words of his book, which follow immediately upon those quoted above, we cannot doubt that he is deprecating, nay condemning, the proud claim attributed to the Pelagians as he writes:

'Then, next after this we must maintain with the utmost firmness this same humility towards God. And this will be fulfilled by us in such a way as not only to acknowledge that we are powerless to accomplish anything relating to the perfecting of virtue without his assistance and Grace, but also to believe honestly that our being deemed worthy to comprehend this is in fact a gift from Him.'

On the other hand Cassian is no supporter of the view of the apparently arbitrary working of divine Grace attributed to St Augustine. One of the serious objections raised by St Augustine's opponents against his theory of 'Predestination' was that it would tend to undermine human effort, and would be calculated to produce spiritual torpor. It is undoubtedly in the light of this contention that we must read the *Institutes*. The whole purpose of the work is to stimulate the Christian, and especially the progressive Christian monks, to patient, life-long effort and endeavour. Perfection must be won with ceaseless toil and pain; but it can be won, and by all, and man's concern is his own part in the struggle. Cassian eschews miracles, and deprecates 'visions', for the ordinary man. He rarely mentions

[1] *Institutes*, XII, xxxii, xxxiii.

Grace; Predestination, never. Poverty, work, obedience, humility, these are the simple and direct avenues which in the *Institutes* he opens to all Christians, and which he promises will lead them to the Heavenly Kingdom.

Already, while writing the *Institutes*, Cassian intended to follow up the work by the *Conferences*, to which he several times refers during the composition of the work, and which, like the *Institutes*, was suggested by Bishop Castor. Unfortunately Castor died – apparently in 425 or 426[1] – before the completion of the first part, so that Cassian does not dedicate it to him. As it stands, the work consists of three parts, each preceded by a preface, the whole comprising twenty-four sections or *Conferences*. Part I (*Conf.* I–X) is dedicated to Leontius, probably the brother of Castor, and the Bishop of Fréjus; and also to Helladius, who is here termed *frater*, but who later became a bishop, and is probably the Helladius or Euladius mentioned in the episcopal list of the see of Arles as the successor to Patroclus, murdered in 426. Part II (*Conf.* XI–XVII) is dedicated to Honoratus and Eucherius, *fratres*. Eucherius was not made Bishop of Lyons till 434; but Honoratus probably became Bishop of Arles early in 428,[2] so that this part of the work cannot have been later than that year. Part III (*Conf.* XVIII–XXIV) is dedicated to Jovinian, Minervius, Leontius, and Theodore, *fratres*, though Theodore succeeded Leontius as Bishop of Fréjus in 432. It is significant that Leontius, who figures so prominently in the dedications, is one of the bishops to whom Pope Celestine had indited the letter in which he censures them for allowing 'presbyters' to dogmatize on matters which he declares to be above their sphere (cf. p. 215). It may be added that the opening chapters of Part I and Part II make it clear that these parts were originally intended to be reversed, while Part III was perhaps[3] the first to be written.

The form of the work is that of a series of dialogues, a form still fashionable at this period. We should describe Cassian's dialogues in modern terminology as 'interviews' between Cassian himself and his friend Germanus on the one hand, and the

---

[1] See O. Chadwick, op. cit., p. 188.

[2] See O. Chadwick, op. cit., p. 188. For a fuller statement of the evidence, see ibid., 'Euladius of Arles', *Journal of Theological Studies*, Vol. XLVI (1945), p. 200 ff.

[3] This is a possible interpretation of what is said in ch. 1, and it is the opinion of Bardenhewer, *Patrology*, p. 516.

monks and anchorites of the desert of Lower Egypt, Nitria, Scete, and the Nile Delta, on the other. These dialogues doubtless reflect in some measure the kind of conversations which actually took place during the writer's ten years' sojourn in Egypt in early life. On the other hand it is a mistake to regard the 'Dialogues' as 'minutes' of actual conversations. Courcelle, Chadwick and others have shown that much of the material is directly based on written sources, and much is again inspired by contemporary religious controversy and discussion within Gaul itself. Moreover, the length of time which separated Cassian's sojourn in Egypt from the writing of the Dialogues precludes any direct verbal record. In addition the plan and arrangement of the work itself are manifestly against such a possibility. A careful reading reveals a literary scheme in which overlapping of subject and treatment in general is carefully avoided, in spite of the length of the work. The author has sought to cover the whole of the ground of monastic life, more especially spiritual life. In accordance with this literary scheme the monks are represented as speaking appropriately, each in character, and there is a certain art or artifice of 'specialization' shown in each monk's selection of his subject and in his treatment of it. Cassian had spent long enough in the desert to have become intimately acquainted with its more outstanding personnel, and his *Conferences* are more properly to be described as 'dramatic dialogues' than actual records.

The work is composed in the first person, the writer, Cassian, representing himself as present at all the dialogues as a listener, while the discourses of the monks are spoken at length in response to questions put to them by Cassian's companion and spiritual brother, Germanus. The unhistorical nature of the actual dialogues, and the deliberate literary artifice are manifest in the way in which the two young men are represented as passing from desert to desert and from one monastic settlement to another, from saint to saint, exactly like modern 'interviewers', questioning their hosts, and drawing from them discourses on various matters of religious interest, but most of all on how best one can make progress in the spiritual life. We know from the diaries and letters of the period that pilgrimages of this kind were becoming fashionable already in the fourth century, and must have been common in the fifth; and we know

P

from the *Conferences* that the multiplicity of visits and the need of offering hospitality to strangers was one of the serious drawbacks to the hermit's life, though nothing on the scale here represented would have been tolerated. Indeed on one occasion we are amused to find Abbot Pinufius[1] endeavouring to persuade the two enquirers to settle in his monastery; but away they go to the next.

The sanity and absence of the extravagant and the miraculous which had characterized the *Institutes* are even more marked in the *Conferences*. In the first chapter of the third part of the latter, Cassian says that the virtues and marvels (*virtutes atque mirabilia*) of Abbot Piamun must be passed over in silence lest he should exceed the plan and limits of his book:

'For we promised to commit to memory what we could recall, not of the miracles of God (*de mirabilibus Dei*), but of the institutes and discipline of the saints, so as to bring before our readers only such instruction as is necessary for the perfect life, and not matter for futile and idle wonder, lacking in any corrective discipline.'[2]

The picture of life in the desert presented by Cassian is in general a dignified and a worthy one, entirely free from extravagance. The daily life, with its stress on the value of manual labour and on a simple and regular régime, though rigorous, is not unhealthy, and one is constantly struck by the long life attributed to the monks. The ordered domestic arrangements of the larger communities were calculated to avoid both waste and want, and at the same time the allocation of specialized work, such as gardening, cooking, etc., would ensure the best results with the minimum loss of time and materials. The attitude towards the aged and the sick is both gentle and sympathetic, and the margin of possibility of real neglect, even of solitary anchorites, is narrowed to the minimum. To the young, and those not yet proved in the rigours of monastic life, the older members are tender and solicitous. It is thus that Abbot Moses 'put a stop to our interview, and urged us, eager though we were and hanging on his lips, to go off and get a little sleep, telling us to lie down on the same mats on which we were sitting, and similarly to put our hassocks under our heads as pillows . . .

[1] *Conferences*, III, xx, 12.
[2] ibid., III, xviii, 1.

And so at length at the bidding of the old man we composed ourselves to be quiet and snatch some sleep, though it was irksome to us, because we were both excited with delight at the conference we had held, and also full of eager anticipation of the discussion which was promised. And so when we had enjoyed our morning sleep and rejoiced to see dawn break at last, we began to ask once more for his promised talk, and the blessed Moses thus began:

' "As I see you inflamed with such an ardent desire that I do not believe that even that smallest possible interval of quiet, which I chose to deduct from our spiritual conference and to give over to your physical refreshment, has been effective in resting your bodies, I feel all the more anxious as I watch your zeal".'[1]

It is interesting to learn that a busy postal system connects the monks with the outside world. In the *Conferences* Cassian tells us that the elders of the monastery of Bethlehem, anxious for the return of Germanus and himself from Egypt, 'had not been at all softened by our very frequent letters to satisfy them.'[2] Elsewhere he speaks of a brother who refused to open 'a great pile of letters' from his friends and relations, declaring that they would awaken disturbing memories and distract his thoughts from the contemplation which he was practising. We may compare what is said in the *Life of St Antony*, of the letters which the saint received from the Emperor Constantine, and also from his sons, Constantius and Constans, and which he was with reluctance persuaded to read.[3]

Indeed these dialogues confirm the impression which we derive both from the *Life of St Antony*[4] and the *Lausiac History*, and from the *Dialogues* of Severus, that monastic retreats are exceptionally active social centres. Patience and forbearance towards the crowds who come to demand interviews, politeness to visitors under all circumstances, are among the virtues for which the desert anchorites are most highly praised.[5] Among their severest trials are reckoned the number of visitors which

[1] *Conferences*, I, i, 23; ii, 1.   [2] ibid., II, xvii, 30.
[3] Athanasius, *Life of St Antony*, ch. 81, English translation by A. Robertson in *Nicene and Post-Nicene Fathers* (Oxford, 1892); and by R. T. Meyer (London, 1950).
[4] See especially caps. 13, 14.
[5] See again the *Life of St Antony*, chs. 14, 72, where Antony's perfect courtesy and grace of bearing and of speech, as well as his civilized appearance and manner in receiving his visitors, are carefully stressed.

exceeds the monks' slender supplies of food, and entails a heavy loss of time from spiritual exercises. The many interviews, and also the hospitality incumbent on the monks, are a source of real suffering to those who have sought the desert, hoping for a life of quiet and contemplation in solitude. We detect a weariness of the visitor who, inspired by vulgar curiosity, wastes the monks' time with idle enquiries, in the anxious question put to Germanus and Cassian by Abbot Piamun as to the reason for their visit:

'For we know that some have come from your country to these parts in order to go round the monasteries just for the sake of getting to know the brethren, not with the intention of submitting themselves to the rules and regulations, for the sake of which they had sought us out, nor to withdraw to the cells and endeavour to carry out in practice what they had apprehended from example or precept.'[1]

At the same time the salutary effect on the mind afforded by change of occupation and companionship when visitors come, and the refreshment brought by conversation with strangers, are fully recognized.[2] The value set on relaxation is delightfully illustrated by the well-known apocryphal story of St John who, when reproved by a passing huntsman for amusing himself by stroking a partridge, replied that his mind would lose its vigour unless relaxed from tension by recreation.[3]

This busy social intercourse, combined with a renunciation of, and freedom from, financial responsibility and civic life, undoubtedly fostered some form of intellectual life, whether stimulated by books or conversation. We have seen that Postumianus assures Severus that his *Life of St Martin* was already being read in the Egyptian desert almost before the ink was dry. And we may be sure that the letters and visitors who flocked to interview the saints did not fail to inform them of the latest events of importance, and of the ideas and questions which were actuating men's minds.

The *Conferences* contain surprisingly little on the whole which dismays the modern reader. There are, as is only to be expected. certain passages which strike us as coming from a strange world

[1] *Conferences*, III, xviii, 2.
[2] ibid., III, xxiv, 19 ff.
[3] ibid., III, xxiv, 21.

of thought, and at which we are somewhat aghast. In particular the second Conference of Abbot Serenus[1] on 'Principalities and Powers' has some strange and terrible things to tell us; for here we learn that 'the atmosphere which occupies the space between heaven and earth is close packed with a dense crowd of spirits, which flit about in it actively and restlessly, so that it is most fortunate Providence has withdrawn them from human sight. For through terror of their onsets, or horror at the forms into which they transform and turn themselves at will, men would either be prostrated by unbearable terror, and collapse, utterly unable to contemplate such things with bodily eyes, or else they would grow worse and worse every day, vitiated by their perpetual example and by copying it.'[2]

And we hear of a truly terrifying vision which appeared one night to a monk in a cave of the desert, in which he saw an immense crowd of demons gathering on all sides and marching towards him, and in their midst the prince, taller and more dreadful than the rest, who seated himself on a throne and began to question each in turn on the extent of the evil which he had been able to effect. Great was the glory which crowned one demon who, after fifteen years of fruitless effort, had at last been successful in seducing a monk.[3]

But in regard to the *Conferences* as a whole – and the extent of the work is very considerable – one is struck by the absence of the extravagant or the fantastic. This is partly no doubt because, as we have already said, the emphasis throughout is on spiritual development rather than on physical austerities. The discipline is contemplative rather than penitential.

No reader, whatever his religious views, whether Catholic, Protestant, or even sceptic, could fail to appreciate the lofty purity of Cassian's teaching. His interpretation of Scripture is wholly free from narrow literalness. Always it is the spirit rather than the letter which he emphasizes. He is at pains to explain that fasting which results from ill temper is not pious but impious; that those who, actuated by hostility for some offence received, goad others on to injure them yet further, in order to display their own patience by contrast, are guilty of grave mis-

[1] *Conferences*, I, viii, 12.
[2] ibid., I, viii, 12.
[3] ibid., I, viii, 16.

conduct. Always as one reads the *Conferences* one is conscious of the wholesome beauty of the Desert Fathers. We hear almost nothing of religious differences, nothing of hatred, or rivalry, or controversy. A quiet dignity of bearing and decorum of conduct go hand in hand with personal simplicity and high endeavour, and with mutual co-operation and loving-kindness. Renunciation and ascetic practices are only means to an end, and their object is a heightened and purified realization of divine perfection. Cassian deprecates any dwelling on one's past sins, even in penitence, regarding such thoughts as unwholesome. In modern phraseology we should say that Cassian always seeks to substitute the positive for the negative in religious life.

No other ancient writer succeeds in conveying as Cassian does the poetry of the desert monasteries, whether small or large. In the *Lausiac History* Palladius writes as a realist, albeit a highly credulous one. Whether from his personal knowledge or from his literary source, he depicts with startling clarity the dangers and difficulties which beset the daily life of the recluse, and he passes in review with unflinching crudity the ignoble jests and pettiness of the less worthy side of community life, where men and women of all classes and every grade of education and ignorance are learning to live together a common life in solitude. Cassian does not ignore such things. He tells of the brother who hid biscuits to satisfy his hunger surreptitiously, and things far worse; but the emphasis is not on these things. They fall into their natural place as the simple human frailties which men take with them into the religious life, but which they outgrow with the help and the kindly sympathy and wise counsel of the men who have grown old in the experience of temptation and self conquest.

The form of the composition – the dialogue, the division into three parts, and the theme of the tour of the two *peregrini* among the monks of Egypt – is reminiscent of Sulpicius Severus. In the work of the latter, however, the dialogue is represented as taking place when the traveller, Postumianus, returns to Gaul, and relates his adventures and his interviews to his friends Sulpicius and the monk Gallus; whereas Cassian takes us into the actual presence of the Desert Fathers, and we are, as it were, present at their dialogues. The *Conferences* recall the *Dialogues* of Severus also in their simple naturalism, and in the

introduction of realistic touches which enable us to picture the
scene in the desert monasteries where the interviews take place.
The brilliance of style of Severus is lacking, and would in any
case have been difficult to sustain in this protracted work;
but Cassian's dialogues have far more life and freshness than,
for example, Palladius's 'Dialogue concerning the Life of Chrysostom'.[1] There is a sense of the spacious and timeless desert,
a fitting background for the old men whose life-long preoccupation has been with spiritual matters. In contrast to their
deep wisdom, the simple naïveté of Germanus's questions are as
freshly conceived as those of *Alice in Wonderland*, from which,
in some queer unaccountable way, this little desert world of the
fifth century strikes the modern reader as not wholly remote.
There is genuine imagination in the picture of the two youths,
over-excited by the talk of Abbot Joseph and unable to sleep in
their cells, stealing out in the silence of the desert night to discuss together, like youthful conspirators, what they ought to do
about their broken promise of a speedy return, given long ago
to the elders of their own monastery.[2]

On the other hand the general avoidance of miracles[3] is in
strong contrast to the account of the Desert Fathers given by
Postumianus; and the persistence with which Cassian adheres
to this abstention, taken in connection with the points of
similarity to the *Dialogues* of Severus in other respects, makes
one wonder if Cassian is writing in deliberate opposition to
Severus. Certain details seem to hint at this. In particular the
story told by Cassian elsewhere[4] of the obedient monk, John of
Lycon,[5] who for 'a whole year' carried water twice a day for
nearly two miles to water a dry stick, which at the end still
proved dry and rotten, is in striking contrast to the same incident related by Postumianus, who, however, gravely assures

---

[1] Migne, *Patrologia Graeca*, XLVII, translated into English by Herbert Moore
(London, 1921).

[2] *Conferences*, II, xvii, 1 f.

[3] A few examples are cited by Cassian. We may instance the raising by Macarius
of the dead man who declared himself to have 'lived under kings of most ancient
date'; but these are accompanied by a warning against the dangers to which
miracles readily give rise. (*Conferences*, III, xv, 3.) Cassian rarely claims to have
witnessed such himself. (cf. p. 226.)

[4] *Institutes*, IV, xxiii f.

[5] Lycon or Lycopolis is situated in the Thebaïd, on the west bank of the Nile.
John of Lycon is apparently a historical character. See Gibson, op. cit., p. 226, n. 5,
and the references there cited.

us that finally the stick burgeoned forth into foliage.[1] The contrast in the two tales is significant. Severus wishes to emphasize the miracle; Cassian, the virtue of unquestioning obedience, the necessity for discipline, and the importance of character.

We have seen that in the *Dialogues* of Severus a marked nationalism was present, an emphasis on the Saint of Tours, whose asceticism and holiness is said to be at least equal to that of the saints of Egypt; an exaltation of the simple Gaulish peasant Gallus, rustic, perhaps, or rather provincial, but not uneducated, and worthy to expound the merits and miracles of Martin and the Gaulish monastery in the presence of Postumianus, who is primed with all the wonderful tales of his travels among the saints. The *Dialogues* are thought to have been published 403–4. Cassian's *Conferences* were published in 426 or shortly afterwards, though they may possibly have been written and even circulated earlier (cf. p. 224). It is almost impossible to doubt that a connection exists between the *Dialogues* and the *Conferences*, despite the interval of time which elapsed between their publication. It is tempting to believe that Cassian wished deliberately to deny Severus's high claims for the prestige of the local national saint, and to insist on the superiority of the saints of Egypt to all others, whether Gaulish or Syrian. This claim to superiority he bases, not on miracles nor divine revelation, nor even on special divine Grace, but on the patience and perseverance of the monks in the discipline of endeavour and obedience, and on the development of character, and the gradual progress of humility and austerity as a means to the attainment of the perfect life.

On the other hand a striking point of agreement between the *Conferences* of Cassian and the *Dialogues* of Severus is the emphasis which both lay on the necessity for modification in the institutes of Egypt when adapting them for use in Gaul. Although in the case of Severus this leniency is accompanied by, though of course not identical with, a spirit of conscious nationalism – Gaul for the Gauls – it is not clear that Cassian was actuated in this matter by any considerations other than those of a severely practical end; but it may well be that he was no stranger to the nationalist feelings so charmingly expressed by Gallus in Sulpicius's *Dialogues*, and they may have played

[1] Sulpicius Severus, *Dialogues* I, 19. Nearly three years is the time mentioned here.

some part in building up the school of thought in the Rhône Valley which did not accord a very ready welcome to the doctrine of Hippo or injunctions from Rome.

I have dwelt on Cassian's teaching because he himself makes it quite clear that the practices and ideals which he introduced into the monastery of Marseilles, and which he recommends to the Gaulish bishops, are in the main those embodied in his writings. But the importance of the works of Cassian is not confined to what they have to tell us of Egyptian thought and the beginnings of monasticism in western Europe. They are concerned with the most important subjects and questions which were exercising the minds of thinking men in Gaul at this period. And by adopting the literary device of dramatic dialogues, the writer has been able to include highly controversial matters without arousing rancour by personal or local allusions.

Among these subjects undoubtedly the most important were the issues under consideration in the Pelagian controversy[1] of which we have made a brief survey at closer range in the preceding chapter. We have already sought (p. 221) to indicate the concern of the *Institutes* with the important issues commonly referred to in the controversy as (divine) 'Grace' and 'Free-Will'. In the *Institutes* the theological aspect of the controversy is rarely brought into the foreground by direct allusion. In the *Conferences*, on the other hand, the fundamental question is more frankly debated, and here Cassian devotes a whole section (*Conference* XIII) of the teaching of the Abbot Chaeremon to a systematic study of the functions of Grace and Free-Will. Elsewhere also he expresses his view with lucidity and decision in a famous passage of the *Conferences* where Abbot Paphnutius discourses[2] on the relationship of divine Grace to Free-Will.[3] The passage on Free-Will occurs in what purports to be the answer to a question put to Paphnutius by Germanus:

'In what, then, does Free-Will consist, and how is it attributed to our own efforts that we are worthy of praise, if God both

[1] A valuable work on Cassian's position in regard to the doctrine of 'Grace' is that of A. Hoch, *Lehre des Johannes Cassianus von Natur und Gnade* (Freiburg im Breisgau, 1895).
[2] I, iii, 11 ff.
[3] For a brief summary of Cassian's theological position, see Harnack, op. cit., Vol. V, p. 247. A fuller and more recent study is that of Chadwick, op. cit., chs. iii and iv.

begins and ends everything in us which leads to our perfection?'[1]
to which Paphnutius replies by pointing out that:

'It is for us to utilize either zealously or negligently the opportunities granted to us by Heaven. . . . But it is well for us to be
sure that, although we practise every virtue with unflagging
efforts, yet we can never attain perfection with all our efforts or
by our own toil; nor is man's own striving sufficient to attain such
lofty recompense of bliss by means of his own efforts, unless we
have secured it by means of the co-operation of the Lord. . . .
No righteous man is able to secure righteousness by his own
power.'

Germanus urges that Scripture, by attributing to us the sin
of disobedience, shows very clearly the freedom of the will,
urging that God shows that the decision to yield or not to yield
lies in our own power.

'How then can it be that our salvation does not lie in our
own hands if God Himself has granted us the power either to
hearken or not to hearken?'[2]

But Cassian leaves his readers under no misapprehension as
to his views on this great question, and Paphnutius dismisses
his young enquirers for the night with these closing words:

'Let no one therefore try by a false interpretation so to twist
the arguments which we brought forward as proving that
nothing can be done without the Lord, nor claim it in support
of Free-Will in such a way as to try to take away from man the
Grace of God and His daily care . . . but let him bear in mind
that just as the power of Free-Will is demonstrated by the disobedience of the people, so the daily care of God, calling upon
him and admonishing him, is also made manifest. . . . We have
no wish to abolish man's Free-Will by the arguments we set
forth, but only to establish the fact that the help and Grace of
God are necessary to it every day and every moment.'[3]

The *Institutes* and the *Conferences*, the two works by which
Cassian is best known, and which embody his views on 'Free-
Will' and Divine 'Grace', had both been published before 429,
the date of Prosper's letter and Hilary's second letter to St
Augustine, which marked the beginning of the Pelagian Con-
troversy in Gaul. Yet curiously enough, no direct reference is

[1] Loc. cit.
[2] ibid., I, iii, 21.
[3] ibid., I, iii, 22.

made to Cassian's works by either Hilary or Prosper, and it is
generally assumed that they were unaware of the existence of
these works at the time. It has been suggested[1] that this is due
to secrecy on the part of the author, that the books were only
privately circulated and not actually published till later, and
that this reticence was due to respect for Augustine's age and
prestige, and for the fight which he had made against Pelagianism. But although some strong arguments have been adduced
in favour of this view, the absence of specific reference by Prosper is fully in accord with the absence of proper names elsewhere in his letter and in that of Hilary. Throughout the controversy, the reluctance of others, as well as of Hilary and
Prosper, to mention Cassian, is very remarkable, and is generally attributed to his high reputation.

It can no longer be claimed that Cassian is a very original
writer in regard to his graded ascetic discipline and the system
of his spiritual teaching. For these he was largely indebted to
Evagrius,[2] a Greek of Pontus, whose works were believed until
recently to have perished, but have been largely recovered
during the present century. Evagrius had been ordained a
reader by St Basil, and a deacon by St Gregory Nazianzene. He
was Archdeacon of Constantinople and had been present at the
great Council in 381, but had later been an inmate of the community of Rufinus and Melania on the Mount of Olives, and
still later he had been in the deserts of Nitria and Cellia in
Lower Egypt. In Cellia he lived for some fourteen years till his
death in 399. His ascetic practices and writings gained him a
high renown as the chief representative and the leading theologian of the ascetic system created by Origen.[3]

The debt of Cassian to Evagrius is paramount both in the
Institutes and the *Conferences*. The literary tone of much of Cassian's material has already been remarked above, and indeed
it could hardly fail to strike anyone who reads the work of
Cassian attentively. It is, however, only comparatively recently
that the literary source of many passages has been demon-

[1] See Fr. M. Jacquin, O.P., *Revue d'Histoire ecclésiastique*, Vol. V (1904), p. 381, and
the evidence which he cites there. Cf. also O. Chadwick, op. cit., p. 114.
[2] For a brief outline of the life of Evagrius and of Cassian's debt, see Chadwick,
op. cit., *passim*.
[3] A recent valuable study of Origen is that of Henry Chadwick, *Origen: Contra
Celsum* (Cambridge, 1953). See also R. P. C. Hanson, *Origen's Doctrine of Tradition*
(London, 1954).

strated,[1] and it is interesting to find that these are in the main the more artificial passages, such as his description of the more important pieces of the dress of a monk and their symbolic meaning; the different exercises of the spiritual life; the divisions of the soul; the technical description of monastic wisdom; the five successive degrees of contemplation; and many other matters.

But the debt of Cassian to Evagrius is far more fundamental than these technical details. It has, indeed, been claimed that Evagrius, under the influence of the Alexandrian fathers, is the chief founder of the spirituality both of East and West, and that he was the principal teacher of Cassian, and chief authority for his ascetical doctrine.[2] Cassian follows Evagrius in what are perhaps the most distinctive features of his directions for ascetic practice – the systematic discipline and the analytical treatment. To Evagrius he is also indebted for the sharp and rigid classification of the vices and the virtues, for the category and classification into what became known later as the 'Seven Deadly Sins'.[3]

It is a curious fact that Cassian nowhere mentions the name of Evagrius. Yet there seems to be no doubt of his influence on Cassian's outline of the discipline of the spiritual life, and on his most characteristic doctrines. On the other hand the influence of earlier ascetic thought on the work of Cassian is not confined to Evagrius. The influence of Origen, of Jerome, of Basil, and of John Chrysostom is also clear. In general the influence of Evagrius on Western thought has been less profound than on that of the East, and in the work of Cassian it has permeated Western ascetic spiritual discipline in a more modified form.

Cassian shares with Faustus of Riez an earnest insistence on the element of combat, on the perpetual conflict of the spirit against sin, as a feature of prime importance in the discipline of the spiritual life leading to contemplation. The theory rests on a conviction of antagonism between flesh and spirit, a conviction which perhaps underlay St Jerome's life of renunciation in the desert. Progress in the contemplative life, at least in the

---

[1] By Dom Marsili, *Giovanni Cassiano ed Evagrio Pontico. Dottrina sulla Caritae Contemplazione* in *Studia Anselmiana*, Vol. V, Rome, 1936. See Courcelle, op. cit., p. 215 f.

[2] Chadwick, op. cit., p. 82 ff.

[3] Evagrius, however, describes the principal sins as eight in number.

more elementary stages of spirituality, is achieved by warfare in the soul, and by the conflict of the spirit against sin.

Cassian, like Faustus of Riez and other writers of this period, makes use of St Paul's figure of the Christians as athletes in this combat. In some measure both the terminology and the conception of the struggle were forced upon them by contemporary conditions. Voices were not wanting in those days of warfare and invasion, accusing the monks and ascetics of shirking their social responsibilities. 'Why return to the desert?' asks Vigilantius; 'this is not fighting, but running away.'[1] To Cassian, as to Faustus, the first step in spiritual progress is to overcome one's sins. 'It is not possible to be victorious without a struggle.'[2]

Cassian was not a great theological thinker. The essentially practical nature of his teaching accounts for the underlying apparent inconsistency of his theory of Free-Will and Grace, and of the absence of logic in his argument – we might almost say the courageous repudiation of logic. His personal adaptation of the teaching of Evagrius and of a modified Origenism, possibly also of his own experience among the monks of Egypt, to the needs of Western ascetic institutions, are essential features of his instructions to the monks of Provence. His modifications to suit local Gaulish conditions may, and probably do, owe something to the *Dialogues* of Sulpicius Severus; but they are integrated in his whole vision of the monastic way of life, which is essentially a balanced one. It is his combination of practical realism with an unfailing conviction of the paramount importance of purity of heart and spirit above all prescribed observances, above all the demands of rigid logic, which have made Cassian the founder of Western monasticism.

His influence was even more immediate in Italy than in Gaul. Cassiodorus urges his community at Vivarium to a diligent study of the *Institutes* and the *Conferences*. The *Rule of St Benedict* enjoins (cap. 42) on the brethren, the reading aloud of the *Conferences*, or the *Vitae Patrum*, or some other edifying work during the time between supper and Compline. His influence on later monasticism has been admirably summarized by Owen Chadwick who opens his study of Cassian with the statement that 'His teaching on the ascetic life and the road to perfection

[1] Jerome, *Adv. Vigil.*, 16.
[2] *Conferences*, XVIII, xiii, 4.

dominated the origins and affected the spiritual ethos of medieval and modern monasticism', and he concludes by pointing out that Cassian interpreted the spirituality of Evagrius to the Middle Ages, and that Benedict could have achieved little without the analysis of the ascetic method proffered by Cassian and Basil.[1]

There are possibly some points in which we may hesitate to agree wholly with Chadwick's views of the ideals of Cassian and of the great contemplatives whom he reverenced. Chadwick has little sympathy for Cassian's distinction between the active and the contemplative life, adopted perhaps from Origen; still less for the conception of spiritual progress as an ascent by graded stages of ascetic discipline. The phrase 'Eastern extravagance', though perhaps just, rings a little harshly as an echo of the names of the Desert Fathers. In the general implications of the work, too, one is led to suspect an underlying censure of the contemplative life. Among the 'defects' of Cassian's work it is claimed (p. 179) that 'The modern test of true contemplation, "effect upon life", is . . . excluded in favour of the unreliable test of spiritual experience;' and both Cassian and Salvian are arraigned before a tribunal which condemns them for concentrating on the things of the spirit while the political and social fate of Europe is being decided by Alaric, Ataulf, Gaiseric. 'The modern instinct inquires whether brotherly love should have driven the better men to support the collapsing bulwarks of society.'

The modern instinct does indeed put this question; but ours is not a contemplative age, and I think that perhaps few who have been privileged to personal intimacy with 'professed' contemplatives would allow that 'effect upon life' is a safe criterion of their progress in the life of prayer and contemplation. So far as we may presume to define this spiritual endeavour, it would seem to consist in a loving attention upon God. The ascetic discipline, and the solitary or the cenobitic life, are simply elements in the relevant discipline to this end, selected and perfected according to the vocation and the means available to the seeker after spiritual perfection.

When, however, we return not a little enviously to Chadwick's learned study, with its clear presentation of Cassian's

[1] Op. cit., p. 178.

spiritual predecessors and preceptors, its firm grasp of their theories of ascetic discipline, and of the conflicting currents of doctrines and of heresies amid which Cassian wrote, we find ourselves in a position to take a sounder view of Cassian's actual achievement than has been possible hitherto. Chadwick's study has taught us that what Cassian had to offer was no mushroom-growth of western Europe, but the fine flower of a long tradition in Mediterranean lands. Cassian has clothed Greek precision of thought and its abstract terminology in a more familiar idiom. He has brought before us the strange Eastern ascetics and their stranger desert life and austerities with a happy naturalism which makes spiritual endeavour and monastic discipline seem a normal and even a homely way of life. His aerial demons and his deadly sins have no home on Gaulish soil, but have crept there like bogeys from the vast spaces of the untenanted deserts of Egypt and the East, the true home of temptation and spiritual warfare, as St Antony and St Jerome knew well. All these varied elements, all this traditional machinery of the ascetic life, fall into place in the pages of Cassian. But Cassian's own personal emphasis throughout is on the validity of human effort, the necessity of divine Grace, and the paramount value of purity of heart and integrity of spirit as the essential elements of the monastic life.

CHAPTER IX

St Germanus of Auxerre and the Growth of Ecclesiastical Biography

IN the preceding chapters we have been in touch with two distinct worlds of thought – the Classical and the Oriental. These two worlds of thought met and contended for mastery in Gaul in the fourth and fifth centuries. The classical survives, and perhaps shows its clearest traces in heresies, the last expression of the old speculative thought of classical philosophy. The Oriental brings with it the mysticism and the high spiritual specialization of constructive renunciation represented by the rise of monasticism, and especially the austere form of monasticism, combined with social democracy.

But although these two spheres of thought were in some measure at variance in Gaul, giving rise to considerable controversy, they must have been mutually beneficial in no slight degree. The spiritual life of Gaul, from whatever quarter it came – whether from Greece, or Syria, or Egypt – is free from the extremes and even extravagances of certain Eastern forms of monasticism. Gaulish monasticism in our period is austere rather than ascetic. The balanced thought and the sense of beauty, which are the product of an education in classical literature, are as evident in the simplicity and quiet of the lives and characters of men like St Martin and St Eucherius as in that of Ausonius; and the sweet and vitalizing humour of Sulpicius Severus and St Paulinus of Nola is no less a product of this same classical tradition than is the farcical burlesque of *Querolus*.

The classical training in relentless logic and scrupulous intellectual honesty and integrity was a beneficial element in both religious teaching and the religious profession. Education in forensic oratory and rhetoric brought the expression of spiritual argument within the type of intellectual experience readily apprehended by the average educated listener or reader, and had a valuable influence on the sermons of the period. It is undoubtedly because they were educated in the classical tradition that the earnest Christians of south-eastern Gaul developed a relatively sober and balanced attitude to the more extreme views of St Augustine. In the writings of Faustus of Riez, and in the anonymous British letters of the period, the modern reader, though not always able to attune himself wholly to the sustained seriousness, not always able to subscribe to the principles inculcated, yet feels himself in a familiar atmosphere, and at ease in his company. The absence of fanaticism has much to do with this congeniality.

So far we have been concerned chiefly with the actual writings of the prominent theological thinkers, or those of their intimates and contemporaries. There is no barrier between ourselves and our subjects, obscuring their true nature by the prejudices and preoccupations of a later age or of a change of outlook. We shall see when we come to consider the writings of the great Bishop of Auvergne, Sidonius Apollinaris, that the same is true there also. He holds us in the classical world, and his outlook and his sense of values and of humour, his directness of vision and freedom from delusion and credulity, are completely congenial to us, and make his writings as fresh to us as if they had been written yesterday.

Nothing could show more impressively the change of atmosphere from the sub-classical world to the Middle Ages than the portraits of the great men of Gaul in our period as they appear in the biographies, written later, and in a different tradition. The contrast is startling. In the later biographies the first thing which strikes us is their comparative puerility, and at the same time their picturesqueness. They abound in the marvellous, are full of miracles. Dignity of thought has given place to homeliness; lofty imagination to simplicity of theme; logical argument and literary expression and illustration to simple and direct narrative; forceful and impressive utterance to a wealth of anecdote and story, with a liberal introduction of direct speech and vivid detail, often also of local colour. The change of tone implies a change of reader or listener. The later biographer has in mind the unlettered congregation or simple devout reader, rather than the cultured Gaul of the country villa, or a public official in the Roman schools.

It is clear that we are no longer primarily concerned with the thinker and writer in his study, but with the popular preacher,

Q

drawing his materials largely from the purveyor of ecclesiastical saga, who in his turn has had his training and experience in a still more popular assembly. This is a point which must be borne in mind in regard to the saints whom we know only from biographies. Fantastic and bizarre as these biographies often are, the early ones sometimes contain a considerable amount of genuine oral tradition, possibly going back to the lifetime of the saint himself. On the other hand this saga tradition is also changing, developing under a new and exacting discipline. It is adapting the technique of the literature of entertainment to the literature of Christian edification. It is learning to adjust itself to the needs of a congregation in Church on the saint's day. This element of edification developed gradually until it became on the one hand a sermon, and on the other a 'type' biography, conforming more or less closely to such earlier biographies as those, for example, of St Antony and St Martin.

It will readily be seen that when the biography was written considerably later than the saint's lifetime, it is not easy to disentangle the saga from the 'type' material. This difficulty is increased by the fact that the idea of a biography is itself the product of a later age. The earliest 'Lives', such as St Hilary's account of St Honoratus, were intended as *exempla*. Their purpose was to recall to their listeners the principal features in the characters and careers of the dead saints who were regarded as worthy patterns to be followed. Historical narrative as such is far from the intention of the writer, who, however, often introduces valuable historical material from saga or personal experience in order to impress and inform his listeners. It thus becomes a matter of paramount importance when we are seeking to reconstruct the life of a saint, first of all to 'unpick' the *Vita*, humbly and with caution, in order to search out any kernel of genuine tradition as distinct from the 'type' features. The failure to detect this element of genuine saga on the one hand, and the tendency to accept uncritically the statements of a *Vita*, provided it be good and early, on the other, are serious defects in many works otherwise scholarly. A sufficiently high standard of critical judgment is not always maintained.

Perhaps even more important than the facts which the biographer asks us to accept are the inferences to be drawn from the milieu in which the saint lived, especially from details of

his family and his circle of friends, his early teachers, and the
nature of their views. It is almost more important still to know
the milieu of the biographer himself, and his own views and
prejudices, his background and probable bias, his temperament
and preoccupations. We want to know the circumstances under
which the biography was written – at whose request and for
what purpose. It is important also to know the literary habits of
the time at which a biography was written, the literary genre at
which the author aimed. In short we must know the motive of
the biographer in undertaking his task, the principle on which
he has selected his materials, and the way in which he has used
them. When we have scrutinized the 'Life' with such questions
as these in mind, we shall be ready to turn with a chastened
spirit to the elements of saga hidden under the 'pious purpose',
as the most valuable element on which the historian can build.

These considerations must be our guide in seeking to reconstruct the career of St Germanus, and to interpret the literary
Vita, which is our main source of information. Germanus is the
most elusive of all the saints who have so far come before us.
The sources are not meagre, but they are of very unequal value.
It will help to assess the relative value of the material if I enu-
merate the sources briefly at this point, before proceeding to discuss in detail the literary Vita of the saint. These sources are of
three kinds: (1) notices in contemporary Gaulish chronicles;
(2) the Latin Vita written in Gaul only about a generation later
than the saint's own time; (3) later traditional matter of doubtful value, claiming to be derived from sources preserved in
Britain in written form.

This does not wholly exhaust our information relating to the
life of Germanus, for we have some highly picturesque details
about his youth and his early relations with St Amator, his
predecessor in the see of Auxerre, and also about the circumstances of his election, in the Vita of St Amator himself, a later
composition commonly regarded as having little or no historical
importance.[1] The extant Vita is almost certainly to be identified[2] with the Vita S. Amatoris[3] known to have been compiled

[1] So W. Levison, 'Bischof Germanus von Auxerre, und die Quellen zu seiner Geschichte', Neues Archiv der Gesellschaft für ältere deutsche geschichtskunde, Vol. XXIX
(1904), p. 158 f.   [2] Levison, op. cit., p. 100, and loc. cit.
[3] The text of this Vita is published by the Bollandists in the Acta Sanctorum, May
1st, s.v. St Amator.

by an African presbyter, Stephen, at the request of Bishop Aunachar[1] of Auxerre about 160 years after the death of St Germanus (see p. 267), that is to say towards the close of the sixth century.[2]

St Amator is well attested from other sources,[3] and there are details in the *Life* which suggest that it contains a certain amount of saga or traditional oral prose narrative, as distinct from either fiction or written Church records. Even if it does not represent a personal tradition, it probably reflects tradition based on historical conditions, and very possibly personal reminiscences preserved in ecclesiastical circles at Auxerre. For this reason I propose to glance briefly at the *Life* by Stephen before proceeding to the more important work of Constantius.

According to the *Life*, Amator belonged on his mother's side to the aristocracy of the Aedui. His father's name is given as Proclidius, and he is described as a citizen of Auxerre. His mother's name was Usiciola. Amator was their only son and the heir to their wealth, which is said to have been very great. He stood high in the favour of St Valerian his bishop; but his parents destined him for matrimony, and he was betrothed to a young maiden named Martha, of eminent parents of the city of the *Lingonices* (of *Lingonica*, the modern Langres). Whether by accident or design, St Valerian, who was performing the marriage ceremony, substituted for the marriage service the service proper for the ordination of priests. Only the bridal couple, we are told, noticed the mistake, and they resolved by mutual consent to live together as brother and sister. At a later date, when St Elladius had succeeded St Valerian, they made their views and their way of life known to the bishop. St Amator was ordained a deacon, and Martha was also consecrated to the religious life. This dénouement, a commonplace of the fashion of the time in which Amator lived, may be historical, though it may possibly be a conventional literary 'property' of Stephen; but neither this nor the rest of the narrative, with its proper

---

[1] Duchesne, *Fastes Épiscopaux*, II, p. 431. His activity covers the years 573–89 (Levison, op. cit., p. 146), and perhaps longer (Duchesne, *Fastes*, II, p. 439 f., cf. p. 427). The letter of Bishop Aunachar to Stephen is still extant, and also Stephen's reply (*Mon. Germ. Epist.*, III, p. 447).

[2] Levison, op. cit., p. 158.

[3] Duchesne, *Fastes Épiscopaux*, Vol. II, pp. 427–46; Baudrillart, *Dictionnaire d'Histoire et de Géographie ecclésiastique*, Vol. II, col. 981.

names, looks like pure fiction. It may be pointed out that an interval would probably elapse between the marriage of the young couple and their public declaration, and such an interval we know to have been usual. Moreover, as Tillemont points out, they seem to have continued to live together, and this also we have seen to be a fashion among the bishops of their time. The words of Constantius imply that the same arrangement was also adopted by Germanus and his wife when Germanus became a bishop – or at least that it was what the standards of fifth-century biography demanded.[1]

The performance of miracles follows as a matter of course, the first being shortly after his ordination, when Amator saved from the attention of devils a wealthy and noble pagan chief of the Aedui named Eraclius, and healed his Christian wife Palladia of a dire disease. It is an interesting story on account of its implications. Palladia had come to dwell in Auxerre, where her family inheritance was situated, taking up her abode in the suburbs; and her husband had evidently joined her on her own patrimony. We shall see Sidonius living on his wife's estate at Avitacum, and other examples show this to have been a common Gaulish practice. On account of Palladia's vain display of ornament she was denied Holy Communion. Offence was taken at this refusal, and Eraclius sought to take vengeance on Amator; but demons made an onset on Eraclius, and Palladia was punished by an attack of paralysis. Incited to penitence by a voice from Heaven, she hastened with her husband to St Amator, and was healed by the aid of his prayers, and Eraclius adopted Christianity.

On the death of Elladius, Amator was elected his successor by popular acclamation and consecrated c. 388. His long episcopate coincided with the onslaught of the Barbarians on Gaul, and he seems to have made a considerable impression by his active and useful tenure of office, performing many miracles, converting the pagans still remaining in the district, and building at least two churches. One incident in particular interests us

---

[1] *Uxor in sororem mutatur ex coniuge* (*Vita*, ch. 2). For a discussion of the whole question of celibacy and marriage in regard to ecclesiastics in the higher orders of the Church, and of the Canon Law regulating procedure, see R. Laprat, 'La Carrière cléricale de Saint Germain et le droit canonique de son temps'; in *Saint Germain et son Temps*, edited by G. Le Bras and E. Gilson (Auxerre, 1950), p. 163, and the references there cited.

· here, however, for it concerns his first relations with St Germanus, who is described as of noble lineage, and as being at that time the Governor of Auxerre.

In Chapter 4, we are told that Germanus was more devoted to hunting[1] than to the works of religion, and that he was in the habit of hanging the heads of the beasts which he killed in the chase from the branches of a beautiful pear tree in the midst of the city to display his prowess. The practice was probably common, for Strabo[2] tells us, on the authority of Posidonius, that it was a habit among the ancient Gauls for successful warriors to hang the heads of the men whom they had killed on the posts of the doors outside their dwellings, as trophies for the display of their prowess. This habit of the young Germanus displeased Amator as being reminiscent of heathenism, and after repeated vain remonstrances, he one day had the tree cut down during Germanus's absence.[3] This greatly incensed the youth, who resolved upon taking the life of his bishop; and the latter, feeling that the time was drawing near when it would be necessary to appoint a successor to himself,[4] set out to the city of Autun, in the territory of the Aedui, where dwelt Julius, Governor of Gaul.[5] Here he was honourably received by the Bishop Simplicius. During his sojourn in the city it was revealed to him from God that Germanus should be his successor, and having obtained the permission of the Governor Julius,[6] to whose jurisdiction Auxerre is said to have been subject, Amator returned to the city. Having collected the people into the *atrium* of his house, he warned them that the end of his life was near, and asked them to choose a successor. When they were silent, he led them to the church, Germanus included, and having made them lay down their arms outside, seized Ger-

---

[1] The account of the hunting episode, and the flight of St Amator to Autun, were formerly thought to be derived from the longer *Life* of St Germanus (see the *Vita S. Amatoris* by Surius, *Acta SS Prima Maii*). More probably the debt should be reversed.

[2] IV, iv, 5; cf. Diodorus Siculus, V, 29; XIV, 115. Cf. also Tacitus *Annals* I, 61.

[3] We may recall St Martin cutting down a tree which had been regarded as divine by the pagan Gauls.

[4] We seem to discern here two quite distinct motives assigned to Amator for his visit to Autun, probably representing two variant traditions.

[5] This detail appears to be quite unhistorical. Autun was never the seat of the *praefectus praetorio Galliarum*, and no prefect of the name of Julius is known from this time. See Levison, op. cit., p. 159, and n. 6.

[6] This would be necessary, since Germanus was already in the service of the State.

manus, tonsured him in the name of God, clothed him in the religious habit, and inducted him into Holy Orders.[1] Shortly afterwards Amator died, having first extracted a promise from his congregation that they would appoint Germanus as his successor.

Apart from the miraculous element there is nothing in this account which is at variance with historical probability. The conditions implied are those of the period to which St Amator is assigned. The bishop is married, as was usual at the time, and with the ascetic practice then fashionable he, like St Paulinus of Nola and St Eucherius of Lyons, resolves to forego the married state, which does not necessarily involve separation from his wife. Autun is still the capital of the Aedui, and an important political centre, to which Auxerre is subject, both politically and ecclesiastically. Amator takes refuge there in time of danger, doubtless because this was the home of his maternal family, where he would, in all likelihood, have been brought up, following Gaulish practice, and where he would be well known and surrounded by friends.

Trees are still held in veneration, as among the heathen Gauls, and Stephen can hardly have invented the characteristic touch of the hanging of the heads of the slain animals as trophies on the tree, reminiscent of what we learn from Strabo. It is characteristic of the bishops of the period that Amator is represented as descended from an old Gaulish family of the local aristocracy. This seems to be the case also with Eraclius and his wife Palladia, his earliest converts; and here we note the high prestige of the wife, a characteristic of Gaulish social life. The love of hunting ascribed to Germanus is wholly in accord with the fashion of the time. It seems probable that Stephen is deriving his materials, at least in part, from ecclesiastical saga, rather than that he is inventing fiction.

---

[1] According to Constantius's *Life of St Germanus*, ch. 2, the latter was elected by the unanimous vote (? acclamation) of clergy, aristocracy, and commons; but the account given in the *Life of St Amator* is fully in accord with contemporary practice, while the statement of Constantius may be merely a general inference. We see the change-over from the old form of election by popular acclamation to the later appointment by consent of the bishops in the letter of Sidonius Apollinaris to his friend Domnulus (IV, 25), and it is to be noted that here it is the metropolitan Bishop of Lyons, Bishop Patiens, who by his vigorous action, substitutes episcopal election for the old popular vote. The passage in the *Life of Amator* again looks like an attempt to reconcile variant traditions. On the current practice, see further H. G. J. Beck, *Pastoral Care of Souls*, p. 15 f.

Turning now to St Germanus, we find our most important evidence in two contemporary notices in Gaulish chronicles. The first is the 'Anonymous Gaulish Chronicle'[1] (entry 114, an. 433), where we read: 'Germanus episcopus Altisiodori, virtutibus et vitae districtiòne clarescit.' ('Germanus, the Bishop of Auxerre, is illustrious for his virtues and for the austerity of his life.').

The second contemporary notice is contained in the Chronicle of Prosper of Aquitaine. Prosper, as we have seen, devoted his energies and his intellect to combating the spread of the Pelagian heresy, and his notice of Germanus is accordingly concerned with his importance in this anti-Pelagian campaign. The passage in the *Epitoma Chronicon*[2] of Prosper, s.a. 429, is as follows:

'Agricola Pelagianus, Severiani episcopi Pelagiani filius, ecclesias Brittaniae dogmatis sui insinuatione corrumpit, sed ad insinuationem Palladii diaconi papa Caelestinus Germanum Autisidorensem episcopum vice sua mittit et de turbatis hereticis Britannos ad catholicam fidem dirigit.'

('The Pelagian Agricola, son of the Pelagian bishop Severianus, corrupts the churches of Britain by the introduction of his doctrine; but at the suggestion of the deacon Palladius, Pope Celestine sends Germanus, bishop of Auxerre, as his own representative, and after the overthrow of the heretics, guides the Britons to the Catholic faith.')

Prosper does not tell us who Palladius was; but again in the same Chronicle, s.a. 431, he writes (ibid., s.a. 431): 'Ad Scottos in Christum credentes ordinatus a papa Caelestino Palladius primus episcopus mittitur.' ('Palladius, having been ordained by Pope Celestine, is sent as the first bishop to the Irish believing in Christ.')

It is generally assumed that the two notices of Palladius have reference to the same person; but, though this is very probable, we have no certainty.

It is clear from what Prosper tells us elsewhere that Pelagianism was especially flourishing in Britain at this time. Prosper refers to the subject again in his famous treatise *Contra Col-*

---

[1] *Mon. Germ. Hist.: Auct. Antiq.*, Vol. IX (ed. T. Mommsen, Berlin, 1892), p. 660.

[2] Ed. cit. (p. 171 f.).

latorem, in a passage following immediately upon his account of Celestine's banishment of Coelestius, Pelagius's disciple, from Italy:

'Nec vero segniore cura ab hoc eodem morbo Britannias liberavit, quando quosdam inimicos gratiae solum suae originis occupantes, etiam ab illo secreto exclusit Oceani, et ordinato Scotis episcopo dum Romanam insulam studet servare catholicam fecit etiam barbaram Christianam.'[1]

('Nor was he less assiduous in freeing the Britains from that same plague, since certain men who were "enemies of Grace"[2] had taken possession of the land of their birth; and he drove them out of that Ocean retreat, and ordained a bishop for the Irish, so that while he was at pains to keep the Roman island Catholic he also made the barbarian island Christian.')

Prosper's preoccupation with the Pelagian question makes him especially interested in Britain and in the mission of St Germanus, which he records in 429. For the same reasons, however, we must be on our guard against placing too much stress on the negative evidence – on what Prosper does not tell us (cf. p. 172). He would not, for example, be likely to take any interest in British affairs other than those which concerned the Pelagian troubles; and if St Germanus had other concerns in Britain we need not look to Prosper for information about them. It may be added here that the account of St Germanus given by Bede (*H.E.*, Book I, chs. 17–21) is of no independent value. It is taken, with the exception of the opening of ch. 17, directly from the *Life* by Constantius. The opening of ch. 17 is derived from Prosper's *Chronicon*.

Who was Palladius, at whose instigation Pope Celestine sent Germanus to Britain in 429? He was a deacon, a member of the third order of the ministry; and he was evidently a man whose opinions in regard to the spiritual needs of Britain were held in high respect in ecclesiastical circles in Rome. He may have been the Palladius consecrated two years later as Bishop to the Irish; but of his subsequent fate nothing is certainly known from ancient sources, and the traditions recorded some two centuries later are confused and unreliable. His identity is quite un-

[1] Prosper, *Liber contra Collatorem*, Migne, *P.L.*, Vol. LI, col. 271.
[2] This is the usual epithet by which the Pelagians were referred to by their opponents.

known.[1] I have suggested elsewhere[2] that he may possibly be the Palladius, son of Exuperantius, referred to by Rutilius Namatianus as having put down revolt among the Armoricans. We shall see that Constantius, the earliest biographer of St Germanus, emphasizes the special interest which the saint took in the fate of the Armoricans throughout his life, and Constantius himself seems to have been well informed in regard to Breton affairs.

It will have been noticed that Prosper does not mention any companion as having accompanied Germanus on his mission; nor does he tell us that Germanus came to Britain a second time. Our only authority for a companion on this visit, and for a second visit by Germanus to Britain at a later date, is the *Life* of the saint by one Constantius, who was probably a presbyter, possibly of Lyons (cf. p. 286). The work was composed at the request of Patiens, who became Bishop of Lyons in 449, and who is known to have been present at the Synod of Arles, along with Faustus of Riez, in or probably shortly before 475. He may have died about 494. The *Life* of Germanus is dedicated jointly to Patiens and Censurius, Bishop of Auxerre, in two prefatory letters which Constantius prefixed to the *Life*. At the time when Censurius received the second letter from Constantius, together with the *Life* (cf. p. 286), Censurius was already Bishop of Auxerre, for he held the see from 472–502. The letters are still extant, and are regarded as genuine. A fuller account of both Patiens and Constantius is reserved for the following chapter. At present I must confine myself to a consideration of the *Life* by Constantius as evidence for the actual life and work of Germanus.

The *Life* by Constantius was probably written about the year 480, or a few years later.[3] Constantius implies in the first prefatory letter that some time had passed since the saint's death (cf. p. 286); but, as Germanus is believed to have died in 448, the interval between the writing of the *Life* and the events to

---

[1] For some suggestions on this subject and further references the reader may consult Bury, *The Life of St Patrick* (London, 1905), *passim*; J. F. Kenney, *The Sources for the Early History of Ireland*, Vol. I (New York, 1929), pp. 165, 169, 327, 334. The subject of his relationship to St Patrick has been discussed recently by L. Bieler, *The Life and Legend of St Patrick* (Dublin, 1949), pp. 83 ff., 94 ff.

[2] *Studies in Early British History* (Cambridge, 1954), p. 223 ff.

[3] See W. Levison, 'Bischof Germanus von Auxerre, und die Quellen zu seiner Geschichte', *Neues Archiv der Gesellschaft für ältere deutsche Geschichtskunde*, Vol. XXIX (1903), p. 97 ff.; *Vita*, p. 231.

which it relates can not have been great. While Constantius was writing this *Life*, Lupus, who, Constantius tells us, was Germanus's companion in the first mission to Britain, was still alive, and in close touch with Constantius's friend, Sidonius Apollinaris. These men were in fact members of the same circle, and Constantius himself was a man of considerable literary gifts. ·

This being so, it is surprising to find that the work abounds in miracles and *fabulae*. Yet we have seen the same features playing an important part in Sulpicius Severus's *Life of St Martin*, which must have been largely written during the saint's actual lifetime; and indeed Constantius seems to have had this work of Sulpicius before him while actually writing.[1] Like St Paulinus and Sulpicius also he had to commend his story to the popular mind by adopting to some extent the manner of the popular story-teller, for which purpose he had a likely subject in the epic achievements of his hero. It is to this popular literary aim that we must attribute the ample detail and the liberal introduction of speeches, such as make the *vitae* of the Middle Ages so lively. This desire to arrest and impress an interested public is responsible for the introduction of such *fabulae* in the work of Germanus as the 'Alleluia Victory', to be discussed later.

The work has come down to us in two versions. The shorter version, which is believed to be the older and the more genuine, has been edited by W. Levison.[2] This is the version which I have followed throughout, though the longer version has also been considered. The longer version, which was edited by Laurentius Surius,[3] has been shown to be less reliable, and to have been interpolated, indeed re-written, somewhat later, and to contain much which is wholly legendary.[4]

---

[1] For a brief account of the nature of the literary indebtedness of Constantius to the *Vita Martini* by Sulpicius, see Levison, *Neues Archiv*, Vol. XXIX, p. 114 ff.; *Vita*, p. 231: 'Constantius non tam biographi quam hagiographi munere fungens *profectui omnium mirabilium exempla largiri sibi* proposuerat.'

[2] *Mon. Germ. Hist:. Script. Rer. Merov.*, Vol. VII (1920), p. 225 ff.

[3] *De Probatis Sanctorum Historiis*, Coloniae Agrippinae 1571–8, Vol. IV, No. XXXI (July), p. 426 ff.

[4] Levison has left us the invaluable results of his critical study of the *Vita* by Constantius, as well as some notes on other works relating to St Germanus, in the notes and preface to his edition of the *Vita*, and also, more fully, in the article on St Germanus cited earlier in this chapter. A useful account in English of the work of the saint, and of our sources of information, is given by Hugh Williams, in his *Christianity in Early Britain* (Oxford, 1912), p. 216 ff. A recent collection of studies has been published under the editorship of G. le Bras and E. Gilson under the title *Saint Germain et son Temps* (Auxerre, 1950).

The shorter version informs us that Germanus was born at Auxerre of noble parents.[1] From what is said later by the author we know that the date was probably c. 378.[2] Germanus was brought up as a Christian, and received a good education from his parents in *studia liberalia*, passing to Rome where he studied Law, and where he pleaded as an advocate before the 'tribunal of the prefecture';[3] but whether the reference is to the *praefectus praetorio* or the *praefectus urbi* is not stated. Whilst thus engaged he married a lady of a noble and wealthy Roman house, and in due course entered the service of the government, becoming *dux* and *vicarius* of the province.[4] Then by a rapid transition he is forcibly consecrated bishop, quite in accordance with what we read elsewhere of current ecclesiastical practice.

At this point the longer *Life* relates the episodes of Germanus's hunting, and of his feud with Amator, and of the flight of the latter to Autun and his subsequent return.[5] The shorter version (ch. 2) has none of these incidents, but passes directly from his offices of *dux* and *vicarius* to his election to the episcopate by popular acclamation. In the account of his election to the episcopate the longer *Life* describes more protracted and quite different proceedings, which are full of interest, comparable as they are with the election of St Ambrose (cf. p. 68, n. 4), and also with that of the Bishop of Châlons as described by Sidonius.[6] In this longer *Life of St Germanus*, as also in the *Life of Amator*, we read that in accordance with the custom of election by popular acclamation,[7] Amator, having called the people together, asked them to name a successor; but as they were silent he led the way to the church, followed by his flock, which included Germanus and apparently his companions in arms. Amator ordered them

---

[1] The ninth-century *Life* of the Saint, written by Heiric (cf. p. 267), gives the names of his parents as Rusticus and Germanilla, and states that they were buried in a church of St Peter on their own estate named *Epponiacus*.

[2] See Levison, *Vita*, p. 251, n. (a).

[3] 'Deinde tribunalia praefecturae professione advocationis ornavit', *Vita*, ch. 1.

[4] 'Quem quidem togae praeconiis praeminentem protinus, res publica ad honorum praesumpsit insignia ducatus culmen et regimen per provincia conferendo.' (ch. 1.)

[5] See the edition of Surius, chs. 2–8 (now believed to be interpolated from the *Life of Amator* by Stephen, chs. 24, 25, 28, 29–32. Cf. Levison, *Vita Germani*, ed. cit., p. 251).

[6] *Ep.* IV, 25.

[7] I confess I find it very difficult to believe that Stephen invented this story, or even that he borrowed it. If he did, his historical sense was admirable; for it is exactly what seems to have been the practice of the fifth century. Cf. p. 291.

to leave their arms outside before entering the church, then, when all were inside and the doors closed, he seized and tonsured Germanus, at the same time stripping off his military insignia and substituting those of an ecclesiastical ordinand.

I shall pass over the austerities[1] attributed to Germanus by Constantius, and his ecclesiastical work in Auxerre, including the monastery which he is said to have founded near the city, on the opposite bank of the River Yonne.[2] The fact of paramount importance in the *Life* is the mission to Britain already referred to by Prosper who, as we have seen, assigns it to the year 429. According to Constantius, Germanus was accompanied in this mission by St Lupus of Troyes, of whom Prosper makes no mention. Prosper tells us that Germanus was sent to Britain by Pope Celestine *vice sua*, 'as his representative', at the suggestion of a deacon, Palladius, to suppress the heresy of Pelagianism which was gaining ground in Britain at this time. Constantius makes no mention of Palladius, but relates (ch. 12) that an embassy was sent to the bishops of Gaul from Britain, bringing information that Pelagianism was undermining the faith among British Christians, and begging help for the Catholic faith. A synod was held in Gaul – so says Constantius, though no such synod has been traced in Gaulish records – and at the request of this synod Germanus was sent to Britain, accompanied by Bishop Lupus of Troyes.

The account of the mission to Britain (ch. 13 f.) given by Constantius is quite fantastic. The journey, we are told, was made in winter, but nothing is said as to where the landing took place. Indeed throughout the *Life*, indications of time, especially in relation to Easter, are more specific than those of place. Nowhere in the *Life* can we identify any place in Britain.

Having reached Britain (ch. 14) the two bishops preached widely, both in the churches and in the open country, spreading the Catholic faith on all sides. Then follows a great discussion, a kind of mass meeting of the Catholics opposed to the Pelagians. 'On this side divine authority, on that human presumption; on this side the Faith, on that delusion; on this side Christ is leader, on that Pelagius. . . . But falsehood is defeated, error is

[1] The most interesting of these is the statement made by Constantius that his wife became to him as a sister, cf. pp. 71, 152.
[2] The foundation seems to be of later date however (see Levison, *Vita Germani*, ed. cit. I, p. 254).

refuted . . . the people as they hearkened could scarcely be restrained; however they proclaimed their decision by acclamation.' The rhetorical style of Constantius has full scope in this chapter, and in the chapter which follows, the triumph of the Roman party is crowned by the miracle of the healing of the blind daughter of an official, somewhat vaguely described as a *vir tribuniciae potestatis* ('a man of tribunician power'). The last doubts are dispersed, and the Catholic faith is accepted.

But this is not the end. After the discomfiture of the Pelagians in this strange form of ecclesiastical council, Germanus and his colleagues take their way to the tomb of St Alban (ch. 16); and again no indication is given as to its locality. Gildas, in his account of the martyrdom of St Alban, does not say that it was at Verulamium, though Bede does, perhaps from conjecture. Gildas's conjecture that it was near the Thames is more likely.[1]

We are now told (ch. 17) that during Lent the Picts and Saxons joined forces against Germanus; but again nothing is said as to the precise locality. The armies met on Easter Sunday. Germanus led the British forces, and – so Constantius tells us – guided them to a valley surrounded by hills, and commanded them all to answer his voice with one shout. The priests now (ch. 18) approach the enemy shouting 'Alleluia' three times, which is echoed by their whole army, and reverberates among the hills. The enemy flee in panic, victory is secured without a blow. The admirable narrative style of Constantius still today succeeds in imposing this fantastic story on our sober historians.

There is nothing improbable in the combination of Picts and Saxons, and a victory by Roman military aid in 429 may well be historical. But the narrative of Constantius is composed purely for edification and obviously in the interests of the anti-Pelagian party in Gaul. Constantius and Prosper had the same interests in view in their notice of this event. The hand of the Church is clear throughout Constantius's entire narrative of the mission, including the coincidence of the activities of the Picts and Saxons during Lent, and the battle on Easter Sunday. But the effective respite which the Gaulish missionary bishop procured for Roman Britain from her Barbarian enemies is very

[1] See C. E. Stevens, 'Gildas Sapiens', *English Historical Review*, Vol. LVI (1941), p. 273.

specifically related and emphasized. It is not impossible that it was the primary object of the expedition.

There follows an interval during which the saint pays a diplomatic visit to Arles to induce the authorities to reduce the taxation of his fellow-citizens (ch. 22), while Hilary is bishop, and Auxiliaris holds the prefecture of the Gauls. The mission is successful, for Germanus heals the sick wife of Auxiliaris, and immediately after the return of Germanus to Auxerre, Constantius relates (ch. 25) the arrival of a second mission from Britain, announcing the revival of Pelagianism and begging the help of Germanus as before. No date is specified, and the indications given by Constantius are vague. He seems to suggest that the second visit probably took place between 441 and 448.[1] The words with which it is introduced in ch. 25, *Interea ex Britanniis nuntiatur* ('Meantime word is brought from the Britains'), occur immediately after Germanus's return from Arles in 441.

According to Constantius he was accompanied on his second visit by a certain Bishop Severus, of whom nothing further is said. Bede states that he was Bishop of Trier and had been a disciple of St Lupus of Troyes;[2] but the *Life of St Lupus of Troyes* makes no mention of the journey of Severus to Britain. The name of Severus is entered in the catalogue of Bishops of Trier on the authority of Bede; but the *exemplaria* of this do not go back beyond the tenth century.[3] As Levison points out,[4] the Severus in question might even be identified with Bishop Severus of Vence in Provence, who took part in the Synods of Riez (439) and Voison (442).

Prosper, as we have seen, makes no mention of this second journey. This is usually attributed to the fact that his Chronicle makes hardly any reference to Gallic affairs after 440, owing to the fact that he had probably left Marseilles by this date, and was acting as secretary (*notarius*) to Pope Leo I. Nevertheless in his new office in Rome he must have had more up-to-date and reliable information of events of outstanding ecclesiastical importance even in Gaul than he could have had in Marseilles.

---

[1] See Levison, *Neues Archiv*, Vol. XXIX, p. 127; cf. C. E. Stevens, 'Gildas Sapiens', *E.H.R.*, Vol. LVI, p. 365, n. 10.

[2] *H.E.* I, ch. 21. Levison regards the *Life of Lupus of Troyes*, ch. 11 (*SS Merov.* III, 124) as Bede's source. See Levison, op. cit., p. 128, n. 6, and cf. his note at *Vita Germani*, p. 268.

[3] See Levison, *Vita Germani*, ed. cit., p. 270, n. 3.

[4] See *Neues Archiv.*, Vol. XXIX, p. 129, and the references there cited.

His omission of all mention of the second visit is therefore remarkable, especially in view of the preoccupation of his Chronicle with heresies.

It must be confessed the second journey looks suspiciously like a duplication of the first, possibly incorporating a variant tradition. The narrative is very summary, nothing specific seems to be claimed as a result of it, and the course of events is strangely reminiscent of the first. In both cases the object is the same, and in both Germanus is accompanied by a fellow-bishop. In both a story is prominent of the cure by Germanus of the young child of a prominent official who apparently held some kind of Roman title. In the first he is merely described as *vir tribuniciae potestatis*,[1] who, together with his wife, presented to St Germanus their ten-year-old blind daughter, whom the saint heals (ch. 15). The incident is represented as taking place immediately (*subito*) after the disputation with the Pelagians, and before the visit to the tomb of St Alban. In the second (cf. 26 f.) a certain (*quidam*) Elafius, whose exact-title is not given, but whose prestige is possibly very high (*regionis illius primus*), also comes forward 'immediately' (*subito*) to present to the saint his son who has been 'stricken with a deplorable disease in the flower of his youth' (*quem in ipso flore adulescentiae debilitas dolenda damnaverat*). This disease, which is said to be caused by a contracted knee, is likewise cured. I submit that the two journeys by the two pairs of bishops, the two prominent officials, with their ailing children and the cures, and the two victories over Pelagianism are probably two variant duplicate accounts, which Constantius has related consecutively. Does not he himself warn us against accepting his narrative too readily, declaring that 'so many years have passed' since the events which he is recording that 'it is difficult to recover the facts from the silence in which they are buried?'[2]

One other point in this apparent duplication calls for comment. In both narratives the nature of the weather during the crossing is especially commented on. In the relatively brief account (ch. 25) of the second visit, the weather is merely stated to be propitious, though it is added that demons preceded

---

[1] On this title see R. G. Collingwood in Collingwood and Myres, *Roman Britain and the Saxon Settlements* (Oxford, 1936), p. 306.

[2] *Tanta enim jam temporum fluxere curricula, ut obscurata per silentium vix colligatur agnitio* (*Vita Germ., Ep. ad. Patientem.*)

the saint and, flying about the whole island, foretold his arrival. In the first account (ch. 13) a terrible storm is said to arise half-way through the voyage, and this is ascribed by Constantius to the instrumentality of the demons. Constantius, as if anxious to assign an important part to St Lupus in the expedition, repre-sents him as arousing the sleeping Germanus who quells the storm by his prayers. It is perhaps worth noting, however, that Germanus is again referred to here as *dux*,[1] which recalls the title *ducatus culmen* of ch. 1. It is just possible that some reminiscence of his early title and office also lies behind the phrase, used of his spiritual leadership in ch. 9, where he is said to visit his church and *monasterium* like a 'general (*dux*) of heavenly hosts'.[2] The figure of a military review seems to rise naturally to the mind of Constantius in connection with Germanus. It may be added that the details of strategical considerations by which Germanus is represented as guided in the disposition of his forces before the battle against the Picts are wholly in accord with military tactics, and carry more conviction than the 'Alleluia Victory'. It is remarkable that Constantius should note these military tactics, and should abstain from ascribing the victory to divine or miraculous agency, though he empha-sizes the coincidence of the battle with Easter.

It is not impossible that Constantius is attempting to weld together two rival traditions, or claims, one from Auxerre, the other from Troyes. The story of Lupus was probably derived from the latter, and seems to have been wholly ecclesiastical in tone. Geographically speaking, Auxerre and Troyes are twin cities, and both lay in the direct jurisdiction of Lyons. It would not be strange, therefore, if Constantius should represent Lupus as accompanying Germanus in an important enterprise, whether his statement is based on tradition or on surmise – or even on a sense of fitness. It has already been mentioned that Constantius represents both Germanus and Lupus as selected for the mission by a Synod of Arles in response to an appeal from the Britons. No such synod can be traced in ecclesiastical records;[3] but Germanus is represented as visiting Arles on a mission shortly before, and as being received there by Bishop Hilary (ch. 23).

[1] The words of the text are: *Et casu dux ipse vel pontifex fractus corpore lassitudine et sopore resolutus est.* For *vel* one MS. has *et*.

[2] *Quasi dux caelestium militum visitare.*

[3] On this subject, see Levison, *Neues Archiv*, Vol. XXIX, 124.

R

It might appear at first sight to be an argument in favour of the participation of Lupus in the mission of 429 that in a letter from Sidonius Apollinaris to Bishop Prosper of Orleans the two bishops are coupled together as models of episcopal excellence. As their sees occupied the two principal sites on the two upper confluents of the River Seine, we cannot attach too much importance to their association in this context. Yet the statement of Constantius deserves weighty consideration from the fact that Lupus was his own contemporary. When great enterprises are attributed to a man during his own lifetime there are good grounds for believing him to have at least had some part in them.

Prosper, on the other hand, in his account of the first mission, makes no mention of the Synod of Arles or of St Lupus. To Prosper, a layman of Marseilles, the Bishop of Troyes may have seemed less important than to Constantius, who was possibly in touch with Lupus personally. Nevertheless since Lupus is referred to by Sidonius[1] as the foremost bishop of his day in Gaul, Prosper could hardly have been ignorant of his participation had this been a fact, and his omission of any reference to Lupus is therefore very puzzling. Was it due to inadvertence?

It can hardly be that the naming of the two bishops together by both Constantius and Sidonius is wholly independent, but it is not easy to see its exact significance. Little help is to be got from dating, since the exact date neither of Constantius's *Life*, nor of the letter in which Sidonius makes mention of Lupus,[2] is known. As Constantius was a close friend of Sidonius, the latter may have coupled the two bishops together on the authority (perhaps verbal) of Constantius; or again because of the geographical proximity of the two sees. On the other hand we cannot dismiss the possibility that Constantius couples the two bishops together on the ground of this letter of Sidonius to himself. This is, however, not very likely; for why should Sidonius call Lupus the foremost prelate in Gaul unless some such exploit as the expedition to Britain were placed to his credit? Troyes was not one of the most important cities ecclesiastically. His high prestige must be due to his personal merit. His literary

---

[1] *Ep.* VIII, 15. Constantius, after all, was a contemporary of Lupus.

[2] The year 478 is tentatively suggested by Dalton as the date of Sidonius' letter; but this is quite uncertain. (*The Letters of Sidonius*, edited by O. M. Dalton (Oxford 1915), Vol. II, p. 172.)

prestige, of which we shall have more to say in the following chapter, would hardly be enough in itself to entitle him to such a high ecclesiastical encomium, even from Sidonius. Whatever the original reason, it seems to have been usual, at least later, to couple Germanus and Lupus together, for in a letter written by Bishop Aunachar of Auxerre to the presbyter Stephen, probably between 573 and 589, we find the three names, Germanus, Hilary and Lupus, grouped together in this order (see p. 267). This may again, however, be due to the influence of Constantius's *Life*.

However we view the first expedition to Britain, whether we regard its object as primarily ecclesiastical, political, or even military; whether we accept Constantius's statement of the participation of Lupus or not – we must, I am convinced, regard the second expedition of Germanus to Britain with great suspicion. A careful comparison in detail of the accounts of the two expeditions as given by Constantius leaves a strong impression that he has given us two versions of the same story. While details of the two passages correspond to a surprising degree, there are also other features of the second expedition which are of very dubious character, such as the absence of any action or narrative of public events in Britain. Nothing is related as happening, nothing is effected. We shall see that this consideration has an important bearing on the apparently somewhat confused chronology of Constantius's narrative.

Immediately after this second journey it is stated by Constantius (ch. 28) that Germanus received a mission from the Armoricans who had been in rebellion against Aetius,[1] and who had been punished by the heavy hand of Gochar[2] (*Gohar, Goar*), the king of the Alani, at that time acting as an ally of the Romans.[3] Gochar (*Gohar, Goar*) is described by Constantius as

[1] For an account of the rebellions of the Armoricans, see Levison, *Neues Archiv.*, Vol. XXIX, p. 139, ff.

[2] This name can only be a further stage in the barbarization of the name which appears in Olympiodorus (*Thebaeus* s.v. 412) as *Goar*. For other forms under which the name occurs elsewhere, see Levison, *Vita*, p. 271, n. 5. For further references see C. Zeuss, *Die Deutschen und die Nachbarstämme* (ed. Göttingen, 1904), pp. 468, 704 f.

[3] When the Alani, Vandals and Suevi crossed the Rhine on their route to Spain in 409, a small part of the Alani, who under Goar had joined the Romans in 407, remained behind, and in 411 united with Gunther, the Burgundian king. Later, in 413, Goar and his Alani seem to have joined themselves to Ataulf and the Goths, and it is doubtless this Goar with whom Paulinus of Pella makes his strange pact during the siege of Bordeaux in 414 (see p. 125). For an outline of his career, see Levison, *Vita Germani*, p. 271, n. 5; *Neues Archiv.*, Vol. XXIX, p. 133 ff.

rex ferocissimus, who is said to have cast greedy eyes on the Armoricans 'with the greed characteristic of barbarians (*aviditate barbaricae cupiditatis*)'.[1] In an important passage (ch. 28) Constantius represents Germanus as setting off at once to meet the king of the Alani, and as opposing himself unarmed to his host, seizing the royal bridle and petitioning the king through an interpreter to desist from his punitive devastation. His appeal succeeded, and it is possible that both the mission from the Armoricans and the success of Germanus on their behalf are to be ascribed to earlier authority *ducatus culmen et regimen per provincias* claimed for him by Constantius (cf., however, p. 263). We are told, however, that Goar, while desisting from his immediate purpose, would only promise a permanent peace for the Armoricans on condition that pardon should be granted by the emperor or by Aetius. Germanus accordingly at once set off to Italy to negotiate the pact (ch. 29 ff.). The course of his journey through Autun and across the Alps, his route through Milan and his sojourn in Ravenna, give Constantius an admirable framework into which to introduce a series of miracles, and an account of the austerities and saintly deeds of his hero, without interrupting the course of his historical narrative; and we cannot but admire the artistic skill with which he carries his story forward, holding an exact balance between the secular and the saintly achievements.

Now it is difficult to see how the expedition to Britain can be separated from the expedition to Armorica and the encounter with Goar. It is clear that Constantius regards them as closely associated, but places the latter immediately after the second expedition. If we dismiss the second expedition, however, we may perhaps look upon the collapse of the Armorican insurrection as brought about by the success of the first expedition to Britain and by the set-back inflicted on the Saxons and their allies in Britain. The narrative of Constantius, apart from its miraculous elements, and apart from the probable duplication of the British expedition, would then give a coherent picture of the part which Germanus plays in the history of the time. Let us follow it further.

It has been mentioned above that Constantius was evidently well informed on Breton events, whatever the source of his in-

[1] Cf. Salvian (*De Gub. Dei*, IV, xiv, 68): *rapacitas Alani*.

formation may have been. In ch. 40 he again reverts to Breton insurgence, informing us that Germanus had obtained from the proper authority the pardon for Armorica which had dictated his journey to Ravenna,[1] where the court was sitting at the time; but that a fresh rebellion broke out 'among that fickle and undisciplined people', led by a certain Tibatto,[2] rendering the mission of Germanus fruitless.[3] This Tibatto is mentioned in the Anonymous Gaulish Chronicle (entry 117, an. 435) as the leader of what appears to be an independence movement set on foot by the *Bagaudae* (cf. p. 166 f.);[4] and again in an. 437 (see entry 119) as being among those captured or slain when the rising was quelled.[5] As Levison points out, there is a difficulty here in regard to date, since Constantius speaks of Tibatto's rebellion in connection with the death of Germanus, which took place at Ravenna between 444 and 450.[6] Levison suggested that this discrepancy might be explained either on the ground that Tibatto may have lived on after the defeat of 437, or Constantius may have confused the leader of an earlier insurrection with another of a later date.[7] My own suggestion is that Constantius, by duplicating Germanus's expedition to Britain, which seems to have shortly preceded Tibatto's rebellion, has been forced to place the latter too late. But however the discrepancy has arisen, it is a comparatively slight matter. The important facts are, first that Constantius has recorded the Armorican insurrections under Tibatto following on St Germanus's British mission or missions; and secondly the important influence exercised by the saint, first in preventing the utmost severity in Goar's punitive measures, and then in his diplomatic activities in Ravenna. It would be interesting to know if there is any

---

[1] Cf. *Vita Germ.*, ch. 35.

[2] *Nisi Tibattonis perfidia mobilem et indisciplinatum populum ad rebellionem pristinam revocasset.*

[3] *Quo facto et intercessio sacerdotis evanuit, et imperialis credulitas circumscriptione frustrata est. Qui tamen pro calliditate multiplici brevi poenas perfidae temeritatis exsolvit.*

[4] *Gallia ulterior Tibattonem principem rebellionis secuta a Romana societate discessit, a quo tracto initio omnia paene Galliarum servitia in Bacaudam conspiravere.*

[5] *Capto Tibattone et ceteris seditionis partim principibus vinctis, partim necatis Bacaudarum commotio conquiescit.*

[6] *Vita Germ.*, ch. 42. Cf. Levison, Introduction to the *Vita*, pp. 226, 229; *Neues Archiv.*, Vol. XXIX, p. 138 f.

[7] For further references to the Armorican rebellion of 437 see Levison loc. cit. Perhaps the most interesting of the references there cited are those of Sidonius (*Carm.* VII, 246) and of Merobaudes (Panegyric on the 2nd – or perhaps the 3rd – Consulship of Aetius).

closer relationship between Constantius's *Life* and the *Anonymous Gaulish Chronicle*. Certainly the latter was also well informed in regard to Breton affairs. Apart from the information which it gives about Gochar, we have seen that it also furnishes a laudatory reference to St Germanus.

Constantius relates the death of Germanus in Chapter 42 immediately after the account of the success of his mission to Ravenna, which was again immediately followed by the news of the fresh outbreak in Armorica. The account of the saint's illness and death at Ravenna is introduced vaguely (ch. 41) by the words *Quadam die*, but it must be assumed to have taken place after only a short interval. Constantius mentions (ch. 35) that Placidia was ruling in Ravenna as regent for her young son, afterwards Valentinian III, and he tells us (ch. 42) that she visited the saint on his sick-bed and draped his body after his death. In due course his remains were honourably conveyed to Gaul, and buried in his own city.

On the whole, when we reflect that Constantius was not primarily composing with a historical end in view, the amount of historical matter which he records is more striking than his omissions or inaccuracies. He has recorded a number of the names of important officials concerned, and their exact functions, and he knows the political situation in Italy. He knows that the Empress Placidia was ruling as regent for her son Valentinian III, and that the court was at Ravenna (ch. 35). He knows that Peter (i.e. Peter II, *Chrysologus*)[1] was Bishop of Ravenna at the time of Germanus's death (see chs. 35, 42). He is familiar with Segisvult, the *magister militum* (ch. 38), and he is only a little premature in attributing to him 'patrician rank'.[2]

In Gaul itself his reference (ch. 24) to Auxiliaris as Prefect of the Gauls is especially interesting, since we know of him elsewhere only from a single inscription on a milestone.[3] He refers (ch. 23) to Hilary, Bishop of Arles. He has remembered Goar (*Gochar*) as *rex ferocissimus Alanorum*, ('the extremely fierce king of the Alani'), and the military subordinate of Aetius, the *vir magnificus* (ch. 28). And he makes mention (ch. 40) of the *perfidia* of Tibatto, the leader of the Armorican rebels, though he has confused the period of his activity. In general it may be said

---

[1] See Levison *Vita*, *M.G.H.* VII, p. 276, n. 1.
[2] ibid., op. cit., p. 278, n. 1. [3] See Levison, op. cit., p. 232.

Constantius has remembered the relative order of events, though he seems to be perhaps slightly inaccurate in his absolute chronology.

Before closing the narrative by Constantius there is one passage which calls for fuller discussion. This is the statement about the saint's early training in the *studia liberalia*, and his promotion to military and civil honours – *ducatus culmen* and the *regimen per provincias*. The passage, however we view it, strikes the key-note to the whole *Life*, and I have left it to the end because I think that we can only hope to interpret it rightly in the light of the saint's career.

The passage is undoubtedly very difficult. The *ducatus culmen* was an essentially military function, and comprised the leadership of the Armoricans and the Nervii, including the coastal districts from the Somme to the Gironde, and the interior of Aquitaine and Lugdunensis I. It would have included the province of Senonia, in which Auxerre stood. Such an office would have made him responsible for the defence of these regions, or, in other words, for the Saxon Shore defences of Gaul, giving him the command of the forces of Lugdunensis II, III, and IV.[1]

On the other hand the office of *regimen per provincias* implies provincial government, and, since the Reforms of Diocletian, military functions could not be undertaken together with a civil career. 'The *cursus honorum* of Germanus constitutes a heresy.'[2]

It cannot be contended that we are here confronted with an abnormality due to the exigencies of the political crisis. The indications are too precise.

In a recent article on the civil career of St Germanus, the French scholar Gaudemet, following on earlier hints by Levison,[3] argues that the three early details of St Germanus's career – his *studia liberalia*, his juridical training, and his military honours – are borrowed from the *Life of St Ambrose* composed by his personal attendant and biographer Paulinus.[4] As early as 1904 Levison had expressed scepticism in regard to Ger-

---

[1] See Tillemont XV, 8; and for the title, see the *Notitia Dignitatum*, ed. O. Seeck (Berlin, 1876), *Occidentalis*, 45, No. XXXVII, p. 205.
[2] Gaudemet, 'La Carrière civile de St Germain', in the volume of studies issued at Auxerre in 1950 by Le Bras and Gilson, *St Germain d'Auxerre et son Temps*, p. 111 ff.
[3] *Vita*, p. 251.   [4] Gaudemet, loc. cit.

manus's legal training, pointing out that it is inappropriate to a bishop, and he had argued that the military functions are even less suited to a lawyer than to a bishop. He was clearly inclined to attach little weight to the testimony of Constantius in this respect, and raised the question[1] as to whether Constantius had read the account of the early career of St Ambrose by his disciple Paulinus.[2]

This technical question regarding Germanus's early offices is one on which I do not feel qualified to pronounce; but it does not seem to me that the literary relationship between the passages in Constantius and Paulinus is a very close one. On the other hand the double functions, civil and military, attributed to Germanus by Constantius, would be entirely in accord with the later career narrated by Constantius – with the military mission to Britain, and the diplomatic missions both to the Alan king, and to Arles and Ravenna. We could better understand Germanus as the leader of a victorious campaign[3] against Picts and Saxons across the channel if he were responsible for the military measures safeguarding the Saxon Shore of Gaul. Military bishops were no novelty in Gaul at that time, as we shall see from the following chapters.

Why is Germanus represented as conducting a military campaign in Britain? The Armorican tract had been a continuous source of trouble since its first revolt in 409 and its brief independence under Honorius. We have already found Rutilius Namatianus referring to a certain Exuperantius as engaged there in trying to restore peace, and to prevent slaves from enslaving their masters (cf. p. 129). In fact this part of Gaul seems to have been the principal area of the activities of the Bagaudae (cf. p. 130, n. 1), who are referred to by Constantius (ch. 40) as 'mobilis et indisciplinatus populus'.[4] There can be no

---

[1] *Neues Archiv.*, Vol. XXIX (1904), p. 117; cf. *Vita*, p. 251, n. 5.

[2] Migne, *P.L.*, Vol. XIV, col. 27 ff. Also *Vita Sancti Ambrosii Mediolanensis Episcopi a Paulino*, text and English translation by Sister Mary Simplicia Kaniecka (Washington, 1928), ch. 2.

[3] I cannot accept C. E. Stevens' estimate of Germanus as an 'amateur general' ('Gildas Sapiens', *English Historical Review*, Vol. LVI (1941), p. 365). R. G. Collingwood recognized the expert nature of the military aid implied by Germanus' campaign, but does not seem to have realized the actual military character and significance of the expedition (see Collingwood and Myres *Roman Britain and the Saxon Settlements*, p. 306 ff.).

[4] For further contemporary references and some discussion, see Levison, *Vita Germani* (ed. cit.), p. 280, n. to ch. 40.

doubt that unrest in Armorica was due in a large measure to the activities of the Saxon pirates along their shores. At the same time we have a clear statement by Zosimus that the people of Armorica were stimulated to rebellion by the example of the insular Britons, who had thrown off the Roman yoke. If Germanus did, in fact, lead an army in Britain in 429, was it primarily to strike at the root of this harm? We know that the command of the Saxon Shore in Britain and in Gaul had been a joint one in earlier times, and we have no grounds for assuming that it had been separated. The reverse is, in fact, more probable.[1]

As regards Germanus's early juridical training, and the civil office which follows as a natural corollary in the narrative of Constantius, it is again not easy to dismiss his statements lightly. Except for the two expeditions to Britain, the saint's activities – apart from his miracles, with which we are not concerned – are wholly devoted to civil negotiations, first at Arles (apparently fiscal), then with the Alan leader, from whose punitive measures he obtains a respite for the rebels; and finally on a formal diplomatic mission to Ravenna, in the course of which he dies. The narrative of Constantius presents us with a flawless consistency. Either he has invented the early military and civil training and offices to account for the saint's later career; or he has developed the later career from some – to us unknown – sources relating to his early offices; or, perhaps he had authority for both. But I do not think he has borrowed anything from Paulinus's *Life of St Ambrose*.

Constantius possessed fine literary gifts, and the *Life of St Germanus* is an admirable production. Bishop Patiens had made an excellent choice in selecting an author for a *Life* of this new saint, and the work of Constantius must have quickly become a serious rival to Sulpicius's *Life of St Martin*. St Martin had been a quiet recluse, the creation of the relatively peaceful conditions of the fourth century. But the fifth century, with Gaul overrun by the Teutonic invaders, called for sterner stuff. Constantius had a high public spirit in addition to his literary gifts. In the chapter which follows we shall see him taking a long and arduous journey in the winter of 473 to help Sidonius, besieged

[1] I have discussed this somewhat more fully in a volume of *Studies in Early British History* (Cambridge, 1954), p. 227 ff.

in Clermont in Auvergne by the Visigoths. He was, in fact, just the man to write a biography which would bring out the heroic qualities in Germanus, and the saint is accordingly shown to us throughout his life in the pages of Constantius as a man of action.

The evidence of the *Life* seems to me to suggest that the reputation of St Germanus was deliberately exploited in Gaul for the following reasons. First of all the Pelagian question was all important. We have a large body of information relating to the controversy in the south, but little for northern Gaul. The *Life* by Constantius is perhaps our most important contribution to the literature relating to the subject for the north.

In the second place it must have been felt desirable to create a new popular saint to rival the cult of St Martin in order to exalt the metropolitan see of Lyons and check the growing prestige of Tours. Finally, by creating a saint who belonged to the local aristocracy, Constantius was ranging himself on the side of Pope Celestine[1] and those Gaulish bishops who sought to check the increasing tendency to elect monastic bishops – *peregrini* of no particular rank or local connection – to fill the sees of Gaul as they became vacant.

It would seem probable that already in his own lifetime Germanus was held in high respect. The references in the contemporary Anonymous Gaulish Chronicle and in the *Epitoma Chronicon* of Prosper have already been quoted (p. 248). Sidonius Apollinaris, writing a generation later, speaks of him as the standard of excellence among bishops (*Ep.* xv). Nicetius, Bishop of Trier, enumerating the Gaulish saints whose tombs were famous for their miracles, names St Germanus first in order after St Martin;[2] and Gregory of Tours bears witness to his miracles both during his lifetime and after his death.[3] His dedications, of whatever date, are very numerous, and Heiric, writing in the second half of the ninth century, even declares that his cult had spread to Britain, for in speaking of Britain he declares: 'Haec beato Germano peculiari devotione submissa.'[1]

---

[1] Cf. his *Letter: Cuperemus quidem* (p. 95).

[2] *Mon. Germ. Hist.: Epist.*, Vol. III (*Epist. Merov. et Karol. Ævi*, Vol. I, Berlin, 1892), p. 121. Nicetius became bishop in 526 or 527 (Duchesne, *Fastes Épisc.*). It is interesting to observe that Nicetius groups Germanus, Hilary and Lupus together, in this order (see above).

[3] See Gregory of Tours (ed. Krusch, *Mon. Germ. Merov.*, Vol. I). *In Gloria Confess.*, ch. 40; *Liber de Virtutibus S. Juliani*, ch. 29. See also his *History of the Franks*, V, ch. 8 (14).

The *Vita* probably spread beyond the limits of Lyons and Auxerre shortly after it was written. The *Life of Epiphanius*, composed between 501 and 504 by Ennodius, Bishop of Pavia, himself a native of Gaul, contains passages which may be verbally reminiscent of it; and the *Vita Radegundis* by Venantius Fortunatus, the contemporary of Gregory of Tours, contains (ch. 16) a reference to Germanus which is also thought to be an echo of the *Vita*.[2]

In a letter which is still extant[3] Bishop Aunachar of Auxerre, whose activity fell between 573 and 589, requested the Presbyter Stephen to write the 'Life of Germanus' in verse, and that of Amator in prose (cf. p. 259). This 'Life of Germanus', if it was ever composed, has not survived; but one day Abbot Lothair of St Germain in Auxerre (864–5), son of Charles the Bald, found the letter of Aunachar and requested the monk Heiric to take the task in hand. Lothair died soon after, but Heiric composed a *Vita* in Latin hexameters in six books,[4] to which he added later two books in prose on the miracles of Germanus.[5] The works add nothing of value to our knowledge of the saint, for though Heiric gives some information not derived from Constantius, his work is too late to have any independent authority.[6]

In one passage of the *Miracula*[7] Heiric gives us some information which has a certain interest, though perhaps rather for what it tells us of Irish *peregrini* of the late eighth century than for St Germanus. The author tells us of an aged and holy man called Marcus, a bishop of Britain, educated in Ireland, who after having exercised his episcopate for a long time in Britain, had come to France in the time of Charles the Bald as a *peregrinus* and was living there as a very holy anchorite in the *coenobium* of SS Medard and Sebastian – presumably Soissons. Heiric claims that Marcus had related to him many acts which St

---

[1] *Miracula Germani*, I, 54, 80.
[2] For these references, see Levison, *Neues Archiv.*, Vol. XXIX, p. 144 f. Cf. his Introduction to the *Vita Germani*, M.G.H.: *Script. Rer. Merov.*, VII, p. 232 f.
[3] *Mon. Germ. Hist.: Epist.* III (*Epist. Merov. et Karol. Ævi*, Vol. I, Berlin, 1892), p. 446 f.
[4] Edited by L. Traube, *Mon. Germ. Hist.: Poetae Latini Ævi Carolini*, Vol. III (Berlin, 1896), p. 421 ff. See also Migne, *P.L.*, Vol. CXXIV, col. 1131 ff.
[5] *De Miraculis Germani*, Migne *P.L.*, Vol. CXXIV, col. 1207 ff.
[6] See Tillemont, op. cit., Vol. XV, p. 7. For some account of the work of Heiric, and of other notices and *Vitae* of St Germanus later than that of Constantius, see Levison, *Neues Archiv*, Vol. XXIX, p. 163 f.
[7] Book I, cap. VIII, par. 80 (cf. also Traube, op. cit., p. 422, n. 3).

Germanus had performed during his sojourn in Britain, and which Marcus had assured him (cf. cap. 82) were still preserved in Britain in a written form. These Heiric claims to have incorporated from the narration of Marcus into his *De Miraculis Germani*. Since Heiric incorporates matter relating to Soissons in his *Annales* of Auxerre which were completed in 875, his statement about Marcus must refer to a date before this year.[1] The passage forms a rider to certain sections of the *Historia Brittonum*, notably chapter 47, in which it is claimed that a written 'Book of St Germanus' (*Liber beati Germani*), which is clearly distinct from that of Constantius, was already in existence in Britain by the eighth century. These passages must now be considered. I shall speak of them only briefly here, referring the reader for fuller details to a recent study which I have made of them elsewhere.[2]

The *Historia Brittonum*,[3] in the form in which it has come down to us, is now known to be the last edition of a compilation from earlier sources. The author's preface to this last version claims to have been made by a certain Nennius, or Nemnivus. On internal evidence its date may probably be placed somewhere c. 800.[4] The version preserved at Chartres[5] is commonly, though not universally, held to be the oldest. It is certainly the oldest known copy, dating from c. 900. The Chartres text is poorly transcribed and fragmentary, and also selective, concerning itself especially with the activities of St Germanus. The deliberate purpose of the selection is made clear by the heading which occurs in the Chartres MS. only, and which is as follows:

'Incipiunt exberta fiiurbagen de Libro Sci Germani inuenta et origine et genealogia Britonum, de Ætatibus Mundi.'[6]

---

[1] See Traube, loc. cit. [2] *Studies in Early British History*, p. 34 ff.

[3] The best editions are those of Mommsen, *Mon. Germ. Hist.: Chronica Minora*, Vol. III, p. 111 ff. and the more recent French edition of F. Lot, *Nennius et l'Historia Brittonum* (Paris, 1934). Important also is the Early Irish Version known as the *Lebor Bretnach*, edited by A. G. van Hamel (Dublin, 1932). A useful English translation of the work, entitled 'Nennius's History of the Britons' is contained in *Six Old English Chronicles*, by J. A. Giles (London, 1848), p. 381 ff.; and a more recent translation has been published by A. W. Wade-Evans (London, 1938). For some discussion, also in English, see Wade-Evans, *Welsh Christian Origins* (Oxford, 1934), p. 63 ff.

[4] For further details, reference may be made to *Studies in Early British History* (edited by N. K. Chadwick), p. 25.

[5] See F. Lot, op. cit., p. 20 ff.; cf., however, H. M. Chadwick in *Studies in Early British History*, p. 23 f. [6] Lot, op. cit., p. 227.

The passage is obscure, but is generally interpreted as suggesting that the text which follows contains 'excerpts'(?) made by the son of Urbgen, which he had found in the *Book of St Germanus*. The Urbgen in question is tentatively identified with the Urbagen (i.e. presumably *Urien*, the lord of Rheged) referred to in Chapter 63 of the *Historia Brittonum* as having besieged the Northumbrians in Lindisfarne. The son mentioned in the heading of the Chartres text as having made the *Exberta* relating to St Germanus is conjectured with some probability to be the *Rum* (? for *Rhun*) *map Urbgen* mentioned in Chapter 63 of the *Historia* as having baptized Edwin, the Northumbrian king, whose conversion is known to have taken place in 627.

The passages in the *Historia Brittonum* relating to the saint are four in number. They are quite distinctive in content, and relate, not to Germanus's strife against the Pelagians, of which we hear from both Prosper and Constantius; or against the Picts and Saxons, of which we hear only from Constantius. None of these are mentioned in the *Historia* in connection with Germanus. The four passages in question relate entirely to his strife against two British princes, one a wicked *tyrannus*, Benli, who lived in a fortress, apparently in Powys on the eastern border of Wales;[1] the other a great prince, Guorthigirn (Vortigern), also ruling in eastern Wales,[2] neither of whom is mentioned by Prosper or Constantius. In these encounters between Germanus and the native British princes as related in the *Historia*, Benli is destroyed on account of his hostile and inhospitable reception of the saint. Vortigern is accused of the sin of incest, and Germanus is represented as trying to convert him, and as pursuing him through Wales till Vortigern finally perished in Pembroke on the River Teifi:

'This is the end of Guorthigirn (Vortigern) as I have found it in the *Book of St Germanus*. Others, however, have said otherwise.'[3]

The whole account is obviously derived ultimately from saga, or oral tradition. Indeed the words of Nennius imply as much, for he gives three variant accounts of the manner of Vortigern's death, adding that the exact end of Vortigern is unknown, but that he died 'without praise', which seems to imply that Nen-

---

[1] *Historia Brittonum*, chs. 32–35.
[2] ibid., chs. 39, 47–49.
[3] 'Hic est finis Guorthigirni ut in illo libro Beati Germani repperi; alii autem aliter dixerunt.'

nius knows of no panegyric poems or elegies such as usually form the basis of later traditions of Celtic and Teutonic princes before the age of written records. Sir Ifor Williams believes that the saga which underlies our narrative relates primarily to Vortigern himself rather than to Germanus;[1] and there must certainly have been in existence a saga of Vortigern, which was probably in circulation throughout the Celtic world in the seventh and following centuries.[2]

On the other hand, the words of Nennius about the *Book of St Germanus*, which he claims as his source, imply that the lost narrative in question related primarily to St Germanus, and I have shown elsewhere[3] that the question of the origin of the story related by Nennius is complicated by the eleventh-century Breton version of the *Life of St Gurthiern* preserved in the cartulary of Quimperlé.[4] The exact nature of the relationship is far from clear, and the evidence is so complicated that I must refer the reader to my previous study for details. It is important to place on record here, however, that the result of a comparison of the various sources would seem to suggest that the cycle of stories of St Germanus, of whatever origin, was originally unconnected with the saga of Vortigern. This may help to account for the fact that in the work ascribed to Gildas there is no reference to St Germanus in connection with the *superbus tyrannus* whose identity with Vortigern has never been challenged; while Constantius, writing his *Life of St Germanus* only about thirty years after the saint's lifetime, has no word of Vortigern. In a word, a comparison of the textual evidence of the sections of the *Historia Brittonum* with the evidence of our other sources appears to militate, so far as it goes, against the historical value of the accounts given in the *Historia Brittonum* of personal contacts and relationship between Germanus and Vortigern.

British theologians of the eighth century gladly seized upon the story of St Germanus as being among the few extant traditions relating to Christianity in our Islands at the close of the Roman period. It helped to bridge the gap between the

---

[1] *Transactions of the Honourable Society of Cymmrodorion* (1946–7), p. 28 ff.; see especially p. 44 f.

[2] See my 'Note on the name Vortigern' in *Studies in Early British History*, p. 34 ff.

[3] Loc. cit.; cf. especially p. 39 ff.

[4] *Cartulaire de l'Abbaye de Sainte-Croix de Quimperlé*, edited by Léon Maitre and Paul de Berthou (Paris, 1896), p. 3 ff.

Roman period and the age of the saints in the sixth century. And the story of a saint from Gaul, coming under Roman auspices, was a valuable weapon of propaganda for the supporters of the union of the Celtic Church – and more immediately the Welsh Church – with the Anglo-Roman Church at the close of the eighth century. It is to this motive that I ascribe the insertion by Nennius or his predecessor into the *Historia Brittonum* of the four sections relating to St Germanus.

Nennius tells us in his Preface that he is writing at the suggestion of Elvodug (*Elvodugus*), the Bishop of Bangor (†809). There can be little doubt that this is the Elbodugus who is stated in the *Annales Cambriae*, s.a. 768, to have been responsible for the acceptance by the Britons (i.e. the Welsh) of the Roman date of Easter. It is significant that Elvodus (*Elfoddw*) is the first Welsh bishop to be styled Archbishop of North Wales in the same annals, s.a. 809. St Germanus, the last great Roman emissary to our Islands, the great saint of fifth-century Gaul, was a hero who would naturally commend himself alike to Bishop Elvodug who sponsored the full inclusion of his Church in the newly introduced Roman Order, and to Nennius, writing, like Constantius, to further the episcopal policy of his metropolitan.

It will be seen that St Germanus resembles his great predecessor St Martin in the early spread of his fame and the prestige which he lent to the church of the city to which he belonged. The cause is probably in both cases to be sought in the excellence of their biographers, and the early date at which the *Vitae* of both saints were put into circulation. I have already given reason to suspect that the *Life* of Germanus was intended to supersede that of St Martin, and there can be no doubt that at least in Britain this end was in fact achieved. It became the fashion for hagiographers to attribute to our British saints a training in Auxerre.[1] An early tradition attributed to St Germanus the education and training of St Illtud.[2] Later tradition

[1] See Hugh Williams, *Christianity in Early Britain*, p. 234.
[2] See the *Life of St. Samson of Dol* (cap. 6), composed possibly in the seventh century. The best edition is that of R. Fawtier, *La Vie de St Samson* (Paris, 1912). The *Vita* has been translated into English by T. Taylor, London, 1925. See further Duine, *Memento des Sources hagiographiques de l'Histoire de Bretagne* (Rennes, 1918), No. 2; and ibid., *Origines Bretonnes* (Paris, 1914). See also the study of *St Illtut* by G. H. Doble (Cardiff, 1944). J. E. Lloyd regards the reference to Germanus as Illtud's teacher as a very early interpolation, observing that 'it raises insurmountable difficulties of chronology'. (*A History of Wales*, Vol. I, London, 1912, p. 144, n. 96).

could not afford to omit the Church of Auxerre from the spiritual education of St Patrick, though St Patrick's Irish biographer, Muirchu, writing shortly before 700, gives a confused account of the relative chronology of Germanus and Amator.[1] We need not take seriously the considerable number of place-names and dedications associated with Germanus (or *Garmon*) in Wales. The name was common, and the philological evidence which is commonly adduced[2] to demonstrate local tradition in Wales for the visit of both Germanus and Lupus will not stand the test of scientific scrutiny.

We have seen that Sulpicius Severus composed his *Life of St Martin* on the model of Athanasius's *Life of St Antony*. We may even suspect that Sulpicius had in view the definite purpose of superseding the *Life of St Antony*, wishing to offer to the Gaulish people as an *exemplum* one who had lived among them, instead of a stranger in remote Egypt. Now the more one studies the *Life of St Germanus* by Constantius, the more one is tempted to suspect that it was intended in its turn to supersede the *Life of St Martin*, and that it was composed primarily to promote the interests of the see of Lyons. To one section of the bishops of Gaul the new monkish ideal, exemplified in the dress and simple habits of Martin, were unacceptable. What Constantius offers them is a direct contrast. In place of Martin, the foreigner of relatively humble origin, a man of wholly democratic ideals, quiet, contemplative, trained in the tradition of Greek monasticism, Constantius offers to his public a man of excellent education who, he claims, had held a high civil post in early life, and who was also a great general, a great Gaulish aristocrat and patriot, and, moreover, a great hero; whose episcopal election was hailed, we are told, by every class of the population with approbation; who defended the Faith against the greatest heresy of the age; who ran every risk to save the people under his charge in Armorica from the barbarities of the Alani, and who met his death on a long journey of intercession on their

---

[1] See Muirchu's *Life*, chs. 8, 9 (edited by Whitley Stokes in *The Tripartite Life of St Patrick*, Vol. II, London, 1887, p. 269 ff.); also in the transcript from the *Book of Armagh*, edited by John Gwynn (Dublin, 1913), fo. 20 a 1; English translation by N. J. D. White, *St Patrick: His Writings and Life* (London, 1920), p. 72 ff. and cf. the Hymn, *Genair Patraicc*: 'He reads the Canons with Germanus; this is what writings relate' (Stokes: *Tripartite Life*, Vol. II, p. 404 f.).

[2] See, e.g. C. Plummer, *Baedae Opera Historica*, Vol. II (Oxford, 1896), p. 32 f.; and A. W. Wade-Evans, *Welsh Christian Origins*, pass.

behalf when they had been in open insurrection against the Roman government.

In effect Constantius offers in Germanus, the noble of Auxerre, a saint acceptable to the Church as a whole, to the aristocratic elements in the population, and to the Gaulish people. Surely a hero and a patriot was the type of saint most needed by a people overrun by Franks, Goths, Alani, Burgundians, rather than a quiet foreigner, a monk who was given to meditation and to prayer, who had abandoned his soldiering in early youth for ever. Can one picture St Martin going boldly up to the conquering lines of the Alani and seizing the bridle of their king, the *rex ferocissimus*,[1] or leading a victorious army in Britain? This was the kind of saint needed by Gaul in the fifth century. St Martin did well enough for the fourth, before the troubles began – so Constantius seems to say.

What do we know of the saint himself as a result of our somewhat protracted study? It must be confessed that we have very little ground for certainty in regard to the facts as a whole. Yet we have seen that neither the miracles nor the *fabulae* ought to take a disproportionate place in our estimate of the historicity of the outline of events recorded by Constantius. We have seen also that despite a regrettable vagueness in regard to precise chronological points, the general relative chronology is fairly sound, if we discount the saint's second expedition to Britain. Again, with the exception of some inaccuracies in detail, the narrative appears to bear a general relationship to historical persons and events, and to the political situation of the period, both in Gaul and Italy. On the whole the work of Constantius has been regarded by competent scholars as based on genuine fact.[2]

The statements of the compiler of the *Historia Brittonum* and the story related by Heiric of the written British *Life* of the saint add nothing to our knowledge in which we can place any confidence. The evidence of place-names and of church dedications in Britain has nothing of value to contribute to our problem. We are thrown back upon the entries in the two contemporary Gaulish chronicles, the one anonymous, the other by Prosper.

---

[1] Is there an intended contrast to Martin's unavailing intercession on behalf of the Priscillianists at the Court of Maximus?

[2] See. e.g. Levison, *Neues Archiv.*, XXIX, p. 124 f.

S

Of these the former merely tells us that at the time of writing Germanus was Bishop of Auxerre, outstanding for virtue and zeal. The latter tells us that he was sent to Britain by Pope Celestine in 429 in consequence of the prevalence of the Pelagian heresy, and that the heretics were quelled. That is really all that we know authoritatively. Prosper appears to have been writing from Provence at the time, though this is not quite certain.

The 'Anonymous Chronicle' appears to have had sources of information which may well have been Breton, and Constantius also seems to have been in touch with Breton affairs, and he emphasizes the lifelong concern of Germanus with Brittany. We have no valid reason for assigning Constantius to Lyons. The *Life* of the Saint of Tours was written in southern Aquitaine, and that of the Saint of Auxerre may well have been written in Southern Provence.[1] We may remember the British or Breton monk who visited Riez and returned with books to his own people, an incident which indicates lively cultural communication between Brittany and Provence. On the whole it would seem probable that contemporary information reached southern Gaul from Brittany, and that such information stressed the political and military activities of Germanus in relation to both Brittany and Britain. It would seem probable also that this was noted at the time by the chroniclers, and written up somewhat later by Constantius, perhaps from the same source of information. A closer study of contemporary references to Breton affairs in the documents of the period, and perhaps also of the period immediately following, may help to narrow the problem still further; but at the moment that is as far as we can take it safely.

[1] The dedication to Bishop Patiens is no guarantee that Constantius was writing from Lyons, though the personal request of Patiens to Constantius that he would write the *Life of St Germanus* of course bespeaks a connection of some kind.

CHAPTER X

The Heroic Age of the Gaulish Church

THE group of ecclesiastics who play a heroic part in the closing days of the Gaulish Church, before the cession of Auvergne, constitute in the main a society with common ideals and a common background. They were not ascetic, either in milieu or outlook, and their sphere lay outside the monasteries, and the monastic movement. They cling tenaciously to the older claims of the Gallo-Roman aristocratic ideal, the old classical tradition; and the extent to which these ideals and traditions permeated their intellectual and spiritual life is perhaps best shown in the perseverence with which they continued to live this cultured inner life, and to exchange these common ideas, while the very foundations of their ancient civilization were crumbling around them. For most of them poetry, philosophy and mythology were everyday preoccupations. Their diction, their allusions, their memories, were stored with the classics, and they could not express themselves in any other idiom, or refresh their minds with any other forms of recreation. Christianity was a new and important spiritual concern; but one feels that for these men it was almost more a profession than a vocation, certainly not an all-pervading spiritual revolution. There is no sign of spiritual clash or conflict, or readjustment. The new religion was blended and harmonized with the standards already set by a classical training, and a balance was maintained. The library of Tonantius Ferreolus at Prusianum (cf. p. 317), which contained the Roman classics on one side of the room, and the works of the Fathers of the Church on the opposite side, was symbolical, and the warm approval which Sidonius expresses for it is no less significant.[1]

Among the men of letters in Gaul who figure in the correspondence of Sidonius as the best classical scholars of the time is Bishop Lupus of Troyes. Three[2] of the letters addressed to him

---

[1] *Ep.*, II, 9.
[2] So according to O. M. Dalton, *The Letters of Sidonius*, translated in two volumes, Oxford, 1915. According to J. Havet, however, there are four letters addressed by Sidonius to Lupus. See *Questions Mérovingiennes* (Paris, 1885), p. 52; republished in *Œuvres de Julien Havet*, Vol. I (Paris, 1896), p. 63 ff; cf. *Spicilegium*, Vol. V, p. 579.

by Sidonius are extant, and he is mentioned with great distinction in a number of other letters by the same author. Reference is also made to him by his contemporary, Constantius, the friend of Patiens in his *Vita S. Germani*. In addition we have extant a letter[1] purporting to be written by Lupus himself, together with Euphronius of Autun, to Bishop Talasius of Angers; and another letter,[2] also extant, and bearing his name, purporting to have been composed for the purpose of congratulating Sidonius on his election to the bishopric of Clermont in 472. The first letter is regarded as genuine; but the second letter is now, as a result of the researches of the French scholar Havet,[3] generally regarded as spurious – perhaps rather too lightly.[4] Havet's objections are based principally – though not wholly – on the rhetorical style in which the letter is written. But is it not possible that this was a deliberate artifice, adopted to suit the taste of the recipient and the nature of the occasion? It is not easy to imagine that any other style would have been acceptable to Sidonius. A congratulatory address by the Public Orator of one of our universities today would have little in common with a letter written by the same man to the same person on a less formal occasion.

We also have a reference to St Lupus in the *Epistola De Laude Heremi* (ch. 42) addressed to Hilary, Bishop of Arles, by Eucherius of Lyons, where the name of Lupus is found among the most honoured of those who had dwelt in the monastery of Lérins, and where it occurs side by side with those of Honoratus, Maximus, and Caprasius. In addition, Dalton points[5] to a passage of Sidonius (*Carmen* XVI, 11), as evidence that Lupus had been Abbot of Lérins. Our most extensive account of St Lupus, however, is an anonymous *Vita S. Lupi*, to which varying dates have been assigned. This *Vita* is extant in two versions, of which the shorter[6] is believed to be the earlier, and consists of twelve brief chapters. The second and 'later' version[7] is substantially in agreement with the shorter version. The shorter version is the

---

[1] Migne, *P.L.*, Vol. LVIII, 66.
[2] Loc. cit., col. 63.
[3] See J. Havet, loc. cit.
[4] This letter is translated into French by Chaix, *Saint Sidoine Apollinaire*, Vol. I (Paris, 1886), p. 442 ff.
[5] Op. cit., Vol. I, p. clxxii.
[6] *Bolland. Acta SS.*, July VII, p. 69 ff.
[7] ibid., p. 72 ff.

one adopted by Krusch, in his critical edition.[1] This is the best edition up to the present time, and the one used by modern scholars.

Krusch holds that the *Vita* was composed in the Carolingian era in the eighth or ninth century. In his view the *Vita* was composed, not primarily in the interest of the cult of St Lupus, but rather in the interest of the temporal possessions of the see of Troyes. On the whole our evidence relating to St Lupus is comparatively full and early, and it is surprising, in view of this, that a certain amount of doubt should still rest on the question of his expedition to Britain, which, if it actually took place, must surely have been the most important event in his life.

Krusch placed no reliance on the *Vita*.[2] His principal objections are based partly on its doubtful chronology, partly on the *fabulae* which it contains. Of the former he writes (op. cit., Vol. III, p. 118): 'Hanc chronologiam falsam esse iudico fictamque totam Vitam inde ab initio usque ad finem,' and of the latter (ibid., p. 119): 'Haec omnia, ut sunt absurda, credi non possunt, Vitaque fabulis fictis adnumeranda est.' Yet Tillemont had written: 'Nous avons l'histoire de sa vie, qui parait écrite avec une entière fidelité: et tout ce qu'on y trouve à redire, c'est qu'elle est trop courte,'[3] and Duchesne writes later: 'Les objections de M. Krusch contre l'antiquité de ce document sont dépourvues de toute valeur.'[4]

We cannot lightly dismiss the judgment of Krusch, which has been accepted by Levison.[5] There are certainly errors of detail in the narrative, such as the statement (ch. 11) that Severus, the metropolitan of Trier in Germania I (*sic*),[6] was one of the saint's disciples. Krusch and Levison regard it as probable that the account in the *Vita Lupi* of the journey to Britain is derived from Bede rather than from Constantius's *Vita Germani*[7], yet

---

[1] *Mon. Germ. Hist.: Script. Rer. Merov.*, Vol. III (1896), p. 120; and in a revised edition, ibid., VII (1920), p. 284 ff.

[2] His argument is given in full in an article, 'Zur Florians- und Lupus-Legende' in *Neues Archiv.*, Vol. XXIV (1899), p. 559 ff.

[3] Op. cit., Vol. XVI, p. 127.

[4] *Fastes Épiscopaux*, Vol. II (Paris, 1899), p. 449.

[5] *Neues Archiv.*, Vol. XXIX, pp. 128, 152; *Vita Lupi*, ed. cit., p. 288.

[6] The biographer was not well informed, being under the impression that the metropolitan city of Trier belonged to Germania I, whereas in fact it belonged to Belgica I. See Levison, *Vita Lupi*, p. 288.

[7] See Krusch, *Neues Archiv*, Vol. XXIV, p. 565; cf. *ibid.*, *Vita Lupi, ed. cit.*, Vol. III, p. 119; cf. Levison, *Neues Archiv*, XXIX, p. 152, and n. 3.

explaining the reference to Severus as Bishop of Trier in Bede (*H.E.* I, 21) as probably due to this passage in the *Vita Lupi*.[1]

We shall see, moreover, that errors occur in the *Vita* in regard to historical facts, notably in connection with Attila's attack, and the part played by Gebavult. How far these errors of detail ought to justify us in dismissing the whole narrative as a product of deliberate fiction is a matter of great doubt. With all deference to the textual erudition of the German editors, it would seem possible that a modicum of genuine tradition remains. This is a subject to which I shall return later in the present chapter.

The account of the saint outlined in the shorter *Vita*[2] is as follows. He was born (ch. 1) at Tullum Leucorum (i.e. Toul) on the headwaters of the Moselle. The date is generally thought to have been about 383. His father was Epirichius, or, more correctly, Pyrrichios (Πυῤῥίχιος),[3] who belonged to a noble family. As he died while Lupus was still young[4] his education was supervised by his father's brother, Lysticius, by whom he was sent to the schools and trained in rhetoric. In due course he gained a reputation for his eloquence. Eucherius tells us that he had a brother Vincent.[5] The family was probably of Aeduan stock, for at a later date, when Lupus was engaged in the sale of his family property, he went for this purpose to the old Gaulish fortress of Matisco, the modern Maçon in Aeduan territory; and in later life he is associated with Euphronius, Bishop of Autun, the capital of the old territory of the Aedui, in writing the letter mentioned above to Bishop Talasius of Angers.

He married Pimeniola, the sister of Hilary, later to become Bishop of Arles; but (ch. 2) after seven years of married life they parted by mutual consent, and Lupus became a monk in Lérins, where Hilary was now a presbyter, and where St Honoratus was still living as head of the community. His brother Vincent was probably also in the monastery, for Eucherius, while praising Lupus as comparable to Caprasius,

---

[1] The name Severus occurs in the *Fasti* of Trier, which, however, do not appear to date from before the tenth century.

[2] Ed. Krusch, *Mon. Germ. Merov.* VII, p. 295 ff.

[3] Krusch, op. cit., p. 295, n. 4.

[4] Is this a conjecture on the part of the biographer? We have seen earlier instances in Gaul during the fourth and fifth centuries of an uncle's responsibility for the education of the sons of his brothers and sisters. Further examples could be added from the literature of other Celtic countries in early times.

[5] *De Laude Heremi*, ch. 42.

the veteran of the monastery and former spiritual guide of Honoratus, praises equally Lupus's brother Vincent as 'a gem shining with a spiritual glory'.[1]

According to the *Vita* (ch. 3) Lupus returned to Mâcon after a year in Lérins, and Tillemont[2] interprets the passage in which Eucherius speaks of Lérins having possessed (*habuit*) both Lupus and his brother Vincent as implying that they probably departed together, or at least at the same time – almost at the same time as Honoratus, who, as we have seen (p. 148) left Lérins to become Bishop of Arles, perhaps in 428. For this reason Tillemont holds that this Vincent cannot be the author of the *Commonitorium* (cf. p. 186 ff.), but regards it as likely that he is identical with a certain Vincent, a monk of Lérins, who became Bishop of Saintes, and whose name, according to Barralis, followed that of St Lupus in an old document of Saintes. It is doubtful, however, if the words of Eucherius can be pressed so far. All that we can say with certainty is that Lupus was in Lérins for a time; that he left behind him there a tradition of great sanctity; and that he had a brother Vincent, also an inmate of Lérins, whose reputation for holiness was no less than his own.

During his absence from Lérins, and while on his visit to Mâcon, where he had gone in order to sell his possessions and distribute his wealth to the poor, he was seized and forcibly made Bishop of Troyes. His consecration probably took place in 426 or 427.[3] According to the *Vita* (ch. 4) he accompanied St Germanus to Britain to combat the Pelagian heresy in the expedition which we must identify with the one recorded by Prosper as having taken place in 429. The *Vita* then proceeds to give an account (ch. 5), derived doubtless from ecclesiastical saga,[4] of the salvation, by the instrumentality of Lupus, of the city of Troyes from the Huns under Attila in 453,[5] and of the conversion of Attila himself to Christianity.

[1] Germanum ejus Vincentium interno gemmam splendore perspicuam (*De Laude Heremi*, ch. 42).

[2] Vol. XVI, p. 128.

[3] Duchesne, *Fastes Épisc.* II, p. 453. Cf. Chaix, op. cit., Vol. I, p. 439.

[4] There is evidence that ecclesiastical saga was widespread and carefully cultivated in regard to the abortive attack of Attila on the cities of Gaul. Krusch (*Neues Archiv* XXIV, p. 560 f.) has enumerated four examples.

[5] The only indication of date given in the *Vita* is contained in the opening words of ch. 5: 'Inter haec nec longa post tempora', following on the narrative of the expedition to Britain related in ch. 4. The intervening period was, in fact, twenty-two years.

According to the story here given, Attila ordered Lupus to go with him as far as the Rhine 'for the sake of his own preservation or the welfare of his army',[1] after which the bishop was allowed to return to Troyes, perhaps with a safe conduct.[2] The city, like so many in Gaul at this time, was undefended by either walls or arms, and Lupus found on his return that the terrified inhabitants, mistrusting Attila's intentions, had dispersed. With the object of re-assembling them he withdrew to the mountain of Lotiscus (mod. *Lassois* in the Côte d'Or) some forty-five miles from the town.[3] But during the two years that he remained there few joined him, and he finally withdrew (c. 433) to Mâçon, where his family property had been, and where his ancestral home was doubtless situated. On the journey his biographer attributes miracles to the saint. We have already seen the biographer of St Germanus making use of a similar literary technique for the introduction of the miraculous element into his narrative.

Krusch rejects[4] the whole story of Lupus's relation with Attila, and emphasizes the silence of Sidonius on the subject. Yet although he here makes use of the *argumentum e silentio* in regard to Sidonius, he refuses to attach value to the credit which Sidonius gives[5] to Bishop Anianus for the immunity enjoyed by Orléans from Attila. He mentions four instances which have come under his notice of 'legends from this same saga cycle of the Huns', namely those of Servatius, Memorius, Anianus, and Lupus. These he regards in the main as 'Carolingian fabrications', which had, however, already begun during the lifetime of Sidonius Apollinaris. The literary evidence cited by Krusch is always important; and he might have added to his examples the mission to Attila with which the *Liber Pontificalis*[6] credits 'Pope Leo'. But Krusch hardly strengthens his case by the arm-chair argument that as Attila had already been defeated on the Campus Mauriacus he could not have been defeated a

---

[1] It is not quite clear whether this refers to their temporal or their spiritual condition. Probably Lupus is regarded on diplomatic grounds as a useful person for the retreating army to have with them. The words are: 'pro incolumitatis suae statu vel exercitus sui salute secum indicit iturum.'

[2] *Iter ostenditur.*

[3] Tillemont points out (Vol. XVI, p. 132) that similar conditions prevailed elsewhere, causing changes in certain episcopal sees, such as Le Puy and Mende.

[4] *Neues Archiv*, Vol. XXIV, p. 560 ff.

[5] *Ep.* VIII, 15 (cf. Gregory of Tours, *Hist. Franc.* II, 7).

[6] Ed. Duchesne, Vol. I (Paris, 1886), p. 239.

second time by the prayers of Anianus. Such embassies as that ascribed by Sidonius to Anianus certainly reflect, even when they do not actually record, the part played by the Church in this period. Moreover Duchesne points out that certain Roman titles, such as *clarissimus*, and certain grammatical and phonological forms found in the *Vita*, are incompatible with the usage of the Carolingian period.

To enter more fully into arguments which might be adduced for and against the authenticity of the details of the narrative[1] would be outside the limits of this brief study. Perhaps it is largely a question of degree. There is nothing inherently improbable in the facts stated. In any case, except for the conversion of Attila, the conditions described are in accord with those known to have prevailed in the period. One cannot help wondering whether a biographer writing in the Carolingian age could have reconstructed these conditions with so scholarly a historical sense?

The passage relating to Higebold, king of the Alemanni – his name is barbarized by Roman writers as Gebavultus[2] and Gibultus[3] – is perhaps on a somewhat different footing. The *Vita* relates (ch. 10) that the Alemanni had made incursions into the neighbourhood of Troyes, and had taken a number of prisoners; but these had been subsequently released by the intercession of the saint, to whom the king accorded a respect similar to that shown by Attila. The localization of the occurrence is inadmissible, and the incident itself bears a close resemblance[4] to the account given by Eugippius in his *Vita S. Severini* (ch. 4)[5] of the release of prisoners by King Gibuldus in the neighbourhood of Batavia (mod. Passau). It is, as Krusch observes,[6] difficult to believe that the same incident can have taken place at approximately the same time in regions so far

[1] Krusch's arguments are partly literary. He refers to the relationship of certain other incidents, such as the narrative of the conversion of King Gebavult, to other hagiological writings.
[2] The form of the name which occurs in the *Vita Lupi*.
[3] The form which occurs in the *Vita* of St Severinus. See below.
[4] It is worthy of note that in both stories the appeal to the king of the Alemanni is made in written form ('*paginola*', *Vita Lupi; epistola, Vita Severini*) through a messenger (*presbyterus, V.L.; diaconus, V.S.*), not by a verbal request. This detail supports the argument in favour of a written relationship between the two *Vitae*.
[5] The text is translated by G. W. Robinson, *The Life of St Severinus* (Cambridge, Mass., 1914).
[6] *Neues Archiv*, Vol. XXIV, p. 556 f.; *Vita Lupi*, p. 287 f. Tillemont himself was in difficulties regarding the passage (op. cit., Vol. XVI, p. 136).

apart, and we may probably postulate a written relationship.

It is, as Tillemont suggests,[1] perhaps during the period of the saint's sojourn in Burgundy that he met St Euphronius of Autun, and that their joint letter to Bishop Talasius[2] (cf. p. 292) was written. Talasius had sent a memorandum on certain difficulties regarding ecclesiastical discipline, to which the letter of Lupus and Euphronius is a reply. The matters touched on are the observance of the principal Church festivals, and the rules regarding the marriage of clerks in the lower Orders. Euphronius was among the most honoured bishops of Gaul in his day, as we gather from Sidonius, who addresses to him, among other letters, one in which, in terms of profound respect, he begs his aid in the election of a new Bishop of Bourges.[3] To Euphronius is ascribed the building of the Church of St Symphorian of Autun, and he is said[4] to have supplied the marble for the covering of the tomb of St Martin.[5] I shall have more to say of him later.

Like his predecessor Constantius, the biographer of St Lupus stresses the asceticism of his hero. It was the fashion in such biographies; but he probably does Lupus no more than justice in this respect, for the saint's training at Lérins, short though it was, and his close family relationship with St Hilary of Arles, would both be consistent with the ascetic habit, or at least the habit of austerity. The latter word would seem to be the more appropriate to Lupus, for he was essentially a cultured ecclesiastic like his contemporary Constantius, and, also like Constantius, an intimate friend of Sidonius Apollinaris, who addresses five letters to him. The last of these in particular (Book IX, 11), makes it clear that Lupus was in the habit of reading and transcribing his friend's work, and that he set great store by it — so that he is piqued when he considers that he has not received enough attention from him. Sidonius evidently held him in high esteem for his literary judgment, and Lupus holds an honoured place in the cultured circle of Gaulish bishops in his own day. Sidonius reminds Lupus that his name appears on the first superscription of his book, 'as befits that of the chief among

---

[1] Op. cit., Vol. XVI, p. 133.
[2] Talasius is believed to have been consecrated in 453.
[3] Ep. VII, 8.
[4] Gregory of Tours, Hist. Franc. II, 15.
[5] Tillemont, Vol. XVI, p. 134 f.

our bishops',[1] and in a letter to his friend Arbogast, the Governor of Trier, he couples Lupus with Auspicius, the Bishop of Toul, and assures Arbogast that however deeply he probes their learning he will not reach its limit.[2]

But Lupus does not owe his pre-eminence among the bishops of his day to his literary gifts alone. He appears in the letters of Sidonius as a practical man whose piety bore fruit in ways most needed in that time of disrupted organization. Sidonius recalls his hard vigils in the spiritual warfare at Lérins, and addresses him in terms of the most unqualified veneration for his goodness of heart and personal integrity[3] – 'They say, veteran leader, that you bring in even the wounded of the enemy'; and he observes that Lupus not only bears in mind the Christians of the highest rank, but that he does not despise the camp-follower or servant, and seeks out with his Gospel teaching even the meanest of the baggage carriers. This is no idle or empty rhetoric, for we have two letters in which Sidonius begs the intervention of Lupus in practical difficulties which have been brought to his notice. One[4] relates to an unfortunate woman who had been kidnapped by the local bandits,[5] and sold into slavery. A man who had been a witness to the contract for the vendors was believed to be resident at the time in Troyes, and Sidonius represents to Lupus that it would prevent matters going from bad to worse if the bishop would use his influence to bring about a measure of compromise satisfactory to both parties. The other letter[6] relates to a certain Gallus who had made an attempt to cut loose from his domestic responsibilities by abandoning his wife, but who had immediately made amends by returning home when Sidonius read to him the letter in which Lupus related his fault. These personal details, no less than the high culture with which Lupus is credited, and the important mission to Britain in which he is stated to have taken part, help us to form a picture of the kind of personality of the man whom Sidonius refers to as *facile principem pontificum Gallicanorum* ('easily the foremost among our Gaulish bishops'),[7]

[1] *Ep.* IX, 11.
[2] *Ep.* IV, 17.
[3] *Ep.* VI, 1.
[4] *Ep.* VI, 4.
[5] The term used is *vargi*, literally, 'wolves'. The word is Teutonic. In Old Icelandic *vargr*, meant 'a wolf', but was also a technical legal term for 'an outlaw'.
[6] *Ep.* VI, 9.
[7] *Ep.* VII, 13.

and whom he couples with Germanus as a model of excellence.[1]

Lupus has become a figure round whom local patriotism has woven a halo of heroic deeds in the midst of the Barbarian Invasions. There may well be a kernel of oral ecclesiastical saga behind these legends; that is to say, of genuine tradition. Traces of such early ecclesiastical saga may help to account for a dedication to a saint of the same name in Brittany; though dedications which modern antiquarians have sought to associate with him in Wales undoubtedly rest on unscientific philological equations. It is perhaps the persistence of this independent heroic ecclesiastical saga more than anything else which makes one hesitate to reject the statement of Constantius about the participation of Lupus in the British mission (cf. p. 258). When a man becomes a figure of heroic legend already in his own lifetime, there is good reason to regard him as a hero.

However we view the actual details of the *Vita*, however legendary certain episodes, the picture which emerges from its narrative, as from the letters of Sidonius, is wholly consistent with our great portrait gallery of fifth-century bishops. Like his friend Sidonius, Lupus combined learning and culture with heroic patriotism and practical administrative ability and a meticulous attention to all questions of discipline, both civil and ecclesiastical, which came within his episcopal jurisdiction. Such a man would not be without diplomatic qualifications, and these he would not fail to use on behalf of the citizens of his open and undefended town. His ancestry among the local Gaulish nobility, and his eminence in Latin letters combine to give him exactly the spirit of devotion and outstanding intellectual ability which marked the leading men of Gaul in its last days. The actual achievements credited to the saint may be partly borrowed from the floating mass of ecclesiastical tradition of the period. The ascetic details and miracles in the *Vita* follow the fashion of the time; but we cannot afford to neglect the *Vita* any more than the *Vitae* of St Martin and St Germanus. In so far as we can check the contents by contemporary records and correspondence, they are typical of the general character and achievements of the outstanding Gaulish bishops of their day.

It is fully in accordance with this historical verisimilitude

[1] *Ep.* VIII, 15.

that we find eloquence stressed as the highest achievement of so many of the great Gaulish churchmen of this period. The victory of Germanus in Britain in his ecclesiastical disputation with the upholders of Pelagianism is ascribed by Constantius chiefly to his eloquence. It is by his eloquence that he is again represented as staying the vengeance of the Alan chief Goar in his punitive expedition on behalf of Aetius against the insurgent Armoricans, and again as pleading on their behalf at a council held in Arles; and finally as winning pardon for the Armoricans in the Imperial Court at Ravenna. Similarly the anonymous biographer of Lupus of Troyes represents his saint as winning immunity for his city against Attila, and even as winning that 'brute' (*feralis*) to Christianity. We shall see later how Sidonius attributes the rally and revival of the defenders of Clermont, beleaguered by the Visigoths, to the presence and eloquent appeals of Constantius, the biographer of St Germanus.

There is something more in all this than mere product of the imagination, which would more naturally have attributed these successes to some form of miracle. Such stories are to be interpreted rather in the light of the impassioned eloquence in extempore preaching ascribed by Sidonius to Bishop Faustus of Riez. Faustus[1] was sent to Rome on a diplomatic mission by the Council of Arles, while the Imperial Government in its turn employed him in its negotiations with the Visigothic King Euric. This persistent tradition of the power of persuasion and argument attributed to the Gaulish bishops of our period is a natural development of the traditional Gaulish eloquence outstanding throughout the Roman world in the preceding century. It has now become disciplined to Christian usage, and is utilized by the Church, and by all who are zealous in the interests of peace, as the most valuable weapon left to an almost defenceless land. Its later developments bear fruit in the great collection of popular sermons of Caesarius of Arles, and the vast sermon literature of the Middle Ages.

We will now consider briefly the person of Constantius, to whom we are indebted for the greater part of our information relating to St Germanus, and himself a contemporary of St Lupus. Our knowledge is chiefly derived from four letters

[1] L. Duchesne, *Early History of the Christian Church*, English translation by C. Jenkins, Vol. III (London, 1924), p. 420.

addressed to him by his friend Sidonius.[1] It appears that he was
a man in Holy Orders,[2] born of a noble family, and possibly
attached to the see of Lyons. He was a man of polished education and strong literary tastes. When Bishop Patiens of Lyons
was about to dedicate a great church which he had built in the
city, Constantius composed an inscription in hexameter verse to
be placed on the walls by the altar, along with those of a certain
Secundinus, while his friend Sidonius composed a set in triple
trochaic to be placed at the far end of the church.[3] We have
seen St Paulinus and Sulpicius Severus similarly composing
verses for the churches of Sulpicius in Aquitaine. It was at the
request of Bishop Patiens that Constantius composed his *Life of
St Germanus*, as he himself states in a letter addressed to Patiens,
which prefaces both the older and the later versions of the *Life*.[4]
He repeats the statement in a second letter addressed to Bishop
Censurius, to whom, at the bishop's request, he sends a copy of
the *Life*.[5]

Apart from this *Life of St Germanus*, and the two letters which
appear at the beginning of the text, little or nothing has survived from Constantius's own hand.[6] The *Life* itself, despite its
excessive concern with miracles, is written in a simple and
polished Latin prose, and shows the author to have possessed a
good narrative style, and to have been well able to utilize the
saga material on which the historical portions are based. We
are best able to gauge his reputation in his own day from the
letters of his friend Sidonius, who evidently entertained the
highest possible opinion of his literary gifts,[7] and of his classical
scholarship and excellent judgment, as well as of his character.
Something of the scope and influence of his literary activity
may be gauged from the fact that it was he who induced
Sidonius to collect and publish his correspondence. Sidonius

---

[1] *Ep.* I, 1; III, 2; VII, 18; VIII, 16.

[2] This would seem to follow from Sidonius's Letters. His rank is not known.
Levison points out (*Neues Archiv.*, Vol. XXIX, p. 108) that the reference to him as
a 'presbyter of Lyons' occurs first in the title to the MSS. of the interpolated *Vita
Germani*. Sidonius makes no reference to it, and for the same reason we may assume
that the title *episcopus* given to him by Isidore (*De Vir. Ill.*, ch. 17) is also erroneous.

[3] Sidonius, *Ep.* II, 10.

[4] See Levison, op. cit., p. 109 f.

[5] Loc. cit.

[6] For further details, see Levison, op. cit., p. 107 f. He is thought to have written
a *Life* of St Remigius of Auxerre, but the extant *Life* is believed to be the work of a
later hand. (See W. B. Anderson, *Sidonius*, Vol. I (London, 1936), p. 330, n. 1.)

[7] *Ep.* II, 10.

dedicated the collection, in eight volumes, to Constantius himself, as we read in the first letter.[1] Although the eighth book, was collected c. A.D. 480 under the stimulus of his friend Petronius, it was also planned to be issued under the auspices of Constantius.[2]

One more fact of importance is known of Constantius. In the winter of 473 the Visigothic King Euric was besieging Clermont-Ferrand, the episcopal city of Sidonius, in Auvergne, and Sidonius was in charge of the defences. From one of his letters[3] we learn that, when the siege was in its most critical state, the fortunes of war were turned by Constantius, who, though now an old man, braved the wintry conditions and bad roads, and made the journey from his home to Clermont to help the besieged citizens. On his arrival he found the walls 'half-demolished' (semirutis moenibus), the buildings 'destroyed by fire', the homes 'half burned down', and the fields strewn with the bones of the unburied dead, much as we have seen conditions at Trier described by Salvian. Nor was this the worst; for the city, we are told, was no less desolated by internal dissensions than by the attacks of the Visigoths.

Constantius seems to have set to work immediately and with vigour, by methods of diplomacy, possibly also by military measures. For the former his polished education in rhetoric and eloquence must have given him admirable qualifications, and his success is proved by the results. We are told that he conciliated and reconciled the garrison, re-manned the walls, and restored unity and concord to the population. The credit for this rally is generally given by historians to Sidonius; but truth to tell, despite his courage and vigour, and the length of time during which he managed to repel the enemy, Sidonius seems to have been losing his control, as he himself generously admits. When he sent for Constantius he must have known him to be a man of vigour and resolution, a man able to grapple with a military crisis. As we read the letter we realize how necessary to an active cleric were the horses and equipment with which Sulpicius Severus taunts the bishops of an earlier day. A busy diplomat and organizer could not easily have travelled through the wintry conditions of the enemy-infested country without

[1] Ep. IX, 16.
[3] Ep. III, 2.

[2] Ep. VIII, 16.

considerable impedimenta, even though Constantius is praised by Sidonius for his moderation – 'coming without ambitious retinues'. We may suspect that it was for his practical knowledge and understanding of affairs, no less than for his literary ability and excellence of character, that Bishop Patiens of Lyons asked him to write the 'Life' of St Germanus. He is believed to have died as a very old man in 488.

The heroic conduct of Sidonius and Constantius at Clermont was in no way exceptional. Though, as we have seen, it is very possible that the wonderful results of patriotism attributed by ecclesiastical tradition to Lupus at Troyes and to Anianus at Orleans (cf. p. 280 f.) may not be strictly historical, these traditions undoubtedly represent conditions very near the truth. What ecclesiastical saga attributes to these men is only a popular version of the kind of patriotic Gaulish resistance to the invader offered by Sidonius in Auvergne, and by Exuperius at Toulouse.[1] In a fragment of a letter of St Paulinus,[2] written c. A.D. 411, and referred to by Gregory of Tours,[3] special mention is made of the courage and patriotism shown by the Gaulish bishops, in particular those of Toulouse, Vienne, Bordeaux, Albi, Angoulême, Clermont, Cahors, and Périgueux. The evidence of the proper names and family histories, as well as details of the correspondence of Sidonius, make it clear that this fortitude and active opposition to the enemy by the Gaulish bishops are the fine fruit of the old Gaulish patriotism, a devotion to the soil and the environment to which these men felt themselves dedicated no less than to their sacred office. Vercingetorix had died a death which discredited his captors, but not the Gaulish hero himself. And his countrymen in later days had lost nothing of their ancient nobility when they entered the Church.

To the list of bishops whose public spirit is extolled by St Paulinus we may add that of Patiens, the great Bishop of Lyons, at whose request Constantius wrote the biography of St Germanus, and of whom Sidonius says that he is 'a man of whom no praise could be excessive'.[4] We know little of him except what we learn from the letters of Sidonius, one of which is addressed

---

[1] Exuperius was Bishop of Toulouse in 405.
[2] Migne, P.L., Vol. LXI, Ep. 48, p. 398, col. 2.
[3] Hist. Franc., Book II, cap. 13.
[4] Ep. IV, 25.

to Patiens himself, while others contain mention of him in the highest possible terms. He succeeded Eucherius (†449) as Bishop of the See of Lyons, though possibly not immediately.[1] He died before 494, since his successor Rusticius (†501) is named in that year.[2] Sidonius himself must have felt a special loyalty to the bishop of his own native city; but even apart from this, it is clear from what he writes that Patiens was a man who would have done credit to the Church in any age, and he must have been a great force for good in that time of disruption and tragedy. His magnanimity, like that of Lupus, extended beyond the immediate sphere of his own jurisdiction. Probably at no period of history has the Christian precept of universal love been practised in the Church with more single-minded devotion than in Gaul during the Barbarian inroads.

Patiens belonged to the class of wealthy bishops which included St Amator, St Germanus, St Lupus, Sidonius Apollinaris, and many others, all of whom belonged to the local landed aristocracy, and were native to the district which they served. They were essentially nobles turned bishops, and in times of danger and devastation they showed to the people of the neighbourhood in which they lived the selfless devotion and generosity which we expect from their class, and which is the chief justification for its existence. Patiens is especially praised and thanked by Sidonius for the open-handed manner in which, in a time of corn famine in 473–4, he threw open his granaries, and distributed his own corn free of charge to the starving people of eight cities, not only in his own diocese, but wherever he knew that the need was great, even himself organizing and bearing the cost of transport. Clermont, the city of Sidonius, had benefited by his kindness, though, as Sidonius observes gratefully, there were no convenient waterways, and the people had no means of making payment for what they had received. At the same time the claims on the great bishop's resources were many and exacting, and Sidonius points out[3] that he combined the virtues of hospitality and asceticism, delighting the Bur-

---

[1] Duchesne, *Fastes Épiscopaux*, Vol. II, p. 163; Cf. p. 158, and cf. W. Levison, *Neues Archiv.*, Vol. XXIX, p. 107, n. 2.

[2] Ennodius, *Vita Epiphanii*, ch. 151 (ed. Vogel, *Mon. Germ. Hist.: Auct. Ant.* VII, p. 103). Chaix places the death of Patiens c. 480 (op. cit., Vol. II, p. 304, n. 1).

[3] *Ep.* VI, 12.

T

gundian King Hilperic, then ruling Lyons, with his table, and the queen with his fasts.

With reference to the wide charity of Patiens, Sidonius tells his nephew that he had delayed reporting to the bishop the fault of some unfortunate peasants whom he accidentally discovered just about to desecrate his grandfather's grave, ignorant of the fact that it was consecrated ground. Sidonius had taken it upon himself to give the poor fellows a trouncing:

'I confess I did wrong; but I could not help punishing them the moment I caught them. . . . I did not refer my cause to the judgment of our bishop, for fear the outcome should be decided rather by his gentleness than by the justice of my plea.'[1]

Patiens appears in the pages of Sidonius as a great ecclesiastic no less than a great Christian. The church at Lyons owed its erection to him. We have already seen reason to think that it was for the opening of this church that Faustus of Riez preached the sermon so highly extolled by Sidonius, who seems to have gone to Lyons himself for the ceremony, and to have met and listened to Faustus on the occasion. It has also been mentioned that Sidonius contributed verses 'in triple trochaic' to be placed at the end of the church, presumably on the wall, and that Constantius, together with a certain Secundinus, also contributed verses 'to adorn the walls by the altar'. The church seems to have been a splendid aisleless basilica, decorated with a wealth of mosaics, and having a fine ceiling, and we are indebted to Sidonius for a detailed description of both the building,[2] and of the opening ceremony (cf. p. 193).

The force and efficiency of Patiens as an ecclesiastical administrator comes out most clearly in the account of the election to the vacant see of Châlons, which probably took place about 470. Sidonius tells us[3] that the election by popular vote being in dispute, and the three candidates unworthy to hold episcopal office, Patiens, together with Bishop Euphronius of Autun, after consulting their fellow bishops in secret conclave, seized and laid hands on an archdeacon, a certain Johannes, a man only in the Second Order, and made him bishop by the sheer force

[1] *Ep.* III, 12.
[2] *Ep.* II, 10. For some comments on difficulties of detail, and further references, see O. M. Dalton, ed. cit., Vol. II, p. 225.
[3] *Ep.* IV, 25.

of their will and vigorous and prompt action. We have seen St Amator acting in a not very dissimilar manner in regard to the election of St Germanus, though in the latter case the biographer attributes the action of Amator to indecision on the part of the populace. It is very possible that the election by popular vote was already becoming out of date, and both Amator – if we may trust the *Life* – and Patiens were making the most of such opportunity as offered to press the claim of the bishops to govern episcopal elections.[1] Patiens evidently held the prestige of the clergy very high, and, notwithstanding his gentleness, took a strong line in establishing electoral procedure in accord with episcopal dignity and the official prerogative of the Church. We find Sidonius Apollinaris conducting the election of the Bishop of Bourges[2] in much the same way, even selecting a layman rather than any of the rival candidates whom he had reason to regard as undesirable; and like Patiens he enlists the co-operation of his fellow bishops to share the responsibility. Here, however, our only knowledge of the procedure is contained in the letters of Sidonius inviting the bishops to come to the election, and we are not told how

[1] A more closely formulated explanation is given by C. E. Stevens in the informative discussion on episcopal elections in his book, *Sidonius Apollinaris* (Oxford, 1933), p. 122 ff. It would seem probable on the whole, however, that the form of elections was still fluid, and that the technical procedure was a matter of controversy. We can trace the growing support given to the bishops in the letters of Popes Leo and Celestine, and the compromise of the Council of Arles in 452. Stevens perhaps takes the evidence of contemporary writings rather too trustfully. When Constantius tells us that Germanus was elected by the unanimous consent of clergy, nobility, and commons, has this really the value of evidence, or does it not rather suggest that Constantius is anxious to claim that the election took place in accordance with the stipulations laid down in the letter of Pope Leo (*Ep.* 10 (6); Migne, *P.L.*, Vol. LIV, col. 634; cf. *Ep.* 40, col. 814)? The *Life of St Amator* would seem to suggest that there was a fuller ecclesiastical tradition extant, which gives a significant picture of the way in which such elections were carried out. The account in the *Life* of St Amator is an interesting supplement to the pictures given by Sidonius of the procedure at Châlons and at Bourges, and implies the injunctions laid down according to the rule of Justinian (I, 3. 41 (42)). Cf. *Novell,* cxxiii, 1; cxxxvii, 2. The modification in the *Life* which represents the congregation as refraining from nominating may or may not be historical; but it is probably introduced to give added weight to the importance of the part played by the bishop. Perhaps the most important contribution to the whole question of episcopal elections in recent times is a note – almost a treatise in itself – by R. Laprat. See his article on 'La Carrière cléricale de Saint Germain' in the volume edited by Le Bras and Gilson, *Saint Germain d'Auxerre et son Temps* (Auxerre, 1950), p. 156, n. 12, and the references there cited. See further an important discussion of the history and proceeding of episcopal elections in Gaul in the fifth and sixth centuries by H. G. J. Beck, *The Pastoral Care of Souls in South-East France during the Sixth Century* (Rome, 1950), p. 15 ff.

[2] *Ep.* VII, 8.

the election itself was actually conducted. One of the two electing bishops is again Euphronius of Autun; the other, Agroecius of Sens.

It is interesting to note what Sidonius tells us[1] of Simplicius, the man whose election to the vacant see of Bourges he succeeded in effecting. He belonged to a local aristocratic family which had produced a number of bishops and prefects.

'So that it had become the custom for his family to voice (*dictare*) the law, both human and divine.'

Both the father and the father-in-law of Simplicius had occupied the see of Bourges with credit in the past, and Sidonius is warm in his praise of the man's personal character. We note that he regards the strong character and personality of his wife as one of his important qualifications for the bishopric. The whole picture which Sidonius presents to us in this letter is significant as illustrating the kind of qualifications valued in a candidate for a vacant see in the fifth century.

There were, indeed, many others, friends and correspondents of our group, who have not left important literary works behind them, but who, like Patiens, gave evidence of their culture by church building. An outstanding example of them is Euphronius, Bishop of Autun, already referred to. He was a friend and valued colleague of both Sidonius[2] and Patiens; and he was also the writer, jointly with Lupus of Troyes, of the letter to Talasius, the Bishop of Angers, on the subject of ecclesiastical discipline (p. 282). If we may believe Gregory of Tours,[3] who had excellent reasons for knowing, he built the basilica of St Symphorian of Autun, and took some part in the ornamentation of the tomb of St Martin at Tours. His friend Perpetuus, Bishop of Tours, also the friend and correspondent of Sidonius, is stated to have rebuilt the basilica of St Martin and to have founded that of St Peter. For the former Sidonius composed a verse inscription.[4]

In addition to the intellectual ecclesiastics of Sidonius's circle there are other cultured men among his correspondents, who were either not in Orders, or at least not primarily engaged in

[1] *Ep.* VII, 9.
[2] We have two letters to him from Sidonius (*Epp.* VII, 8; IX, 2).
[3] *Hist. Franc.* II, 15.
[4] *Ep.* IV, 18.

pastoral work. Such would seem to be a certain Johannes, of whom little is known[1] apart from a single letter addressed to him by Sidonius.[2] He evidently belonged to the same cultured milieu as Constantius and Sidonius, and in the letter referred to, written perhaps in 478, Sidonius congratulates him in the warmest terms on his literary excellence. His achievement, if we could trust the rhetoric of Sidonius, is nothing less than a small scale classical revival.

'In this storm of War which has brought shipwreck to the Roman forces, you are the only master in Gaul who has guided the Latin tongue into port.'

He goes on to speak of him as one who will appear to after ages as a new Demosthenes or Tully. It is clear that, however much allowance we make for polite hyperbole, Johannes was a man of high culture, and, it would seem, vigorous in his efforts to restore the educational standard of the past. It is the evident belief of Sidonius that Johannes was the founder of a new school of learning at Châlons. 'Since degrees of rank have now disappeared, by which high and low were wont to be distinguished, henceforth education will be the only criterion of nobility. I am, indeed, more beholden to your teaching than anyone', and he adds that he will be indebted to the School and to his teaching for his future readers.[3]

It is not easy to be certain whether Sidonius has in mind, as he writes, the political activities which were disturbing Gaul, 'seeking to place the slaves above their masters' (cf. pp. 125, 130); or whether he is thinking of the monastic movements now gaining ground in Gaul, with their international democratic influence. Either would represent tendencies disintegrating to the old order which he loved so dearly, and of which the distinguishing features are classical culture and love of letters.

As yet monasticism had made comparatively little headway in Gaul. The group of correspondents with whom we have been concerned seem to have been primarily scholars and men of action, whether administrators or soldiers. Our records of Germanus, Lupus and Constantius represent them as in some

---

[1] According to Dalton (op. cit., Vol. I, p. CLXX) he was a grammarian teaching in Aquitaine under Visigothic rule. Dalton does not state his evidence, but the tenor of the letter would favour this.

[2] *Ep.* VIII, 2.

[3] Loc. cit.

measure soldiers and travellers, and also diplomats. Sidonius was first and foremost a busy Roman official, and later a conscientious bishop. Patiens was an active church builder and ecclesiastical organizer and social worker. None of these men were monastic in their way of life. Constantius is at pains to assure us that Germanus lived an ascetic life; but it does not appear from the narrative that he was a recluse, and the contrary is clearly implied. It is not at all likely that he had any monastery (cf. p. 253). The biographer of Amator adds the professional touch about the celibacy adopted by the bishop and his wife, and embellishes it with a picturesque story of the wrong marriage service. Lupus is equally credited with ascetic practices. These are the stock properties of ecclesiastical biographers, and represent a fashion spreading from the East. The facts of the careers, and the letters of Sidonius, tell a different story – of vigour and activity; of charity and hard work; of travel in winter; of fighting for the Faith, but still more for the old civilization and the land in which it had taken root; of councils and diplomatic missions on behalf of the Christians of Gaul, but still more on behalf of the Gaulish people, irrespective of their religious views or their political parties.

Undoubtedly the greatness of the ecclesiastics of Gaul in this period lies in the fact that they were able to combine great deeds with a high standard of intellectual culture. The combination is rare; and in those unsettled days we feel as we read the pages of Salvian how little peace of mind or quiet study the conditions of the age can have offered to its busy officials. Yet we find Sidonius sending copies of the works of Orosius and Eusebius to Euric's general Namatius as he patrolled the Straits of Dover on the watch for Saxon pirates. We shall see Sidonius himself venturing out of Clermont, to give chase to the monk Riocatus for the sake of a coveted book, risking the skirmishers of the Gothic armies in the open country. Our evidence for the intellectual pre-eminence of Lupus and Constantius is at least as substantial as our records of their heroic achievements. Record and tradition alike credit all the most intellectual names in Gaul with brave deeds and great enterprises. The standards of the age, standards set by the conduct of the Gaulish noble families, demanded that every member of the old aristocracy should be both a man educated in the Roman tradition and a man actively engaged in public life, whether ecclesiastical or civil; and, in addition, if necessity required it, a great soldier in the fullest sense of the word.

CHAPTER XI

Sidonius Apollinaris

WE are especially intimate with the great Gaulish nobles and prelates of the closing years of Roman Gaul, partly owing to the growth of ecclesiastical biography, and perhaps even more to the wide prevalence of letter writing, and to the fashion of collecting and publishing correspondence – one of the most valuable survivals in this period from the literary practice of earlier times. The letters of the ecclesiastics of eastern Gaul, such as Eucherius, Salvian and Faustus, bring us into direct touch with the daily life of the ecclesiastic of the age, and with his spiritual aims and ideals. The correspondence of Sidonius Apollinaris in particular, even allowing for his heavy debt to the letter writers of an earlier age, is a mirror of the changing conditions and fluctuating currents of thought during the period of the Barbarian conquests. The consciousness of representing the old classical culture which they saw disappearing drew his correspondents together in a common literary fellowship, and goes far to account for the eagerness with which they received one another's works, and for the hyperbolical praises which they heaped on literary mediocrity.

The ease of communication and the relatively short distances in eastern Gaul must have been a great factor in this common intellectual life and the exchange of letters. Sidonius and Constantius, Lupus, Patiens, Faustus, Claudianus Mamertus and many others were not only known to one another personally, but they lived near enough to one another to be able to meet from time to time, and to exchange messages, books and poems. In the letter to his friend Rusticus, Sidonius, while regretting that the distance which separates them renders the exchange of letters a rarity, refers nevertheless to the arrival of personal messengers from Rusticus, bringing verbal communications from his friend. Sidonius himself was able to carry on a lively communication with many of his friends and fellow bishops, not only in eastern Gaul, but as far afield as Bayeux in the northwest, and Bordeaux and Bazas in the west and south-west, even

Rheims and Trier in the north. It has been remarked[1] how rarely we hear of letters failing to reach their destination, and how little apprehension seems to have been entertained of this, which must have encouraged and facilitated the exchange of ideas among our busy scholars and ecclesiastics.

The greatest literary bishop of Gaul whose work has come down to us from the closing years of the Roman Empire is Gaius Sollius Apollinaris Sidonius, the Bishop of Clermont-Ferrand in Auvergne. Both his poems and his letters bring us into close contact with the leading persons and events of the time. The literary merit of his works may not be of the highest order, and that of the poems is certainly not. But both his poetry and his letters are of great interest, because the author participated in the principal events of a very stirring period, and had close and interesting contacts with the leading personalities of his day, especially in Gaul.

We are especially fortunate in having a wealth of information, regarding not only Sidonius himself, but also his immediate ancestors and descendants. As a recent biographer has pointed out,[2] we have the history of a great Gallo-Roman family in this important period of history, from the lifetime of his great-grandfather, the prefect of the Gauls under Theodosius, down to his great-granddaughter, Placidina, the wife of Leontius II, Archbishop of Bordeaux under the son of Clovis. We are able to trace, from generation to generation, the effect of the rapidly changing course of public events on the life of the individual. The first of the Apollinares known to us is a pure Roman, and still a pagan. Sidonius himself is one of the last representatives of Roman culture, but at the same time a Christian bishop of high ideals, and with a deep sense of responsibility both to Gaul and to Rome. But he lived to see the Dark Ages setting in, and his son is already half-barbarized. The history of his family is an epitome of the history of Gaul from the Roman era to the beginning of the Middle Ages.

For these reasons Sidonius has been more carefully studied than any other writer of the period, and from almost every angle. The bibliography relating to both the man and his writings is enormous. The reader will find admirable studies in

[1] Stevens, *Sidonius Apollinaris* (Oxford, 1933), p. 77.
[2] Henry Légier Desgranges, *Les Apollinaires* (Paris, 1937), p. 6.

French by Chaix,[1] and later by Desgranges[2] and by more recent writers; in English by Bigg,[3] Dill,[4] Hodgkin,[5] and also in the valuable Introduction by Dalton to his translation of the letters of Sidonius.[6] An excellent modern scholarly monograph by C. E. Stevens[7] contains in addition a valuable critical bibliography.

For the text of the works of Sidonius I have used the edition by Paul Mohr, published at Leipzig in 1895; and the edition of the poems and of the first two books of the letters by W. B. Anderson (Loeb Classical Library), Vol. I, 1936. The poems, and the letters in this volume by Anderson are also translated into English. A complete English translation of the letters is published by Dalton in the work cited above, which contains in addition some useful notes and a biographical list of Sidonius's correspondents and persons mentioned in the letters. For the convenience of English readers I have followed the numbering of the poems in Anderson's edition, and of the letters in the English translation by Dalton.

The immediate ancestry of Sidonius is an interesting chapter in the unwritten history of the Gaulish nobility. The actual origin of the family is unknown, but its members seem to have been allied to the principal aristocratic families of Lyons, Auvergne and Velay. In one of his letters[8] he speaks of the many friends, kinsfolk and acquaintances, who greeted him on his journey all along the way from Lyons. His great-grand-father, who was still a pagan, had been Prefect of Gaul under Theodosius I.[9] His grandfather Apollinaris had been made Praetorian Prefect of Gaul by Constantine, and had been sent later on a successful expedition to Spain with the young Constans, Constantine's son, after which he retired into private life. He was the first member of the family to become a Christian, which is the more surprising because Christianity had been first introduced into Gaul some three centuries earlier. But the new

[1] L. A. Chaix, *Saint Sidoine Apollinaire et son Siècle* (Clermont-Ferrand, 1866).
[2] Henry Légier Desgranges, *Les Apollinaires*, ed. cit.
[3] C. Bigg, *Wayside Sketches in Ecclesiastical History* (London, 1906).
[4] Sir Samuel Dill, *Roman Society in the Last Century of the Western Empire*[2] (London, 1933), p. 187 ff.
[5] Thomas Hodgkin, *Italy and Her Invaders*, Vol. II, Oxford, 1892.
[6] O. M. Dalton, *The Letters of Sidonius* (Oxford, 1915), 2 vols.
[7] *Sidonius Apollinaris and His Age* (Oxford, 1933).
[8] *Ep.* I, 5.
[9] See *Ep.* I, 3.

faith was slow to obtain universal recognition, and there were still heathen temples dedicated to various divinities at Narbonne in Sidonius's lifetime. Most of what is known of him is derived from the epitaph composed on him by Sidonius himself, which is contained in *Ep.* III, 12.

Sidonius was born at Lyons c. 430. His father, like his grandfather and great-grandfather, held the office of Praetorian Prefect in Gaul, and Sidonius speaks, in one of his rare references to his youth, of being present at Arles when, in the year 449, his father was presiding over the tribunals of the Gauls, and the Consul Astyrius opened the year with the customary ceremonies.[1] His mother's name is unknown; but she was still living on in her home in Lyons in 474 with her daughters, and Sidonius confided to them the education of his children. We recall the childhood of Ausonius in the house of his maternal grandmother and aunts, and again we are led to surmise that the true nucleus of the family and the home in these great Gaulish households were the women on the maternal side of the family. His cousin Eulalia was married to Probus, a learned man of letters, of a very noble family, and the son of Magnus of Narbonne who was consul under Majorian. We have already spoken of Sidonius's allusion to a brother at Lérins (p. 150), though we are not told his name, and it is uncertain whether Sidonius means us to understand that he was a true brother, or only a brother in religion, though the former is perhaps the more probable.

The principal events of Sidonius's life are well known, though considerable uncertainty hangs over many of the details. He was born in 430, 431 or 432[2] at Lyons. Both his mother and his wife Papianilla belonged to the family of Avitus, a former Prefect of the Gauls, and later emperor. In his train Sidonius went to Rome, and his first panegyric was composed in the new emperor's honour. On the death of Avitus he returned to Lyons and took part in the unsuccessful Gaulish revolt against Majorian; but by a panegyric on Majorian,[3] and a special brief poetical petition also addressed to him,[4] he probably succeeded in obtaining the pardon of the people of Lyons. Shortly after,

[1] *Ep.* VIII, 6.
[2] See Desgranges, op. cit., p. 7; cf. Stevens, op. cit., p. 1 and n. 3.
[3] *Carmen* V.
[4] ibid., XIII.

sent to Rome on a mission by his compatriots, he composed a panegyric on the Emperor Anthemius by whom he had been welcomed, and from whom he received the title of Prefect of Rome. He returned to Gaul at the close of his period of office and retired to his wife's estate[1] at Avitacum,[2] and for some years devoted himself to the life of a literary country gentleman.

Meanwhile Gaul had been largely lost to the empire. The most formidable of the occupying forces were the Visigoths, whose power extended from the Loire to the south of Spain. Many of the Roman officials entertained relations with them, among others the Aviti; and it was largely by Visigothic support that Avitus himself, the father-in-law of Sidonius, had been made emperor. At this point (c. 469 or shortly after),[3] on the death of Eparchius, Bishop of Clermont-Ferrand, the chief city of the Arverni, Sidonius was raised to the episcopate. His position must have been one of great difficulty and delicacy, for Auvergne was devoted to Rome and dreaded the Arian Goths, and his own sympathies were whole-heartedly with the Arverni. He and his nephew Ecdicius were, in fact, the true leaders of the resistance, and for three years he successfully held the city of Clermont against a more or less continuous blockade[4] by the Visigoths under their king Euric.[5] When this district, which Euric had not succeeded in reducing, was finally ceded to the Goths by treaty in 475, Sidonius was imprisoned for nearly two years[6] at Liviana[7] on the River Aude, between Carcassonne and Narbonne; but he obtained his release by the good offices of his friend Leo,[8] who acted as Euric's minister, although Leo himself was a Roman and a Catholic. Later Sidonius made his way to Euric's court at Bordeaux as a suppliant in a legal dispute about land, and, perhaps as a result of yet another panegyric, a poem in fifty-nine verses on the Arian conqueror which

[1] *Ep.* II, 2. But see Stevens, op. cit., p. 20, n. 2.
[2] The site is unknown. For a discussion, see Stevens, op. cit., Appendix B, p. 185 f.
[3] For a discussion of the date, see Stevens *op. cit.*, p, 205 f.
[4] For a discussion as to the exact nature of the Gothic operations in Auvergne, see Stevens, op. cit., p. 130 ff.
[5] A brief summary of Euric's career is given by W. B. Anderson, *Sidonius, Poems and Letters*, Vol. I, p. xxvii ff.
[6] See Stevens, op. cit., p. 163, and the references there cited.
[7] Now Capendu (Stevens, op. cit., p. 162).
[8] *Ep.* VIII, 3. Leo was a native of Narbonne, and a poet and lawyer, as well as a man of wide culture.

Sidonius enclosed in a letter to his old friend the poet Lampridius,[1] he was permitted soon afterwards to take up again his episcopal duties at Clermont and to retain them till his death in 488. It is customary for critics to smile at the facility with which the panegyrics of Sidonius were composed for contending parties of totally opposed political views;[2] but they are, after all, little more than official journalism, and it will be conceded that a fanatical Arian ruler who allows a Catholic bishop, after a three-years' military resistance, to return quietly to his episcopal duties is not undeserving of such a graceful form of thanks.

The importance of the Gaulish background shows itself in many ways in the personal and the family life of Sidonius. Not only does Sidonius confide the early training of his own children to his mother and sisters at Lyons; we also find his daughter Alcima and his daughter-in-law Placidina virtually undertaking responsibility for Arcadius, the son of Apollinaris, Sidonius's grandson.[3]

Another feature in which Sidonius appears to follow Gaulish custom is his choice of his wife's property for his home. We have seen that in our period it is by no means rare for the husband on his marriage to go to live on his wife's estate. We have seen Sulpicius Severus receiving at least a part, if not the whole of his subsistence from his mother-in-law Bassula. Paulinus of Nola went to live on the estate of his wife Therasia in Spain. Paulinus of Pella, after his marriage, at once set about the care of his wife's estate. We have seen how, in the tradition contained in the *Life of St Amator*, a certain Eraclius, a wealthy and noble pagan chief of the Aedui, accompanied his wife Palladia to live on her inherited estate in the suburbs of Auxerre. The same custom seems to be reflected in regard to Sidonius who, though he had a town house at Lyons, lived by preference on his wife's estate at Avitacum.

---

[1] He was murdered later by his slaves, and the news of his death caused Sidonius grave consternation (see p. 310).
[2] A particularly notable case is perhaps that of the *vobis regia virgo regius ille mihi* in *Carmen* II, 485.
[3] See Dalton, Vol. I, pp. xiv f.; li, nn. 2, 3. See also Gregory of Tours, *Hist. Franc.*, III, 2; and for the later Placidina, daughter of Arcadius, see Venantius Fortunatus, *Carmen* XV, 93, where she is mentioned in the laudatory fashion of the time, as first the wife, and later the spiritual 'sister', of Leontius, Bishop of Bordeaux.

This close cohesion of Gaulish family life must have done much to explain the survival of Gaulish patriotism and love of home, even after the political and intellectual union with Rome had long been complete. The Romanized Gauls looked to the family dwelling and the family estate as to their permanent home, irrespective of all political vicissitudes. We have seen superannuated Gauls, after a lifetime spent in the Roman civil service, returning to their estates, as a Scotsman returns to his village or glen, to spend the evening of his life at 'home'. Sidonius reminds his brother-in-law Ecdicius that 'the country which gave us birth has a right to hold the highest place in our affection'.[1] This love of home and Gaul is seen in its most striking form among the Aviti of Narbonne, the family to which belonged Ecdicius himself, and also Sidonius's mother and wife, the family which even gave an emperor to Rome. It has been fairly claimed for Ecdicius and Sidonius that they were the heart of the resistance movement in the last stand made in Gaul against the Visigoths. The public spirit and high standards of life and thought of this great family can be traced even down to the time of Venantius Fortunatus (cf. p. 301, n. 3).

The noble Gaulish patriotism and love of his native land which Sidonius shares with his compatriots is closely bound up with his devotion to all that was best in classical, and especially Roman culture. To the Gallo-Roman nobility the defence of Gaul against the Teutonic invaders meant the defence of all that remained of classical literature and learning. The settlement of the Burgundians and Visigoths in Gaul involved not only in some measure[2] the loss of the Gaulish land and homes, but the loss of civilization and intellectual life, of that culture so passionately loved, both for its own sake, and because it furnished a spiritual retreat, a refined mental world to which only the best spirits had the entrée, and where they met with the secure confidence of friends.

Sidonius was never without a present consciousness of the declining culture around him, and the deterioration in the standards of education, especially among the middle classes. In

[1] *Ep.* III, 3.
[2] Dill was of the opinion that the nobility were for the most part left in undisturbed possession; but this, as we have seen in Chapters V and VII, is only true to a very limited extent and in some areas. See Sir S. Dill, *Roman Society in Gaul in the Last Century of the Western Empire*[2], p. 372 ff.

a letter to Claudianus Mamertus[1] he complains of the crude style of oratory of the middle class, and elsewhere he wistfully addresses his friend Sapaudus, a rhetor of Vienne, as probably the last worthy representative of Roman eloquence.[2] Elsewhere to his friend Hesperius[3] he stresses the growing indifference to the purity of the Latin language, and the beauty of its traditional diction, and he notices with dismay the prevalent tendency to barbarisms. His letter written in 478 to his friend Johannes[4] compliments him on reviving a literature which was 'almost dead and buried', and declares that Latin is being destroyed by the storm of war which has wrecked the Roman power. As we have seen already, the writer expresses the view that now that class distinctions have disappeared, the only standard of nobility in future will be a polite education.

For his brother-in-law Ecdicius he has warm praise because he not only instilled the love of eloquence and poetry into the nobles of Gaul, but also because he credits him with having induced them to abandon 'the barbarous Celtic dialect'.[5] In a letter to his friend Placidus of Grenoble he makes reference to 'the splendour (*pompa*), the fine quality (*proprietas*) of the Latin tongue',[6] almost with the affection he would accord to a living being.

It is undoubtedly this passionate clinging to an old and stable culture, the outcome of his training in Roman schools and a Roman education, which accounts for the excessive adulation which Sidonius metes out to those of his friends who still wrote good Latin, and who still composed verses in the classical tradition. His own intellect was not of the highest order, and his critical faculty would seem to be defective if we judge him by the hyperbolical praise lavished on the indifferent writings of his friends. All this is now a commonplace of literary history, and there is nothing remarkable in it. What is very astonishing is the tenacity with which he and his fellow 'Romans' in Gaul – Mamertus, Faustus, and others – devote their leisure, and perhaps more than their leisure, to the pursuit of literature, while the enemy are closing in on this last little group of lovers of old-style poetry left to the empire in Europe.

---

[1] *Ep.* IV, 3.
[2] *Ep.* V, 10.
[3] *Ep.* II, 10.
[4] *Ep.* VIII, 2.
[5] *Ep.* III, 3.
[6] ibid.

The poems of Sidonius were probably published in 468, some years before the first book of the letters. They were composed at various periods from his earliest years, and circulated privately among his friends, though he probably kept careful copies, perhaps with a view to ultimate publication. In a letter to his friend Tonantius, who has asked for some poems from his pen, he replies: 'You see, while looking for something for you to sing, I have sung something myself instead. I bring to light scraps like these from the depths of my desk, where they have lain hidden for about twenty years, gnawed into holes by the mice.'[1] There is no evidence that any of his letters were published before the complete collection which is still extant,[2] and which is divided into two parts, perhaps originally published separately. The first part consists of panegyrics, with their dedications and prefaces; the second, of his earlier poems. The entire collection is dedicated[3] to his old school friend, Magnus Felix of Narbonne, of whom we shall have more to say later.

The poems are not inspired by lofty imagination. But his literary integrity, his love of classical learning, and his intellectual refinement give a certain distinction to all that he wrote, even the panegyrics. To classical scholars whose standards are set by the reading of a lifetime in the works of the greater poets of Greece and Rome the poems of Sidonius come as poor stuff, 'a most miserable style';[4] but his mastery of oratorical technique and gift of phrase have created many forcible descriptions which would have called forth thunderous applause in a public speech, and their pith and vigour are not in any way diminished when they are coloured by the expression of his personal attitude to his subject. I may refer, e.g. to his description of Bishop Patiens's new church at Lyons, and of the eloquence of Bishop Faustus's dedicatory sermon, and the incidental references to Faustus's work in organizing the nursing of the sick and the burial of the dead (cf. p. 193 f.).

It is largely to the Roman education in rhetoric, as well as to the influence of the spoken word and the technique proper to it, that we must ascribe those features of the poetry of Sidonius which offend modern literary taste. To the student of oral

[1] *Ep.* IX, 13.
[2] See W. B. Anderson, *Sidonius, Poems and Letters*, Vol. I, p. lii.
[3] *Carmen* IX.
[4] T. Hodgkin, *Italy and her Invaders*, Vol. II (Oxford, 1892), p. 320.

literature he is particularly interesting for the intermediate position which he holds between the native Gaulish panegyrist, whose function it is to compose oral poetry with all its traditional technique, but clad in a Roman dress; and the Roman classical poets whose original stimulus is fading after a late spring on Gaulish soil. He cannot be judged by classical standards; still less is his poetry barbaric. It resembles the work of an expert equestrian riding two steeds simultaneously in the circus, and precariously commanding our admiration rather by his bizarre and uncanny confidence and technical dexterity than by the serious beauty of true horsemanship. It is trick riding.

The results are nevertheless of great interest, and merit a closer study from the point of view of the oral technique. For our present purpose, however, the chief value of the panegyrics of Sidonius lies, not in their felicity of expression, or their unusual and interesting diction and metrical forms, but their close contact with, and inspiration by, the immediate events of his own day which called them forth. A recent French critic has observed that to annotate the *Panegyrics* of Sidonius is actually to live again half a century of the history of Gaul at the time of the Great Invasions.[1] Students of Early Teutonic literature in particular cannot be sufficiently grateful for his vivid contemporary verse sketches of the Teutonic invaders who were rapidly bringing to a close the culture which Sidonius prized so highly. These minute and accurate descriptions are perhaps the most interesting passages in his poems, and the side-lights on the Teutons with which they present us, supplemented by others in his letters, have left us a little portrait gallery of contemporary Barbarians worthy to rank with Ausonius's professors of Bordeaux in another field.

Sidonius had particularly good opportunities of watching the Teutonic peoples at close quarters, and a neat facility in hitting them off. Yet he probably obtained his detailed descriptions mostly from hearsay, at any rate his lists or 'runs'. If so they are all the more valuable, because they must have been truthful enough to have gained general acceptance. And though every

---

[1] 'Commenter les Panégyriques de Sidoine, c'est en réalité retracer un demi-siècle d'histoire de la Gaule à l'époque des Grandes Invasions.' A. Loyen, *Recherches historiques sur les Panégyriques de Sidoine Apollinaire* (Paris, 1942), p. 20.

historian of the period sighs for the vast amount of information
which Sidonius has withheld from us, we must be thankful for
many a telling picture neatly sketched in a few lines of swift
delineation in his letters and poems. Such is the little poetical
inventory of the Teutonic envoys at the court of the Visigothic
king Euric, which he gives us in his letter to the rhetor Lampridius,[1] where we read of the blue-eyed Saxon, at home on the
sea, but not on land, whose peculiar way of shaving the head
well back from the brow enlarges the face and makes the head
seem smaller. There strolls one of the tribe of the Heruli, dweller
in ocean's most remote creeks, and of the same complexion
with its weedy depths; and the seven-foot stature of the Burgundian is insisted on both here and elsewhere.[2] Here even the
Ostrogoth pays homage, and, by a grand hyperbole, the Sas-
sanian Shah of Persia seeks aid of Euric against the foes menac-
ing his capital of Susa on the far Euphrates. This last daring
utterance makes us pause – but it would sound well declaimed
in a public speech.

It is by just such a few happy strokes of his pen that in a letter
to his friend the Gaulish admiral, Namatius, we catch a glimpse
of an official of the Visigothic king patrolling the Straits of
Dover against Saxon pirates, and begging Sidonius to send him
Varro and Eusebius to read in his leisure moments. Again
Sidonius hits off the Saxon, 'the most ferocious of all foes':

'He attacks unexpectedly; if one is prepared, he slips away.
Resistance he slights, rashness he beats down. If he pursues he
catches; if he flees he escapes. He has no fear of shipwreck, it
merely exercises him. He not only knows the dangers of the sea –
he is familiar with them. A storm puts those who are to be
attacked off their guard, and prevents the attackers from being
seen beforehand. In the hope of making a surprise attack he
cheerfully risks his life amid rough seas and sharp rocks.'[3]

The Saxons seem to have made the deepest impression of all
the Barbarians on Sidonius. He refers to them in the *Panegyric
on Avitus* as 'the Saxon pirate who looks on it simply as play to
plough the British waters with leather craft, cleaving the grey
sea in a curragh.'[4]

Doubtless these catalogues of Barbarians were the common-

---

[1] *Ep.* VIII, 9.
[3] *Ep.* VIII, 6.
[2] *Carmen* XII, 11.
[4] *Carmen* VII, 369 ff.

places of contemporary rhetoricians, for they occur elsewhere in the poems of Sidonius also. There is one in the *Panegyric on Avitus*, where a short list is given,[1] and where the mention of every tribe is followed by a brief note indicating their outstanding characteristics. Thus we are told that the Herulian found in Avitus his match in speed, the Hun in javelin-throwing, the Frank in swimming, the Sauromatian in the use of the shield, the Salian in marching, the Gelonian in using the scimitar. Such rhetorical 'runs', once established, die hard. It is not impossible that even the descriptive epithets of Barbarians had already become stereotyped in the technical equipment of the rhetoricians. The Burgundians are referred to as 'seven-foot high', both in the inventory of Barbarians at Euric's court and in the little poem addressed to a certain Senator Catullinus.[2] The Goths are generally 'skin-clad'. In the poems, indeed, the Barbarian tribes are generally mentioned each with his appropriate opprobrious epithet[3] – the 'savage' (*trux*)[4] and 'fierce' (*ferox*)[5] Aleman, the 'corpulent' (*pinguis*) Vandal,[6] the 'skin-clad' (*pellitus*) Goths, whom he erroneously calls *Getae*.[7]

But Sidonius must have had more direct information, both from personal knowledge and from eye-witnesses, than was furnished by such trite catalogues. His famous full-length description of the Gothic king, Theodoric,[8] in the letter to his brother-in-law Agricola; his detailed account of the Huns in the *Panegyric on Anthemius*;[9] the pictures of the Barbarian mourning, and of the little Frankish wedding feast so pitifully ruined by Majorian;[10] of the Franks themselves, 'whom death may overcome, but not fear,' and 'whose courage almost outlives their lives,'[11] – all these must surely be based on personal observation, whether by Sidonius or his informant. Here the per-

---

[1] *Carmen* VII, 230 ff.
[2] ibid., XII, 11.
[3] We occasionally find simple catalogues, however, without descriptive epithets, e.g. *Carmen* V, 474 ff., VII, 321 ff.
[4] ibid., V, 375.
[5] ibid., VII, 373.
[6] ibid., V, 390.
[7] ibid., V, 562; VII, 349; 450 ff. Cf. *Ep.* I, 2.
[8] *Ep.* I, 11.
[9] *Carmen* II, 243 ff. I cannot agree with Prof. Anderson that the description of the Huns by Sidonius is imitated from Claudian, *In Rufinum* I, 323 ff. The two passages have hardly anything in common, and the description given by Sidonius is much fuller and more interesting.
[10] *Carmen* V, 218 ff.   [11] *Carmen* V, 251-3.

sonal appearance and dress and military technique of the
Franks are particularly informing. Again in the little poem
XII addressed to Catullinus, the senator already referred to,
Sidonius tells us categorically that he has himself 'endured
Teutonic speech among long-haired hordes', and that he has
had to applaud unwillingly the Burgundian harps resounding
to the plectra,[1] while his eyes and nose are offended by the rank
butter on their hair and the coarseness of their food.

To historians of the fifth century the great importance of
Sidonius lies even more in his letters than in his poems. The
letters, as stated above, were collected and compiled at the suggestion of Constantius, to whom they are dedicated. It is not
known when Sidonius began to prepare them for publication,
but the date 469 has been suggested.[2] They were not published
all together, but at different periods, perhaps each book separately; and the earliest collection seems to have been supplemented and enlarged from time to time. Certainly the eighth
and the ninth books were added to the original collection later,
and not both at once.[3] The individual letters are often difficult
to date, but the majority seem to have been written within a
comparatively short period, perhaps during the last twenty
years of his life.

It is almost certain that we have not got the letters in their
original form. Following earlier models, especially those of the
younger Pliny,[4] and also Symmachus,[5] Sidonius has clearly
touched up and worked over his original correspondence for
purposes of publication.[6] There are also clear indications of
artificial grouping and arrangement in the letters themselves.
The whole of Book VI, and the majority of the letters of Book
VII, for example, consist of letters to bishops. It is thought that
Sidonius aimed in some measure, perhaps not very whole-

[1] *Barbaricis abacta plectris . . . Thalia* (*Carmen* XII, 6 ff.). The exclusive use of
stringed instruments at the Gothic court is specifically mentioned in the account of
Theodoric (*Ep.* I, 2). This preference for the harp among the Teutonic peoples is
fully borne out by references in Anglo-Saxon and Early Norse poetry relating to
our period.

[2] Anderson, ed. cit., p. lx.

[3] ibid., loc. cit. For some discussion of the general history of the publication, see
Stevens, op. cit., p. 168 ff.

[4] 'Ego Plinio ut discipulus assurgo', *Ep.* IV, 22.

[5] Careful study has been made of the literary debt of Sidonius to the classics in
his letters. See Stevens. op. cit., p. 174 f., and the references there cited.

[6] We may refer to his introductory letter to Constantius, Book I, 1. For some
discussion of this subject, see Anderson, op. cit., p. lxii.

heartedly, at including one letter only to each of his correspondents. If so we have need to be thankful that he did not
adhere strictly to his purpose.

These indications of plan and purpose, however, must have
had some more serious object than superficial literary form.
They suggest that Sidonius, by publishing his correspondence,
was aiming deliberately at what, in fact, he has in a very considerable measure achieved, namely, holding up a mirror to
contemporary Gaul. By address and allusion, not rarely by
deliberate description, he presents us with a series of miniatures
of his friends and contemporaries, a series of vignettes of current
events. The excellence of the letter as a literary form for his purpose is that it allows his personal gifts and his individual view-
point the freest scope, especially his gift of brilliantly crystalliz-
ing the broad essentials of peoples and situations in a brief
phrase, often with a touch of humour.

We recall the letter to his brother-in-law Agricola, in which
he makes reference with wry and wistful merriment to the doctors from whom he is fain to bear off his sick daughter Severiana
into the country, because 'with their attendance and disagree-
ments, their ignorance, and constant attentions, they over-
anxiously kill off many patients'.[1] Or there is the allusion to
himself and his young son reading Terence and Menander
together – 'reading and appreciating the play and enjoying the
humour. The play charmed him, and he me, and we were both
equally captivated'.[2] Even in his description of the solemn
Rogations instituted by Mamertus, his humour bubbles up as
he recalls the vivid contrast of public prayers as they had
previously been conducted – 'often interrupted for refreshment'; and he adds lightly with reference to these earlier
prayers: 'They were chiefly for showers or fine weather, so
the potter and the gardener could never decorously attend
together.'[3]

It is perhaps this power of detached observation and humorous summary which more than all his other gifts makes Sidonius
seem very modern to us. The lightness of touch, the power to
play at being in earnest, the pleasure of laughter for its own
sake, are themselves sure indications of an active intellectual life

---

[1] *Ep.* II, 12.
[2] *Ep.* IV, 12.
[3] *Ep.* V, 14.

and a refinement of perception. The deep seriousness which guided his purpose as Bishop of Auvergne, and inspired his courage in the last days, is nowhere allowed to obtrude itself. He is as far as possible from the austerity or the penitential asceticism of later medieval religious discipline. One gets an impression from the letters that he would regard the subjects on which he feels most deeply as unsuitable for conversation or letter, much as people do today. Indeed one feels as one reads Sidonius that, had the Barbarian Invasions not occurred, we should have by-passed the Middle Ages altogether in Gaul and passed straight from the Roman era into the modern world.

It is accordingly in his lighter moments and his happy social contacts that we find Sidonius at his best as a letter writer. We can enjoy his gift of bright and vivid presentation undisturbed by deeper emotional implications. His little gems of wit and humour show a keen observation of the significant details which go to make up the more studied descriptions, both of personalities and scenes, when he is working on a larger canvas. Perhaps the most famous, and certainly the most important, of his full-length portraits, is his account of the Visigothic king, Theodoric II, Euric's predecessor, in which he describes the king's person minutely, if perhaps a trifle conventionally, and in which he also gives us a valuable account of his daily routine, and of his bearing and his recreations.[1] A more lively and personal portrait is that of the Gaulish poet and orator Lampridius of Bordeaux,[2] the old friend of Sidonius who was murdered by his slaves c. 480 (cf. pp. 301, 326) – a man, so Sidonius tells us, passionate and impulsive, but without malice or meanness; one to whom 'no one was sufficiently distasteful to call forth his curses, yet no one congenial enough to escape his abuse', superstitious and given to consulting astrologers, yet reading the ancients with perseverance and reverent admiration, at once a polished and fluent speaker and one of the most accomplished among the Gaulish poets of his day.[3]

In strong contrast to these two widely differing portraits is the more intimate study of the scholar and presbyter Claudi-

---

[1] *Ep.* I, 2.

[2] *Ep.* VIII, 11.

[3] He obtained the favour of Euric, and probably helped Sidonius to regain his liberty when the latter was detained by Euric at Bordeaux. See *Ep.* VIII, 9; and cf. p. 326.

anus Mamertus of Vienne,[1] whom we have already seen in a
previous chapter (cf. p. 209 ff.) assisting his brother the bishop
in his episcopal duties, looking after his business affairs, accompanying him on his journeys, helping him in Church matters,
and – most interesting of all – training his choir (whatever that
means). We have seen him corresponding with Sidonius on
literary matters, and as the author of a philosophical religious
work on the nature of the soul. And finally, most gratifying and
rare of all these glimpses of fifth-century intellectual and
spiritual life, we have seen Mamertus in his little academy of the
young intellectuals of Vienne, a beloved teacher whose only
fault is the sympathetic tolerance and courtesy with which he
treats the least promising of their group.

As one turns the pages of the letters, and the great figures of
the century file past, one feels the illusion of a pageant. It is not
that all the characters are equally life-like by any means. Some
of them are poor stuff, especially when the writer squares his
elbows to do his work thoroughly. His studied account of
Tonantius Ferreolus[2] is a lifeless inventory – it is only incidentally, in the account of the visit of Sidonius to Ferreolus's country
house Prusianum[3] that the man comes to life. Again the 'type
character' sketch of an immoral person,[4] and the hardly more
acceptable picture of the typical well-preserved Germanicus,[5]
are only redeemed by the relentless scrutiny to which every
feature, physical, moral and personal, is subjected by the
writer.

Yet what a range and variety of types and classes, what a
number of peoples and nationalities, what a jostle of bishops and
presbyters, poets and orators, kings and emperors, statesmen
and husbandmen, Jews and merchants, fugitives and refugees,
he brings before us! Chaucer's range is narrow beside it. And
then there is the wealth of scenes, the pageantry of Roman and
Barbarian at close quarters, marrying, fighting, hating, coming
to close grips – personal, military and diplomatic. Not the least
valuable aspect of these letters, both to us and to historians, is
the sense of integrity which they impress on the mind of the
reader of our own day. A range so wide and so varied might

---

[1] *Ep.* IV, 11.
[2] *Ep.* VII, 12. See also *Carmen* XXIV, 34 ff.
[3] *Ep.* II, 9.
[4] *Ep.* III, 13.   [5] *Ep.* IV, 13.

easily have slipped into a series, into a kaleidoscopic effect, into a 'collection'. In these letters, on the contrary, the same persons appear and reappear with all the naturalism of the incidents and accidents of life. A personality may be himself the recipient of a letter; or he or his affairs may be referred to in more or less detail in a letter to a mutual friend; or again he may never take a leading part, and yet by various references or allusions we know both him and his milieu. Partly by Sidonius's wide circle of contacts with the leading men of Gaul, partly by his own craving for intellectual contacts, partly again by the difficulties of the times, which precluded frequent personal visits and substituted the interchange of letters, Sidonius has rendered his country in his own lifetime articulate and living to us today.

It has already been hinted that the letters are not so spontaneous as the writer would have us believe. Undoubtedly they owe something to famous letter-writers of the past – to the younger Pliny in particular, to Symmachus, to Cicero, as Sidonius tells us himself, and to others. It is not always easy to gauge how far specific passages are reminiscent of earlier models, how far inspired by social conditions which reflect the classical past. It may be confidently suggested that one of his letters, written while on a temporary visit to Langon on the Garonne, near Bordeaux, to his friend Trygetius in Bazas, contains echoes of the letters of Ausonius to his friend Theon of Médoc (cf. p. 319); and examples of such echoes could easily be multiplied. The enchanting picture of Claudianus Mamertus and his little academy in Vienne (cf. p. 208) is not without echoes of Plato. But was not the whole ideal and practice of Claudianus himself in all probability indebted to such classical predecessors as the academy? Again the somewhat unedifying letter of the scandal at Arles, and the emperor's dinner party,[1] may owe something in its style to Athenaeus; but one cannot doubt that the scene described actually took place. The account of the journey of Sidonius over the Alps from Lyons to Rome,[2] written as he was resting on his couch in the inn before entering the Imperial City, is perhaps influenced in style by the *De Reditu Suo* of Rutilius Namatianus (cf. p. 126 ff.); but the journey is overland, and made by an observant writer with an eye for detail quickened by his reading of Virgil, which gives it a value inde-

[1] *Ep.* I, 2.   [2] *Ep.* I, 5.

pendent of any models; and the closing portion, in which he touches lightly on the sounds and spectacle of the great city, given over to carnival on the marriage of the Suevian patrician Ricimer to the emperor's daughter Alypia, is inspired directly by his personal experience, and is of interest in its own right.

Many of the scenes in the letters are deployed with elaborate art. The account of the trial of Arvandus[1] is a masterpiece in its way, describing in a letter to his friend Vincentius the whole sorry business, step by step, including the vivid trial scene, and the 'traitor's' humiliating condemnation. Even today it is impossible to read the scene unmoved; and we find ourselves searching in our minds, as every historian since has searched, for the reason which can have inspired such unbounded confidence in a man on trial for high treason. What could have led Arvandus to his unhesitating admission of his authorship of the incriminating intercepted letter? And equally we wonder at Sidonius's complacent attitude to the man. Is it possible that the motives of Arvandus may have been other than treasonable? It would almost appear from Sidonius's letter that, after Arvandus had admitted authorship, any further defence was shouted down, and he was haled away to the common jail. Yet the advice of Arvandus to Euric to attack the Bretons north of the Loire might perhaps be construed as patriotic strategy rather than treason.[2] At the time (A.D. 468) the Bretons were in a state of rebellion against Rome under their king, Riothamus.

It would be tedious to detail the many scenes on which we would gladly linger, but in conclusion one of his little glimpses – alas, all too few! – of Barbarian pageantry calls for a special note. It is the letter to a friend Dominicius,[3] written c. 470, in which he gives a minute inventory of the dress and equipment of the young Barbarian prince Sigismer, whether Frank or Burgundian, on his way, probably through the town of Lyons, to wed a Burgundian princess – perhaps the daughter of Hilperic.[4] The description is so detailed that it has arrested the attention and interest of all social historians of the period. The style nevertheless is artificial and rhetorical, and though we

[1] *Ep.* I, 7.
[2] The death sentence pronounced on Arvandus was afterwards commuted to sentence of banishment.
[3] *Ep.* IV, 20.
[4] Dalton, op. cit., Vol. I, p. xciii; II, p. 233.

cannot doubt that here, as elsewhere, Sidonius is describing a scene which he has himself witnessed, the literary form of the passage is following well-worn models.

Not the least interesting class of people who flit through the letters are the letter carriers themselves – a more varied, if less picturesque class than those who carried letters to and fro between St Paulinus at Nola and his friends in Gaul. For the most part the 'postmen' employed by Sidonius sound casual enough. Sidonius begs his friend Magnus Felix to send him a letter by 'some traveller'.[1] Claudianus Mamertus refers to himself as having to 'search everywhere for some kind of person whose goodwill or necessities' will induce him to carry a letter to Sidonius.[2] To his kinsman Simplicius he sends by a man who, he declares, is of a type who are quite despicable; but he adds, significantly enough, that friends who are dependent on letters for their intercourse cannot be too particular about the messenger.[3] Many of the writers, as we should expect, send letters by members of their domestic or official staffs, to whom also Sidonius frequently entrusts his replies. Euric's admiral Namatius naturally employs a courier.[4] Sidonius, writing to his friend Rusticus, refers to his messengers in whom he noted the good effect of their master's training, and the influence of his unassuming manners.[5] His brother-in-law Agricola sends his message of invitation by his boatmen.[6]

It is perhaps somewhat surprising to find how few of the letter carriers are men in Orders. One letter is sent to kinsmen of Sidonius, Simplicius and Apollinaris, by a certain Brother Faustinus, for whom he expresses great veneration.[7] A letter is conveyed to Bishop Euphronius of Autun, the colleague of St Lupus (cf. p. 282) by the priest Albiso and the deacon Proculus.[8] The Bishop Principius sends his clerk Megethius,[9] and Sidonius refers to him as 'our old messenger',[10] suggesting that his services were regularly employed. The only letter which we hear of as 'lost' had been entrusted to a Reader named Constans.[11] The relatively small proportion of letters carried by ecclesiastics in

[1] *Ep*. III, 7.
[2] *Ep*. IV, 2.
[3] *Ep*. IV, 7.
[4] *Ep*. VIII, 6.
[5] *Ep*. II, 11.
[6] *Ep*. II, 12.
[7] *Ep*. IV, 4.
[8] *Ep*. IX, 2.
[9] *Ep*. VIII, 14.
[10] *Ep*. IX, 8.
[11] *Ep*. IV, 12.

this period is in striking contrast to the correspondence of St Paulinus of Nola and his friends in Gaul, a large part of which, it will be remembered, was regularly carried by the monk Victor, and the exorcist, Cardamas.

It is interesting on the other hand to find Jews not rarely employed in the capacity of letter carriers. Sidonius seems to have been peculiarly enlightened in his attitude to Jews and to have held them in high regard. Between himself and his old school-fellow, Magnus Felix of Narbonne,[1] a Jew was employed who is described as a 'dependent' (*cliens*) of the latter. Sidonius also commends a Jew who carries a letter to Bishop Eleutherius,[2] and sends a letter to Bishop Nunechius of Nantes by the hand of Promotus, a converted Jew.[3]

The prominence of Jews as letter carriers is perhaps not unconnected with the appearance of the trader in the same capacity. The only full-length portrait of a letter carrier which Sidonius has left us is that of Amantius,[4] a small trader of Marseilles, whose native city was Clermont, and who seems to have carried letters regularly between Sidonius and Bishop Graecus of Marseilles. The man was evidently something of an adventurer, even a bit of a rogue,[5] but industrious and engaging withal. He managed to impose on Sidonius, as he did on everyone else; and it is a tribute to his genius that Sidonius, again like everyone else, continued to countenance him and even employ him after finding himself duped.

In the first letter in which Sidonius refers to Amantius,[6] he commends him to Graecus as a Reader of the Church, to whom he has given both a letter of introduction and a canonical letter, and he expresses warm hope of a brilliant mercantile career for the man. At the same time he stresses his good qualities. The man, he tells us, has become known as an agent and trader, but although he inspires general confidence, the profit goes to others; and Sidonius adds that his honesty stands so high in the general opinion that, despite his lack of capital, people trust him enough to lend him money without insisting on any further security. He adds moreover that these facts have only just come to his notice, but that this does not prevent his asserting them

[1] *Ep.* III, 4; IV, 5.
[2] *Ep.* VI, 11.
[3] *Ep.* VIII, 13.
[4] *Ep.* VII, 7; IX, 4; Cf. VI, 8.
[5] *Ep.* VII, 2.
[6] *Ep.* VI, 8.

with confidence on the authority of common acquaintances.

Disillusionment is frankly avowed in the next letter,[1] and Sidonius finds himself obliged to apologize to Graecus for having misinformed him as to the man's character and standing. At the same time it is clear that he got a good deal of pleasurable amusement from the fellow. – 'It makes', he assures Graecus, 'a good story', and he proceeds to relate it with gusto, assuring the good bishop that he will not report anything of the rogue which will offend his ear, or impose on him a second time. He then relates with some insight how the man's father, a very respectable man in a small way in Clermont, had ruled his son for his good, but with a somewhat over-firm hand, so that the youth ran away to Marseilles. Here he managed to ingratiate himself with the citizens and even the local authorities. He also succeeded in marrying a rich heiress, though he had little more to recommend him than an adroit address and his own sharp wits. These seem, however, to have imposed not only on the people of Marseilles and the bride's mother also, but even on Sidonius;[2] and though the latter refers later to the man's marriage settlement as an imposture and a swindle, the two bishops continued to make use of his services whenever he passed between their cities, which was not rarely.[3] The whole story of this Gaulish Hajji Baba is related by Sidonius[4] with piquancy and great good humour. Sidonius may be suspected of liking the rogue, for his next letter to Graecus begins jauntily enough.

'Here is Amantius again, the bearer of my trifles, off to his Marseilles as usual to bring home his gatherings from the city.'[5]

A large proportion of Sidonius's correspondents are men of Gaulish family, owning what must have been hereditary Gaulish lands and estates. In the poem (XXII) addressed to his friend Pontius Leontius of Bordeaux – elsewhere[6] referred to by Sidonius as 'easily the foremost of the Aquitanians' – he has left us a detailed and delightful account of the home of the family to which Paulinus of Nola had belonged. It is referred to

---

[1] *Ep*. VII, 2.
[2] *Ep*. VI, 8.
[3] See, e.g. *Ep*. VII, 2; VII, 10; IX, 4.
[4] *Ep*. VII, 2.
[5] *Ep*. VII, 7; cf. *Ep*. IX, 4.
[6] *Ep*. VIII, 12.

as *Burgus*, and is generally identified with Bourg-sur-Garonne. The place was evidently a fortified and impregnable castle, perched on a high rock at the confluence of the Garonne and the Dordogne, and it is undoubtedly the focus of the *regna* which Ausonius attributed to St Paulinus. The arresting and romantic opening lines of the description[1] introduce us to the fullest account which we possess of a cantonal military stronghold of the fifth century with all the amenities and refinements of a Gallo-Roman nobleman's country house – its great granaries and store-houses, its porticos, its baths and summer and winter apartments, its spinning-room, the private apartments of its owner, the crude log fire heating in winter, even its frescoed walls depicting in unfading colours – we remember that the family had long been Christian – the early history of the Jews.[2]

One of the most interesting of the letters, written to his friend Donidius, describes his visit to Prusianum, the estate of Tonantius Ferreolus, and to Vorocingus, or Voroangus, the estate of Apollinaris, both close together, near Nîmes. Apollinaris is a relative of Sidonius, and Ferreolus is related, through his mother Papianilla, to the great family of the Aviti; and in the account of his visit Sidonius pictures for us the genial country, the great villas, that of Ferreolus containing the library of classical and Christian authors already referred to (p. 275), and the amusements and amenities of these great homes of two nobles whom Sidonius describes as 'the flower of the nobility who are our contemporaries'. The Donidius to whom this letter was written was himself living on his ancestral estate at Eborolacum,[3] and we hear in another letter of his attempt to recover a part of it which had been lost to him in the Visigothic Invasion.[4] Sidonius's most-favoured residence – much loved, it would seem, by his daughter also[5] – was his wife's hereditary estate of Avitacum.[6]

His friend Consentius[7] is a typical example of the Gaulish nobility, a combination of high-minded statesman, cultured man of letters, and zealous agriculturalist. He lived on his

---

[1] *Carmen* XXII. See more particularly 101 ff.
[2] *Recutitorum primordia Judaeorum*, ibid., 201.
[3] *Ep.* II, 9. *Eborolacum* is Ebreuil, near Gannat, in the valley of the Sioule.
[4] *Ep.* III, 5; cf. VI, 5.   [5] *Ep.* II, 12.
[6] *Ep.* II, 2.   [7] *Ep.* VIII, 4.

estate, the Villa Octaviana between Narbonne and Béziers, which he had inherited from his father, a distinguished citizen of Narbonne, and a man of intellectual distinction. Sidonius writes with enthusiasm of the charm of the estate – its situation near town and sea and river, the beauty of its architecture, the white colonnade of the chapel, the baths, evidently something of a landmark, its fields and waters, its vines and olives, the beauty of its setting in hill and plain, its splendid library, and, most characteristic touch of all, its master dividing his time between agriculture and writing, so that one is in doubt as to whether his mind or his estate enjoys the finer culture. Yet Consentius had been in the Imperial Service in early life, and had been entrusted by the Emperor Valentinian III with missions to Constantinople, and had held the office of Prefect of the Palace under Avitus.[1]

Another correspondent of Sidonius of the same class is his old school-fellow, Magnus Felix of Narbonne, to whom he dedicated his poems.[2] His father Magnus had been a senator of Narbonne, and consul in 460 and Prefect of Gaul in 469; a man of high honour enjoying a wide reputation for his ability. Sidonius makes a reference to his fine library.[3] His elder brother Probus,[4] who had married Sidonius's cousin Eulalia, was also a man of literary taste and ability. Sidonius evidently holds the opinion of Magnus Felix on political matters in high esteem, for he writes[5] begging news of the newly appointed quaestor Licinianus. But Magnus Felix is evidently deeply absorbed in life on his country estate, for Sidonius upbraids him for his dilatoriness as a correspondent, and accuses him of burying himself in his office or library. We may contrast the approval which he repeatedly expresses towards his father-in-law, the Emperor Avitus, who, while devoting himself to country life, had never given way to idleness or unwarlike sloth, but had continued his military studies and his pursuit of martial exercises.[6] In truth every Gallo-Roman, whatever high office he might hold, was at heart a country gentleman.

---

[1] Dalton, op. cit., I, p. clxiv.
[2] See *Carmen* XXIV; cf. ibid., IX.
[3] *Carmen* XXIV, 92.
[4] See *Carmen* XXIV, 92 f.; cf. IX, 332 f.
[5] *Ep.* III, 7.
[6] *Carmen* VII, 316 ff.; cf. ibid., 369 ff.; 460 ff.

Similarly devoted to his country estate is Trygetius of Bazas,[1] to whom Sidonius writes a playful invitation during his sojourn near Bordeaux, which surely owes something to the invitations of Ausonius to his friend Theon of Médoc, also of Bazas (cf. p. 312). Sidonius upbraids his friend for being indifferent to the attractions of Bordeaux, with its succulent oysters, and to the mullets of the Garonne, and asks if Bazas 'built on dust', and fields 'as sandy as Syrtes', 'shifting soil and sands tossed by this wind and that' hold such a charm for him as to keep him back from the twelve miles journey to Bordeaux. We have seen that this region amid the sandhills held a similar strange attraction for Ausonius's whimsical friend. 'Or is it,' again asks Sidonius, 'that the uncertainty of the winter roads makes you hesitate, because the whirling winds of Bigorre obliterate the tracks of the shifting banks so that you are afraid of a kind of shipwreck while making a land journey on foot'.

This hint of fear is, however, only a pretext for the introduction of a list of the high enterprises in Spain – at Cadiz and Gibraltar – which evidently lie to the credit of Trygetius, and of which we would gladly have heard more.[2]

It is evident that Sidonius regards this love of the soil, and of a cultured life of calm routine on the ancestral estate, as a serious menace to the effectiveness of his fellow countrymen, and inimical to the best spirit of Gaulish patriotism. Again and again we find him urging the young nobles to leave their cherished country life and enter the service of the State. It is in the strongest terms that he writes to his friend Eutropius, appealing to him to enter the Imperial Service:

'You are full of life at home; but when you have to set about a distant journey a heavy despair fills you with panic.'[3] And he urges his friend to visit Imperial Rome, 'O, for shame if you abandon yourself among rustic herdsmen or grunting swine-herds, as if it should be the height of your bliss to break up the ground with your quivering plough, or to bend over your curved scythe and deflower the meadow of its splendour, or to stoop as a

---

[1] *Ep.* VIII, 12. On Trygetius, see Chaix, *Saint Sidoine Apollinaire et Son Siècle*, Vol. I (Clermont-Ferrand, 1866), p. 225.

[2] For other possible political or diplomatic enterprises of Trygetius, see Dalton, op. cit., I, p. clxxxii.

[3] *Ep.* I, 6.

labourer and hoe your vineyard, heavy with young growth.
... It behoves a man of your descent to cultivate himself no
less than his estate.'

And when he writes later to congratulate Eutropius on
becoming Prefect of Gaul, he reminds him of the letter of exhor-
tation which he had written previously, urging him to accept
office:

'But how hardly were you persuaded to combine the office of
prefect with the pursuit of philosophy!'[1]

Another letter to his friend Syagrius, who is busying himself
on his estate at Taionnacus near Autun, is an impassioned
appeal to him to abandon the plough for pursuits more worthy
of his ancestors.

'Tell me, flower of our Gallic youth,' he begins, 'how long
your country pursuits will hold you indifferent to those of the
town?' And he continues, 'How much longer will your estate of
Taionnacus weary you – a scion of patrician stock now turned
husbandman? . . . How much longer will you work your heavy
hoe already blunted, and the rows still not completely dug?
. . . Desist from shaming your noble birth by playing the
rustic.'[2]

As one studies the letters of Sidonius, and the family history
and background of his contemporaries and those who come
within his orbit, one is more and more impressed by the importance of the native Gaulish background, both as a formative
element in their literary education, and as a direct inspiration
of their life work. Especially this seems to be true of men like
Syagrius, whose homes or ancestral lands were in the old territory of the Aedui, and the upper waters of the rivers draining
from this area, a kind of Highland zone. Yet these men were
among the most cultured of their age, the most devoted classical scholars of the closing years of the empire. Syagrius was
equally master of Latin and of Burgundian.[3] The combination
of passionate devotion to the actual land of one's birth, with a
complete assimilation of the culture of a more advanced nation,
is comparable to the conditions prevalent in Scotland today.
And the way in which we have seen old Gauls return to settle on

[1] *Ep*. III, 6.
[2] *Ep*. VIII, 8. For Syagrius, see also *Ep*. V, 5.
[3] *Ep*. V, 8.

their native soil when their term of foreign service has expired is similarly Scottish in character.

With Sidonius the love of home and country was inseparable from love of Rome and Roman culture; and this was natural, for Gaul had long been the chief home of that culture. Sidonius hated the Barbarians as being alien to both. He sneers at the want of culture of the Visigothic court. When asked by Evodius[1] to compose verses to be engraved on a silver cup for Euric's queen, Ragnhild, he remarks: 'In such a forum or such an Athenaeum[2] your vellum will get the praise rather than my inscription.'[3] We have seen him sneering at the skin-clad Goths (*pelliti*), and the great height of the Burgundians (cf. p. 307), and he hates the roughness of the Celtic dialect.[4] He is astounded at his friend Syagrius who, after having had his Virgil 'driven into him with the cane' in youth, could now bring himself to master the German tongue, and he adds lightly:

'It is almost inconceivable how tickled we all are to hear that in your presence a Barbarian is terrified of committing a barbarism in his own language.'[5]

To his friend Philagrius he writes, 'You shun barbarians because they have a bad reputation'; and he adds, characteristically enough, 'I avoid them, even when they have a good one.'[6]

And when the end came, his bitterest memory of his prison at Liviana[7] is of two old Gothic women established near to the window of his room, who, when he retired at night, began their chatter, 'more quarrelsome, drunken, and revolting creatures than any we shall ever see again'.[8]

In the later letters, written from the heart of Auvergne while the Gauls were making their last starving resistance to the

---

[1] A petitioner at Euric's court.

[2] In the Athenaeum at Rome authors read or recited their compositions, and similar institutions were founded in the provincial capitals, such as Lyons. See Dalton's note, op. cit., Vol. II, p. 224. The point of Sidonius' sneer is that in the Barbaric court the silver will be appreciated, not the inscription engraved on it.

[3] *Ep.* IV, 8.

[4] *Ep.* III, 3.

[5] *Ep.* V, 5. Syagrius was secretary to the Burgundian king. [His great-grandfather had been consul in 381, and a friend of both Ausonius and Symmachus. See O. Seeck, *Symmachus*, p. cix; Dill, op. cit., p. 376.

[6] *Ep.* VII, 14.

[7] After the cession of Auvergne to Euric, Sidonius was imprisoned for some time at Liviana near Carcassonne.

[8] *Ep.* VIII, 3.

Y

Goths, we hear a new and deeper note of earnestness than in the earlier correspondence. A greater capacity for emotional suffering and steadfast endeavour rings through the letters, till even his literary style changes in response to his overcharged feelings, and the old tricks of rhetoric give place to a style rendered vivid by the nature of its subject. Writing to summon his brother-in-law Ecdicius c. 470 he cries excitedly:

'It is for you that the last breath of freedom is waiting, drawn by the citizens in their dying agonies. Whatever we have to look to – whether hope or despair – still our resolve is to have you among us to be our leader.'[1]

How nobly Ecdicius answered the appeal may be gathered from the letter which Sidonius wrote to him in 474. The letter is one of the freshest and most charming in the collection. Sidonius recalls the heroic dash made by Ecdicius and a little band of eighteen commandoes through the Gothic lines to come to the aid of the beleaguered city; and he described the scene which follows, when a crowd of both men and women of every rank and age lined the ruinous walls to watch him cross the ground between the city and the enemy, 'At midday, and right through the open you crossed with a mere troop of eighteen cavalry through some thousands of Goths.'

In the ovation which greeted the heroes from the people of Clermont we seem to have the last breath of ancient epic poetry, a little fifth-century *Iliad* in prose:

'Some kissed away the dust from you, some seized the bridles smeared with foam and blood, some inverted the saddles soaked with sweat, others unbuckled the clasps to remove the cheek-pieces of your helmet to enable you to take it off. Others were busy unlacing your greaves; others again were counting over the notches in the edges of your swords dinted in the fray, and yet others measuring with envious fingers the holes pierced in your corslet by cut and thrust . . . you endured graciously the platitudes of their excessive congratulations while you were torn this way and that by the crowd hurling themselves at you to embrace you.'[2]

It is largely this love of country and readiness to sacrifice all

[1] *Ep.* II, 1. [2] *Ep.* III, 3. With this picture of the unarming of Ecdicius we may compare the little inventory of the arms and armour of Avitus in the *Panegyric* addressed to him, *Carmen* VII, 241 ff.

rather than suffer a Barbarian domination which endears Sidonius to us today. His deep earnestness of purpose, his reso- lute defence of the city entrusted to his care, his noble appeals to his fellow bishops to resist the Arian Visigothic king Euric, are far removed from either the Roman official or the medieval churchman, and ring with a peculiarly modern note. In 472–3 he wrote to Bishop Basilius of Aix:

'It must be confessed that however formidable the Gothic king, because of his mighty deeds, I dread his attacks on our Christian laws even more than on our Roman defences.'[1]

On hearing a rumour that the Goths have occupied Rome, he writes from Clermont in 474 to Bishop Mamertus of Vienne:

'We unhappy people of Auvergne are always their thorough- fare for these incursions';[2] but he adds that they mean to resist with spirit and courage, though they realize the odds against them and place no confidence in their city walls charred by fire, or their decayed stockades, or their ramparts, worn down by the breasts of the sentries on guard.

Writing the same year to his old friend, Magnus Felix of Narbonne, with reference to the newly appointed quaestor, Licinianus, he wistfully enquires whether he is likely to open a door of safety to the beleaguered city, so that 'our men may pause to take breath from their unbroken watch. Neither a snowy day nor a night moonless and stormy tempts them to abandon guard upon the walls.'[3]

And to Bishop Graecus of Marseilles, the same year:

'I am within the little space of the half-burnt ruins of a totter- ing wall, shut in by the terror of the war which is actually upon us, so that I am never able to satisfy my longing for you.'[4]

It is a sorry end to the bright hopes expressed in the *Pane- gyric on Majorian*[5] that the devastated land of Gaul, with its proud and gallant nobility prostrate and despised, would be led to a victorious peace by the new emperor.

Sidonius lived to see peace concluded; but the peace brought only disappointment and bitterness. It was bought at the cost of the cession of Auvergne to the Goths. The Roman power in Gaul was at an end, and the Gaulish people and the classical

---

[1] *Ep.* VII, 6.   [2] *Ep.* VII, 1.
[3] *Ep.* III, 7.   [4] *Ep.* VII, 10.
[5] *Carmen* V, 350 ff. Cf. ibid., 574 ff.

culture which they had so nobly made their own passed under Barbarian domination. The privations of war, starvation, isolation, deadly peril were over; but a numbness almost more deadly had set in – the apathy which supervenes when a supreme effort has been made, and supreme sacrifice has ended in utter failure, utter loss. Sidonius writes to Graecus once more: 'We are all agreed that war conditions were less wretched than these of peace.'[1]

Sidonius has sometimes been accused of insufficient seriousness of purpose.[2] His balanced outlook and wide range of social contacts, and the rarity with which he expresses himself with emotional intensity, combined with a lightness of touch and a certain urbane blitheness of expression, are perhaps too near to those of modern civilized standards to be justly appreciated by modern critics. We miss the austerity of the great churchman, the epic achievements of the great soldier, the profound philosophy, the deep sense of underlying tragedy, the passionate clinging to human relationships which impress the modern imagination. It is only in this last letter[3] to his old friend Bishop Graecus, on the conclusion of the peace which he hated and despised, that the intensity of his passionate feelings breaks the slender meshes of his self-imposed standards of good taste.

'It is then,' he cries in agonized despair, 'in expectation of this glorious peace that we tore out the plants growing in the crannies of the walls for food, often through our ignorance infected by poisonous weeds, which our hands, as green as they through famine, often plucked. . . . I implore you to repudiate this treaty, which is without either value or honour. The negotiations pass through your hands.'

Bishop Graecus of Marseilles, to whom the letter is written, was one of four bishops entrusted with the drawing up of the terms of peace with the Visigoths under Euric, involving the cession of Auvergne in 475. The other three bishops were Basilius of Aix, Faustus of Riez, and Leontius of Arles. Sidonius evidently regarded Graecus as chiefly responsible for the ignominy, for in the same letter he continues:

---

[1] *Ep.* VII, 7.
[2] T. Hodgkin's estimate (*Italy and her Invaders*,[2] Vol. II, p. 318 f.), friendly and sympathetic though it is, does Sidonius far less than justice, even in his episcopal capacity.
[3] Loc. cit.

'In the absence of the governor, not only are the peace terms already negotiated placed in your hands, but even those not yet ratified are referred to you,' and he goes on to say that if they have been betrayed it is due to the cowardice of Graecus and his colleagues.

Then in a passage for which even his severest critics exonerate him from lack of fervour he cries, 'O, break off by some means these shameful peace negotiations. If need be we would gladly prolong the siege and go on fighting and starving.'

In the closing lines a softer light falls, as his thoughts turn from bitterness and reproaches to a tender solicitude for his people, rendered homeless, exiles, even captives. In his mind he probably saw once more the hated scenes he had described in his letter to Pannychius of Bourges, in reference to the miseries brought upon the population by the hated official Seronatus,[1] 'the certain sign of whose immediate arrival in whatever direction he goes', he declares, 'is gangs of prisoners of war, being dragged along, and dragging their chains with them', and he beseeches Graecus in a last appeal to take steps to provide for the displaced population:

'The other regions ceded expect only servitude, but Auvergne must expect punishment. If you are powerless to save us in our extremity . . . make arrangements about land for our exiles, ransom for the captives, provision for the displaced population. Even though our wall now lies open to the enemy, do not let yours be shut against those in need of hospitality.'[2]

The same appeal, the same solicitude, which Salvian voices in his book *Ad Ecclesiam*, the same problem of hungry homeless masses, moving southward, Sidonius now faces and seeks to bring home to others. It is the tragedy which Faustus seeks in his sermons to impress on the consciousness of the monks of Lérins, as he warns them against a spiritual apathy born of a sense of their island security. Similar tragedies and similar problems fifty years earlier had drawn the Roman official Rutilius Namatianus back to his Gaulish estates after the devastation of Provence, that he might build temporary dwellings for his

---

[1] *Ep.* V, 13. Seronatus was probably the Governor of Aquitania Prima under Roman rule. He was convicted of treason and excessive oppression, and the people of Auvergne ultimately brought him to justice. He suffered the death penalty. See Dalton, I, p. xxxviii, n. 2, and the references there cited.

[2] *Ep.* VII, 7.

tenants whose homes had been burnt and destroyed. Sidonius, while he himself is led captive to the fortress at Liviana, begs practical help from his old friend Graecus, the Bishop of Marseilles, for the people of Auvergne who are evacuating their lands and homes on the entry of the triumphant Goths.

The detention in Liviana was probably not of long duration, and the liberation of Sidonius was probably due to his friend Leo, Euric's cultured minister, who was a descendant of the great orator Fronto, and a member of an aristocratic family of Narbonne.[1] From Liviana Sidonius seems to have gone to Bordeaux, where he is concerned to recover an estate which had come to him through his wife. Perhaps Avitacum itself had been appropriated during his absence.[2] While in the neighbourhood of Bordeaux he wrote to his friend, the poet and courtier Lampridius, the famous letter containing the panegyric on Euric which was probably largely instrumental in the reinstatement of Sidonius in his bishopric. The following years were devoted to his ecclesiastical duties, and it is probably during this period that he collected and polished his letters for publication. An account of his death is given by Gregory of Tours,[3] but the actual date is unknown.[4]

The catastrophe and the evacuation of Auvergne are only the last of a long series, the immediate result of the Barbarian Invasions which had been hurling themselves like great breakers over the whole of southern and western Europe. We have seen Palestine and Egypt flooded with the population fleeing from Italy before the oncoming invaders; we have seen the population of western Gaul fleeing to Marseilles and to North Africa before the Vandals and the Visigoths. We cannot doubt that many would take ship from Bordeaux to the safer ports of our islands, where we know they were not wholly strangers. We have seen that already in 384 the poet Latronian, the Spanish bishop Instantius, and other educated members of the Priscillianist group had been banished to the Scilly Isles. We know that Coelestius, the friend and disciple of Pelagius, was an Irishman. And we have seen that evidence is not wanting throughout our period of a more or less continuous intellectual

[1] See Dill, op. cit., pp. 369, 375 f., and the references there cited.
[2] *Ep.* VIII, 9. See also Dill, op. cit., p. 369.
[3] *Hist. Franc.* II, 23.
[4] For a discussion of this subject, see Stevens, op. cit., pp. 179, 211 ff.

contact between the Continent and the British Isles. It is impossible to doubt that this contact would be speeded up under
the stimulus of the Barbarian Occupation of Gaul, and that the
current would set strongly for the British Isles, not only as being
the farthest from the storm centre, but also as being a fertile
country well able to support an increase of population. It is
doubtless to the upheavals of Gaul that we owe much of the
great intellectual stimulus to which Irish learning in the Dark
Ages bears witness, and which Ireland, as the last outpost of
classical culture, cherished and handed back to its Continental
home in a later age.

INDEX

Etheria, *or* Eucheria, 17
Eucheria, see Etheria
Eucherius, St, Bishop of Lyons, 77, 87, 112, 149–59, 163, 168 f., 187, 194, 200, 203, 210, 212, 224, 240, 247, 276, 278 f., 289, 296; works of, 152–9; artificial style of, 158 f., 189
Euchrotia, poetess and wife of Delphidius of Bordeaux, 18, 33 f., 36, 41, 43, 45
Eugippius: *Vita S. Severini*, 281
Euladius, Bishop of Arles, 148, 179 181 f., 224
Eulalia, cousin of Sidonius, 299, 318
Eumenius of Autun, 27 ff., 30
Eunomia, 21
Euphronius, Bishop of Autun, 276, 278, 282, 290, 292, 314
Euric the Visigoth, 198, 285, 287, 294, 300, 306 f., 310, 313, 321, 323 f., 326
Eusebius, Bishop of Caesarea; *Chronicle of*, 16, 79, 105; *History of Christian Church*, 105; works of, 142, 294, 306; priest, 103
Eustachius, Bishop of Marseilles, 206
Eustathius, American bishop, 146
Eustochium, daughter of St Paula, 16, 20 f., 144
Eutropius, friend of Sidonius and Prefect of Gaul, 319 f.
Eutyches, presbyter and abbot of Constantinople, 173
Evagrius, of Pontus, works of, 157, 169, 206, 235–8; priest, 92
Evil, problem of, 165, 167
Evodius, Bishop of Uzala, 177 f.; petitioner at Euric's court, 321; Prefect, 42
Exorcist, 82 f., 98, 315
Exuperantius, relative of Rutilius Namatianus, 129 f., 264
Exuperius, Bishop of Toulouse, 113, 288

Fabiola, 194
Faustinus, Brother, 314
Faustus, 'the Briton' *or* 'Breton' abbot of Lérins, and then Bishop of Riez, 16, 151 ff., 160, 163 f., 192–207, 210, 236 f., 241, 250, 285, 290, 296, 303 f., 324 f.

Favorinus of Arles, 25
Felicissimus, 43
Felix, St, 64, 70, 74, 83 ff., 88, 133; monk of Hadrumetum, 177 f.
Ferreolus, Tonantius, friend of Sidonius, 275, 304, 311, 317
Florentinus, 131
Florentius, Bishop of Cahors, 82
Florus, monk of Hadrumetum, 177 f.
Franks, 122, 127, 129, 131, 167, 191, 307 f.
Freebooters, 55 (n. 2)
Free will, 174, 175, 177, 233 f.
Fronto, orator, 326
Furia, 18

Gaiseric, 238
Galla, wife of Eucherius, Bishop of Lyons, 87, 151 f., 169
Gallican Church, 205 f.
Gallinaria, island of, 98, 118, 143
Gallus, friend of Sulpicius Severus, and disciple of St Martin, 108 f., 110, 115, 121, 230, 232 f.; 'a certain', 283
Garonne, river, 48, 55, 126; mullets of, 319
Gaudemet, J., 263
Gaul, Celtic influences in, 23, 25; culture of, 35, 108, 140 f., 157, 320; early Christianity in, 90, 298; end of Roman power in, 324; government of, 22, 298 f.; pre-Roman, 24; Romanization of, 22 f.; saints with tombs famous for miracles, 266
Gauls, family feeling among, 302; nationalism of, 232; patriotism of, 111, 302, 320 f.; revolt against Majorian, 299
Gavidius, Bishop, 107
Gebavult, King, 278, 281 (n. 1); *see also* Higebold
Gelasius, monk, 87
Gelonian, 307
General Council, 189
Gennadius, presbyter of Marseilles, 91, 93, 96, 121, 150, 153 f., 161 f., 165, 170, 172, 186 ff., 198 f., 200, 206 ff., 216; *De Viris Illustribus*, 206

Date Due

CPSIA information can be obtained
at www.ICGtesting.com
Printed in the USA
BVHW050106080223
658119BV00002B/89